Community Mental Health

Challenges for the 21st Century

SECOND EDITION

Edited by Jessica Rosenberg
& Samuel J. Rosenberg

 Routledge
Taylor & Francis Group

NEW YORK AND LONDON

Second edition published 2013
by Routledge
711 Third Avenue, New York, NY 10017

Simultaneously published in the UK
by Routledge
27 Church Road, Hove, East Sussex BN3 2FA

Routledge is an imprint of the Taylor & Francis Group, an informa business

First edition published by Routledge 2006

Library of Congress Cataloging-in-Publication Data
A catalog record for this book has been requested

ISBN: 978–0-415–88740–3 (hbk)
ISBN: 978–0-415–88741–0 (pbk)
ISBN: 978–0-203–83433–6 (ebk)

Typeset in Perpetua and Bell Gothic by
by Florence Production Ltd, Stoodleigh, Devon

Printed and bound in the United States of America
by Edwards Brothers, Inc.

Contents

CONTENTS

About the Editors

Jessica Rosenberg is Associate Professor of Social Work, Long Island University, where she also is Director of University–Community collaboration to support grandparents raising grandchildren. She holds an MSW from Hunter College School of Social Work and a Ph.D. from Wurzweiler School of Social Work, Yeshiva University. She is the former Assistant Director of the New York City Chapter of the National Association of Social Workers (NASW), where she worked on passage of the New York State social work licensing law and facilitated the NASW/1199–SEIU Alliance. Dr. Rosenberg is active in her labor union and faculty senate. She sits on the Advisory Board of the Heights-Hill Mental Health Service South Beach Psychiatric Center Community Advisory and the Kincare Task Force Advisory Board. She practiced for over 15 years with clients with serious mental illness in community mental health agencies. Dr. Rosenberg has published numerous articles on issues related to mental health, stigma, immigration, serious mental illness, and labor unions. Her book, *Working in Social Work: the Real World Guide to Practice Settings*, is a comprehensive guide to the field for students and new social workers. Most recently, she edited an innovative online curriculum designed to enhance skills and knowledge about working with clients impacted by the recession. Her current research is in the area of community mental health practice in a post-recession world.

Samuel J. Rosenberg is Dean, School of Social Science and Human Services and Professor of Social Work and Sociology at Ramapo College of New Jersey. Dr. Rosenberg administers seven undergraduate programs: Sociology, Social Work, Psychology, Teacher Education, Law and Society, Environmental Studies, Social Science, and three graduate programs: Master's in Educational Technology, Master's in Educational Leadership and Master's in Sustainable Development, and he has responsibility for a division of 100 faculty and 1,600 students, curriculum and program development, scheduling, advising, and developing general education courses. Dr. Rosenberg has been a scholar and direct practitioner for over 25 years. He has taught at State University of New York, City University of New York, Brooklyn College, and The New York State Office of Mental Health Intensive Case Manager Program. Dr. Rosenberg was the Director of the Heights Hill Mental Health Service of the South Beach Psychiatric Center, New York State Office of Mental Health. Dr. Rosenberg has written numerous articles on issues concerning providing mental health services and diversity, psychoeducation, immigration, and professional concerns of mental health professionals. Dr. Rosenberg was the recipient of a grant from the New York Community Trust for the production of the groundbreaking educational video *The Whole Family*, a psychoeducational film for Latino families and consumers. *The Whole Family* is used at colleges and universities throughout the United States, Europe, and Latin America. He serves as a College Liaison for faculty development to the Faculty Resource Center, New York University. In September 2011, he received the Distinguished Alumnus Award from the Silver School of Social Work at New York University.

Contributors

David E. Biegel is the Henry L. Zucker Professor of Social Work Practice and Professor of Psychiatry and Sociology at the Mandel School of Applied Social Sciences, Case Western Reserve University. He currently serves as Associate Dean for Research and Training of the Mandel School and as Co-Director of the School's Center on Substance Abuse and Mental Illness. In addition to previously serving as Chair of the Doctoral Program, he has served as the founding director/co-director of a number of research centers at the Mandel School including: the Center for Practice Innovations, Alzheimer's Disease Caregiving Institute, and the Cuyahoga County Community Mental Health Research Institute. Dr. Biegel teaches research and policy courses in the Mandel School's Master's and Doctoral degree programs. Together with Dr. Elizabeth Tracy, he is co-editor of the *Evidence-Based Practices* Book Series, with volumes published by Oxford University Press. Dr. Biegel is a member of the Board of Directors of the Alcohol, Drug Addiction, and Mental Health Services Board of Cuyahoga County. He has been involved in research for the past two decades pertaining to the impact of chronic illnesses on families. Dr. Biegel's publications focus on family caregiving with individuals with co-occurring mental and substance use disorders, with severe and persistent mental illness, and with the frail elderly.

Anne Bingham is a graduate student in the clinical doctoral psychology program at Drexel University.

Leopoldo J. Cabassa is an Assistant Professor of Clinical Psychiatric Social Work at the Department of Psychiatry at Columbia University and the Assistant Director of the New York State Center of Excellence for Cultural Competence at the New York State Psychiatric Institute. Dr. Cabassa received his MSW and Ph.D. from the George Warren Brown School of Social Work at Washington University in St. Louis. Prior to joining the faculty at Columbia, Dr. Cabassa was an Assistant Professor at the University of Southern California (USC) School of Social Work and at the USC Keck School of Medicine Department of Psychiatry and Behavioral Sciences. His research focuses on understanding the causes of racial and ethnic disparities in health and mental health care and in developing and implementing culturally tailored interventions aimed at reducing these inequities in care. His work has been supported by the New York State Office of Mental Health and the National Institutes of Health.

Alma J. Carten is an Associate Professor of Social Work at New York University. She has held a number of faculty appointments, including director and chair of a CSWE-accredited undergraduate social work program, Adjunct Professor for the Hunter College School of Social Work, teaching in the School's Distance Learning Program for city employees, and Visiting Professor with the Behavior Science Department of the New York City Police Academy. She has conducted research and published on family preservation programs, maternal substance abuse, child survivors of HIV/AIDS, independent living services for adolescents, child maltreatment and Caribbean families, and neighborhood-based services. She was a member of the Administration for Children's Services Commissioner's Task Force on Minority Agencies. She served as President of the New York City Chapter of the National Association for Social Workers from 2000 to 2002.

Patrick Corrigan is Distinguished Professor and Associate Dean for Research in the Institute of Psychology at the Illinois Institute of Technology. Prior to that, Corrigan was Professor of Psychiatry and Executive Director of the Center for Psychiatric Rehabilitation at the University of Chicago. Corrigan is a licensed clinical psychologist setting up and providing services for people with serious mental illnesses and their families for more than 30 years. Corrigan has been principal investigator of federally funded studies on rehabilitation and consumer operated services. Ten years ago, he became principal investigator of the Chicago Consortium for Stigma Research, the only National Institute of Mental Health (NIMH)-funded research center examining the stigma of mental illness. More recently, the Chicago Consortium evolved into the National Consortium on Stigma and Empowerment (NCSE), supported by NIMH as a developing center in services research. Centered at IIT, NCSE includes co-principal investigators from Yale, the University of Pennsylvania, and Rutgers. One recent study supported by the National Institute on Alcohol Abuse and Alcoholism (NIAAA), NIMH, and The Fogarty Center examined the stigma of mental illness endorsed by employers in Beijing, Chicago, and Hong Kong. In the past few years, Corrigan has partnered with colleagues from the Department for Veteran Affairs and Department of Defense to develop and evaluate anti-stigma programs meant to help soldiers returning from Iraq and Afghanistan seek out services for Post-Traumatic Stress and other disorders, when needed. Corrigan is a prolific researcher, having published 11 books and more than 250 papers. He is editor of the *American Journal of Psychiatric Rehabilitation*.

Marilyn L. Flynn is Dean of the School of Social Work at the University of Southern California in Los Angeles. She was appointed in 1997 by the President of the University as the seventh Dean in the 90-year history of the School. Dean Flynn is widely regarded as one of the most innovative leaders in graduate social work education. Since assuming her role as Dean at USC, she has doubled graduate enrollment in Ph.D. and MSW programs to nearly 1,000 students at four academic centers throughout the southern California region. Dean Flynn is also nationally recognized for her leadership in establishing the first graduate military social work specialization in a major civilian research university. She has recruited faculty with extensive service experience, including deployment, from the Army, Navy, Marines, and Air Force to direct and teach in this effort. She is also currently working to engage community programs in the Los Angeles and southern California region in a common effort to improve the reintegration of service members as they return from combat. The Center for Innovation and Research on Veterans and Military Families (CIR) in the School has currently received more than $12 million from the Department of Defense to support components of this initiative. Dean Flynn received her Ph.D. from the University of Illinois at Urbana with specialization in economics and social policy. Dean Flynn has spent her academic career in the study and evaluation of community organizations, public–private partnerships, public income transfer systems, and program design for special populations.

Michael B. Friedman is an Adjunct Associate Professor at Columbia University Schools of Social Work and Public Health. Born in 1943, Michael Friedman came of age in the 1950s and 1960s when America was undergoing a cultural revolution. He studied and taught philosophy for several years, but was quickly drawn to the challenges of mental illness. He worked as a mental health practitioner, administrator, and advocate for over 40 years before retiring in July of 2010. At that time, he was Director of The Center for Policy and Advocacy of the Mental Health Association of NYC, a center that he founded in 2003. In that role, he also founded the Geriatric Mental Health Alliance of New York and, most recently, the Veterans' Mental Health Coalition of NYC. Over the years, he has served on numerous planning and advocacy groups at the federal, state, and local level. Currently, he teaches health and mental health policy at Columbia University and writes frequently about policy and about aging. He has spoken and led workshops at numerous professional conferences, and he is the author of numerous articles on such topics as geriatric mental health, child mental health, psychiatric rehabilitation, mental health policy and finance, health policy reform, and more. His writings are available at www.michaelbfriedman.com

Lisa Furst is the Director of Public Education of the Mental Health Association of New York City (MHA of NYC) and Director of Education for the Geriatric Mental Health Alliance of New York. She received her MSW degree from the Hunter College School of Social Work and is a licensed social worker in New York State. She is co-author of the book *Depressed Older Adults: Education and Screening*, published in August 2010 by the Springer Publishing Company.

Anthony M. Hassan was appointed Clinical Associate Professor at the University of Southern California School of Social Work in 2009, serving as the inaugural Director of the CIR on Veterans and Military Families. Dr. Hassan is a retired Air Force officer who brings 25 years of experience in military social work and leadership development. He previously served as Deputy Department Head of the Leadership Directorate and Director of the Master's Degree Program in Counseling and Leadership at the United States Air Force Academy in Colorado Springs. He transformed the graduate program's curriculum, ensuring quality education for over 80 top-tier Air Force commanders and improving cadet leader development and squadron organizational performance. At the Academy, Dr. Hassan also helped develop a Defense Health Program research project to study factors promoting resiliency in the Army National Guard. Prior to the Air Force Academy, he was the CEO of a military community mental health center that ranked 1st of 10 Community Mental Health Centers in the region for productivity and "best clinic." Dr. Hassan served during Operation Iraqi Freedom in 2004 on the first-ever Air Force combat stress control and prevention team embedded in an Army unit. He was also hand-selected to assist and educate East African countries in 2006 with capacity building for disaster response. Adding to his work abroad, he led the largest military substance abuse and family advocacy programs in the Pacific, which were recognized as benchmark programs and training sites for all other Pacific bases.

Kirk Heilbrun is currently Professor and Head, Department of Psychology, Drexel University. He received his doctorate in clinical psychology in 1980 from the University of Texas at Austin, and completed postdoctoral fellowship training from 1981 to 1982 in psychology and criminal justice at Florida State University. His current research focuses on juvenile and adult offenders, legal decision-making, and the evaluation and interventions associated with such decision-making. He is the author of a number of articles on forensic assessment, violence risk assessment and risk communication, and the treatment of mentally disordered offenders, and has published seven books in these areas. He is the Co-Director of the Pennsylvania Mental Health and Justice Center of Excellence, having previously served as president of both the American Psychology–Law Psychology/APA Division 41, and the American Board of Forensic Psychology. He received the 2004 Distinguished Contributions to Forensic Psychology award and the 2008 Beth Clark Distinguished Service Contribution Award from the American Academy of Forensic Psychology.

Christian Huygen is a clinical psychologist and the executive director of Rainbow Heights Club, a groundbreaking, publicly funded psychosocial and support agency specifically serving lesbian, gay, bisexual, and transgender people living with mental illness. Rainbow Heights Club now serves over 500 members, nearly 90% of whom state that they are able to stay free of hospitalization and in the community because of the support that they receive there. Dr. Huygen designed and implemented a cultural competency program on LGBT mental health issues for mainstream care providers, which has now been presented to over 3,000 individuals in 200 agencies, universities, hospitals, and clinics. He has served as provider co-chair of the LGBT Citywide Committee of the Federation of the New York City Department of Health and Mental Hygiene since 2006, and was the lead organizer for two citywide E/Quality Care Conferences on LGBT affirming mental health, MR/DD, and substance abuse and alcoholism services. He co-chairs the Technical Assistance Committee of the Empire State Pride Agenda's LGBT Health and Human Services Network, and helped to oversee a statewide assessment of the health and human service needs of LGBT New Yorkers, as well as a blueprint for Meeting LGBT Health and Human Service Needs in New York State.

Emily Kidder is a Public Health Specialist in the Specialty Marketing unit of Ogilvy CommonHealth Worldwide. Prior to joining Ogilvy CommonHealth Worldwide, Emily worked as a Program Association with the Geriatric Mental Health Alliance, under the leadership of Kimberly Williams, Michael Friedman, and Lisa Furst. She received her Master's in Public Health from Columbia University in May 2011.

Eileen Klein has been working in public mental health as an administrator and supervisor for over 30 years. She was the Deputy Director of Operations at South Beach Psychiatric Center. She has had extensive experience with mentally ill consumers, both in clinical treatment, supervision, social policy development, and advocacy. She has been extensively involved in program planning, grant writing, and development for a variety of patient populations throughout her career. She is currently a Professor at Ramapo College of New

Jersey. In addition, she has been an Adjunct Professor at New York University, Hunter School of Social Work, and Long Island University in their Master of Social Work programs. Dr. Klein specializes in teaching issues and publications related to community mental health, working with vulnerable populations and policy implementation and administration. Dr. Klein has published several articles on working with LGBT mental health consumers, stigma, community mental health, and engaging outpatients in treatment that is directed by consumer choice.

Lenore A. Kola is Associate Professor of Social Work at the Mandel School of Applied Social Sciences, Case Western Reserve University, and co-director of the Center for Evidence-Based Practices (CEBP), which is a partnership between the Mandel School and the Department of Psychiatry at the Case School of Medicine. She is also former Dean of the School of Graduate Studies. In an academic career spanning over 35 years, Dr. Kola has developed and implemented more than 10 different training and fellowship programs for Master's students and professionals funded by federal, state, and county agencies, as well as by charitable foundations. These programs have helped advance the knowledge, skills, credentialing, and professional development of social workers and chemical-dependency counselors alike. Dr. Kola was the founding Chair of the NASW Section on Alcohol, Tobacco and Other Drugs and founding Editor of the award-winning NASW ATOD newsletter, *Issues of Substance*. Dr. Kola has published on the topics of alcohol and other drugs and the elderly and, more recently, on integrated treatment for co-occurring mental illness and substance use disorders; supported employment; evidence-based practices; and implementation science (or technology transfer)—the translation of research evidence into service-systems change, organizational change, and clinical change.

Kathryn Krase is a social worker, lawyer, and social work educator. Dr. Krase is an Assistant Professor of Social Work at Ramapo College of New Jersey. She has previously served as a law guardian and guardian *ad litem* representing children in New York City Family Court for the New York Society for the Prevention of Cruelty to Children. Dr. Krase also served as the Associate Director of Fordham University's Interdisciplinary Center for Family and Child Advocacy and the Clinical Social Work Supervisor for the Family Defense Clinic at New York University Law School. She has co-authored "Mandated Reporting of Child Abuse and Neglect: A Practical Guide for Social Workers."

Ric Kruszynski has developed clinical, supervisory, and training expertise on the topic of dual disorders over the past 26 years, in both mental health and substance abuse treatment facilities. He is a Licensed Independent Social Worker and a Licensed Independent Chemical Dependency Counselor. Ric currently serves the CEBP at Case Western Reserve University (formerly known as the Ohio Substance Abuse and Mental Illness Coordinating Center of Excellence—Ohio SAMI CCOE) as Director of Consultation and Training. He consults with Ohio's County Mental Health and Substance Abuse Boards and provides training as part of the Center's effort to implement effective treatment for co-occurring substance abuse and mental disorders across Ohio. He has provided consultation and training in co-occurring disorders treatment nationally with programs in nearly 20 states, as well as with several international programs in that role. Ric has been training in the areas of substance abuse prevention, assessment, and treatment since 1986. His work with

Integrated Dual Disorder Treatment (IDDT) was featured in the November/December 2008 issue of *Social Work Today*. He served as a consultant on the 2009 SAMHSA publication "Integrated Treatment for Co-occurring Disorders: The Evidence."

Eun-Jeong Lee is an Assistant Professor in the Institute of Psychology at Illinois Institute of Technology. Dr. Lee received her Ph.D. in Rehabilitation Psychology from the University of Wisconsin-Madison in 2007. She completed a one-year pre-doctoral psychology internship in the Charles G. Matthews Neuropsychology Lab at the University of Wisconsin Hospital and Clinics and the Mendota Juvenile Treatment Center of the Mendota Mental Health Institute. She also worked for four years as a psychologist in Korea after receiving her Master's degree in Developmental Psychology from the Catholic University of Korea. Her research interests are in the areas of the cognitive vulnerability model of depression for people with disabilities, stigma and the help-seeking behavior model for people with disabilities from racial and ethnic minority background, research methodologies, and neurorehabilitation. She has written several rehabilitation-related articles and book chapters. Lee is a current member of the Satellite Center on Adherence and Self-Determination.

Russell F. Lim is a Health Sciences Clinical Professor at the University of California, Davis School of Medicine (UCD SOM), Department of Psychiatry and Behavioral Sciences, and Medical Director of Turning Point Integrated Services Agency. He is the editor of *The Clinical Manual of Cultural Psychiatry*, published by American Psychiatric Press, Inc. (APPI) in 2006. He has been the course director of a Continuing Medical Education course on Cultural Psychiatry at the American Psychiatric Association (APA) Annual Meeting for 16 years. Dr. Lim was the Association of Academic Psychiatry's Teacher of the Year in 2008 for Region X. In his role as Chair of the Diversity Advisory Committee (DAC), founded in 1999, he received the American College of Psychiatrists' (ACP) Award for Creativity in Psychiatric Education in 2007. Dr. Lim's four-year resident curriculum on Cultural Psychiatry was recognized by the American Association of Directors of Psychiatry Residency Training as a model curriculum in Cultural Psychiatry in 2010. He has been a board member of the American Association of Community Psychiatrists since 1998. He has published over 30 articles and book chapters, and was co-editor with Francis Lu, MD, of the July/August 2008 issue of *Academic Psychiatry* on Psychiatric Education and Culture.

Francis G. Lu is the Luke & Grace Kim Endowed Professor in Cultural Psychiatry, Director of Cultural Psychiatry, and Associate Chair for Medical Student Education in the Department of Psychiatry & Behavioral Sciences at University of California, Davis since July 2009. He is also Assistant Dean for Faculty Diversity for the School of Medicine. As a Distinguished Fellow of the APA, Dr. Lu has contributed to the areas of cultural psychiatry, psychiatric education, media and psychiatry, and the interface of psychiatry and religion/spirituality through his presentations and more than 70 publications. He has participated on expert panels and advisory committees on diversity, cultural competence, and mental health disparities sponsored by the APA, the Office of the Surgeon General, HHS Office of Minority Health, HRSA, SAMHSA Center for Mental Health Services, the California Endowment, the Templeton Foundation, the California State Department of

Mental Health, and UCSF. For example, Dr. Lu has served on the California State Department of Mental Health Cultural Competence Advisory Committee since 1996. The APA awarded him the 2001 Kun-Po Soo Award for his work in integrating Asian issues into psychiatry; in 2002, he received a Special APA Presidential Commendation from President Richard Harding for his work in cross-cultural psychiatry. From 2002 to 2007, Dr. Lu chaired the APA Council on Minority Mental Health and Health Disparities. In 2008, the American Psychiatric Foundation awarded him one of its Advancing Minority Mental Health Awards. In 2008, the Association for Academic Psychiatry awarded him its Lifetime Achievement Award.

Sarah P. Lynch is a graduate of Columbia University School of Social Work. She is currently the Clinical Team Leader at the PIER Program at Maine Medical Center, an early intervention treatment program and research study for adolescents and young adults with early symptoms of psychosis. Sarah has been co-facilitating psychoeducational multifamily groups for eight years and currently supervises the PMFG component of the EDIPPP multi-site study. She is a Senior Trainer at the PIER Training Institute and has trained and supervised clinicians nationwide on the PMFG model.

Nelma A. Mason is a graduate of the University of Southern Maine School of Nursing, with more than 30 years of experience. She has worked almost exclusively in the area of mental health/psychiatric nursing and has been certified by ANCC as a Psychiatric and Mental Health Nurse since 1988. She has worked across the spectrum of mental health service settings. She has been employed at Maine Medical Center in the PIER Program for three years and is a co-facilitator of a psychoeducation multifamily group. She was first trained as a facilitator in 2000 while working for an agency providing residential and support services to people with persistent and severe mental illness.

William R. McFarlane received his MD from Columbia University, College of Physicians and Surgeons, and completed his residency and fellowship at Albert Einstein College of Medicine. He is Director of the Center for Psychiatric Research at Maine Medical Center in Portland, ME, and a Professor at Tufts University School of Medicine. His areas of research and practice include family psychoeducation and other psychosocial interventions for severe psychiatric disorders, as well as pioneering efforts in the area of early detection and intervention of psychotic disorders in youth and young adults. Dr. McFarlane teaches family therapy and the psychobiology of mental illnesses to medical students and residents at Maine Medical Center in partnership with the Tufts University School of Medicine and the University of Vermont.

John J. McLaughlin is currently an Assistant Professor of Social Work at Ramapo College in New Jersey and specializes in community mental health. He received his MSW from Hunter College, CUNY, in 1979 and then worked for 30 years at South Beach Psychiatric Center, a NY State Office of Mental Health facility that serves the seriously mentally ill in New York City. At South Beach, Mr. McLaughlin worked in a number of different positions, including several administrative ones, and in both inpatient and outpatient settings. Of note, he served as Director of Social Work, co-founded South Beach's Critical Incident Response Team, and implemented and supervised South Beach's first assertive community treatment (ACT) team. He is a member of the National Alliance on Mental Illness (NAMI).

Steven Miccio is the Executive Director of People, Inc., in Poughkeepsie, NY, a consumer-operated mental health advocacy organization. A consumer leader, Steve has recently been developing a white paper authorized by over 200 consumers in New York State that demands quality services and renewed values in mental health services. Steve was diagnosed with bipolar disorder in the 1990s and has been an advocate for eliminating stigma and discrimination for many years.

April Naturale is a traumatic stress specialist with a 25 year history in health/mental health administration. She received her Master's in Social Work from Columbia University and her doctorate in Clinical Social Work from New York University. She directed Project Liberty, the NY 9/11 disaster mental health response and spent several years in the Gulf Coast after the large-scale hurricanes that devastated the area. Dr. Naturale has provided disaster consultation and training throughout the United States and internationally across three continents. She helped launch SAMHSA's National Suicide Prevention Lifeline and recently directed the BP Deepwater Horizon Oil Spill Distress Helpline network, as well as the 9/11 10th Anniversary Healing and Remembrance program. Dr. Naturale currently works with ICF International, where her primary responsibility as is a Senior Advisor to the Substance Abuse and Mental Health Services Administration's Disaster Technical Assistance Center.

Richard Pulice has had over 30 years of experience in mental health, working for state and local governments, not-for-profit agencies, and in private practice. He has published many articles regarding services for the seriously mentally ill, in both the popular press and in professional journals, and is a frequent speaker at state, national, and international conferences, advocating for persons with a mental illness. Formerly an Assistant Professor at the University at Albany and SUNY Empire State College, he is now Profesor and Chair of the Social Work Department and the Director of the Institute for Community Research and Training at the College of Saint Rose in Albany, NY.

Robert J. Ronis is the Douglas Danford Bond Professor and Chairman of the Department of Psychiatry at University Hospitals Case Medical Center/CWRU School of Medicine, and Co-Director of the Center for Evidence-Based Practices at Case Western Reserve University. A CWRU School of Medicine graduate, Dr. Ronis completed his residency in Psychiatry at University Hospitals. As a National Health Services Corps volunteer, he was the first full-time psychiatrist in southeastern Ohio, before returning to Case to develop its Community Psychiatry program in 1990. He was Residency Training Director and Vice Chair from 1996 to 2004. Dr. Ronis was co-founder of the Public Academic Liaison (PAL) Program, a collaboration for clinical service and community-based research with Cuyahoga County Community Mental Health Board. Among his other innovations are the biennial All-Ohio Institute on Community Psychiatry and the Mental Health Executive Leadership Programs in collaboration with the Weatherhead School at CWRU. Dr. Ronis was named a Distinguished Fellow of the APA in 1996 and an Exemplary Practitioner by the NAMI in 2002. He is a Past President of the Ohio Psychiatric Association and has served on the Assembly of the APA and on the board of the American Association of Community Psychiatrists. In January 2010, he was elected as a Director for the American Board of Psychiatry and Neurology.

W. Patrick Sullivan serves as Professor at the Indiana University School of Social Work. He also served as Director of the Indiana Division of Mental Health and Addiction from 1994 to 1998. While earning a Ph.D. at the University of Kansas, Sullivan helped develop the Strengths model of social work practice and has extended the model in mental health and addictions treatment. He has over 70 professional publications on a diverse range of topics. He received the Distinguished Hoosier award from Governor Frank O'Bannon in 1997 and earned the Sagamore of the Wabash from Governor Joseph Kernan in 2004.

Philip E. Thomas is a licensed clinical social worker, Department of Veteran Affairs, and VISN 11 Network Homeless Coordinator for the Veterans Health Administration. He holds an MSW from Indiana University and has over 25 years' experience in community mental health. He has published on issues related to homelessness and social work practice and theory. He frequently presents on topics related to ending veteran homelessness. He currently is involved in policy development and oversight as it relates to interagency plans to end homelessness.

Hendry Ton received his BA degree in Psychology and Molecular Cell Biology at the University of CA, Berkeley. He graduated from the UC Berkeley–San Francisco Joint Medical Program where he attained an MS degree in Health and Medical Science, a Division of Public Health and an MD degree and completed his residency at UC San Francisco. Currently, Dr. Ton is an Associate Clinical Professor of Psychiatry and Director of Education at the Center for Reducing Health Disparities at UC Davis, where he has authored a curriculum for health care leaders entitled "Providing Quality Health Care with CLAS: A Curriculum for Developing Culturally and Linguistically Appropriate Services." This program has lead to culturally and linguistically appropriate system changes at academic, county, and state health organizations in California. He is also a co-founder and the medical director of the Transcultural Wellness Center, a community clinic that specializes in serving the mental health needs of Sacramento's diverse Asian and Pacific Islander communities. He has received the UC Davis Chancellor's Achievement Award for Diversity and Community in 2005 and the 2007 Dean's Award for Excellence in Community Engagement for his work with communities, ethnic minorities, and cultural competence. Dr. Ton is also the Psychiatry Clerkship Director and he leads the UC Davis medical school curriculum on cultural competence and professionalism. This effort helped the Department of Psychiatry receive the prestigious ACP's Award for Creativity in Psychiatric Education for its work on cultural competence in resident and medical student education. Dr. Tonhas has presented nationally on the topics of cultural competence and curricular development and has also received teaching awards for his work with medical students, residents, and faculty.

Kathleen West is a public health professional with expertise working with programs serving at-risk families, maternal and child health, intergenerational trauma, and public mental health and addiction issues. For more than three decades, Kathleen has worked with systems of care that serve high-risk families while based in Los Angeles and Geneva, Switzerland. Her particular interest is in multidisciplinary interventions that focus on developmental and mental health issues related to trauma exposure. Her educational background includes degrees in biology and anthropology from Kalamazoo College, and Master's and doctoral degrees from the UCLA School of Public Health. Dr. West's extensive consulting experience spans 30 years and includes prevention, secondary intervention, and treatment programming, evaluation and data design, policy development and implementation, research, advocacy, training, and technical assistance. She has authored a number of articles and chapters, including WHO monographs. She is affiliated with the Center for Innovation and Research on Veterans and Military Families, USC School of Social Work, as a Research and Policy Analyst.

Kimberly A. Williams is the Director of the Center for Policy, Advocacy, and Education at the Mental Health Association of New York City (MHA-NYC). In this role, she directs the Geriatric Mental Health Alliance of New York, an advocacy and education organization with over 3,000 members, which she co-founded in 2004. She also oversees the work of the Veterans' Mental Health Coalition of New York City, which was co-founded by MHA-NYC in 2009. She is an adjunct lecturer at the NYU Silver School of Social Work. Ms. Williams received her Master's degree in Social Work from Columbia University, where she was a founding member of the Student Social Workers' Alliance for a Progressive Society.

William H. Wilson is Professor of Psychiatry at the Oregon Health & Science University, where he teaches and practices patient-centered psychiatry. A graduate of the University of Pennsylvania School of Medicine, he completed residency training in psychiatry at the University of Wisconsin–Madison. He has served on the faculties of the University of Wisconsin, University of Pittsburgh, and the Medical College of Pennsylvania. Previously he has designed and directed treatment programs and served as principal investigator in NIMH-sponsored research regarding pharmacological treatment of schizophrenia. He is a Distinguished Fellow of the APA and is listed in *U.S. News'* "Top Doctors," the *Best Doctors in America*, and *Who's Who in America*. Recognition includes the "Exemplary Psychiatrist Award" from the National Alliance for the Mentally Ill, State of Oregon's "2000 Mental Health Award for Excellence" from the state of Oregon, and "Nancy C. A. Roeske, MD Certificate of Recognition for Excellence in Medical Student Education" from the APA. Interests outside of psychiatry include his family, social justice, animal rights, vegetarianism, the environment, and the performing arts.

Preface

This book builds upon its predecessor, *Community Mental Health: Challenges for the 21st Century*, and provides the most up-to-date research and treatment models in the field. The first edition distinguished itself as one of the most comprehensive books about community mental health. In this edition, readers will find that over two-thirds of the chapters are new, and all of the chapters have been updated to reflect emerging trends and research. An important dimension of this book is the focus provided by multiple disciplines: the breadth of the contributors represents a wide range of professions: nursing, social work, psychology, psychiatry, public health, sociology, and the law. The inclusion of so many diverse perspectives is central to the creation of a nuanced and comprehensive analysis of community mental health, and this text is relevant for students and practitioners from across disciplines. This book is a resource for students preparing to become mental health professionals, for individuals currently working as practitioners in community mental health settings, and for policy planners and advocates engaged in the evaluation and development of programs in the human services.

Central to the overarching framework of the text is its focus on the recovery philosophy. This book, as with the first edition, locates issues of serious mental illness within the context of the recovery movement, a paradigm shift in community mental health that challenged destructive and stigmatizing stereotypes of mental illness and infused treatment and research with principles based on hope, respect, and a commitment to humane treatment.

When we published the first edition of this text in 2006, we examined how the events of September 11, 2001 changed the world. In the wake of 9/11, post-traumatic stress disorders became part of the lexicon of everyday life, as the consequences of that attack destabilized the world and extended the concept of vulnerable to the entire population. At the writing of this book, we note the effect of the economic crisis on mental health and well-being. The global economic crisis that began in 2008 has had a significant impact on community mental health services. Many Americans are experiencing emotional distress as they struggle with poverty and unemployment, and the recession has forced financial concerns front and center and created a class of the "new poor"; in 2010, 46.2 million people were officially classified as being in poverty, the highest number ever recorded. At the same point in time, funds for services have been slashed. A recent report issued by the NAMI cites severe funding cuts between 2009 and 2011 resulting in diminished services for vulnerable individuals. Today, the social context for community mental health services is stressed and stretched to the limit, and yet community mental health has never been more important or more necessary.

The book is divided into six parts. Part One, entitled "From Stigma to Recovery" provides the overarching philosophical orientation for the book, which is a commitment to recovery as the guiding perspective that informs best practices in this field and which serves as the focal point for diverse stakeholders, including consumers, policymakers, advocates, practitioners, educators, families, and friends. The first chapter, "Recovery and Stigma in People with Psychiatric Disabilities," is authored by two leading scholars in the field. It provides a relational analysis of stigma and recovery and examines the intersection of these two concepts. The chapter explicates and advances the theoretical development of the recovery model and proposes suggestions to promote recovery and confront stigma. Chapter 2 is entitled "Marginal No More: Serious Mental Illness, Sexual Orientation, and Gender Preference." Noting that members of marginalized communities confront multiple layers of stress and stigmatization on a daily basis, the chapter provides an analysis of the dynamics of the dual stigma of being an LGBT person living with a major mental illness, and describes an innovative community mental health program, the Rainbow Heights Club, that was developed to address the unique psychosocial needs of this population. The third chapter in this part, entitled "Where do we go from here? The Mental Health Consumer Movement in the United States," contextualizes the discussion historically within the policy concerns leading to the passage of the Community Mental Health Act of 1963 and the subsequent advances in policy and practice. It discusses the advent and development of self-help groups and peer support and documents the progress that has been made in meeting the needs and desires of those recovering from mental illness.

Part Two of the book is "Emerging Trends in Community Mental Health" and is comprised of two new chapters. The first of these, Chapter 4, is about one of the most important areas in community mental health: the treatment needs of our military veterans and their families. We now know that the wars in Iraq and Afghanistan have taken a tremendous toll on the psychological well-being of hundreds of thousands of veterans. This chapter, entitled "Emerging Community Mental Health Challenges: Meeting the Needs of Veterans and Families Impacted by Military Service," is written by an outstanding team that includes a social work educator who is a retired Air Force officer, a public health practitioner and scholar, and the Dean of the School of Social Work at the University of Southern California. Key elements include the historical context for mental health care to the military, the influence of military culture, stigma, and the special treatments needs of this population. The second chapter in this part, "Community Mental Health: Innovations in Diversion from Prosecution of People with Mental Illness," addresses one of the most important concerns in mental health today: the issue of forensic mental health. The prison system has replaced the asylum as society's method of large-scale institutional warehousing, with estimates that over 1.25 million inmates suffer from serious mental health problems. This chapter provides an informed and well-substantiated discussion of innovative models to promote community mental health treatment as an alternative to criminal prosecution for persons with mental illness.

Part Three of the book, "Community Mental Health across the Life Cycle," contains three chapters, all of which are new. The first of these three chapters, entitled "Community Mental Health with Children and Youth," is written by a social work educator who is also a lawyer. It is an excellent discussion that identifies the psychosocial risk factors for childhood mental illness and provides a historical analysis of social responses to childhood mental health needs.

The chapter examines a number of serious public health concerns, such as bullying, and explicates best-practice models. The second chapter in this section is entitled "Family Psychoeducation in the Treatment of Mental Illness: Historical Context, Current Practice and Future Directions." This chapter, authored by a distinguished and interdisciplinary team that includes one of the pioneers of multi-family groups with serious mental illness, describes the use of multi-family psychoeducation groups, a treatment approach that helped to usher in a paradigm shift in the field that has moved away from a perspective that located the "blame" for mental illness on the family to embracing a philosophy that joins with families in working toward recovery. Chapter 8, which is the third chapter of this section, is entitled "Meeting the Mental Health Challenges of the Elder Boom." It is an excellent discussion of the mental health needs of older adults. Written by leading advocates for aging and mental health issues, it combines the authors' passion about the well-being of older adults with comprehensive research and is a very strong addition to this edition. Readers will get an excellent overview of the policy and practice implications related to the mental health needs of the fastest-growing segment of the American population, older adults.

Part Four is entitled "Diversity and Community Mental Health" and contains four chapters, three of which are new to this book. The first chapter of the section is about African–Americans and mental health. Authored by a scholar from NYU's School of Social Work, it presents a comprehensive discussion of the intersection of racism and mental health care in American history and provides an incisive analysis of the relationship of white privilege to mental health problems. The Anti-Racist Model, a promising treatment model to address institutional racism and personal bias, is described, along with implications for best practices. The next chapter, "Community Mental Health Services to Asian–Americans," is authored by a team of psychiatrists who have expertise in issues of culture and diversity. This chapter provides an extremely useful analysis of culturally competent community mental health care, examines the prevalence of mental health diagnoses among Asian–American Pacific Islanders, barriers to services, stigma, and cultural and linguistic challenges. Readers will significantly extend their knowledge base about the cultural health beliefs and mental health needs of Asian–Americans. The third and final chapter in this part is about community mental health services to Latinos. The chapter presents an overview of the sociodemographic diversity of the Latino population, reviews current epidemiological studies documenting the prevalence of mental health disorders in Latino adults, discusses mental health care disparities, provides examples of culturally competent mental health treatments, and presents public policy recommendations for community mental health care delivery to Latinos. The final chapter of this part, Chapter 12, is entitled "Community Mental Health: Cross-Cultural Mental Health Response in Disasters." The author has national and international experience in disaster relief and she is the former Director of Project Liberty, New York's 9/11 disaster mental health response. In this chapter, she shares her knowledge and experience providing mental health services around the world and examines challenges in implementing cross-cultural community mental health initiatives.

Part Five is entitled "Best Practices in Community Mental Health" and is comprised of four chapters, each of which provide the most up-to-date research on best practice treatment models in community mental health. The first chapter in this part, "Assertive Community Treatment: An Evidence-Based Practice and Its Continuing Evolution," examines the development and application of ACT in the treatment of severe and persistent mental illness. ACT teams have been shown to promote psychiatric stabilization with persons who have serious mental illness and to enable them to live independently in the community. The next chapter in this part is "Evidence-Based Treatment for Adults with Co-occurring Mental and Substance Use Disorders: Current Practice and Future Directions." Authored by an interdisciplinary team that brings together expertise in psychiatry, social work research, and substance abuse training, this chapter is an immensely readable and well-argued paper that provides considerable support for the use of an integrated treatment model for clients with co-occurring mental illness and addiction. "Neuropsychiatric Perspectives on Community Mental Health: Theory and Practice" is the next chapter in this part. The author is a psychiatrist who is committed to person-centered psychiatry and to the application of neuropsychiatry in the context of treating the whole person. The chapter provides an excellent and very readable overview of psychiatric disorders and the psychiatric tools that are available to treat them. This chapter will be immediately useful for all students and practitioners in this field. The part concludes with a chapter entitled "The Practice Effectiveness of Case Management Services for Homeless Persons with Alcohol, Drug, or Mental Health Problems." The relationship of homelessness and mental illness is well known, with estimates by the Substance Abuse and Mental Health Services Administration that approximately 20–25% of the homeless population in the United States suffer from some form of severe mental illness. Authored by a highly experienced practitioner/scholar in community mental health, this chapter is a comprehensive analysis of practice and policy considerations with this population and discusses evidence-based case management models and approaches for homeless individuals with substance use and mental-health disorders.

The final part of the book is Part Six, "Community Mental Health: Organizational and Policy Issues," and consists of two chapters. The first of these, "Community Mental Health: Policy and Practice," is written by an educator with over 25 years of policy and practice experience with clients with serious mental illness. This chapter serves as an excellent bookend for the text, as it weaves together the policy and practice considerations that are presented throughout the book. Students and practitioners seeking a comprehensive synthesis of the relevant issues, including important historical developments in community mental health, will find it in this chapter. The final chapter of the text is entitled "Mental Health Leadership in a Turbulent World." It provides an incisive analysis of the challenges of providing community mental health services in a post-recession world. Community mental health services have been badly battered by the funding cutbacks in the wake of an unstable economy that went into free-fall in 2008. While elected officials play politics with government funding streams, and various stakeholders, including consumers and policymakers, advocate for humane mental health care, the day-to-day community mental health enterprise is recreated in new and emerging formations. Leadership is a central factor in successful program design and delivery. This chapter raises the essential questions that define skilled and creative leadership in these turbulent times.

In conclusion, this text contains eighteen chapters, all of which bring together cutting-edge research, policy analysis, and practice models in the planning and delivery of community mental health services. The breadth of topics covered, the inclusion of multiple disciplines, and the varied expertise of the many contributors—practitioners, educators, consumers, policymakers, and advocates—enriches the book. We are confident that readers will find this volume to provide a timely and challenging collection of readings for students and practitioners of community mental health.

Acknowledgments

Throughout many years, as mental health practitioners and as educators, we have seen that the field of community mental health attracts a special kind of person: passionate, curious, adventurous, and fueled with a fire to bring about positive change. Community mental health is a tough field in which to work; it is not glamorous, and the demands are considerable. Fiscal constraints and bureaucratic requirements create pressure, and, although people do get better, progress can be slow and uneven. Despite these challenges, the best community mental health professionals bring a message of hope and optimism and a deep commitment to promoting the self-determination and dignity of persons who struggle with serious mental illness. This book is in appreciation of all of those individuals who make a difference in the lives of others.

The authors express their deep gratitude to Dana Bliss, Senior Editor of Routledge Mental Health, whose encouragement, and guidance made this edition possible. The ongoing support from Diana Alspach, Zewde Petros, Vicki Shonbrun, Toni deLorge, and Jan Orzeck was invaluable. We dedicate this book to Daniel, Adrienne, Silvia, and Elizabeth: You are always with us on this path, illuminating it with love.

Part One

From Stigma to Recovery

Chapter 1

Recovery and Stigma in People with Psychiatric Disabilities

Patrick Corrigan and Eun-Jeong Lee

INTRODUCTION

The ideas of recovery and stigma have mutual effects on each other. Recovery has reintroduced goal directedness, hope, and self-determination into comprehensive discussions about mental health and its service system. Scholarly discussion about "recovery" seems to be entering its second generation, seeking better definition with empirically sound proxies as a base for understanding strategies meant to enhance it. Stigma is a major hurdle to recovery. People with serious mental illness are sometimes unable to achieve important life goals when the public endorses stereotypes about their disorders and discriminates against them as a result. Ironically, just as stigma impedes recovery, so recovery challenges stigma. Stigma is being squelched, as all stakeholders come to understand and adopt the principles of recovery. This chapter is a brief introduction into the intersection of the two ideas. It begins with the most contemporary definitions of recovery, leading to directions for further theoretical development. Social cognitive models of the stigma of mental illness are then discussed, outlining where definitions of recovery and stigma intersect. The second half of the chapter proposes ways to deal with these ideas: to promote recovery and confront stigma. Note that this chapter is about people with serious mental illnesses, perhaps more accurately defined as psychiatrically disabled. The chapter concerns itself with psychiatric disability; as a result of these kinds of illness, people are unable to achieve major life goals such as working in a meaningful job, living independently, and enjoying intimate relationships.

HISTORICAL AND THEORETICAL OVERVIEW OF RECOVERY

As outlined in Table 1.1, recovery has been described in two ways. First, recovery is understood in terms of *outcomes*; people with significant psychiatric disability are able to totally overcome or learn to live with psychiatric symptoms and dysfunctions (Ralph & Corrigan, 2005). As a result, they are often successful in such important life goals as full-time employment and independent living. In addition, recovery is seen as a *process*. As such, recovery has reintroduced such important processes as hope and well-being into rehabilitation.

Table 1.1 *Elements of the Two Definitions of Recovery*

Recovery as outcome	Recovery as process
Benchmarks of outcome	Important benchmark processes
Relief from psychiatric symptoms	Hope about the future
Independence in matters related to housing	Psychological well-being
At least halftime work or school	Goal orientation
Regular social and recreational activities	Personal empowerment

To put these definitions into perspective, we begin back to the turn of the 19th century when early perspectives on diagnosis and prognosis were being formed. Emil Kraepelin, the German psychiatrist and father of modern psychopathology, first gave voice to the pessimistic ideas about serious mental illness that affected almost a century of subsequent ideas and services. According to Kraepelin (1919), the prognosis of people diagnosed with schizophrenia and other psychoses is expected to be marked by a progressively degenerative, downhill course that is unresponsive to treatment. This perspective was evident in earlier versions of the *Diagnostic and Statistical Manual* (*DSM*). Consider how this prognostic paradigm might play out in long-term follow-up research. If Kraepelin were correct, following people diagnosed with schizophrenia between the ages of 20 to 30 years should yield the same decrepit end point: overwhelmed by psychotic symptoms and unable to maintain major roles in such important life domains as work, housing, and relationships. Researchers began just this line of research in the 1950s (cf. Corrigan & Calabrese, 2005, for a more thorough discussion of long-term follow-up research). Briefly, these studies identified adults who met diagnostic criteria of the time for schizophrenia and who were relatively young. They then repeated regular assessments to determine what became of these individuals. At the 20- and 30-year marks, they roughly found a rule of thirds (Ciompi, Harding, & Lehtinen, 2010; Harding, 1988). About one-third of the sample seemed to have moved beyond the mental health system entirely and was pursuing life in what might be construed as "normal": competitive jobs, independent housing, and long-term relationships. About one-third of the sample achieved a semblance of these goals with the support of a competent mental health system. About one-third of the sample seemed to show a continued undulating course marked by periods of symptoms and significant disabilities interspersed among periods of relative remission. Note that only a third of this last third (or one-ninth of the entire sample) needed regular hospitalization to manage their illness. Hence, only about 10% of the group that Kraepelin predicted would end up demented actually showed any syndrome that approximated this endpoint. It is the rule, and not the exception, that people with the most serious of mental illnesses do recover.

Recovery as Process

One of the purposes of recovery as a movement that emerged from consumers, survivors, and ex-patients was to reject pessimism and re-inject hope into their lives. As a result, recovery from this perspective is less concerned about outcomes—whether the person achieves some kind of symptom- and disability-free endpoint—and more about processes (Davidson, Tondora, Lawless, O'Connell, & Rowe, 2009; Silverstein & Bellack, 2008). Recovery is more about how a person with mental illness would pursue a meaningful life. What actions and activities foster an environment where a person's search for this kind of life can be supported? The wisdom of leaders in the consumer movement illustrates what is meant by a meaningful life.

> Recovery is a process, a way of life, an attitude, and a way of approaching the day's challenges. It is not a perfectly linear process. . . . The need is to meet the challenge of the disability and to re-establish a new and valued sense of integrity and purpose within and beyond the limits of the disability; the aspiration is to live, work, and love in a community in which one makes a significant contribution.
>
> (Deegan, 1988)

> Having some hope is crucial to recovery; none of us would strive if we believed it a futile effort . . . I believe that if we confront our illnesses with courage and struggle with our symptoms persistently, we can overcome our handicaps to live independently, learn skills, and contribute to society, the society that has traditionally abandoned us.
>
> (Leete, 1988)

An essential element of recovery as a process is empowerment. People must have the power to act on decisions that produce an optimistic future which reflects their personal goals (Corrigan, 2002). Research has shown empowerment to be a complex phenomenon that includes a sense of personal control over one's environment and a feeling of agency in one's world (Rogers, Chamberlin, Ellison, & Crean, 1997; Segal, Silverman, & Temkin, 1995). Studies have also indicated that these forms of empowerment are highly correlated with measures of recovery that reflect process (Corrigan, Giffort, Rashid, Leary, & Okeke, 1999; Corrigan, Salzer, Ralph, Sangster, & Keck, 2004).

WHAT ARE THE HARMFUL EFFECTS OF STIGMA?

Although the quality and effectiveness of mental health treatments and services have improved greatly over the past 50 years, many people who might benefit from these services fail to complete the recovery process, either by not obtaining needed services or not fully adhering to treatment regimens. Stigma is a complex phenomenon, and so we adopt a cognitive behavioral model of stigma and argue that individuals with mental illness may have varied responses to stigma, depending on the parameters of the situation.

Cognitive Behavioral Model of Stigma

Stigma associated with mental illness is multidimensional and based on a complex process. This complexity can be best described using a cognitive behavioral model that has three components: cognition, affect, and behavior (see Figure 1.1). First, *stereotypes* can be understood as a cognitive component in this model. Stereotypes are knowledge structures that the public

5

has learned about a marked social group (Augoustinos, Ahrens, & Innes, 1994; Esses, Haddock, & Zanna, 1994; Hilton & von Hippel, 1996; Judd & Park, 1996; Krueger, 1996; Mullen, Rozell, & Johnson, 1996). They are often framed as seemingly fact-based beliefs, with a negative evaluative component. For example, commonly held stereotypes about people with mental illness include violence (people with mental illness are dangerous), incompetence (they are incapable of independent living or real work), and blame (because of weak character, they are responsible for the onset and continuation of their disorders) (Brockington, Hall, Levings, & Murphy, 1993; Corrigan et al., 2000; Hamre, Dahl, & Malt, 1994; Link & Phelan, 2001). People learn stereotypes about people with mental illness through contact or exposure, such as images or information provided by the mass media. *Prejudice* is the affective reaction regarding a particular group based on endorsing stereotypes about that group. Dangerousness is strongly associated with fear and, in this case, can be exacerbated by beliefs that people with mental illness are unpredictable. Negative emotions lead to discrimination, which is understood as the behavioral result of prejudice in the cognitive behavioral model (Crocker, Major, & Steele, 1998).

Discriminatory behavior manifests itself as negative action against the outgroup or exclusively positive action for the ingroup. Most notably, outgroup discrimination may appear as avoidance—i.e., not associating with people from the outgroup. In order to escape potential danger, members of the general public will seek to avoid them. Avoidance is probably most

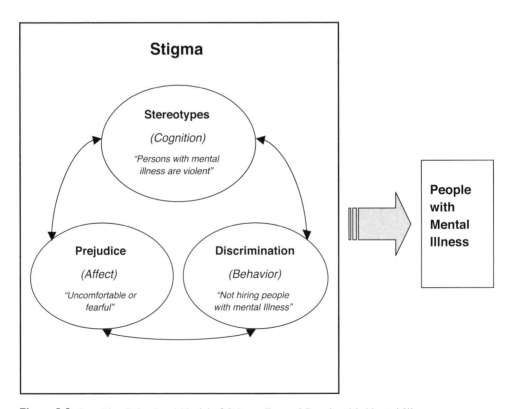

Figure 1.1 *Cognitive Behavioral Model of Stigma Toward People with Mental Illness*

egregious when acted on by employers and landlords, because this discrimination is punitive in form and experienced as taking away rightful opportunities (choosing not to hire anyone from the group considered dangerous) or reacting to them aversively (agreeing with locking individuals with mental illness in isolated place). Research has identified a variety of prejudices and discriminations that reflect the stigma associated with mental illness. Some of these are listed in Table 1.2, including those most commonly observed in the research literature (Corrigan & Wassel, 2008; Peluso Ede & Blay, 2009).

Types of Stigma

The convergence of research has led to four types of stigma relevant to health conditions and especially mental illness. We have distinguished two primary forms of stigma, namely *public stigma* (what a naïve public does to the stigmatized group when they endorse the prejudice of that group) and *self-stigma* (what members of a stigmatized group may do to themselves if they internalize the public stigma) (Corrigan & Penn, 1999; Corrigan & Watson, 2004). In this chapter, we will introduce two additional types of stigma: *label avoidance* and *structural stigma*.

Public stigma occurs when members of the general population endorse prejudice and act in a discriminating manner (Corrigan & Penn, 1999). It represents what the public does to people known to have mental illness. The prejudices and discriminations in Table 1.2 serve as an aggregation of instances that might harm a person with mental illness. For example, individuals described as seeking assistance for depression were rated as more emotionally unstable, less

Table 1.2 *Stereotypes/Prejudices of Mental Illness and the Resulting Discrimination*

Stereotypes/prejudices	Discriminations
Dangerousness	Avoidance and withdrawal
People with mental illness are unpredictable and dangerous	Employers do not hire
Those with mental illness are violent	Landlords do not lease
	Members of the community do not socially interact
Responsibility	Coercion
Blame and shame	Outpatient commitment
Onset responsibility	Forced medication
Offset responsibility	
Character/moral weakness	
Incompetence	Segregation
People with mental illness can't work or live independently	State hospitals
Those with mental illness can't function as members of the community	Mental health ghettoes

interesting, and less confident than people with back pain and people not seeking help for depression (Ben-Porath, 2002).

Self-stigma occurs when people internalize the prejudice and discriminate against themselves. Self-stigma has been divided into progressive stages known as the "three As": *aware*, *agree*, and *apply* (Corrigan & Calabrese, 2005; Corrigan, Watson, & Barr, 2006). Applying or internalizing stereotypes has two harmful effects. Cognitively and emotionally, internalizing stigma can hurt self-esteem ("I am not a good person; I am not keeping up with my other workers because I am mentally ill.") and lessen self-efficacy ("I can't keep up with my workers because I have schizophrenia."). Behaviorally, the three As lead to the "why try" effect (Corrigan, Larson, & Rusch, 2009). "Why should I try to get a promotion? I am not worthy of it." Or alternatively, "Why try to seek out a training program? I am unable to be successful."

Label avoidance refers to a third type of stigma that blocks service use for people in need of psychiatric care. One way in which people are publicly labeled is by associating with a mental health program ("Hey, that's Ms. Jones. She is coming out of that psychiatrist's office. She must be nuts!"). To avoid labeling, some people refrain from seeking services that would be helpful, or do not continue to use services once initiated. Some people call this nonadherence: namely, the person does not follow medical or other psychotherapeutic directions as prescribed by a professional (Lacro, Dunn, Dolder, Leckband, & Jeste, 2002; Velligan et al., 2006). Adherence is actually a complex construct affected by stigma (Ayalon, Areán, & Alvidrez, 2005; Corrigan, 2004; Sirey et al., 2001), but also by other issues including poor mental health literacy and absence of culturally sensitive services (Jorm, 2000).

Structural stigma is defined one way as the absence of appropriate services for people with mental illness. The idea mostly evolved from the field of sociology and manifests itself in two ways: (1) policies of private and governmental institutions that intentionally restrict the opportunities, and (2) policies of institutions that yield unintended consequences which hinder the options of people with mental illness (Corrigan, Markowitz, & Watson, 2004; Pincus, 1996, 1999a, b). Intentional institutional discrimination manifests itself as rules, policies, and procedures of private and public entities in positions of power that consciously and purposefully restrict the rights and opportunities of minority groups. For example, Jim Crow Laws were largely enacted by Southern states to explicitly undermine African–American rights in such vital areas as employment, education, and public accommodation. An example related to mental health would be statutes that restrict a person's parental rights because of past history of mental illness (Corrigan et al., 2005).

WHAT IS THERE TO DO ABOUT RECOVERY?

Many would say recovery has become the first principle in psychiatric rehabilitation programs. A panoply of values and directions have emerged to guide people to a recovery-based service system. Less obvious, however, is direction about what to do about recovery. What skills, for example, might people use to promote their recovery? Or, more broadly put, what approaches and strategies might a program include to facilitate consumer recovery? We briefly review the status of acknowledged evidence-based practices (EBPs), as well as the ongoing dynamic for identifying other approaches with a putative evidence base. We then list specific skills that providers might adopt to actualize EBPs and their positive effects.

Evidence-Based Practices

There are costs and benefits to EBPs. In terms of benefits, a focus on evidence-based approaches assures that consumers will be involved only in services that have been shown to be effective. EBPs help all stakeholders choose which practice will be more effective, as well as diminish unintended egregious effects. In addition, facing ever-restricted budgets that fail to sufficiently fund mental health service needs, public administrators can now decide to invest their resources in proven services (Goldman et al., 2001). Disadvantages in an evidence-based approach to identifying effective services have also been cited. Some advocates have noted that the criteria for classifying a service as effective and worthwhile—an empirical evidence base—reflects the priorities of the research community, but not necessarily of the community of consumers, survivors, and ex-patients (Fisher & Ahern, 2002; Frese, Stanley, Kress, & Vogel-Scibilia, 2001; Marty, Rapp, McHugo, & Whitley, 2008). In particular, traditional empirical research does not necessarily include the kinds of epistemology that led to the development of such important ideas of the consumer movement as empowerment and recovery (Van Tosh, Ralph, & Campbell, 2004). Moreover, empirical research approaches do not easily crosswalk with more ethereal constructs such as spirituality (Plante & Sherman, 2001; Weisman de Mamani, Tuchman, & Duarte, 2010), a construct that has a central role in many consumer conceptions of recovery. Finally, the excitement about evidence-based initiatives puts several possible intervention programs for people with mental illness into limbo, because definitive research has yet to be concluded. A prominent example is consumer-operated services; although both consumer and mental health advocates have endorsed this approach as a fruitful avenue for meeting some of the needs of people with serious psychiatric disorders, research that meets standards for EBPs still seems lacking (Davidson et al., 1999; Goldstrom et al., 2006).

Two consensus-based efforts informed the EBPs listed below. The first, called Implementing Evidence-Based Project, was sponsored by four groups including the Robert Wood Johnson Foundation and the Center for Mental Health Services (Drake et al., 2001; Mueser, Torrey, Lynde, Singer, & Drake, 2003; Torrey et al., 2001). The project sought to improve service access through development of standardized implementation packages, created in concert with different stakeholders including, consumers, family members, providers, and administrators. The second review, called the Patient Outcomes Research Team, sought similar goals by extensively reviewing the research literature on treatments and services for people with schizophrenia (Lehman et al., 2004). Six EBPs have been identified: illness management skills (Mueser, Corrigan, Hilton, & Tanzman, 2002), assertive community treatment (Phillips et al., 2001), supported employment (Bond et al., 2001), family psychoeducation (McFarlane, McNary, Dixon, Hornby, & Cimett, 2001), integrated treatments for mental illness and substance abuse (Drake et al., 2001), and medication therapies (Kopelowicz & Liberman, 2003; Mellman et al., 2001).

Illness management and recovery describes a collection of interventions that seek to achieve a broad set of goals (Mueser et al., 2002; Salyers et al., 2009). These interventions include social skill and other psychoeducational programs, coping skills training, and non-pharmacologic treatment for cognitive disabilities. *Assertive community treatment* (ACT) is an especially well-studied service that helps people with serious mental illness accomplish independent living goals (Coldwell & Bender, 2007; Phillips et al., 2001). It may include symptom monitoring and medication management, management of entitlements, housing assistance, financial

9

management, health promotion, and activities related to daily living. There are no time limits to services.

Supported employment yields measurable increments in new work compared with sheltered workshops and transitional employment (Bond, Drake, Mueser, & Becker, 1997; Burns et al., 2009; Twamley, Jeste, & Lehman, 2003). Four defining principles are listed here (Bond, Drake, & Becker, 2008): (a) competitive employment is the goal, not prevocational treatments; (b) supported employment starts off with repaid, real-world job search; (c) rehabilitation and mental health treatments are provided by an integrated team, not separate services; and (d) support is time-unlimited. Mental illness and disability issues do not end when beginning a job. In fact, the person's need for services might increase during the year after going back to work.

Families of people with psychiatric disorder are impacted by the disorder (Pilling et al., 2002). Family members also play a central role in their relative's recovery from mental illness. Current evidence has supported several principles that describe effective *family interventions* (Pilling et al., 2002): include family members as equal partners in the intervention; be flexible in approaching the family; help the family to learn communication skills; provide training in problem-solving strategies; and help family members expand their support network. Finally, *integration of services* for mental health and substance abuse disorders needs to be the norm rather than the rarity. Traditionally, problems related to substance abuse were addressed by a completely separate system from mental health providers. Researchers maintain that this kind of artificial split undermines recovery for the person with dual disorders (Essock et al., 2006).

Moment-to-Moment Skill Sets

EBPs provide the big-picture perspective on services that facilitate recovery. These rest on a few basic skills that are fundamental to all human services. We call these the moment-to-moment skills, on which counselors rely to do the business of consumer recovery and which are divided into two groups in Table 1.3. First are the "fundamental two," the base for almost every counseling effort: reflective listening and support. These are the epitomes of person-centered psychotherapies, about which Carl Rogers (1951, 1980) eloquently wrote, and rest on three principles: (a) *genuineness*: Counselors must remain true to their beliefs and not attempt to frame interaction in any other light; (b) *empathy*: People benefit immensely from the counselor who understands and then reflects back their gut-level emotions and belief; and (c) *unconditional positive regard*: Despite whatever the person might have said or done, he or she is respected as a person ("I may not agree with what you believed or how you behaved, but I value you nonetheless").

Two Fundamental Skills

Reflective listening skills are frequently hailed as the foundation of engaging interactions. Important here is providing a quiet place and time for the person to tell his or her story of the moment. The counselor should avoid barriers to communication such as asking too many questions or diverting to an issue that is not important to the exchange. Wait and listen to what the person is saying. And, especially important, reflect back the person's message. The

Table 1.3 *Moment-to-Moment Skill Sets that Guide Providers in Helping People Recover*

Two fundamental skills	
Reflective listening	The skills that guide the provider to be genuinely present and to help
Interpersonal and instrumental support	
Four additional tool sets	
Motivational interviewing	Person-centered consideration of costs and benefits of individual decision
Shared decision-making	A free and open exchange for consumer and service provider, especially regarding treatment options
Steps to personal and interpersonal problem solving	Defining a goal, listing strategies for attaining goals, considering pros and cons of strategies, developing plan of action
Relapse prevention and advanced directives	Plan while in a good state how to handle future problems

counselor listens for the processes that underlie the message. What might be the person's goals for what has been said? How might the person feel when relaying this message? Reflective listeners do not limit attention to words. Counselors also consider the context of the message, other people participating in the exchange, and subtle communication portrayed by the lilt of the voice or subtle cues in eye contact and body language.

Also included in the Rogerian principles is the idea of support. With support comes commitment: recognition that ample time and perhaps a quiet place are needed for these kinds of exchange. There are two types of support: interpersonal and instrumental. *Instrumental support* is *in vivo* and goal-directed to help the person accomplish daily goals in real-life settings. These may include such practical things as grocery shopping, totaling the checkbook, cleaning one's home, or traveling to the dentist. The challenge in this kind of support is to balance the need for assistance with the attempt to be independent. Independence goals are owned and addressed by the consumer, not the service provider. *Interpersonal support* is more what Rogers (1959) had in mind. People are fundamentally social beings, with a deep-seated need for social exchange. It can be as mundane an effort as being "nice," or more purposeful, as reflective listening. The extent of interpersonal support can be difficult to sort out for service providers. There is a professional ethic to avoid dual roles. Service providers should not be the person's counselor *and* friend. This was a much easier ethic to observe when interventions were limited to the 50-minute weekly session in a therapist's office. However, the heart of EBPs is in the world with the person. These are nebulous areas that challenge definition. Still, there are interactions where dual roles are clear and concrete. Dating or establishing other intimate relationships with the person is clearly taboo. What about having a cup of coffee after work hours? The idea of dual roles is more complex when considering peers as service providers, people who, by virtue of their recovery, have deeper understanding of the person's current joys and concerns.

An Additional Set of Tools

The bottom half of Table 1.3 lists four other tool sets that are frequently basic to the EBPs: motivational interviewing, shared decision-making, problem solving, and relapse prevention.

Motivational Interviewing

Substance abuse providers developed *motivational interviewing* as a way to help people take stock of their addictions (Miller & Rollnick, 2002). The approach has since been extended as a systematic way for people to consider any significant life decision: whether to take an antipsychotic medication, move into one's own apartment, or break up with one's spouse (Arkowitz, Westra, Miller, & Rollnick, 2008). Fundamental to the task is helping the person understand the costs and benefits of a specific decision. Motivational interviewing is not meant to be mechanical, however. It is important to express empathy, to understand and reflect back to the person his or her perspective on the decision. It is hard to do this and avoid what is often the hidden agenda in motivational interviewing: for example, to convince the addict to stop using heroin. Added to empathy is the need to develop discrepancy (understand how a specific decision is hindering a broader goal), roll with the resistance (do not fall into the trap of proving a specific decision is right or wrong by arguing with any consequence), and support self-efficacy (identifying the little steps the person is taking to accomplish those broader goals).

Shared Decision-Making

Drake, Deegan, and Rapp (2010) have held up shared decision-making (SDM) as a first principle for building goal-oriented and successful working relationships between the person with mental illness and his or her service team. It commonly includes three parts: (1) Influence decision-making by helping the person examine the costs and benefits of specific health decisions or behavior. (2) This kind of assessment is facilitated by providing information so that the person better understands the disease process and corresponding treatment. The education process requires development of meaningful and user-friendly information channels. These might include face-to-face, classroom kinds of endeavor. Online technologies have also moved into this arena, including interactive websites, teaser videos on YouTube, Facebook pages, and Twitter (Owen et al., 2010). (3) Health-related decision-making is fundamentally social intercourse, and so we come back to reflected interviewing and interpersonal support.

Problem Solving

There are two kinds of problem solving: personal and interpersonal (Nezu, Nezu, & D'Zurilla, 2007). The first provides tools to help the person overcome difficulties that are largely his or hers alone; the second is a problem that is shared with another. The *interpersonal* problem solving may be a bit confusing, because people frequently play a role in personal problems. For interpersonal problem solving, problems are meaningfully shared among two or more people. For example, two roommates do not agree about the noise level at night. Or, two business partners disagree about the need to work overtime.

Commitment is a key ingredient to addressing interpersonal problems. The people pursuing interpersonal problems need to determine whether it is worth the effort to work together to resolve the problem. Interpersonal problem solving also differs from personal problem solving in that all steps must be addressed consensually. Problem solving of both kinds involves five steps: (1) Identify the problem. Specify the who, what, when, and where of a problem. (2) Brainstorm solutions. Do not censor solutions. Shoot for at least eight, so participants really push themselves to identify creative, maybe even silly, possibilities. (3) Evaluate individual solutions. Weigh the pros and cons of brainstormed solutions. (4) Pick one or a small mix of solutions and plan it out. Who will be involved in implementing the solution, when and where will it occur, and what will be done? (5) Evaluate the solution. Problem-solving participants need to make sure they provide time to follow up and check on the planned solution's impact. If successful, the person(s) continues with the plan. If not, they might revisit the plan for a tune up or retreat to the original list of brainstormed solutions to consider others.

Relapse Prevention and Advanced Directives

Relapse is very common in people with psychiatric disabilities. Relapse prevention seeks to teach people ways to cope with relapses during periods when the person is thinking clearly and is not overwhelmed emotionally (Marlatt & Donovan, 2005). When participating in relapse prevention programs, people learn how to recognize environmental triggers and early-warning signs of relapse. They then pair identification of these cues with a behavioral-response plan: for example, a person who recognizes when she becomes anxious has decided to pair this with a brief walk around the office building to calm down. Advanced directives are more formal examples of these, typically developed in relation to significant relapse leading to more invasive therapies (Atkinson, 2007; Swanson, Swartz, Ferron, Elbogen, & Van Dorn, 2006). The person, for example, might make decisions about when to be rehospitalized, where might the person go, what are med changes the person is willing to entertain, and who in the person's support network should be notified about the relapse.

CONFRONTING THE STIGMA OF MENTAL ILLNESS

As previously discussed, mental illness stigma can have significant constricting effects on recovery, preventing people with mental illness from participating fully in their communities. On the basis of the literature review, Corrigan and Penn (1999) grouped the various approaches to changing public stigma into three groups: protest, education, and contact. Protest is a strategy that highlights the moral injustices of stigma, chastising offenders for their believing and acting in a socially iniquitous way (Corrigan, 2006). For example, an anti-stigma program using protest might present the varied ways in which people with mental illness are disrespected in the media (e.g., banner headline: "Freed Mental Patient Kills Mom"), followed by the message to "STOP!": stop thinking or engaging in behaviors that disrespect people with mental illness. The NAMI developed StigmaBusters in 2000 partly for this purpose. It played a prominent role in getting ABC television to cancel the program *Wonderland*, about a New York-based, forensic program that portrayed persons with mental illness as unpredictably dangerous (Corrigan & Gelb, 2006). StigmaBusters' efforts not only targeted the show's producers and several management levels of the network, they encouraged communication with commercial sponsors, including the CEOs of Mitsubishi, Sears, and the Scott Company. ABC took the show off the air rather than risk sponsors' boycotts. Although organized protest can be a useful tool for convincing television networks to stop running stigmatizing programs (Wahl, 1995), it may produce unintended "rebound" effects, because people react in an obverse manner to what they are told to do (Macrae, Bodenhausen, Milne, & Jetten, 1996; Penn & Corrigan, 2002).

Education is another strategy to reduce mental illness stigma by challenging inaccurate stereotypes about mental illness, replacing them with factual information. Public service announcements, books, flyers, movies, videos, and other audiovisual aids have been used to dispel myths about mental illness and replace them with facts (National Mental Health Anti-Stigma Campaign, 2006; Page, 1983; Smith, 1990). Some benefits of educational interventions include relatively low costs and capability of reaching large audiences. Research suggests educational strategies have moderate success. For example, Spagnolo, Murphy, and Librera (2008) reported a medium effect size ($d = 0.43$) for a public education program among high-school students. It is important to note, however, that, though education produces short-term improvements in attitudes (Corrigan et al., 2001; Corrigan et al., 2002; Morrison & Teta, 1980; Penn, Kommana, Mansfield, & Link, 1999; Pinfold et al., 2003), the magnitude and duration of improvement in attitudes and behavior may be limited (Corrigan & McCracken, 1998; McCracken & Corrigan, 2004).

Contact is the third strategy for reducing stigma and has long been considered an effective means for reducing intergroup prejudice between majority and minority groups (Pettigrew & Tropp, 2000). According to Allport (1954/1979), contact strategies are optimized when they contain four key elements: (1) equal status between groups; (2) common goals; (3) no competition; and (4) authority sanction for the contact. Several studies specifically focusing on contact's effect on mental illness stigma have produced promising findings. Corrigan and colleagues (2001) found that contact with a person with mental illness produced greater improvements in attitudes than protest, education, and control conditions. In a subsequent study, contact again produced the greatest improvements in attitudes and participant willingness to donate money to a mental health advocacy group (Corrigan et al., 2002). Improvements in attitudes seem to be most pronounced when contact is with a person who moderately disconfirms prevailing stereotypes (Reinke, Corrigan, Leonhard, Lundin, & Kubiak, 2004; Rusch, Kanter, Angelone, & Ridley, 2008).

Resolving Self-Stigma

Self-stigma is believed to mediate the relationships between public stigma and recovery. There are two major approaches to reduce self-stigma: (1) facilitating change in self-stigmatizing cognitive schemata and (2) fostering personal empowerment (Corrigan & Calabrese, 2005).

Self-Stigmatizing Cognitive Schemata

Cognitive therapy has been shown to be an effective strategy for helping people change cognitive schemata that lead to anxiety, depression, and the consequences of self-stigma (Chadwick, Birchwood, & Trower, 1996; Garety, Fowler, & Kuipers, 2000). The primary targets of this approach have been the cognitive schemata underlying delusional beliefs and attributions regarding auditory hallucinations. Changes in these schemata have been shown to yield improvement in psychiatric symptoms. The most promising studies of this line of research in relation to stigma were initiated by two other British researchers, David Kingdon and Douglas

Turkington (1991, 1994). They expanded cognitive therapy for psychosis beyond the content of specific symptoms, also targeting catastrophic interpretation of one's symptoms and the stigma attached to mental illness generally.

Personal Empowerment

Personal empowerment is the exercise of one's own sense of will and determination and is very prominent in the consumer recovery literature (Jacobson & Greenley, 2001; Ralph, 2000). Anthony (1993, 2000) and Jacobson and Greenley (2001) suggest a high level of empowerment is associated with greater recovery. Therefore, reducing self-stigma and facilitating empowerment will likely be important for the recovery process among people with mental illness (Corrigan & Calabrese, 2005; Speer, Jackson, & Peterson, 2001). For example, active participation and engagement in all aspects of care make an ideal approach to increase empowerment; consumer-operated self-help services are another good example of practices that facilitate empowerment (Davidson et al., 1999).

Empowerment has significance both for individuals with mental illness and for the larger groups to which they belong. For the individual, empowerment is thought to require the general qualities of self-determination (encompassing a sense of personal agency), personal competence (including acceptance of illness and positive self-esteem), and social engagement (which includes social advocacy for self and others; Dickerson, 1998). Politically, empowerment represents an effort on the part of consumers as a disenfranchised group to play a larger role in mental health-care policy development and service delivery. Contemporary examples of consumer political empowerment include consumer-directed research, consumer mental health-care policy lobbying, and consumer-run clubhouse programs (Dickerson, 1998). Such initiatives may be empowering whether they are met with support or resistance on the part of mental health-care providers and policymakers. In contrast to a paternalistic system in which power is granted by a ruling elite, individual consumers and consumer groups are thought to be empowered by the very process of asserting themselves or their agenda in the interpersonal and/or political arena.

SUMMARY

The purpose of this chapter was to introduce the intersection of recovery and stigma. The definitions and key elements of recovery and stigma were discussed. The ideas of recovery and stigma have a mutual effect on each other. People with serious mental illness are sometimes unable to achieve important life goals when the public endorses stereotypes about their disorders and discriminates against them as a result. Recovery reminds everyone that people with mental illness are just that, people with the same aspirations as other people.

In this chapter, we also attempted to propose practice and strategies to promote recovery and confront stigma. The status of evidence-based practices related to recovery was discussed. Illness management and recovery, assertive community treatment, supported employment, family interventions, and integration of services were identified as evidence-based practices. Protest, education, and contact were reviewed as major strategies to change public stigma. Cognitive behavioral therapy was introduced as an effective strategy to change self-stigmatizing thoughts. Empowering people with serious mental illness in the community plays a critical

15

role in confronting stigma, as does being main agents in their own recovery processes. People with serious mental illness are able to work in a meaningful job, live independently, and enjoy intimate relationships, as people without mental illness do.

DISCUSSION QUESTIONS

1. This chapter examines issues related to stigma and recovery and identifies four distinct forms of stigma. Among them is *public stigma,* which involves negative and biased portrayals of the mentally ill by the public. In what ways do you think the media (movies, TV shows, ads) contribute to public stigma toward mental illness? What other forms of public stigma toward mental illness can you identify?

2. How does the process of self-stigma (internalized negative self-perceptions) affect a person who struggles with an illness or disability?

3. Discuss the following concept: "Recovery is not a linear process. It is a way of life." What does this mean to you? How might this relate to people who struggle with mental illness?

LEARNING ASSIGNMENT

Class Project

As part of a class effort, develop a plan to form an anti-stigma campaign that protests negative images in the media that portray people who are psychiatrically disabled. What kinds of strategy would your program employ?

SUGGESTED READINGS

Corrigan, P.W. (Ed.) (2005). *On the stigma of mental illness: Implications for research and social change.* Washington DC: American Psychological Association Press (343 pages).

Corrigan, P.W., & Lundin, R.K. (2001). *Don't call me nuts! Coping with the stigma of mental illness.* Tinley Park, IL: Recovery Press (446 pages).

Ralph, R.O., & Corrigan, P.W. (Eds.) (2004). *Recovery in mental illness: Broadening our understanding of wellness.* Washington DC: American Psychological Association Press (282 pages).

INTERNET RESOURCES

Center on Adherence and Self-Determination: www.adherenceandselfdetermination.org

National Consortium on Stigma and Empowerment: www.stigmaandempowerment.org

REFERENCES

Allport, G. (1954/1979). *The nature of prejudice*. New York: Doubleday Anchor Books (original work published 1954).

Anthony, W.A. (1993). Recovery from mental illness: The guiding vision of the mental health service system in the 1990's. *Psychosocial Rehabilitation Journal, 16*(4), 11–23.

Anthony, W.A. (2000). A recovery-oriented service system: Setting some system level standards. *Psychiatric Rehabilitation Journal, 24*(2), 159–168.

Arkowitz, H., Westra, H.A., Miller, W.R., & Rollnick, S. (2008). *Motivational interviewing in the treatment of psychological problems*. New York: Guilford Press.

Atkinson, J. M. (2007). *Advance directives in mental health: Theory, practice and ethics*. London: Jessica Kingsley Publishers.

Augoustinos, M., Ahrens, C., & Innes, J. (1994). Stereotypes and prejudice: The Australian experience. *British Journal of Social Psychology, 33*(1), 125–141.

Ayalon, L., Areán, P. A., & Alvidrez, J. (2005) Adherence to antidepressant medications in black and Latino elderly patients. *American Journal of Geriatric Psychiatry, 13*, 572–580.

Ben-Porath, D.D. (2002). Stigmatization of individuals who receive psychotherapy: An interaction between help-seeking behavior and the presence of depression. *Journal of Social and Clinical Psychology, 21*(4), 400–413.

Bond, G.R., Becker, D.R., Drake, R.E., Rapp, C.A., Meisler, N., Lehman, A.F., et al. (2001). Implementing supported employment as an evidence-based practice. *Psychiatric Services, 52*(3), 313–322.

Bond, G.R., Drake, R.E., & Becker, D.R. (2008). An update on randomized controlled trials of evidence-based supported employment. *Psychiatric Rehabilitation Journal, 31*(4), 280–290.

Bond, G.R., Drake, R.E., Mueser, K.T., & Becker, D.R. (1997). An update on supported employment for people with severe mental illness. *Psychiatric Services, 48*, 335–346.

Brockington, I., Hall, P., Levings, J., & Murphy, C. (1993). The community's tolerance of the mentally ill. *British Journal of Psychiatry, 162*, 93–99.

Burns, T., Catty, J., White, S., Becker, T., Koletsi, M., Fioritti, A., et al. (2009). The impact of supported employment and working on clinical and social functioning: Results of an international study of individual placement and support. *Schizophrenia Bulletin, 35*(5), 949–958.

Chadwick, P.D.J., Birchwood, M., & Trower, P. (1996). *Cognitive therapy for delusions, voice and paranoia*. New York: Wiley.

Ciompi, L., Harding, C.M., & Lehtinen, K. (2010). Deep concern. *Schizophrenia Bulletin, 36*(3), 437–439.

Coldwell, C.M., & Bender, W.S. (2007). The effectiveness of assertive community treatment for homeless populations with severe mental illness: A meta-analysis. *The American Journal of Psychiatry, 164*, 393–399.

Corrigan, P.W. (2002). Empowerment and serious mental illness: Treatment partnerships and community opportunities. *Psychiatric Quarterly, 73*, 217–228.

Corrigan, P.W. (2004). How stigma interferes with mental health care. *American Psychologist, 59*, 614–625.

Corrigan, P.W. (2006). Language and stigma: Comment. *Psychiatric Services, 57*, 1218.

Corrigan, P.W., & Calabrese, J.D. (2005). Strategies for assessing and diminishing self-stigma. In P.W. Corrigan (Ed.), *On the stigma of mental illness: Practical strategies for research and social change* (pp. 239–256). Washington DC: American Psychological Association.

Corrigan, P.W., & Gelb, B. (2006). Three programs that use mass approaches to challenge the stigma of mental illness. *Psychiatric Services, 57*, 393–398.

Corrigan, P.W., Giffort, D., Rashid, F., Leary, M., & Okeke, I. (1999). Recovery as a psychological construct. *Community Mental Health Journal, 35*(3), 231–239.

Corrigan, P.W., Larson, J.E., & Rusch, N. (2009). Self-stigma and the "why try" effect: Impact on life goals and evidence-based practices. *World Psychiatry, 8*(2), 75–81.

Corrigan, P.W., Markowitz, F.E., & Watson, A. (2004). Structural levels of mental illness stigma and discrimination. *Schizophrenia Bulletin, 30*, 481–491.

Corrigan, P.W., & McCracken, S.G. (1998). An interactive approach to training teams and developing programs. *New Directions in Mental Health Services, 79*, 3–12.

Corrigan, P.W., & Penn, D.L. (1999). Lessons from social psychology on discrediting psychiatric stigma. *American Psychologist, 54*, 765–776.

Corrigan, P.W., River, L.P., Lundin, R.K., Penn, D.L., Wasowski, K.U., Campion, J., et al. (2001). Three strategies for changing attributions about severe mental illness. *Schizophrenia Bulletin, 27*, 187–196.

Corrigan, P.W., River, L.P., Lundin, R.K., Wasowski, K.U., Campion, J., Mathisen, J., et al. (2000). Stigmatizing attributions about mental illness. *Journal of Community Psychology, 28*, 91–103.

Corrigan, P.W., Rowan, D., Green, A., Lundin, R., River, P., Uphoff-Wasowski, K., et al. (2002). Challenging two mental illness stigmas: Personal responsibility and dangerousness. *Schizophrenia Bulletin, 28*, 293–310.

Corrigan, P.W., Salzer, M., Ralph, R.O., Sangster, Y., & Keck, L. (2004). Examining the factor structure of the Recovery Assessment Scale. *Schizophrenia Bulletin, 30*(4), 1035–1041.

Corrigan, P.W., & Wassel, A. (2008). Understanding and influencing the stigma of mental illness. *Journal of Psychosocial Nursing and Mental Health Services, 46*, 42–48.

Corrigan, P.W., & Watson, A.C. (2004). Stop the stigma: Call mental illness a brain disorder. *Schizophrenia Bulletin, 30*, 477–480.

Corrigan, P.W., Watson, A.C., & Barr, L. (2006) Understanding the self-stigma of mental illness. *Journal of Social and Clinical Psychology, 25*, 875–884.

Corrigan, P.W., Watson, A.C., Heyrman, M., Warpinski, A., Gracia, G., Slopen, N., et al. (2005). Structural stigma in state legislation. *Psychiatric Services, 56*, 557–563.

Crocker, J., Major, B., & Steele, C. (1998). Social stigma. In D.T. Gilbert, S. Fiske, & G. Lindzey (Eds.), *The handbook of social psychology* (Vol. 2, 4th ed., pp. 504–553). New York: McGraw-Hill.

Davidson, L., Chinman, M., Kloos, B., Weingarten, R., Stayner, D., & Tebes, J.K. (1999). Peer support among individuals with severe mental illness: A review of the evidence. *Clinical Psychology: Science and Practice, 6*(2), 165–187.

Davidson, L., Tondora, J., Lawless, M.S., O'Connell, M.J., & Rowe, M. (2009). *A practical guide to recovery-oriented practice: Tools for transforming mental health care*. New York: Oxford University Press.

Deegan, P.E. (1988). Recovery: The lived experience of rehabilitation. *Psychosocial Rehabilitation Journal, 11*(4), 11–19.

Dickerson, F.B. (1998). Strategies that foster empowerment. *Cognitive and Behavioral Practice, 5*, 255–275.

Drake, R.E., Deegan, P.E., & Rapp, C. (2010). The promise of shared decision making in mental health. *Psychiatric Rehabilitation Journal, 34*(1), 7–13.

Drake, R.E., Goldman, H.H., Leff, H.S., Lehman, A.F., Dixon, L., Mueser, K.T., et al. (2001). Implementing evidence-based practices in routine mental health service settings. *Psychiatric Services, 52*, 179–182.

Esses, V., Haddock, G., & Zanna, M. (1994). The role of mood in the expression of intergroup stereotypes. In M. Zanna & J. Olson (Eds.), *The psychology of prejudice: Vol. 7. The Ontario Symposium* (pp. 77–101). Hillsdale, NJ: Lawrence Erlbaum Associates.

Essock, S.M., Mueser, K.T., Drake, R.E., Covell, N.H., McHugo, G.J., Frisman, L.K., et al. (2006). Comparison of ACT and standard care management for delivering integrated treatment for co-occurring disorders. *Psychiatric Services, 57*, 185–196.

Fisher, D.B., & Ahern, L. (2002). Evidence-based practices and recovery. *Psychiatric Services, 53*, 632–633.

Frese, F.J., Stanley, J., Kress, K., & Vogel-Scibilia, S. (2001). Integrating evidence-based practices and the recovery model. *Psychiatric Services, 52*, 1462–1468.

Garety, P., Fowler, D., & Kuipers, E. (2000). Cognitive-behavioral therapy for medication-resistant symptoms. *Schizophrenia Bulletin, 26*, 73–86.

Goldman, H.H., Ganju, V., Drake, R.E., Gorman, P., Hogan, M., Hyde, P.S., et al. (2001). Policy implications for implementing evidence-based practices. *Psychiatric Services, 52*, 1591–1597.

Goldstrom, I.D., Campbell, J., Rogers, J.A., Lambert, D.B., Blacklow, B., Henderson, M.J., et al. (2006). National estimates for mental health mutual support groups, self-help organizations, and consumer-operated services. *Administration and Policy in Mental Health and Mental Health Services Research, 33*(1), 92–103.

Hamre, P., Dahl, A.A., & Malt, U.F. (1994). Public attitudes to the quality of psychiatric treatment, psychiatric patients, and prevalence of mental disorders. *Nordic Journal of Psychiatry, 48*, 275–281.

Harding, C.M. (1988). Course types in schizophrenia: An analysis of European and American studies. *Schizophrenia Bulletin, 14*(4), 633–643.

Hilton, J., & von Hippel, W. (1996). Stereotypes. *Annual Review of Psychology, 47*, 237–271.

Jacobson, N., & Greenley, D. (2001). What is recovery? A conceptual model and explication. *Psychiatric Services, 52*, 482–485.

Jorm, A.F. (2000). Mental health literacy: Public knowledge and beliefs about mental disorders. *British Journal of Psychiatry, 177*, 396–401.

Judd, C., & Park, B. (1996). Definition and assessment of accuracy in stereotypes. *Psychological Review, 100*, 109–128.

Kingdon, D., & Turkington, D. (1991). The use of cognitive behavior therapy with a normalizing rationale in schizophrenia: a preliminary report. *Journal of Nervous and Mental Disease, 179*, 207–211.

Kingdon, D. G., & Turkington, D. (1994). *Cognitive-behavioral therapy of schizophrenia*. New York: Guilford Press.

Kopelowicz, A., & Liberman, R.P. (2003). Integration of care: Integrating treatment with rehabilitation for persons with major mental illnesses. *Psychiatric Services, 54*, 1491–1498.

Kraepelin, E. (1919). *Dementia praecox and paraphrenia*. Huntington, NY: Krieger.

Krueger, J. (1996). Personal beliefs and cultural stereotypes about racial characteristics. *Journal of Personality & Social Psychology, 71*, 536–548.

Lacro, J.P., Dunn, L.B., Dolder, C.R., Leckband, S.G., & Jeste, D.V. (2002) Prevalence of and risk factors for medication nonadherence in patients with schizophrenia: A comprehensive review of recent literature. *Journal of Clinical Psychiatry, 63*, 892–909.

Leete, E. (1988). A consumer perspective on psychosocial treatment. *Psychosocial Rehabilitation Journal, 12*, 45–52.

Lehman, A.F., Kreyenbuhl, J., Buchanan, R.W., Dickerson, F.B., Dixon, L.B., Goldberg, R., et al. (2004). The schizophrenia Patient Outcomes Research Team (PORT): Updated treatment recommendations 2003. *Schizophrenia Bulletin, 30*(2), 193–217.

Link, B.G., & Phelan, J.C. (2001). Conceptualizing stigma. *Annual Review of Sociology, 27*, 363–385.

McCracken, S.G., & Corrigan, P.W. (2004). Staff development in mental health. In H.E. Briggs & T.L. Rzepnicki (Eds.), *Evidence-based social work practice* (pp. 232–256). Chicago, IL: Lyceum Books.

McFarlane, W.R., McNary, S., Dixon, L., Hornby, H., & Cimett, E. (2001). Predictors of dissemination of family psychoeducation in community mental health centers in Maine and Illinois. *Psychiatric Services, 52*, 935–942.

Macrae, C.N., Bodenhausen, G.V., Milne, A.B., & Jetten, J. (1996). Out of mind but back in sight: Stereotypes on the rebound. In S. Fein & S. Spencer (Eds.), *Readings in social psychology: The art and science of research* (pp. 30–43). Boston, MA: Houghton, Mifflin and Company.

Marlatt, G.A., & Donovan, D.M. (2005). *Relapse prevention: Maintenance strategies in the treatment of relapse prevention*. New York: Guilford Press.

Marty, D., Rapp, C., McHugo, G., & Whitley, R. (2008). Factors influencing consumer outcome monitoring in implementation of evidence-based practices: Results from the National EBP Implementation Project. *Administration and Policy in Mental Health and Mental Health Services Research, 35*(3), 204–211.

Mellman, T.A., Miller, A.L., Weissman, E.M., Crismon, M.L., Essock, S.M., & Marder, S.R. (2001). Evidence-based pharmacologic treatment for people with severe mental illness: A focus on guidelines and algorithms. *Psychiatric Services, 52*, 619–625.

Miller, W.R., & Rollnick, S. (20002). *Motivational interviewing: Preparing people for change.* New York: The Guilford Press.

Morrison, J.K., & Teta, D.C. (1980). Reducing students' fear of mental illness by means of seminar-induced belief change. *Journal of Clinical Psychology, 36*, 275–276.

Mueser, K.T., Corrigan, P.W., Hilton, D.W., & Tanzman, B. (2002). Illness management and recovery: A review of the research. *Psychiatric Services, 53*(10), 1272–1284.

Mueser, K.T., Torrey, W.C., Lynde, D., Singer, P., & Drake, R.E. (2003). Implementing evidence-based practices for people with severe mental illness. *Behavior Modification, 27*(3), 387–411.

Mullen, B., Rozell, D., & Johnson, C. (1996). The phenomenology of being in a group: Complexity approaches to operationalizing cognitive representation. In J.L. Nye, A.M. Brower, et al. (Eds.), *What's social about social cognition? Research on socially shared cognition in small groups* (pp. 205–229). Thousand Oaks, CA: Sage Publications.

National Mental Health Anti-Stigma Campaign (2006). Retrieved September 3, 2010, from www.whatadifference.samhsa.gov

Nezu, A., Nezu, C., & D'Zurilla, T. (2007). *Solving life's problems: A 5-step guide to enhanced well-being.* New York: Springer.

Owen, J.E., Boxley, L., Goldstein, M.S., Lee, J.H., Breen, N., & Rowland, J.H. (2010). Use of health related online support groups: Population data from the California Health Interview Survey complementary and alternative medicine study. *Journal of Computer-Mediated Communication, 15*(3), 427–446.

Page, S. (1983). Psychiatric stigma: Two studies of behaviour when the chips are down. *Canadian Journal of Community Mental Health, 2*, 13–19.

Peluso Ede, T., & Blay, S.L. (2009). Public stigma in relation to individuals with depression. *Journal of Affective Disorders, 115*, 201–206.

Penn, D.L., & Corrigan, P.W. (2002). The effects of stereotype suppression on psychiatric stigma. *Schizophrenia Research, 55*, 269–276.

Penn, D.L., Kommana, S., Mansfield, M., & Link, B.G. (1999). Dispelling the stigma of schizophrenia: II. The impact of information on dangerousness. *Schizophrenia Bulletin, 25*, 437–446.

Pettigrew, T.F., & Tropp, L.R. (2000). Does intergroup contact reduce prejudice: Recent meta-analytic findings. In S. Oskamp (Ed.), *Reducing prejudice and discrimination* (pp. 93–114). Mahwah, NJ: Lawrence Erlbaum Associates.

Phillips, S.D., Burns, B.J., Edgar, E.R., Mueser, K.T., Linkins, K.W., Rosenheck, R.A., et al. (2001). Moving assertive community treatment into standard practice. *Psychiatric Services, 52*, 771–779.

Pilling, S., Bebbington, P., Kuipers, E., Garety, P., Geddes, J., Orbach, G., et al. (2002). Psychological treatments in schizophrenia: I. Meta-analysis of family intervention and cognitive behavior therapy. *Psychological Medicine, 32*, 763–782.

Pincus, F.L. (1996). Discrimination comes in many forms: Individual, institutional, and structural. *American Behavioral Scientist, 40*, 186–194.

Pincus, F.L. (1999a). The case for affirmative action. In H.J. Ehrlich (Ed.), *Race and ethnic conflict: Contending views on prejudice, discrimination, and ethnoviolence* (pp. 205–222). Boulder, CO: Westview Press.

Pincus, F.L. (1999b). From individual to structural discrimination. In H.J. Ehrlich (Ed.) *Race and ethnic conflict: Contending views on prejudice, discrimination, and ethnoviolence.* Boulder, CO: Westview Press.

Pinfold, V., Toulmin, H., Thornicroft, G., Huxley, P., Farmer, P., & Graham, T. (2003). Reducing psychiatric stigma and discrimination: Evaluation of educational interventions in UK secondary schools. *British Journal of Psychiatry, 182*, 342–346.

Plante, T.G., & Sherman, A.C. (2001). *Faith and health: Psychological perspectives*. New York: Guilford Press.

Ralph, R. (2000). Recovery. *Psychiatric Rehabilitation Skills, 4*(3), 480–517.

Ralph, R.O., & Corrigan, P.W. (Eds.) (2005) *Recovery in mental illness: Broadening our understanding of wellness*. Washington, DC: American Psychological Association.

Reinke, R.R., Corrigan, P.W., Leonhard, C., Lundin, R.K., & Kubiak, M.A. (2004). Examining two aspects of contact on the stigma of mental illness. *Journal of Social and Clinical Psychology, 23*, 377–389.

Rogers, C. (1951). *Client-centered therapy: Its current practice, implications and theory*. London: Constable.

Rogers, C. (1959). A theory of therapy, personality and interpersonal relationships as developed in the client-centered framework. In S. Koch (Ed.), *Psychology: A study of a science. Vol. 3: Formulations of the person and the social context*. New York: McGraw-Hill.

Rogers, C. (1980). *A way of being*. Boston: Houghton Mifflin.

Rogers, E.S., Chamberlin, J., Ellison, M.L., & Crean, T. (1997). A consumer-constructed scale to measure empowerment among users of mental health services. *Psychiatric Services, 48*, 1042–1047.

Rusch, L.C., Kanter, J.W., Angelone, A.F., & Ridley, R.C. (2008). The impact of In our voice on stigma. *American Journal of Psychiatric Rehabilitation, 11*(4), 373–389.

Salyers, M.P., Hicks, L.J., McGuire, A.B., Baumgardner, H., Ring, K., & Kim, H.W. (2009). A pilot to enhance the recovery orientation of assertive community treatment through peer provided illness management and recovery. *American Journal of Psychiatric Rehabilitation, 12*(3), 191–204.

Segal, S.P., Silverman, C., & Temkin, T. (1995). Measuring empowerment in client-run self-help agencies. *Community Mental Health Journal, 31*(3), 215–227.

Silverstein, S.M., & Bellack, A.S. (2008). A scientific agenda for the concept of recovery as it applies to schizophrenia. *Clinical Psychology Review, 28*(7), 1108–1124.

Sirey J.A., Bruce M.L., Alexopoulos, G.S., Perlick, D.A., Friedman, S.J., & Meyers, B.S. (2001). Stigma as a barrier to recovery: Perceived stigma and patient-rated severity of illness as predictors of antidepressant drug adherence. *Psychiatric Services, 52*, 1615–1620.

Smith, A. (1990) Social influence and antiprejudice training programs. In J. Edwards, R.S. Tindale, L. Heath, & E.J. Posavac (Eds.), *Social influence processes and prevention* (pp. 183–196). New York: Plenum.

Spagnolo, A.B., Murphy, A.A., & Librera, L.A. (2008). Reducing stigma by meeting and learning from people with mental illness. *Psychiatric Rehabilitation Journal, 31*(3), 186–193.

Speer, P.W., Jackson, C.B., & Peterson, N. (2001). The relationship between social cohesion and empowerment: Support and new implications for theory. *Health Education & Behavior, 28*, 716–732.

Swanson, J., Swartz, M., Ferron, J., Elbogen, E., & Van Dorn, R. (2006). Psychiatric advance directives among public mental health consumers in five U.S. cities: Prevalence, demand, and correlates. *Journal of the American Academy of Psychiatry and the Law, 34*(1), 43–57.

Torrey, W.C., Drake, R.E., Dixon, L., Burns, B.J., Flynn, L., Rush, J., et al. (2001). Implementing evidence-based practices for persons with severe mental illnesses. *Psychiatric Services, 52*, 45–50.

Twamley, E.W., Jeste, D.V., & Lehman, A.F. (2003). Vocational rehabilitation in schizophrenia and other psychotic disorders: A literature review and meta-analysis of randomized controlled trials. *Journal of Nervous & Mental Disease, 191*(8), 515–523.

Van Tosh, L., Ralph, R., & Campbell, J. (2004) The rise of consumerism. *Psychiatric Rehabilitation Skills, 4*, 383–409.

Velligan, D.I., Lam, Y.F., Glahn, D.C., Barrett, J.A., Maples, N.J., Ereshefsky, L., & Miller, A.L. (2006) Defining and assessing adherence to oral antipsychotics: A review of the literature. *Schizophrenia Bulletin, 32*, 724–742.

Wahl, O.F. (1995). *Media madness: Public images of mental illness*. New Brunswick, NJ: Rutgers University Press.

Weisman de Mamani, A.G., Tuchman, N., & Duarte, E.A. (2010). Incorporating religion/spirituality into treatment for serious mental illness. *Cognitive and Behavioral Practice, 17*(4), 348–357.

21

Chapter 2

Marginal No More

Serious Mental Illness, Sexual Orientation, and Gender Preference

Jessica Rosenberg, Samuel J. Rosenberg, Christian Huygen, and Eileen Klein

INTRODUCTION

Members of marginalized communities contend with multiple layers of stress and stigmatization. When such people are also struggling with mental illness, their situation presents great challenges. Interventions specifically designed to address and ameliorate stigma can have a powerful positive impact. Revising and revisiting this chapter, originally published in 2006, affords us the opportunity to present empirical evidence that bears out our anticipated outcomes. In the earlier version of this chapter, we had proposed that interventions specifically directed at stigmatized and marginalized individuals would dramatically improve quality of life, social support, and treatment compliance, and significantly reduce the use of emergency services such as psychiatric hospitalization. The empirical evidence of consumer survey data bears out these anticipated outcomes. The present chapter examines an innovative response to the needs of lesbian, gay, bisexual, and transgender (LGBT) mental health consumers. In mainstream settings, LGBT consumers are often marginalized or poorly understood; they frequently react to this situation by not disclosing or discussing their LGBT identities, or the conflicts and challenges that they experience, either internally or interpersonally, because of their sexual orientation or gender identity. Rainbow Heights Club was designed to be a safe and non-stigmatizing environment in which LGBT mental health consumers could form a community of mutual support and advocacy. The present chapter makes connections to recent work on stigma and how it operates, and documents Rainbow Heights Club's impact and effectiveness. Although Rainbow Heights Club focuses on consumers' sexuality and gender identity, we believe that it can serve as a paradigm for better meeting the needs of numerous marginalized and stigmatized communities of mental health consumers.

In building effective community mental health responses to the specific needs of marginalized populations, we must begin by considering those needs. The treatment needs of LGBT individuals who suffer from serious mental illness are generally overlooked (Rosenberg et. al., 2005). Research suggests that the mental health needs of this population differ from those of the heterosexual seriously mentally ill, and that mainstream mental health-care systems may not fully address their concerns (Cochran, 2001).

The LBGT seriously mentally ill individual, if untreated, is at increased risk for a host of co-occurring disorders and related problems, including substance abuse, HIV/AIDS, and involvement in the criminal justice system (Cochran, Sullivan, and Mays, 2001; Fergusson, Horwood, and Beautrais, 1999; Sandfort et al., 2001). Fergusson et al. (1999) found that, by age 21, LGBT individuals were at increased risk for major depression, conduct disorders, substance abuse and/or dependence, suicidal ideation, and suicide attempts. The pattern holds at midlife as well. Cochran et al. (2001) found evidence that lesbian, gay, and bisexual respondents to the National Survey of Midlife Development in the United States showed increased risk for psychiatric disorders as compared with heterosexual women and men.

Similarly, Hellman et al. (2002) found higher rates of bipolar and depressive disorders in LGBT males than in control males; however, that study found no significant differences between LGBT and control females.

LGBT individuals with serious mental illness live with a double burden of stigma. Society discriminates against their sexual and gender identity, as well as their mental health status. This means that, in mental health settings such as inpatient units and outpatient treatment settings, they often attempt to hide their sexual or gender identity; conversely, when interacting with members of the LGBT community, they are often reluctant to disclose their mental health status. This often means that they lack any safe context in which they can articulate and manifest the full range of challenges and obstacles that affect their lives. The fact that the field of mental health has in the past conflated these two stigmas by defining homosexuality itself as a kind of mental illness is a particularly corrosive aspect of the situation in which LGBT consumers often find themselves.

This chapter will present an overview of the dynamics of the dual stigma of being an LGBT person living with a major mental illness. It will discuss an innovative community mental health program, the Rainbow Heights Club, which was developed to address the unique social needs of this population and help them to participate maximally in the community.

STIGMA

As noted above, LGBT individuals with serious mental illness are subject to dual stigma that stems from societal discrimination toward same-sex preference and bias against mental illness.

In the classic perspective elaborated by Goffman (1963), stigma is conceptualized as an "attribute that is deeply discrediting" and that reduces the bearer "from a whole and usual person to a tainted, discounted one" (Goffman, 1963, p. 3). Persons who are stigmatized possess characteristics that position them outside of the expectations established by socially accepted norms. Stigma represents a relational attribute, a "mark," associated with a person that links him/her to undesirable stereotypical characteristics (Link and Phelan, 2001). Stigma is not merely a label, but, rather, directs social attention to something "in the person" that inherently makes the person tainted. As such, the victims of stigma are blamed for "being" socially unacceptable. Whereas individuals diagnosed with cancer are referred to as "having cancer," individuals diagnosed with schizophrenia are seen as "being schizophrenic." Research shows that stigma is a central process that has serious consequences in shaping the pursuit of activities related to life chances: occupation, education, health, and general well-being. In the case of

23

LGBT persons with severe mental illness, this becomes compounded by the duality of the stigmatization process and the spillover into all areas of social and subjective experience.

The process of stigmatization unfolds when five critical components converge: (1) labeling; (2) stereotyping; (3) separating "us" from "them"; (4) status loss and discrimination; and (5) an imbalance of power (Link & Phelan, 2001).

Labeling

LGBT sexual and gender identity is labeled as different from the heterosexual norm. Similarly, the condition of mental illness is marked as a difference from the presumed norm of mental health.

Linking Human Difference With Negative Attribute

Once LBGT persons who are seriously mentally ill have been socially labeled as "different," the second step in the stigmatization process is to assign these differences a negative attribute. As such, gays and lesbians are perceived to be different in negative ways, as amoral or deviant. In addition, their mental illness leads to further social exclusion owing to societal attitudes toward mentally ill persons, including the belief that the mentally ill are dangerous and bizarre.

Them and Us

LGBT persons are denied access to basics such as housing and employment. The mentally ill experience a similar situation when confronted with the NIMBY (not in my backyard) phenomenon, when residential programs seek to develop housing or there is a rehabilitation program featuring supported employment. There is a denial of access and in extreme cases, when a stigmatized group becomes dehumanized, they can become victims of fatal violence.

Status Loss and Discrimination

Once the process of stigma construction evolves to the point where negative associations are group specific, members of such groups experience downward mobility and status loss and, owing to their negative stereotype, become the subject of discrimination. Low social status engenders low self-esteem. For those who are chronically mentally ill, a process of self-designation evolves where clients refer to themselves as *having become a schizophrenic*, rather than *having schizophrenia* (Estroff, 1981). Their illness defines who they are and evolves into a loss of social roles and identity. Identification with the LGBT sexual minority population further complicates this loss of social acceptance. The comparatively higher incidence of substance abuse and suicide among LGBT adolescents attests to the deleterious effects of stigma (Fergusson et al., 1999).

Stigma: An Imbalance of Power

The ability to construct a complex system such as stigma is dependent on an imbalance of power: Those who actively participate in stigmatizing others must have the power to proceed unchecked, and victims of stigma must lack sufficient power and recourses to counter and oppose status loss, marginalization, and a reduction in life chances. In effect, the process of social stigmatization rests on social, economic, and political power over the populations designated for stigma. Despite the demographic incidence of homosexuality (estimated at 4–10% of the population, often higher in large metropolitan areas), LGBT people remain a socially marginalized population that does not readily self-identify, particularly when in positions of power such as elected officials, corporate executives, and professionals. Similarly, the mentally ill are equally underrepresented in positions of social and political power. Whereas they are overwhelmingly dependent on social programs for their subsistence, they have not become a political voting block capable of influencing the political process.

The dual stigmatization of LGBT consumers is visible in many aspects of popular culture. In numerous popular movies such as *Silence of the Lambs*, the sadistic, psychotic serial killer is often homosexual, and, routinely, in movies as well as in life, the parents of people who disclose a same-sex sexual orientation instantly ask themselves and one another, "what they did wrong." Combined with the misguided insistence of certain political groups that homosexuality is a "lifestyle choice" rather than an inalienable, inherent aspect of a human being, this can give rise to the sense, on the part of an LGBT person living with mental illness, that he or she is somehow to blame for his or her condition, and that they do not deserve competent or culturally sensitive treatment.

Thus, in the field of mental health, stigma constitutes a psychosocial stressor that warrants the attention of mental health practitioners and planners as a public health matter. In this light, the development and implementation of Rainbow Heights Club exemplify a community mental health response to a targeted population. The challenge was to create a program that would confront the manifold stresses created by stigma and provide an affirmative atmosphere for psychological, social, emotional, and physical well-being. The staff developed and, through grant funding, implemented their idea to create Rainbow Heights Club, a supportive, sensitive place to affirm one's identity as an LGBT consumer of mental health services.

PROGRAM DESCRIPTION

Rainbow Heights Club is a psychosocial support and advocacy program that serves LGBT people, age 21 and up, who have a past or present Axis I diagnosis; are lesbian, gay, bisexual, or transgender; and are currently in psychiatric treatment. (If prospective clients of the agency are not currently in treatment, referrals are provided.) The emphasis is on creating a safe space within which members can disclose and discuss both their sexual and psychiatric issues, find social support and acceptance, feel like a welcomed member of a community, and find that they can offer support and acceptance to others. A range of support and activity groups is offered each day; attendance, as well as participation in all groups, is voluntary; all services are provided free of charge; and a highlight of each day is the evening meal, which members can help to plan, shop for, prepare, serve, and clean up after.

With the support of the New York City Department of Health and Mental Hygiene, Rainbow Heights Club opened its doors in September 2002. At first, the agency had a membership of 15 people, and a daily census of 4 or 5 people. As of December 2010, the club had over 500 members, with about 100 more joining every year; daily attendance is between 30 and 45. The club's growth was facilitated through extensive outreach, as well as word of mouth.

In 2009, in response to extensive requests from consumers, the agency successfully applied for additional funding to extend its 25 hours a week of afternoon services into weekday evenings. Support from the New York State Department of Health enabled the agency to extend its programming, which is now offered 12:30—8:30 p.m., five days per week.

Ongoing consumer input is a cornerstone of the work at Rainbow Heights Club. Because attendance and participation are voluntary, members only participate in programming that directly meets their interests and needs. Staff solicit consumer input in weekly community meetings and monthly consumer advisory board meetings. Members give input on staffing and programming and propose new activities and groups. Members organize special events, excursions, and outings—and they also plan and carry out fundraising events, such as bake sales and talent shows, to finance these special events.

Updating this chapter in early 2011 gives us the opportunity to comment on the consumer input the agency solicited during the budget crisis, and the impact it had on Rainbow Heights Club members. In 2010, the agency experienced the loss of 15% of its annual funding, as did many agencies like it. Rather than attempting to cope with this difficult situation alone, staff communicated openly with consumers in community meetings about the exact amount of funding that was being lost, and requested input regarding the areas of the budget that most directly impacted on consumers' experience.

One might assume that consumers would be distressed or dismayed at being included to such a degree in decisions about agency budgeting. However, the opposite was the case. Consumers expressed gratitude and relief that these disclosures were made to them, and that their input was sought in these decisions. "We know there's a budget crisis happening. Sometimes other programs just downsize or even close up, and we never get told anything," one consumer said. "So it feels good that you were honest with us about what's going on."

Other than staff salaries, and non-negotiable expenses such as required insurance and audit fees, the main areas that impact consumers' experience at Rainbow Heights Club are the evening meal program and a small stipend ($2 daily) that is given to members who participate in the day's programming, to assist them in meeting the cost of the subway ride home. Members unanimously stated that they could easily accept a 30% reduction in the food budget, that they could readily accept menus featuring simpler fare, and that they would contribute more effort to helping prepare food in-house. However, they stated overwhelmingly that, without the daily $2 transportation stipend, many of them who live on disability support and are unable to work would simply be unable to afford transportation to the club. Staff responded by implementing the recommended reduction in the food budget, but respected consumers' need for the transportation stipend and did not make reductions there. As a result, the agency weathered a round of significant budget cuts with open communication and improved morale. Although it may seem either trivial or counterproductive, the approach taken with these budget-related conversations is typical of the consumer-oriented attitude at Rainbow Heights Club and appears to be central to the significant positive impact the agency has on its members' lives.

It is one of Rainbow Heights Club's fundamental tenets that everyone has the right to explore and express their sexual orientation and gender identity however they see fit. There is no right or wrong way of being an LGBT person at Rainbow Heights Club. We realize that some members benefit greatly from being open and "out of the closet" about their sexual orientation or gender identity, whereas, for others, choosing to maintain their privacy is vitally important. Although we facilitate open conversations about disclosing one's identity to others, staff do not pressure or even encourage members to disclose if it is not their own decision to do so.

This breadth of acceptance of members' expression (or non-expression) of their identities is particularly important for people who are on the transgender continuum. Many members of Rainbow Heights Club would not be able to pass the psychiatric evaluation that is required for those who wish to receive hormone therapy or gender-affirming surgeries. Others would not be able to afford the expense of such interventions. Still others choose not to alter their bodies in any way, but still inhabit their preferred gender role as either a public or a profoundly private experience of deep personal conviction. Regardless of the degree to which a given member's gender identity is something that other people can see, both staff and members affirm each member's chosen gender identity by using the name and pronoun that support that identity. This simple gesture of freedom, dignity, and acceptance can have powerful effects, and we recommend it to all clinicians and recovery communities.[1]

RESULTS OF RAINBOW HEIGHTS CLUB CONSUMER SURVEY

Twice each year, Rainbow Heights Club requests feedback from its consumers in the form of an anonymous consumer survey that assesses members' satisfaction with the agency's services, as well as the agency's impact on members' well-being and quality of life. The results of this survey demonstrate the effectiveness of the agency's interventions. They are documented in detail in Hellman, Klein, Huygen, Chew, and Uttaro (2010). As the present chapter focuses on stigma and its amelioration, we will briefly summarize recent survey results that highlight these issues.

Eighty-seven members took part in the June 2010 consumer survey. Many completed the survey online; members could also complete the survey on paper, or, if their reading or writing skills were a barrier for them, they could request to take the survey as an interview, with a staff member writing down their responses. The results show that 88% of members were free of psychiatric hospitalizations in the past year; 84% were free of hospital admissions for medical reasons; 79% of members who expressed an opinion felt that being a member of Rainbow Heights Club helped them to remain free of psychiatric hospitalization; and 85% of members who did experience psychiatric hospitalization in the past year felt that Rainbow Heights Club helped them to be psychiatrically hospitalized less often, or for a shorter time, than they would have been otherwise.

Rainbow Heights Club members showed very strong treatment compliance: 80% of members who have a psychiatrist, and 98% of those who have a therapist, saw these care providers in the previous month; 83% who take psychiatric medications take them "always," and another 11% take them "often," for a total of 94%; and 71% say they are more consistent with their treatment since joining Rainbow Heights Club.

27

Of members expressing an opinion, 85% say they have more hope since joining Rainbow Heights Club; 75% have better self-esteem; and 85% have more social support. These figures underline the impact of a program designed to address and ameliorate the mechanisms of stigma.

As a side note, the demographics of Rainbow Heights Club are highly diverse: 37% are African–American, 21% are Latino, 4% are Native American, 3% Asian–American, 16% identify as "other," and 37% are white. A full 30% of active members are transgender or gender-nonconforming: 14% are transgender male-to-female, 3% are transgender female-to-male, 8% identify as gender nonconforming, and 4% identify as "other."

In closing, we would like to offer some suggested guidelines toward effective and culturally competent treatment with LGBT mental health consumers.

LGBT consumers report numerous barriers that make it difficult for them to find and access effective care (Lucksted, 2004). Even if their care providers do not openly discourage them from discussing issues relating to their sexual orientation or gender identity—which they often do—consumers may simply assume that, in keeping with the mental health field's long tradition of pathologizing same-sex sexual attraction and nonconforming gender identity, their care providers will follow suit. It is vital that we take the first step in letting consumers know that we want to be affirming and accepting of all of our clients, and that we want to hear about the full range of their experience.

Use Inclusive Language

Many of us unknowingly give LGBT clients the impression that we are not prepared to hear about their experience. For example, if we innocently ask a female client, "Are you married, or do you have a boyfriend?" we have excluded the possibility that she may have a same-sex partner. For a client who is already apprehensive about making such a disclosure, such language may cause her to give a simple concrete answer, "no," rather than making the effort to make an anxiety-provoking disclosure that seems to be outside her care provider's frame of reference. Asking, instead, "Are you in a relationship right now? What kind of people do you usually have relationships with?" is a simple way of opening a door and letting our clients know that we want to hear from them.

Make Your Office and Environment LGBT-Inclusive

If you have a bulletin board featuring community resources, including a flyer or brochure from a local LGBT community center or group makes a statement, and LGBT clients are likely to take note. Many LGBT people lose the support of friends, family, or religious communities after disclosing their LGBT status. As a result, many are vigilant in seeking clues about whether or not it will be safe to disclose in a given context. A flyer, a brochure, or an LGBT magazine included with the other materials in an office or waiting room is a simple way of sending LGBT clients the message that they have a right to express themselves and find support.

Welcome and Normalize Consumer Disclosures

All clients struggle with the issue of discussing their sexual relationships, feelings, conflicts, hopes, and fears with care providers. All clients—especially LGBT ones—would benefit from the reassurance of a simple "I'm glad you told me that," in response to a disclosure about their identity, relationships, or feelings. Care providers can demonstrate their openness by following up on disclosures with simple, normalizing questions, such as, "What's he like?" and "Where did you meet him?" Those simple questions demonstrate that the relationship being discussed is real, is important to the care provider, and is appropriate for discussion with the care provider. Showing this openness can have a tremendous, positive effect on the working alliance and undo some of the estrangement from the mental health establishment that many LGBT consumers experience.

Avoid Both Overpathologizing and Underpathologizing

Many care providers pathologize any aspect of a consumer's expression of his or her sexual or gender identity, interpreting it as further evidence of the person's illness. However, LGBT consumers' efforts to express their sexuality and find connections with others are often the locus of a great deal of creativity, resilience, courage, and even playfulness. Conversely, it is not helpful to assume that every expression of a consumer's sexuality or gender identity is to be celebrated. LGBT people can make decisions that are harmful to themselves and/or other people, just like anybody else. Any such activity should be pragmatically evaluated in terms of its effect on the consumer's physical and emotional health, self-esteem, and relationships.

For each club member, the benefits of participation in the club are different. Some enjoy the possibility of having friends who are also LGBT consumers. Others take advantage of the chance to develop a budding repertoire of social skills in a safe and supportive environment. Still others focus on the chance to express themselves artistically or in writing. Along the way, they are all learning to be more comfortable telling their stories, and they are all learning how universal many aspects of their stories can be.

The two following vignettes vividly illustrate the many and varied ways that the Rainbow Club members have benefited from this program:

Laura

"Laura," a member of Rainbow Heights Club, is a Latina lesbian who wears her hair in a short crew cut, never wears makeup, and prefers masculine clothing. On her first day at a new mental health clinic, she was sitting in the waiting room when a staff member walked through the room and said, to the receptionist, "*Mira esa puta* (look at that dyke)." The man turned out to be her therapist. When staff asked her whether she had told the man she had understood perfectly well what he had said, she replied, "No! I had a lot of stuff I had to get off my chest." She added that she avoided talking about her sexuality or her relationship in her treatment. This story demonstrates the lengths to which LGBT people with mental illness feel they must go in order to get some vestige of assistance from a system they believe fundamentally does not care about them. Laura's story also shows that many LGBT people with mental illness remain in the closet, even with their therapists; and that they often do not believe that they deserve, or have the right to demand, competent and respectful treatment. Participating in Rainbow Heights Club helped Laura to realize how central her identity and relationships are to her recovery. She came to realize that she deserved and needed a therapist who would support and affirm her. Rainbow Heights Club staff were able to refer her to more supportive treatment, and since that time she has returned to work and has remained free of hospitalization.

Steven

"Steven" is a 60-year-old Caucasian male with a history of numerous psychiatric diagnoses, treatment with an extensive array of medications, and numerous hospitalizations over the past 30 years. He rarely participates in structured support or activity groups at the club, but instead makes extensive use of opportunities for informal socializing with other club members in the safe environment the agency provides. He is currently stable, entirely free of medications, and has not been hospitalized since he started attending the club five years ago. He is a valued member of the Rainbow Heights Community: he is a source of playful humor as well as thoughtful advice. He credits the support and encouragement of club members with enabling him to make these changes in his life.

CONCLUSION

Rainbow Heights Club has consistently helped nearly 90% of its members remain free of psychiatric hospitalization every year. When we consider that all Rainbow Heights members are diagnosed as severely mentally ill, and that the majority of them have a history of repeated psychiatric hospitalizations, it is clear that the support provided by the club is making a significant difference in keeping this population stable and in the community. This outcome demonstrates the importance of providing culturally sensitive and specific psychosocial support and advocacy services, within a peer-based environment. We feel strongly that mental health consumers who are members of a number of marginalized, oppressed communities can benefit from the establishment of similar agencies addressing their particular needs.

DISCUSSION QUESTIONS

1. Discuss dual stigma as it relates to LGBT individuals with serious mental illness.

2. Brainstorm and list on the blackboard examples of how people in our society are stigmatized.

3. In what ways do the mental health needs of the LGBT population differ from those of the heterosexual seriously mentally ill? In what ways are they similar?

LEARNING ASSIGNMENT

Identify groups in the United States that have suffered from stigma. What steps can you think of to reduce stigma.

SUGGESTED READINGS

Estroff, S. (1981). *Making it crazy: An ethnography of psychiatric clients in an American Community*. Berkeley, CA: University of California Press.

Goffman, E. (1963). *Stigma: Notes on the management of spoiled identity*. Englewood Cliffs NJ: Prentice Hall.

Lucksted, A. (2004). Lesbian, gay, bisexual and transgender people receiving services in the public mental health system: Raising issues. In R.E. Hellman & J. Drescher (Eds.), *Handbook of LGBT issues in community mental health*. Binghamton, NY: The Haworth Press.

INTERNET RESOURCES

Association of Gay and Lesbian Psychiatrists: www.aglp.org

The Gay, Lesbian and Straight Education Network: www.glsen.org

Rainbow Heights: www.rainbowheights.org

NOTE

1   We realize that some mental health-care providers struggle with the issue of endorsing a client's chosen gender identity when doing so appears to reinforce a gender identity disorder currently pathologized in the present edition of the *Diagnostic and Statistical Manual of Mental Disorders*. However, we strongly recommend that care providers use transgender clients' chosen name and pronoun, in the privacy of the consulting room, and then simply observe the results. If the client becomes more related and open; if he or she shows a greater degree of self-esteem, insight, and judgment; if the therapeutic alliance tangibly improves—then recognizing and respecting the client's preferred gender role would seem to be a beneficial and therapeutic intervention. Conversely, refusing to recognize a client's preferred gender can be experienced by transgender clients as abusive and rejecting, and often results in the client breaking off treatment, or requesting a different care provider.

REFERENCES

Cochran, S.D. (2001). Emerging issues in research on lesbians' and gay men's mental health: Does sexual orientation really matter? *American Psychologist, 56*, 931–947.

Cochran, S.D., Sullivan, J.G., & Mays, V.M. (2001). Prevalence of psychiatric disorders, psychological distress, and treatment utilization among lesbian, gay, and bisexual individuals in a sample of the U.S. population. Unpublished manuscript (Available from Susan D. Cochran, Department of Epidemiology, School of Public Health, University of California, Los Angeles, Box 951772, Los Angeles, CA 90095- 1772).

Estroff, S. (1981). *Making it crazy: An ethnography of psychiatric clients in an American community.* Berkeley, CA: University of California Press.

Fergusson, D.M., Horwood, L.J., & Beautrais, A.L. (1999). Is sexual orientation related to mental health problems and suicidality in young people? *Archives of General Psychiatry, 56*, 876–880.

Goffman, E. (1963). *Stigma: Notes on the management of spoiled identity.* Englewood Cliffs, NJ: Prentice Hall.

Hellman, R.E., Klein, E., Huygen, C., Chew, M., & Uttaro, T. (2010). A study of members of a support and advocacy program for LGBT persons with major mental illness. *Best Practices in Mental Health: An International Journal, 6*, 13–26.

Hellman, R.E., Sudderth, L., & Avery, A.M. (2002). Major mental illness in a sexual minority psychiatric sample. *Journal of the Gay and Lesbian Medical Association, 6*, 97–106.

Link, B., & Phelan, J. (2001). *On stigma and its public health applications.* Paper presented at Stigma and Global Health: An International Conference, Bethesda, Maryland.

Lucksted, A. (2004). Lesbian, gay, bisexual and transgender people receiving services in the public mental health system: Raising issues. In R.E. Hellman & J. Drescher (Eds.), *Handbook of LGBT issues in community mental health.* Binghamton, NY: The Haworth Press.

Rosenberg, S., Rosenberg, J., Huygen, C., & Klein, E. (2005). No need to hide: Out of the closet and mentally ill. *Best Practices in Mental Health: An International Journal, 1*, 72–85.

Sandfort, T.G.M., de Graaf, R., Bijl, R.V., & Schnabel, P. (2001). Same-sex sexual behavior and psychiatric disorders: Findings from the Netherlands mental health survey and incidence study (NEMESIS). *Archives of General Psychiatry, (58)*, 85–91.

Chapter 3

Where Do We Go From Here?

The Mental Health Consumer Movement in the United States

Richard Pulice and Steven Miccio

As we move into the second decade of the 21st century and take stock of the community mental health landscape, a mixed picture emerges: Stigma against persons with mental illness persists, and poverty, despair, and the lack of treatment for persons with a disability define the reality for millions of people. Community mental health programs are reeling from the impact of the economic downturn and the recession of 2008, and cutbacks to social programs abound, often at the expense of the most vulnerable. However, at the same time, the struggle for social justice and civil rights continues, with some notable achievements, primarily through legislative reforms, advocacy, and court interventions. Although it would be heartening to be able to state that stigma and discrimination against persons with a disability have subsided, and that poverty, despair, and a lack of appropriate treatment are no longer an issue, we are unable to do that. However, we can identify a number of examples of positive changes in community mental health. This chapter examines the transition of persons suffering from mental illness from patient to client to consumer and then system survivor. Finally, it considers the role of self-help and peer support as a model for continued positive change.

HISTORICAL OVERVIEW: FROM INMATE TO CONSUMER

The treatment of persons with serious mental illness has evolved considerably since its brutal beginnings in early American history, a period in which people who were judged as "mentally ill" were viewed as inmates, often housed in jails or prison-like environments, and afforded the same level of treatment as criminals. Later, they assumed the role of hospital patient, and were given treatments that ranged from lobotomies and sterilization to heavy doses of medication and electro-shock therapy. Large, impersonal, state facilities housed hundreds of thousands of people, often for their entire lives. The 1960s and 1970s ushered in an era of deinstitutionalization and, with that, the label of clients, with the implication that they could make choices about the treatment they receive. Finally and most recently, persons suffering from a mental illness are called consumers and have a role in policy and program planning, as well as advocacy and service delivery.

THE CONSUMER MOVEMENT IS A CIVIL RIGHTS MOVEMENT

The civil rights movement in the United States, although a long struggle, came to a peak in the 1960s, first addressing issues of race and later those of ethnicity and sexual discrimination. As part of this effort, disability rights were also included as components of the social justice movement; the first gains were made in the area of developmental disabilities, then called mental retardation. Progress in the care of persons with a mental illness was achieved as well, albeit more slowly and with more societal resistance. Often unsupported by family and communities, mental health consumers had to fend for themselves.

The mental health consumer movement that came to fruition in the 1970s was a civil rights entity for people who have suffered from a serious mental illness and who alleged to have been oppressed, overmedicated, incarcerated, and coerced for many years, in mental health facilities in the United States and around the world. The movement was made up of people who believed that they were dehumanized by psychiatrists and other mental health providers owing, in large part, to the belief that people with mental illness could not or would not recover to a life of independence and self-determination. The consumer movement put forward the theory that recovery was possible. The people that started the movement became more self-determined and independent and were, in fact, recovering from what seemed to be a life-long debilitating illness. Through the consumer movement, people realized that they did not have to accept a life of low expectations and minimal achievements. People involved in the movement learned from each other how to become less reliant on the mental health system as it existed and moved to demand rights and respect from a system that was based on a foundation of long-term institutionalization and total dependence. The mental health consumer movement gave birth to self-help and peer support approaches, which have been responsible for the growth of peer-operated services. It has also been a catalyst for the recovery of thousands of people who may have never achieved their full potential if the mental health system did not adapt to a more recovery-oriented structure. The following pages trace the history of the consumer movement and the role that self-help and peer support plays in the recovery of many.

A HISTORY OF THE MENTAL HEALTH CONSUMER MOVEMENT (1868 TO THE PRESENT)

Why go back and examine history? What can we learn from the past? Can understanding the past help us avoid recreating the same mistakes in the future? Can mental health professionals be part of positive change? Understanding history is one way to impact positive change.

To understand the mental health consumer movement, one needs to go back in history to 1868, when Elizabeth Packard, a former psychiatric patient, founded the Anti-Insane Asylum Society. Packard wrote articles and books and pamphlets that described her experiences while committed to an Illinois insane asylum. As one of the first consumer advocates in mental health, she met great opposition during that time, as people had many fallacious beliefs about mental illness, including that it was the result of demonic possession. As a consequence, her activism was largely ignored.

In 1908, Clifford W. Beers, also a former psychiatric patient, founded the National Committee on Mental Hygiene. This committee later became what is known as the National Mental

WHERE DO WE GO FROM HERE?

Health Association, whose work was pioneering in supporting the causes of those with a mental illness. Beers' mission was to improve the life and treatment of people with mental illness, not through organizing people but through connections and networks he developed in the community. Beers knew that the world was not ready for organized activism and knew that he could better serve the mentally ill by using the influence of other people in the community. Although Beers was relatively successful in his mission to improve the mental health system, he too continued to meet with great opposition. Despite some efforts to protect the rights of the mentally ill and to have services offered in the community, the 1920s and 1930s continued to be a time of significant growth of large psychiatric institutions.

In the 1940s, a group of former mental patients formed WANA (We Are Not Alone). Their goal was to help others make the transition from inpatient hospitalization to community living. These efforts led to the establishment of Fountain House. The members of Fountain House supported one another in a mutual setting and promoted meaningful work and social relationships. This model contributed greatly to peer support and self-help, which will be discussed later in this chapter. Fountain House still exists today in New York City as a model psychosocial rehabilitation program.

THE ERA OF DEINSTITUTIONALIZATION

The 1950s ushered in the era of deinstitutionalization. This led the way for what is today's current consumer movement. The impetus behind deinstitutionalization was, primarily, an economic one, designed to create cost savings for the states, disguised as a social movement whose stated aim was putting people back into community settings. For example, the resources, both financial and programmatic, to serve those persons who were released from New York City institutions did not follow them into the community. This early effort resulted in many people falling through the cracks and promoted re-admittance (recidivism) back into psychiatric hospitals, and some would hypothesize that it resulted in more people with mental illness ending up homeless or in jails and prisons. The money that was saved by reducing the cost of inpatient care did not get fully reinvested in the form of community services, resulting in service gaps in housing, clinical, social, and health services. One positive outcome of deinstitutionalization, however, was that some of the people who were released from the large institutions were witness to the civil rights movements taking place. Small groups began to gain a voice in regards to the treatment of people in the hospitals. Throughout the years, ex-patients began to find their voice and stood in opposition to the poor, inconsistent, and often inadequate treatment that they were receiving from the mental health community.

In the 1960s and 1970s, the mental health consumer movement began to gain momentum. Interestingly, the movement made its mark inside psychiatric institutions in the United States, as patients began to protest the poor or disrespectful treatment that they were receiving. During this time, deinstitutionalization was in full swing. This furthered the mission of the consumer movement through the development of mutual support groups and the beginnings of consumer-run services in the community. Deinstitutionalization highlighted the need for community-based services to address re-entry into the community in terms of adequate housing, meaningful work, effective treatment, and the development of social relationships.

As mental health services in the communities grew, they illustrated the need for public policy change to meet the demands put on community-based services. This public policy change fueled the consumers/survivors/ex-patients and mental patients to form mutual support groups in community settings. Sally Zinman, a self-described ex-mental patient and consumer leader wrote a "how-to" book with former patients, which educated others on how to start support groups (Zinman et al., 1987).

The unrest among former mental patients in the United States gave root to several consumer support groups that developed unique and different philosophies and missions. As the result of these differing opinions and philosophies, the anti-psychiatry movement began. In fact, three distinct groups of ex-patients evolved. One group sought to abolish psychiatry and the mental health system, owing to alleged forceful coerciveness and poor treatment of people. A second group of ex-patients attempted to reform the mental health system in concert with concerned professionals and policymakers. Finally, a third group continued to believe in, and rely on, traditional mental health services. The group that believes that the current mental health system is "okay" can best be described as individuals who have been in the system for a very long time, have been told again and again that they will never recover, and are so fearful of the system that they will not stand up or voice opinions owing to fear of retribution.

Although this group is in decline today, there is still a presence of people who remain compliant to the system and lack self-determination and self-esteem. This is not a criticism of any particular group; it is just a reality of the perception of the antiquated mental health system that continues to be held by people who could possibly have a better quality of life with improved education and greater self-esteem. The differing philosophies among these groups still continue, yet it is clear that recovery from mental illness is possible if individuals have the proper supports in place.

On the other end of the spectrum, during the 1970s, a social justice movement began that worked against forced treatment and promoted client self-determination. Groups emerged calling themselves by names such as Mad Pride, Network Against Psychiatric Assault, On Our Own, The Insane Liberation Front, and the National Association for Rights and Protection and Advocacy. They were led by consumers who had been in the system and were now demanding "Nothing about us without us" from the policymakers of the mental health system. What this meant was that consumers believed that they knew what was best for them in their recovery from mental and emotional problems. Consumers wanted a place at the table of policy-making and to reform the mental health system. Consumers insisted that the traditional model of mental health services did not take into account that people with mental illness were whole people, and not just the symptoms recognized by many in the mental health system. This brought critical attention to how people were consistently and historically treated symptomatically, with medication, psychotherapy, electro-shock therapy, or long-term warehousing in large institutions or acute-care settings.

As deinstitutionalization continued, and advocacy groups continued to grow into the 1980s, consumer-operated groups began to organize in a more formal way. Many obtained official status as IRS 501(C) 3 not-for-profit organizations[1] and began to receive funding from federal and state governments. Services they provided included advocacy, as well as peer support and mutual support groups. The consumer movement received recognition and support regarding the value of peer support, advocacy, and self-help. This was acknowledged by governments and policymakers. Today, many consumer run organizations are "at the table," deeply involved in policy-making and systems advocacy. Many have even become mental health service providers, offering housing, vocational assistance, and peer case management services. As a result of consumers becoming paraprofessionals in the mental health system, restlessness and disagreement have developed among consumers across the nation. Some groups feel that the consumer/providers have been co-opted by the mental health system and thus cannot promote change in the system that financially feeds them. The groups that are today called the more radical anti-psychiatry movement refuse to accept funds from any government source and continue to fight at the grass-roots level, with limited support and organization. Consumer groups that work within the mental health system accept local and government funding, and work to partner with mental health professionals in changing the culture of managing mental illness to managing wellness. The approach is to create a more efficient and effective mental health system through self-help, person-centered treatment and proactive treatment. Although the consumer community continues to be fragmented at times, one thing is clear: consumer-operated services have been and continue to be a vital part of the mental health service system. As more research is completed that examines the efficacy of consumer-operated services, the mental health system should continue to promote a culture shift that will move from illness-based management to wellness-based management. The mental health system needs to be proactive in the recovery of individuals and less reactive to the incidents of crisis that occur today. The majority of today's mental health consumer movement is focused on developing the partnership model between providers and consumers and creating change that is needed to infuse the philosophy of recovery. The consumer movement must work with policymakers at the state and federal levels to promote reform that will empower and promote consumers of services having a choice in treatment options.

SELF-HELP/PEER SUPPORT

Can people with a disability such as a serious mental illness help each other in a meaningful way? What is the effect of that support on the quality of a person's life? Self-help or peer support, once called a "partnership model," is a process by which people voluntarily come together to help each other in a group or individual setting by addressing common concerns and issues. Support groups constitute an intentional effort where people share their personal experiences with others to increase a person's understanding of a given situation. "Peer support is a system of giving and receiving help founded on key principles of respect, shared responsibility and mutual agreement of what is helpful" (Mead, Hilton, and Curtis, 2001). In the 1970s and 1980s, self-help/peer support began in the large psychiatric centers and concentrated on changing attitudes and behaviors on the psychiatric units. In California, a group called We C.A.N. (Client Advocacy Now) started support groups on the hospital units and began to play out real-life situations in the hospital by mimicking staff, through acting out their perceptions of patient care. The first skits were born. Consumer groups got the attention of the hospital staff and became an integral part of staff training. This initiated a change in the attitudes of the staff and eventually became instrumental in getting the training out to the local county hospitals. This helped staff understand how they were being perceived and in turn changed behaviors of staff from seemingly insensitive treatment to respectful treatment of patients. As the skits continued, consumers began to return to the original model of support groups, and more and more ex-mental patients wanted to learn more about self-help. This was the beginning of formalizing self-help support groups, which differed from the traditional medical-model support groups that were run by professional therapists. One of the differences between professional support groups and groups run by peers is that consumer participation is completely voluntary. There is also no hierarchy in the peer support group, and no one pretends to have all of the answers. As there is no professional in a support group, it tends to promote independence, which in turn promotes higher self-esteem, stronger self-determination, and better recovery outcomes. Hope is elevated to a level that many professionals rarely attain with "patients."

Although support is not therapy in the traditional sense, it can often result in better rewards, either in concert with traditional therapy or, sometimes, other than therapy, as it offers comfort, support, and a friendly ear that will intently listen to and validate the feelings of fellow participants. It also builds relationships, which, in the traditional sense, are often absent or limited, as today's therapists have very limited time to build healing relationships. In many cases, staff retention is a difficulty with therapists, as a result of job movement or positions laid victim to funding cuts. It is difficult for a consumer to build a trusting relationship if therapists do not retain their positions, and an individual may have two or several therapists in a single year. The support groups offer stability, time, and the ability to foster strong relationships, which often grow into natural social relationships. Support groups are very comforting to people who have experienced similar situations, and have been effective in helping people get beyond issues that have prevented forward progress towards recovery.

There are a few rules that most support groups follow. They include, but are not limited to:

- No street drugs or alcohol may be used or carried on a person during scheduled activities.
- No violence, verbal or physical will be permitted.
- Intolerance will not be tolerated.
- In return for support, members are expected to respect the needs of those supporting them and to be considerate of each other.
- Do Not Commit! Unless expressly and freely told to do so by him/her in writing.
- Confidentiality is a must.

Peer support can be done in a group setting or can be done one to one with individuals. Either way, it is effective, and people can easily choose which format they would like that promotes recovery and comfort. Peer support is characterized by its effective use of mutual aid, social interaction, and companionship that encompasses all aspects of people's lives, such as work and recreation.

Support groups are usually the best means for individuals to learn new information on local programs, such as coping strategies or alternative treatments. Support groups educate individuals on local advocacy efforts, other support groups, and vital information related to entitlements. Support groups can include tasks that educate others on how to address problems and issues, through modeling, teaching, learning, and problem-solving skills discussion.

According to many consumers, the focus of the traditional mental health system is on symptom reduction. Consumers believe that this method of treatment does not take into account that people with mental illness are whole people. By only focusing on the symptoms, normative treatment is ignored. This results in limited discussion of personal interests, personal goals, and personal feelings beyond symptoms, and it limits social support networks. Supports promote personal interest discussion, as it promotes participants to move beyond symptomatic examination toward self-determination and empowerment, which are vital for successful recovery (Chamberlin, 1995). The traditional medical model also looks to reduce hospitalizations for individuals, but does not take into account that a reduction in hospitalization does not necessarily mean a better quality of life. A person may be able to stay out of a hospital, but may be sitting in a room with a TV, chain smoking cigarettes, and drinking large amounts of coffee (Deegan, 1992). These are topics that are often discussed in support groups, and these are the tools that help people get beyond illness and on a road to recovery. This is not to say that there are no valid or acceptable traditional models of mental health care. It is to say that there needs to be a balance of treatment that looks at all aspects of one's life.

One of the more positive benefits of support groups is in the area of social integration. Support groups afford people the opportunity to participate in all aspects of community life. The groups promote voluntary relationships, valued social roles, and life-enriching activities. At a peer-operated organization called PEOPLE, Inc., many of the support groups have turned into additional groups that focus on recreational activities and community participation activities. Individuals from several support groups have started jewelry-making, craft, and music groups. Some groups plan weekly shopping outings together, or go to movies together, or even plan cooking events where each person brings ingredients, and culinary delights are created. It is all self-perpetuated by participation in original support groups, and the participants drive the activities in a collaborative partnership. The longer a support group continues to meet, the stronger the relationships, and the more valued the social networks become. Studies have shown (Corrigan & Jacobson, 1997) that continued group membership can result in improved self-esteem, better decision-making skills, and improved social functioning (Carpinello, Knight, & Janis, 1991).

In more recent years, support groups have become increasingly popular on the Internet, including many listserves, chat rooms, and bulletin boards. There are also national and local self-help clearinghouses that disseminate information about existing self-help groups. The bottom line to peer support and self-help is that these activities focus strongly on recovery outcomes and solutions for individuals. These groups are powerful tools in many aspects of one's life, and yet remain underutilized and under-researched in the scientific field.

PRACTICE AND POLICY CONSIDERATIONS

As new consumer leaders emerge in the consumer mental health movement, they are working to collaborate and partner with the mental health systems in their respective regions to reform the mental health system and develop better outcomes for individuals. It is more of a proactive approach, which is different from the original advocates who believed that they had to be adversarial to create change. As education is increasing, consumers and non-consumers, providers and family members understand the issues facing the mental health system a little better today, but there is a long way to go in reforming a system that is underfunded and under-researched. It is time to raise the bar on local, state, and federal accountability, and it is time to reform the vision of what mental health services should look like. Recovered

39

consumers see the value in peer support and self-help and are demanding, not only to sit at the table, but also to lead the way, or partner, in reforming services that are helpful for all individuals and see individuals as whole people, with needs, goals, and dreams.

As practitioners in the mental health system, it is important that we learn from history and apply the lessons learned in a positive way. How will you work with consumers of mental health services? What are the mutual roles of professional and consumers? Although there are no simple and fixed practice answers, it is clear that an attitude and approach of mutual respect is essential. How to implement this in practice is very individualized and requires an ongoing evaluation of self and your place in the cycle of care and support and recovery.

Changes in mental health policy over the last decade have also provided support to the mental health consumer movement and contributed to the progress that has occurred. Parity in insurance, assuring that mental health services are paid for in the same way that health care services are paid for, is now the norm in many states and for federal employees. Health-care reform, passed by the Congress in 2010, will also play a role in this parity, although, at the time of writing, the effect of challenges to this legislation and the impact of post-recession fiscal constraints are unclear. Other legislative efforts, some viewed as positive, some as negative, that assure access treatment and a safe environment have also been implemented in the last few years. As practitioners at all levels, we must be aware of these policies and their impact on practice.

SUMMARY

This chapter examined the history and development of the mental health consumer movement in the United States. It looked at the change in social status and acceptance of a disability group who, as a result of a lack of a strong advocacy base, often suffered from substandard and dehumanizing living conditions. As history has shown, mental health consumers have come forward to advocate for themselves and those who will need services in the future. This advocacy, coupled with the emergence of self-help groups and peer support efforts, has made great strides in bringing the needs and desires of those recovering from a mental illness to the forefront. Finally, the role of practitioners in this movement was considered, with an eye toward understanding and being a part of a mutually respectful process in which influencing policy and practice plays a role in the overarching goal of recovery.

DISCUSSION QUESTIONS

1. This chapter addressed issues related to consumers of mental health services. What other groups can you think of in the United States that have had a similar kind of history? What is your impression of their past and current situation? What "lessons learned" can we apply from this reading to your identified group(s)?

2. Stigma (thinking or acting negatively) about a person or group is still a big problem throughout the world. How can you combat stigma, both in your own thinking and actions and in those of others?

3. A big fear of many persons in the community is that persons with a mental illness are violent. Is this true? What can we do to educate others about this issue?

LEARNING ASSIGNMENT

Class Project

As part of a class effort, research what consumer or peer organizations are in your area. Have a group from class visit them to talk about what they do, who they serve, etc. Present your information in class with an eye toward the readings and how you, as mental health professionals, can support their mission.

SUGGESTED READINGS

Beam, Alex (2001) *Gracefully insane: Life and death inside America's premier mental hospital*, Public Affairs.

D'Antonio, Michael (2004) *The State Boys Rebellion*, Simon & Schuster.

Whitaker, Robert (2002) *Mad in America: Bad science, bad medicine, and the enduring mistreatment of the mentally ill*, Perseus Press.

INTERNET RESOURCES

The National Alliance for the Mentally Ill: www.nami.org

The National Association of State Mental Health Program Directors: www.nasmhpd.org

The National Institute for Mental Health: www.nimh.nih.gov

NOTE

1 The IRS offers a number of not-for-profit designations, the most common of which is called 501(C) 3. This allows for exemption from taxes and for charitable donations to the organization to be tax deductible.

REFERENCES

Carpinello, S.E., Knight, E.L., & Janis, L. (1991). A study of the meaning of self-help, self-help groups processes and outcomes. Proceedings: 1992 NASMHPD Research Conference. Alexandria, Virginia, 37–44.

Chamberlin, J. (1995). Rehabilitating ourselves: The psychiatric survivor movement. *International Journal of Mental Health, 24*(1), 323–346.

Corrigan, P.W., & Jacobson, N.S. (1997). Considerations for research on consumer empowerment and psychosocial interventions. *Psychiatric Services, 48,* 347–352.

Deegan, P.E. (1992). The Independent Living Movement and people with psychiatric disabilities: Taking back control over our own lives. *Psychosocial Rehabilitation Journal, 15,* 3–19.

Mead, S., Hilton, D., & Curtis, L. (2001). Peer support: Theoretical perspective. *Psychiatric Rehabilitation Journal, 25*(2), 134–139.

Zinman, S., Harp, H.T., & Budd, S. (Eds.) (1987). *Reaching Across: Mental health clients helping each other.* Riverside, CA: Self-Help Committee of the California Network of Mental Health Clients.

Part Two

Emerging Trends in Community Mental Health

Chapter 4

Emerging Community Mental Health Challenges

Meeting the Needs of Veterans and Families Impacted by Military Service

Marilyn L. Flynn, Anthony M. Hassan, and Kathleen West

INTRODUCTION

During the past century, the United States has been almost continuously at war, with the Iraq and Afghanistan conflicts the longest in our nation's history. It is now apparent that psychological and personal stresses for service members and their families are more prevalent and powerful than previously understood. The transition from life as a warfighter to civilian life is difficult and not always negotiated successfully. Community mental health programs and the recovery philosophy have never been more crucial to resolution of these hardships and to restoration of human potential.

This chapter describes the special history and context for delivery of mental health services to military service members, veterans, and their families, with a general profile of service member characteristics. The influence of military culture is explained as a mediating factor in outreach and treatment, and challenges to mental health for service members are described, with attention to those especially at risk for depression or anxiety reactions. A brief overview is provided of evidence-based interventions now widely employed in treatment. Finally, present issues in systems of care and the problem of stigma are addressed.

EVOLUTION OF COMMUNITY MENTAL HEALTH CARE IN THE MILITARY

Separate health and mental health provisions for veterans and active military personnel date back to the creation of Hand Hospital in Pittsburgh, Pennsylvania, during the War of Independence in 1778. During the more than 200 years since, two distinct systems for care of injured veterans have evolved—one for those on active full-time duty, and a second to assist veterans following their separation from service. Families and dependents of veterans were excluded, however, until 1966—almost 180 years later, when they were first granted limited eligibility through a Department of Defense (DoD) supported provider group insurance. The extent of their participation and inclusion has gradually increased since that time. Today, this medical care program is called TRICARE and it provides care for active-duty service members and their families, retired service members and their families, National Guard/reserves and their families, survivors, and others entitled to DoD medical care.

The DoD and related congressional committees that oversee appropriations have historically had very little interaction with veterans' health and mental health, today overseen by the Veterans Health Administration (VA). The result has been a serious disjuncture in continuity of care and transfer of patient records that has only recently been addressed. The role of civilian community mental health agencies, public and private, independent of those contracting with DoD or the VA as service providers, has never been separately analyzed as a critical part of the total care network. Yet, in the Iraq and Afghanistan conflicts and in future regional wars, local mental health clinics, school mental health programs, hospital emergency rooms, and other mental health-affiliated agencies have constituted and will continue to constitute a third pillar on which recovery and veterans' support will rest. All providers, not just those in the military, will need an awareness of the needs in this special population.

The primary purpose of the DoD military health system is to ensure that service members are maintained in, or rapidly restored to, readiness for active service, although increasingly it has been recognized that combat-related disorders are persistent and may require years of subsequent attention. VA programs, by contrast, focus on restoring functions impaired by war, protecting those who cannot function through various forms of long-term care or community-based services, and assisting with transition to community life.

During the 1980s, the community mental health movement in the United States exercised a substantial impact on the then-VA Department of Medicine and Surgery. New policies calling for deinstitutionalization of veteran patient populations and creation of new community-based clinics were adopted. Today, VA health programs include all levels of care, through community veterans' clinics and medical campuses directly operated by the VA to Veteran Centers helping service members with adjustment to civilian life following war. Veteran Centers offer both counseling and outreach services to veterans and their families. For those veterans living in the community, the VA offers support through contracted community-based outpatient clinics, operated by civilian practitioners under local governmental or nonprofit jurisdiction. Veterans' service organizations (VSOs) buttress these efforts through voluntary activities and as subcontractors for the DoD and VA. The myriad of VSOs across the country vary greatly in size, effectiveness, quality assurance, and professionalism, but are an expression of the personal urgency many feel and the desire to form a more welcoming society for those who have served.

THE CONTEXT FOR MILITARY SERVICE

Organization and Demographic Characteristics

The United States armed forces are divided into five branches: Army, Navy, Marines, Air Force, and Coast Guard. Each service also recruits reservists and National Guard members from among civilians. That National Guard and the state militias trace their roots to the earliest days of colonization, whereas the reserves were formally organized during the past century. Since 2001, both the reserves and the Guard have been given expanded responsibilities that include both protection of life and property at home and integrated participation in wars abroad. In 2011 alone, more than 94,000 guards and reservists had been activated for service, and over 50,000 are serving in Iraq and Afghanistan.

According to the Government Accountability Office, the composition of the armed forces roughly mirrors that of the United States population, with a slight over-representation of African–Americans. About 36% of service members identify as members of ethnic or racial groups other than Caucasian, with 16.8% African–American, 10.4% Hispanic, 3.8% Asian/Pacific Islander, and 1.5% other. Women now comprise 14.4% of the total force, which represents the greatest proportion in United States military history. Whereas only 7,494 served in the Vietnam War, more than 200,000 have now served in Operation Enduring Freedom (OEF) and Operation Iraqi Freedom (OIF).

Beyond race and gender, diversity can be found across age, geographic location, family composition, and religious background. Among all branches, the average active-duty member is 28 years old, with the youngest average of 25 years in the Marine Corps, and the highest of 29.6 years in the Air Force. The majority are married, 55.2%, and 43% have children, two on average. Many active-duty members have children who are 5 years or younger (41%). Children may attend school on base or in the community. Even when located near large military bases, community schools are often inattentive to the reactions of children to the deployment or death of a parent, creating an area of unmet need in school mental health programs.

Among the National Guard and reserves, the population is older, with an average age of 34 in the reserves and more than a quarter over 41. Almost half (49%) are married, with a wide range among branches, from 30.8% of Marine Corps reservists to 60.6% of Air Force reserves. Relatively few reservists have children (25.1%), compared with the National Guard (41.6%) and others with active-duty status. As might be expected, children in reserve families are generally older, with half between the ages of 6 and 14 years.

Although active-duty service members hail from all 50 states, over half (54.5%) of the forces are stationed in just six states—California, Virginia, Texas, North Carolina, Georgia, and Florida. Upon separation from military service, many veterans and their families remain or return to communities where they were previously based. As a consequence, these six states also have large numbers of veterans. Reserve and National Guard members are concentrated in just 11 states—California, Virginia, Texas, North Carolina, Georgia, Florida, Pennsylvania, New York, Ohio, Alabama, and Illinois. With war waged thousands of miles away and the home military presence limited to only 11 states, Americans are unusually distanced psychologically from the consequences of battle and deployment.

In terms of religious affiliation, the number of military personnel who identify as secular/no religious affiliation, Muslim, Jewish, Buddhist, Hindu, or other non-Christian faiths has grown almost twofold over the past decade. This religious profile is a reflection of the trend in civilian society, but represents a departure from past military populations. It has produced a mismatch today between the military chaplaincy and the personnel they serve. Although only 3% of active-duty service members belong to an evangelical congregation, 33% of military chaplains are members of such denominations. Despite these issues, the chaplains play a crucial role in strengthening the resiliency and morale of service members and are important to their successful reintegration into civilian life.

Military Culture

As recently noted by prominent journalists, the level of public attention to one of the longest running wars in U.S. history has been very low (Brokaw, 2011; Woodward, 2011). Part of this is accounted for by the fact that less than 1% of the American population has served as part of the professional, active-duty, local Guard or reserve forces in Iraq and Afghanistan (United States White House, 2011). For the majority of urban Americans who do not live near a military installation, there is little opportunity to directly observe or personally experience the consequences of this conflict. In smaller, rural communities, where people are more socially connected, the loss of a resident is more keenly felt, but localized all the same.

Equally significant is the gap between civilian and military culture, which is much more pronounced in a nation without universal conscription. As in all cultures, the military has developed its own language, symbols, distinctive norms for behavior, systems for rewards and punishment, and internal institutions to reinforce expectations. Sequestered life on military bases, with schools, hospitals, religious leaders, shopping facilities, and all the other accoutrements of communal life, strengthens internal ties and a sense of being different. Although this kind of socialization promotes unity and preparation for the rigors of war, it also can leave career service members and their families less equipped and less comfortable in a civilian environment. At the same time, it may mean that community mental health professionals, among others, are less effective in communicating with military families, less prepared to recognize the constraints service members face, and less able to choose interventions that are meaningful and feasible.

The United States military is acknowledged worldwide for its professionalism. Preparation for military service involves repeated emphasis on the values of duty, honor, and integrity in personal relationships and teamwork, unit cohesion, and self-sacrifice at the group level. These guidelines are used by service members to evaluate themselves, are tools for survival in combat, and represent points of distinction for the unit itself. The traditions and missions of each branch of the armed forces differ and become part of a service member's identity. Although these ethical standards and traditions are respected in principle by the civilian community, they carry added meaning that is not always recognized in a therapeutic encounter and can alter the success or failure of a therapeutic alliance.

At the same time, the "military" is not a unidimensional entity but a collection of subcultures and subgroups. Sources of internal diversity include rank, the occupational specialty to which an individual has been assigned—which may or may not correspond to their civilian training— and branch of service. As true of the larger society, other salient influences on military experience are defined by race, gender, sexual orientation, primary language and ethnicity, citizenship status, spirituality, age, life stage, and family composition. In general, because of the need for unity and a common sense of mission, the military focuses least on sources of difference and individuality.

One apocryphal story demonstrates this point. A soldier requested new boots.

"What size do you wear?" the solider was asked.
"Why, size ten, sir—the same as everyone else," he replied.

Moving from this mentality or coming to terms with it can be a thorny path for service members, their families, and community mental health professionals.

The strict segregation of civilian and military health-care systems has been eroding for the past three decades. Community-based services of necessity nudged the two sectors into closer connection, especially with the widespread phenomena of homelessness, drug abuse, and mental illness among Vietnam veterans. Perhaps the most important factor, however, has been the shift toward a volunteer army over the decade of warfare in the Middle East that began in 2002. Higher proportions of reserve and National Guard members, sometimes as high as 40%, have been brought into combat; volunteers in the regular forces have separated in greater numbers following their terms of duty; and women have enlisted at the highest rates in history. These groups return, on the whole, much more rapidly to civilian life, lack the organized support that a military base gives to its residents, and bring experiences with them that cannot be easily shared with their neighbors, friends, employers, or family.

THE CHALLENGES TO MENTAL HEALTH

Studies reveal that a high proportion of Iraq and Afghanistan war veterans suffer with mental illness. In a recent study conducted by the Veterans Health Administration, more than one-third of nearly 300,000 veterans had been diagnosed with mental health problems, typically depression or PTSD (Hoge, Auchterlonie, & Milliken, 2006).

Combat Stress and Signature Injuries

By 2011, over 2 million American troops had been deployed as part of OEF in Afghanistan and in OIF. Almost one-third of the 1.4 million members of the National Guard and reserves have served in Iraq or Afghanistan, a number unprecedented compared with previous wars. Thousands of these service members have subsequently come home and honorably separated from service. Thousands more have deployed and continue to serve in the National Guard or Reserve; they therefore can be called to duty again at any point (Schell & Tanielian, 2011).

The demanding operational tempo of two challenging combat theaters, coupled with the nature of the nation's all-volunteer force, has meant that many service members have been deployed two, three, four, or more times since 2001. It should be noted that American soldiers serve longer deployments than their counterparts in the Coalition forces—up to twice as long—and, often, they are allowed very brief rest periods at home between deployments.

In the unique conflicts at the center of the global war on terror, 97% of those sent to fight return home—an unprecedented figure in military history. Although this is good news, the attendant consequences will require society's support for decades to come. Approximately 10–20% of returning warriors will exhibit symptoms of combat trauma; virtually all will require a "step-down" period of readjustment, as will their families. Unlike previous wars, where fighting men and women had as much as two weeks aboard ship before arriving home, service members are now moved rapidly by airplane, with only three to six days in transit. Equally unique, they are not returning from a "front," but rather a combat zone of continuous threat, in city streets and countryside alike, improvised explosive devices murderously hidden in the soil and snipers on rooftops or knolls, and noise everywhere. Not every service member undergoes this psychological pounding, but sometimes the prospect is as daunting as the reality.

The number of surviving service members with permanent disabling injuries surpasses that of any previous modern conflict. In World War II, the survival rate for those suffering physical damage was 2:1; it is now 8:1. Signature wounds of the Iraq and Afghanistan wars include loss of limbs and digits, facial wounds, hearing damage, and traumatic brain injury (TBI), principally from encounters with improvised explosive devices. Improvements in armored protection have gradually reduced the numbers of service members with these physical injuries, although the danger has remained imminent.

The invisible wounds of war have finally been acknowledged by the DoD, Congress, and the general public as legitimate and serious. Psychological response to extreme stress has been reported among soldiers even in the earliest accounts of Greek warfare. Known as "soldier's heart" in the Civil War and "shell shock" in World War II, an organized description was first formulated for American troops following the Vietnam War. The extent of psychological damage was never publicly reported, however, because breakdown or paralysis under stress was either denied or seen as a failure of character.

This response is now known as PTSD, and the first systematic study of prevalence was made by RAND Corporation in 2008. Symptoms include hypervigilance, sleeplessness, irritability, withdrawal, and inability to concentrate, and are sometimes associated with domestic violence, child abuse, and risk-taking behavior. RAND estimated that approximately 30% of all returning veterans were affected with the disorder. Subsequent studies in Israel, Great Britain, and the United States have lowered this figure to perhaps 10 or 15%, with rates rising according to a number of factors, including length of time in theater and role in combat. Risk also seems to be higher among those with prior trauma experiences, such as physical abuse or exposure to excessive aggression (Charuvastra & Cloitre, 2008; Koenen, Moffitt, Poulton, Martin, & Caspi, 2007; Tolin & Foa, 2006). Individuals with such histories include veterans with prior involvement in violence who received criminal-background waivers. Approximately 125,000 so-called "moral waivers" were granted to this group by the DoD between 2003 and 2006 alone.

Diagnosis and treatment of PTSD is particularly difficult for a number of reasons. Service members have little incentive to acknowledge symptoms, even when interviewed in theater or after return to base, as this may mean a delay in discharge and, worse, labeling and stigma. It is also true that veterans may not manifest disabling effects of trauma for a year or more after homecoming.

Finally, experience from the Israeli Defense Force and survivors of the Yom Kipur War in 1973 reveals that PTSD can be a lifetime affliction, requiring decades of attention and medication. Thus, the 300,000–500,000 service members who may have combat-stress reactions stemming from deployment to Iraq or Afghanistan could present demands on the community mental health system lasting well into old age. Anecdotal evidence from the VA suggests that some veterans from World War II, the Korean War, and Vietnam show clear evidence of PTSD even today.

PTSD has dominated public dialogue, but other mental health problems of veterans are equally grave. Suicide and depression have climbed to historic highs in the Army, Marine, reserves, and National Guard. Historically, the armed services have experienced fewer suicides than among civilians, but, in 2009, for the first time rates of suicide in the American military exceeded those of civilians. Investigators were disconcerted to find that service members took their own lives at all stages of military processing: pre-deployment, during deployment, and following deployment. The youngest and least educated persons in the Army and older men from the National Guard and reserves appeared to be most vulnerable (Kang & Bullman, 2008; Miller et al., 2009). It should be mentioned that failed suicide attempts have caused life-long impairment, and those who attempt suicide once often are subject to recurring depression or other mental disorders that place them at increased risk for future suicide attempts. Suicide, more than death from natural causes, produces complicated grief and guilt among surviving family members. Members of a soldier's military unit also seem to be disproportionately affected by a suicide (Farberow, Gallagher-Thompson, Gilewski, & Thompson, 1992; Institute of Medicine [IOM], 2010). Large-scale studies by the DoD are currently underway to understand better how depression can be detected and treated earlier, but many questions remain.

Substance Abuse

Returning veterans are at increased risk for other self-inflicted and other-directed harms. These include tobacco use, hazardous drinking, drug use, and accidental overdose. Based on studies from past conflicts, combat exposure is associated with high arrest rates and convictions, although several variables contribute to this problem. One current large-scale study has shown that PTSD symptoms, combat exposure, younger age, and divorce are all strongly associated with antisocial behavior, defined as drug and alcohol abuse, confrontations with police, and other misconduct (Black et al., 2005; Booth-Kewley, Larson, Highfill-McRoy, Garland, & Gaskin, 2010; Kulka et al., 1990).

The U.S. Centers for Disease Control and Prevention has noted that perpetrators of violent crimes are more likely to have a TBI history, often co-occurring with PTSD. They are more prone to become victims of violence themselves as a consequence of anger management problems and uninhibited, confused, or agitated behaviors (Centers for Disease Control and Prevention, 2006). For example, in 1988, nearly half of male Vietnam combat veterans with PTSD had been arrested or incarcerated at least once, and 11% had been convicted of a felony (Kulka et al., 1990).

The Institute of Medicine (IOM) has documented an association between deployment to war zones and alcohol and drug abuse or dependency (IOM, 2008). An excellent example is provided by a recent study in Travis County, Texas. Researchers found that 40% of all alcohol and substance abuse charges in the area had been filed against veterans aged 20–29 who had served in OEF and OIF. Other charges involved aggravated kidnapping and aggravated sexual assault, both in the context of family-related violence and often committed under the influence of alcohol as well. Although 85% of this study population was eligible for VA services, 65% had received no attention, and community-based mental health or substance abuse treatment programs were found to be inadequate for veterans' needs (Travis County, Texas, 2009).

A study of nearly 300,000 Iraq and Afghanistan veterans by the VA is illustrative. This survey found that more than one-third had been diagnosed with mental health problems, typically depression or PTSD (Hoge, Auchterlonie, & Miliken, 2006). Moreover, the number of mental health problems rose steadily, the longer veterans were out of service. These observations were consistent with a DoD Task Force on Mental Health report (2007a), which suggested that 33% of all service members were likely to report problems of substance abuse, depression, combat-related post-traumatic stress, and other anxiety reactions.

PROBLEMS OF SPECIAL POPULATIONS IN THE ARMED FORCES

Gays and Lesbians in the Service

The ambivalent and inconsistent policies applied to gay and lesbian service members have been followed closely by the military. Following a survey of the armed forces by the Joint Chiefs of Staff, the government formally repudiated past practices in favor of a policy of nondiscrimination. Military law, pension policies, and other aspects of military life will be changed in fundamental ways over coming years. Chaplains in the evangelical tradition have already expressed concern about the divergence between their beliefs and new military policy, and other forms of tension are inevitable. However, a more normalized work environment for gays and lesbians should promote mental health and unit morale, with fewer ruined careers and undeserved dishonor.

Psychological Injuries to Women

Ten percent of personnel who have served in Iraq and Afghanistan are women. They may be more susceptible to combat stress, express health problems in unique ways, and have high exposure to sexual assault. (It should be noted that male soldiers have also been victims of sexual violence.) Recent studies show that between two-thirds and three-quarters of military women have been exposed to sexual harassment, and 25–43% have been attacked through sexual assault, rape, or attempted rape (Bastian, Lancaster, & Reyst, 1996; Fontana & Rosenheck, 1998). These alarming rates of sexual violence against women service members are particularly worrisome, because harassment and assault under conditions of deployment are associated with a five-times-greater risk of developing PTSD. This is an even higher risk for this disorder than combat itself confers (Kang, Dalager, Mahan, & Ishii, 2005). Although the causes of this association are not well understood, it is clear that women who enter the military have higher rates of *previous* trauma exposure (17–68%) than the general population (17% lifetime prevalence) (Hidalgo & Davidson, 2000; Merrill et al., 1999; Rosen & Martin, 1996).

The concept of "moral injury" as an element in many PTSD diagnoses may be useful in work with veteran women, as it helps to explain the harm caused by military sexual assault. By definition, moral injury is caused by a "violation of values and/or a betrayal of trust," and "causes damage to individuals' conceptions of themselves, other people, and important institutions" (Nash et al., 2010.) Women expect that their comrades "have their back" and "cover them," according to the ethos of military culture. With camaraderie and loyalty to fellow service members highly valued, military sexual assault has especially pernicious meanings. When assault or attempted rape is committed by a superior officer, the psychological complications are compounded further.

In addition to a work environment that is sometimes hostile or threatening, women must also resolve personal and family issues that involve family role reversal, separation from very young children, and unpredictable periods of absence. Although men also have their share of relationship stressors, there is less social sanction and social support in the case of new wives or young mothers. For example, single mothers have reported greater disruption to their families when they leave their children in the care of others, through pre-arranged family care plans that are sometimes in a different geographic location. This adds another transition for the whole family and additional strains on community reintegration (Kelley, 1994).

Military women have less martial stability than their male counterparts, with divorce rates that are 2.5 times the national average (Department of Defense Task Force on Mental Health, 2007b; Harrell & Miller, 1997; Williamson & Mulhall, 2009). Because women generally undertake more household management responsibilities and are primary caregivers for children and aging parents, regardless of employment—or deployment—status, they are likely to come home to face an overwhelming array of expectations (Coltrane, 2000).

The Reserve and National Guard

The National Guard and reserves, who comprise at any given time between 26% and 40% of the force in Iraq and Afghanistan, are disproportionately at risk for breakdown in mental health. Even after adjusting for age, health, and a range or other factors, data show that reservists are more likely than regular armed forces to develop symptoms of PTSD and major depression. Reservists are in fact twice as likely to demonstrate need for mental health services following deployment, based on screening criteria used by the military (Castaneda et al., 2008; Schell & Marshall, 2008). Several factors are thought to contribute to these comparatively poor outcomes. Most reservists live far from military facilities and therefore have little identity as a military family. They lack access to the supportive services and network found at or in military installations. With an average age of around 38, mobilization orders disrupt careers and affect families' lives, not only through the reservist's absence, but also by changes in income and medical insurance providers. One deployment can disrupt an individual's relationship with his or her employer; several deployments can bring loss of job, marriage, and family connections (Castaneda et al., 2008; Defense Centers of Excellence, 2009; MacReady, 2008; Schell & Marshall, 2008).

The strain felt by reservists is heightened by their over-representation in the rank of individual augmentees (IAs), who fill shortages in military units or provide specialized skills on individual assignments, apart from the reserve unit to which they belong. In the OEF/OIF conflicts, IAs have primarily been allocated to the Army and may be sent across service branches to units that have previously bonded and by whom the augmentee may be viewed as an outsider. Currently, more than 55,000 Navy reservists alone have served as augmentees, mostly with the Army (Defense Centers of Excellence, 2009). Because all reservists and Guard members live in the community rather than on base, it is in general difficult for them to reconnect with the unit members with whom they served during deployment. IAs are even more isolated, and an absence of support from people who have shared the deployment experience can intensify the pain of transition from war theater to home.

Military Families and Children

Families of deployed service members have always been expected to be encouraging and protective, but their own needs and reactions to deployment have often been understudied or ignored, especially by civilian institutions. By and large, military children and families are largely resilient, characterized by an ability to adapt, take advantage of adversity, and change to learn new skills. A website devoted to, and developed by, "military brats" illustrates the positive aspect of coping (www.militarybrats.com; Ender, 2002; Wertsch, 1991). On the other hand, not all families display these qualities of durability. "Secondary" PTSD has now been identified as a serious and real threat to spouses, children, and others who must adapt to the disordered behavior of a veteran family member (Figley, 1998). Under circumstances in which a returning service member cannot sleep, turns day into night, reacts with unpredictable hostility to daily events, cannot maintain work, and cannot focus, every family member is thrown of balance. This is especially true if appropriate support is not available in schools or mental health clinics, the family is otherwise isolated, or PTSD symptoms co-occur with TBI, substance abuse, depression, or other diseases.

Research is beginning to take shape on OEF/OIF spouses and children (Department of Defense, 2010; Flake, Davis, Ellen, Johnson, & Middleton, 2009; Mansfield et al., 2010). The cumulative impact of multiple deployments is associated with more emotional difficulties among military children and more mental health diagnoses among spouses (Lester et al., 2010). Although service member spouses display equivalent levels of anxiety or other mental health problems when compared with the deployed service member population, spouses feel fewer stigmas and are more willing to seek help (Eaton et al., 2008). Even couples and families who are resilient and find supportive relationships to sustain them through deployments face challenges at reintegration (Bowling & Sherman, 2008).

Nearly 2 million children have a parent serving in the military. Their range of reactions varies widely, based on age, developmental stage, gender, and temperament. Caregiver, family, and community-specific factors also influence their ability to adapt. Because studies of OIF/OEF families are comparatively new, evidence is mixed regarding effects of deployment. For families living on base, resilience in the face of separation seems to be higher, but for others, outside the base, results are more worrisome. Children manifest distress through poor school performance, strained family and peer relationships, bullying, and depression. In the youngest children, these symptoms seem to last longer than expected, even months after the parent has returned. Absence of a parent for military children is more than separation; fear of death and permanent loss are always lurking behind. Thus, parental combat deployment has a cumulative effect that lingers and is manifested in changing symptoms, depending on the child's age and development (Chandra et al., 2010; Department of Defense, 2010; Hall, 2008; Lester et al., 2010).

Schools, community mental health programs, and other child-serving agencies are, as a rule, not oriented to secondary PTSD or other symptoms that children with deployed parents present, leaving them in unsympathetic or uncomprehending environments, despite the best intentions of professionals (Military Child Education Consortium, 2003).

SERVICE SYSTEMS: RELEVANCE, ACCESSIBILITY, AND ADEQUACY

It is difficult to make comparisons among veterans of the major 20th- and 21st-century conflicts, owing to differences in public policy, service availability, problem definition, and data collection. Apparently, OIF/OEF veterans are even less likely than previous generations of service members to make use of veterans' medical services, including mental health support, through the VA. As many as 40–60% of veterans from the current war either do not seek health care through the VA or discontinue treatment shortly after their first appointment. For those with PTSD or lagged reactions to combat, this means that civilian agencies, especially community mental health programs and hospital emergency rooms, very likely become the primary resource. Reasons reported by disappointed patients for avoidance of the military medical system include long waiting lines, lack of personalized interest, the geographic isolation of some VA medical facilities, unwelcome reminders of military culture, and absence of helpful interventions. Instances of deficient physical plant, insufficient trained personnel, and medical neglect in the VA system have also received high-profile media attention.

In a recent New York State study of veterans' access and utilization of military medical programs, Schell and Tanielian (2011) painted a daunting picture of stumbling blocks for veterans. They were often unaware of available services, unsure of whether the service would be helpful for their specific problems, lacked information about service locations, were uncertain of eligibility requirements, and did not know how to apply. Although there is likely to be variability across other states, the New York State example raises troubling questions (Burnam, Meredith, Tanielian, & Jaycox, 2009; DoD Task Force on Mental Health, 2007a; Tanielian & Jaycox, 2008).

At the same time, data indicate that positive VA medical care outcomes exceed those for the average civilian facility. The number of social workers, psychologists, psychiatric nurses, and trained paraprofessionals is growing, and some facilities offer outstanding programs. Schnell and Tanielian (2011) see the basic problem in the following way:

[There is a] fundamental gap in our knowledge about the needs of veterans returning from Iraq and Afghanistan, the adequacy of the care system available to meet those needs, and the experiences of veterans and service members who use these systems.

The importance of achieving greater coordination between the Department of Defense, the VA, and civilian mental health agencies in the transfer of patient records, shared knowledge of efficacious and effective interventions, workforce development, and building of community collaborations to serve the family unit would seem paramount. In the past, military and civilian cultures existed on parallel tracks; today, they are intertwined as never before.

STIGMA IN SERVICE REFERRAL AND UTILIZATION

The recovery model in modern community mental health involves full commitment to reduction of stigma and individual empowerment. In civilian society, some states—notably California and Wisconsin—have taken the lead in implementing these principles. The military, too, has sought to decrease stigma and alter policies that label service members or veterans as diseased, deficient, or even unpatriotic. For example, the Army has substituted the term "behavioral health" for mental illness and has created several training programs that address the topics of suicide prevention and PTSD. Soldiers are advised to find help and given training sessions to understand better what benefits treatment can confer. More mental health providers are available both on base and in the community. Positive steps have been taken, without question.

Unfortunately, DoD and armed-services policies have undermined these good intentions, and it is still not clear which policies might generate more desirable effects. One example, the Deployment Limiting Psychiatric Conditions policy that was adopted in 2006, was designed to prevent service members from being taken from psychiatric hospitals and sent to war. According to this requirement, a service member taking medication must be medically stable for three months before deployment. An exception to the policy can only be granted by senior-level command leadership. Service members affected by these rules do not deploy with their unit, may lose opportunities for promotion, and conceivably might lose their post. It is not surprising that troops steer clear of treatment under these conditions.

EVIDENCE-BASED INTERVENTIONS

Peer-to-Peer Mentoring and Counseling

Considerable weight has been placed in this chapter on the meaning of shared values and experience in the military. It is not surprising, therefore, that peer-to-peer counseling programs have emerged as one widely adopted intervention method. In some communities, mental health agencies have well-established training protocols; elsewhere, volunteers are recruited with little formal preparation. Training helps volunteers understand how to establish boundaries and limits in their relationships with peers, how to listen, how to recognize warning signs of depression or danger to others, and how to make referrals—among other skills. Some programs, such as "Vet-2-Vet" in New Jersey, have gained congressional attention for their widespread impact.

The scientific foundation for peer counseling is growing. Pfeiffer et al. (2011) conducted a meta-analysis of seven randomized studies comparing peer support and cognitive behavioral therapy (CBT) care in the treatment of depression. Results indicated that peer counseling was superior to usual care and seemed to produce benefits that were equivalent to CBT. Peer counseling interventions would thus seem especially compatible with newer approaches in community mental health that stress self-help and organization by consumers in their own interests.

Cognitive Behavioral Therapy and Prolonged-Exposure Therapy

CBT and a closely related intervention, prolonged-exposure therapy, constitute the most widely used methods for treating symptoms of PTSD in veterans. A service member with PTSD is repeatedly disturbed by flashbacks and nightmares or other reminders of upsetting experiences in the theater. The trauma may be related, not only to a direct action such as killing one of the enemy, but sights associated with war—dead children, dismemberment of buddies, and other shocks. Exposure programs seek to neutralize these memories through "imaginable exposure," in which the veteran is asked to revisit the troubling memory, talk about it, and discuss the aspects that were most horrifying. A second element of the intervention involves requiring the veteran to go back in real life to situations that evoke troubling memories—large crowds, for example—and to do this again and again. Finally, where depression is a component of the veteran's symptoms, there is strong encouragement for reengagement in pleasurable activities.

Approximately 20 years of research have consistently validated the utility of prolonged-exposure therapy, though there is variation within patient subgroups. Eighty percent of patients show significant reduction in psychological disturbance in response to this method (Eftekhari, Stines, & Zoellner, 2006). In 2007, the IOM reviewed 53 research reviews of pharmaceutical treatment and 37 studies of psychotherapy in an effort to understand which might be most efficacious. The IOM concluded that, "Exposure therapies—such as exposing individuals to a real or surrogate threat in a safe environment to help them overcome their fears—are effective in treat people with PTSD." However the Institute was cautious to say that prolonged-exposure therapy should not be regarded as the only treatment, nor should any others be discontinued.

Other Therapies

Most veterans are not permanently traumatized by war. They do hurdles in reconnecting with spouses, children, employers, educational institutions, and community life. They are also impatient. Long-term interventions are not tolerated; some evidence shows that service members are most comfortable with one to three visits. Although CBT in its traditional form is adaptable to short-term treatment, there is currently exploration of alternative approaches. Arthur Nezu, a noted American psychologist, has developed an approach called "Problem-solving therapy" that is highly efficacious in civilian populations and is now being tested for the first time with veterans within several VA hospitals across the country. The value of this method is that it helps to reduce stress and permits veterans and their families to tackle multiple practical challenges in transition to civilian life. Because of the preventive character of this approach, it fits well with recovery philosophy and present perspectives in community mental health.

Interventions with service members and their families are still being conceptualized and tested. Greater concentration on elements in the transition from military to community life will be critical. Community-based groups will play a key role, because the adjustment of service members and their families may be compromised for months, and even years. Community consequences of PTSD are today reflected in rising rates of homelessness among OEF/OIF veterans, both male and female, and persistent rates of unemployment that exceed those of the civilian population. Post-discharge suicides, premature aging, and failed relationships are more prevalent among community-dwelling veterans. The need for research that advances evidence-based practice is acute.

SUMMARY AND CONCLUSIONS

A small number of Americans are now serving in the military—fewer than 1%. Some are looking for direction; others are inspired by a sense of patriotism; and others just want to continue the family tradition of military service. Whatever their reason is for joining, they enter the ranks prepared to give their life for their country. Despite this heroic calling, they have undoubtedly grown tired and weary after a decade of war. The persistent high operational tempo, development of invisible wounds, and experience with the many reintegration challenges has clearly taken a toll on them. Compounding matters is the long-standing stigma within the military associated with seeking help for those wounds affecting both the service member and/or their family members.

As mentioned, the key psychological issues affecting the approximately 2 million American troops deployed to Iraq and Afghanistan since 2001 are TBI, PTSD, substance abuse, depression, anxiety, marital discord, and suicide—and the diagnoses overlap. It is then reasonable to expect an uptick in these mental health issues as our troops return from these war zones. Additionally, it is not uncommon for these mental health conditions to surface months and even years after redeployment, rather than just after homecoming. As we have learned, a false homecoming can deceive health-care workers and family members into a perception that all is well among members of the military reentering communities stateside.

The plight of Vietnam veterans has taught us that the only thing that happens after returning from combat is that the problems increase. The longer people are back, the more people come forward as potentially struggling. The influx of Iraq and Afghanistan veterans into the U.S. mental health system has yet to peak, but is clearly underway. There is concern that the mental health-care system is not prepared to handle the care of returning veterans. The IOM (2010) report clearly indicated a shortage of mental health professionals competent to meet the demands of those returning from war.

It is unlikely that the mental health of veterans and their families, the quality of, and access to, care, or the lack of qualified providers will be adequately addressed without local, state, and federal agencies joining forces. Therefore, we need to bring together a diverse set of resources, identify new opportunities across the public and private sectors, and lay the foundation for a coordinated approach to supporting and engaging veterans and their families for many years to come. Given the current and future mental health challenges facing our veterans and their families, community mental health programs and the recovery philosophy have never been more crucial to resolution of these hardships and to restoration of human potential for veterans and their families. The brave men and women who wear the uniform in combat deserve our deepest gratitude and support.

DISCUSSION QUESTIONS

Please answer one of the following questions below:

1. Do you believe there are parallels between working with military populations and other types of population? What are the similarities? What are some differences?

2. After reading this chapter, how have your thoughts, feelings, assumptions, beliefs, values, or attitudes changed toward working with the military populations? If they have not changed, explain why this may be the case.

3. What were the strengths and limitations of the material covered in this chapter? What are the implications for you in your practice?

LEARNING ASSIGNMENT

Group project options:

1. Identify programs in or near your community that serve veterans and their families. Contact them to explore ways your group can support their work.
2. In small groups, develop visual presentations (e.g. video, posters, or PowerPoint presentations) for the class on the subject of reintegration of veterans into civilian society today. For example, a video could depict a role-play of a veteran in a job interview confronting employer discomfort or lack of knowledge about the military; a poster collage could show conflicting images of the OIE/OEF wars and civilian society's response; a PowerPoint presentation could go into further depth on any one of the topics discussed in this chapter.

SUGGESTED READINGS

Department of Defense Task Force on Mental Health (2007). *An Achievable Vision: Report of the Department of Defense Task Force on Mental Health*. Falls Church, VA: Department of Defense.

Institute of Medicine (2010). *Returning Home from Iraq and Afghanistan. Preliminary Assessment of Readjustment Needs of Veterans, Service Members, and Their Families*. Washington, DC: The National Academies Press.

Tanielian, T., & Jaycox, L. (2008). *Invisible Wounds of War: Psychological and Cognitive Injuries, Their Consequences, and Services to Assist Recovery*. Arlington, VA: Rand Corporation.

INTERNET RESOURCES

United States Department of Veterans Affairs: Benefits: www.vba.va.gov/VBA

Defense Centers of Excellence for Psychological Health and Traumatic Brain Injury (DCoE): dcoe.health.mil

The Center for Innovation and Research on Veterans and Military Families (CIR): cir.usc.edu

REFERENCES

Bastian, L., Lancaster, A., & Reyst, H. (1996). Department of Defense 1995 Sexual Harrassment Survey. Department of Defense. Retrieved from www.dtic.mil/dtfs/doc_research/p18_11.pdf

Black, D., Carney C., Peloso, P.M., Woolson, R.F., Letuchy, E., & Doebbeling, B.N. (2005). Incarceration and veterans of the First Gulf War. *Military Medicine, 170,* 612–618.

Booth-Kewley, S., Larson, G.E., Highfill-McRoy, R.M., Garland, G.F., & Gaskin, T.A. (2010). Factors associated with anti-social behavior in combat veterans. *Aggressive Behavior, 36,* 330–337.

Bowling U., & Sherman, M. (2008). Welcoming them home: Supporting service members and their families in navigating the tasks of reintegration. *Professional Psychology: Research and Practice, 39,* 451–458.

Brokaw, T. (2011). The bravest families in America. Reported on the Oprah Winfrey show. Retrieved from Oprah.com

Burnam, A.M., Meredith, L.S., Tanielian, T., & Jaycox, L.H. (2009). Mental health care for Iraq and Afghanistan war veterans. *Health Affairs, 28,* 771–782.

Castaneda, L.W., Harrell, M.C., Varda, D.M., Hall, K.C., Beckett, M.K., & Stern, S. (2008). *Deployment experiences of guard and reserve families.* Santa Monica, CA: RAND Corporation.

Centers for Disease Control and Prevention (2006). See www.cdc.gov/TraumaticBrainInjury/severe.html

Chandra, A., Lara-Cinisomo, S., Jaycox, L., Tanielian, T., Burns, R.M., Ruder, T., & Han, B. (2010). Children on the homefront: The experience of children from military families. *Pediatrics, 125,* 16–25.

Charuvastra, A., & Cloitre, M. (2008). Social bonds and posttraumatic stress disorder. *Annual Review of Psychology, 59,* 301–328.

Coltrane, S. (2000). Research on household labor: Modeling and measuring the social embeddedness of routine family work. *Journal of Marriage and Family, 62,* 1208–1233.

Defense Centers of Excellence (2009). Special challenges for reservists. Retrieved from www.med.navy.mil/sites/nmcsd/nccosc/serviceMembers/Pages/returningFromDeployment/specialChallengesForReservists.aspx

Department of Defense (2010). *Report on the impact of deployment of members of the armed forces on their dependent children.* Washington, DC: Department of Defense.

Department of Defense Task Force on Mental Health (2007a). *An achievable vision: Report of the Department of Defense Task Force on Mental Health.* Falls Church, VA: Department of Defense.

Department of Defense Task Force on Mental Health (2007b). *Demographics 2007: Profile of the military community.* Washington, DC: Department of Defense.

Eaton, K., Hoge, C., Messer, S.C., Whitt, A.A., Cabrera, O.A., McGurk, D., Cox, A., & Castro, C.A. (2008). Prevalence of mental health problems, treatment need, and barriers to care among primary care-seeking spouses of military service members involved in Iraq and Afghanistan deployments. *Military Medicine, 173,* 1051–1056.

Ender, M. (2002). *Military brats and other global nomads: Growing up in organization families.* New York: Greenwood Publishing Group.

Eftekhari, A., Stines L.R., & Zoellner, L.A. (2006). Do you need to talk about it? Prolonged exposure for the treatment of chronic PTSD. *The Behavior Analyst Today, 7,* 70–83.

Farberow, N., Gallagher-Thompson, M., Gilewski, M., & Thompson, L. (1992). Changes in grief and mental health of bereaved spouses of older suicides. *Journal of Gerontology, 47,* 357–366.

Figley, C. (1998). Burnout in families: The penultimate fatigue of family relationships. *The Family Digest, 10,* 1–6.

Flake, E., Davis, B.E., Johnson, P., & Middleton, L. (2009). The psychosocial effects of deployment on military children. *Journal of Developmental and Behavioral Pediatrics, 30,* 271–278.

Fontana, A., & Rosenheck, R. (1998). Duty-related and sexual stress in the etiology of PTSD among women veterans who seek treatment. *Psychiatric Services, 49,* 658–662.

Hall, L.K. (2008). *Counseling military families.* New York: Taylor & Francis.

Harrell, M., & Miller, L. (1997). *New opportunities for military women: Effects upon readiness, cohesion, and morale.* Santa Monica, CA: Rand Corporation.

Hidalgo, R., & Davidson, J. (2000). Posttraumatic stress disorder: Epidemiology and health-related considerations. *Journal of Clinical Psychiatry, 61,* 5–13.

Hoge, C.W., Auchterlonie, J.L., & Milliken, C.S. (2006). Mental health problems, use of mental health services and attrition from military service after returning from deployment to Iraq or Afghanistan. *Journal of the American Medical Association, 295,* 1023–1032.

Institute of Medicine (2008). *Gulf War and health: Physiologic, psychologic, and psychosocial effects of deployment-related stress.* Washington, DC: The National Academies Press.

Institute of Medicine (2010). *Returning home from Iraq and Afghanistan. Preliminary assessment of readjustment needs of veterans, service members, and their families.* Washington, DC: The National Academies Press.

Kang, H.K., & Bullman, T.A. (2008). Risk of suicide among US veterans after returning from the Iraq or Afghanistan war zones. *Journal of the American Medical Association, 300,* 652–653.

Kang, H., Dalager, N., Mahan, C., & Ishii, E. (2005). The role of sexual assault on the risk of PTSD among Gulf War veterans. *Annals of Epidemiology, 15,* 191–195.

Kelley, M. (1994). The effects of military-induced separation on family factors and child behavior. *American Journal of Orthopsychiatry, 64,* 103–111.

Koenen, K., Moffitt, T., Poulton, R., Martin, J., & Caspi, A. (2007). Early childhood factors associated with the development of post-traumatic stress disorder: results from a longitudinal birth cohort. *Psychological Medicine, 37,* 181–192.

Kulka, R., Schlenger, W., Fairbanks, J., Hough, R., Jordan, K., Marmar, C., Weiss, D., & Grady, D. (1990). *Trauma and the Vietnam War generation: Report of findings from the National Vietnam Veterans Readjustment Study.* New York: Brunner/Mazel.

Lester, P., Peterson, K., Knauss, L., Glover, D., Mogil, C., Saltzman, W., Pynoos, R., Wilt, K., & Beardslee, W. (2010). The long war and parental combat deployment: Effects on military children and at-home spouses. *Journal of the American Academy of Child & Adolescent Psychiatry, 49,* 310–320.

MacReady, N. (2008). Coming home. *The Lancet, 372,* 703–704.

Mansfield, A.J., Kaufman, J., Marshall, S.W., Gaynes, B.N., Morrissey, J., & Engel, C.C. (2010). Deployment and the use of mental health services among U.S. military wives. *New England Journal of Medicine, 362,* 101–109.

Merrill, L.L., Newell, C.F., Thomsen, C.J., Gold, S.R., Milner, J.S., Koss, M.P., & Rosswork, S.G. (1999). Childhood abuse and sexual revictimization in a female navy recruit sample. *Journal of Traumatic Stress, 12,* 211–225.

Military Child Education Consortium (2003). How to prepare our children and stay involved during deployment. Retrieved from militarychild.org

Miller, M., Barber, C., Azrael, D., Calle, E.E., Lawler, E., & Mukamal, K.J. (2009). Suicide among US veterans: A prospective study of 500,000 middle-aged and elderly men. *American Journal of Epidemiology, 170*(4), 494–500.

Nash, W., Litz, B., et al. (2010). Moral injury: What leaders need to know. Presentation at the Navy and Marine Corps Combat & Operational Stress Conference 2010. San Diego, California.

Pfeiffer P.N., Heisler, M., Piette, J.D., Rogers, M.A.M., & Valenstein, M. (2011). Efficacy of peer support interventions for depression: A meta-analysis. *General Hospital Psychiatry, 33,* 29–36.

Rosen, L., & Martin, L. (1996). The measurement of childhood trauma among male and female soldiers in the US Army. *Military Medicine, 161,* 342–345.

Schell, T.L., & Marshall, G.N. (2008). Survey of individuals previously deployed for OEF/OIF. In Tanielian, T. & Jaycox, L.H., Eds., *Invisible Wounds of War: Psychological and Cognitive Injuries, Their Consequences, and Services to Assist Recovery.* Retrieved from www.rand.org/pubs/monographs/2008/RAND_MG720.pdf

Schell, T., & Tanielian, T. (Eds.) (2011). *A needs assessment of New York State veterans. A final report to the New York State Health Foundation.* Retrieved from www.rand.org/pubs/technical_reports/TR920.html

Tanielian, T., & Jaycox, L. (2008). *Invisible wounds of war: Psychological and cognitive injuries, their consequences, and services to assist recovery.* Arlington, VA: Rand Corporation.

Tolin, D., & Foa, E. (2006). Sex differences in trauma and posttraumatic stress disorder: A quantitative review of 25 years of research. *Psychological Bulletin, 132,* 959–992.

Travis County, Texas. (2009). Veterans Intervention Project: Jail Survey Report. Travis County, Texas.

United States White House (2011). White House Report on Strengthening Military Families. Meeting America's Commitment. Retrieved from www.defense.gov/home/features/2011/0111_initiative/strengthening_our_military_january_2011.pdf

Wertsch, M. (1991). *Military brats: Legacies of childhood inside the fortress.* New York: Harmony Books.

Williamson, V., & Mulhall, E. (2009). Invisible wounds: Psychological and neurological injuries confront a new generation of veterans. Retrieved from http://iava.org/files/IAVA_invisible_wounds_0.pdf

Woodward, B. (2011). The bravest families in America. Reported on the Oprah Winfrey show. Retrieved from www.oprah.com

Chapter 5

Community Mental Health

Innovations in Diversion from Prosecution of People with Mental Illness

Kirk Heilbrun and Anne Bingham

INTRODUCTION

The last two decades have witnessed a number of important advances in forensic mental health. In this chapter, we summarize three of the most important of these advances in the community: (1) the *Sequential Intercept Model* (SIM) (Munetz & Griffin, 2006), a conceptual framework for describing how people with mental illness become involved with the criminal justice system—and how they may be diverted from standard avenues of criminal prosecution; (2) *specialized police response* to individuals with behavioral health problems, with the Crisis Intervention Team (CIT) the most widely recognized of such approaches; and (3) *problem-solving courts*, beginning in 1989 with a single drug court and growing into an array of courts to which justice-involved individuals with particular problems (ranging from substance abuse to mental health to veterans' issues) can be diverted as an alternative to criminal prosecution, with this diversion including treatment for such problems. We offer an overview and describe the history and research support for each of these advances, followed by consideration of the implications of each for practice and policy.

OVERVIEW OF INNOVATIONS

Sequential Intercept Model

The SIM (Munetz &Griffin, 2006) is a conceptual framework that describes five points in the criminal justice system that are particularly relevant for possible "interception" from prosecution of people with mental illness. These five stages are as follows: (1) law enforcement and other first responders; (2) initial detention and hearings; (3) jails, courts, and forensic evaluations; (4) re-entry programs; and (5) community corrections and support. Each point encompasses a set of justice-related procedures and describes a stage at which alternatives to standard prosecution may be developed. For example, the first point (law enforcement and other first responders) describes the initial interaction in the community between a police officer (or other first responder) and an individual with mental illness. Traditional police training and practice emphasize the importance of appropriate response to police authority and arrest of those who do not respond appropriately—resulting in arrests of those who otherwise might be questioned, cautioned, and released. Individuals with severe mental illness are less likely to behave in conventional fashion during encounters with the police, placing them at greater risk for arrest under some circumstances. Later in this chapter, we describe in more detail what can result when police are trained to recognize the signs of behavioral health disorders and respond in a way that might be seen as less threatening to such individuals—without putting officers at greater risk of harm.

As a second example, there will always be instances in which individuals with severe mental illness or substance abuse problems, or veterans with post-traumatic stress disorder, are arrested. Following this arrest, however, a community with at least one specialized problem-solving court can screen this individual to decide whether referral to the specialized court, rather than traditional criminal justice prosecution and possibly incarceration, would be in the mutual interests of both that individual and the larger community. We describe problem-solving courts, which constitute a major part of this intercept, in more detail later in this chapter.

Communities that are just beginning to consider such diversionary alternatives can use the SIM in developing new policies regarding diversion from prosecution or treatment and other services during the re-entry process (returning from jail or prison incarceration into the community). Communities that have more experience in the implementation of specialized policies in these areas tend to practice the interception of people with mental illness at earlier points in the process (Munetz & Teller, 2004).

Specialized Police Response

Police officers are often the first professionals to have contact with a person with mental illness, with up to 10% of police calls involving mental health issues (Demir, Broussard, Goulding, & Compton, 2009). In order to reduce the risk of harm to both the officers and the individual being arrested, many police departments have developed specialized police responding. The most widely recognized model of such specialized police response is the CIT (Dupont & Cochran, 2002). CIT-trained officers are able to recognize the signs of mental illness and assess the possible value of mental health treatment as an alternative to arrest on a case-by-case basis. Police departments have also begun to offer less intensive training (CIT training typically takes 40 hours) to other officers who are not part of the CIT, so these officers can increase their awareness of the symptoms of mental illness and possible responses—as it is unlikely that CIT officers will ever be so frequently trained and widely available that they can handle every call involving a mentally ill person (Watson, Morabito, Draine, & Ottati, 2008).

Problem-Solving Courts

Specialty courts such as drug courts and mental health courts are not adversarial in the same sense that traditional criminal courts are, relying instead on behavioral contracting and participation in treatment as conditions of remaining under their jurisdiction. (In addition to receiving treatment, those defendants in specialty courts may have the substantial incentive of having their arrest or conviction expunged from their record, if they successfully complete the requirements of the specialty court.) These courts first appeared in the 1990s and have proliferated rapidly, even serving as models for newer courts such as veterans' courts. Some have described the expansion of drug courts in the United States as one of the "major justice reforms of the last part of the 20th century" (Goldkamp, White, & Robinson, 2001, p. 27). In the problem-solving court model of jurisprudence, the judge is a central figure for both encouragement and sanctions (Wilson, Mitchell, & Mackenzie, 2006). These courts also recognize that judicial sanctions alone may not be effective if underlying issues such as mental illness and substance abuse are not addressed and resolved, however, so they require concurrent participation in treatment (Gottfredson, Najaka, & Kearley, 2003).

HISTORY AND EMPIRICAL SUPPORT

Sequential Intercept Model

In 2002, the United States surpassed Russia in the rate at which citizens were incarcerated, with the U.S. rate at that time totaling 701 per 100,000 (Munetz & Teller, 2004). Such incarceration is expensive. Many jurisdictions have welcomed the prospect of incarcerating fewer individuals when both public safety and individual rehabilitation are better served with an alternative disposition of criminal charges. The SIM (Munetz & Griffin, 2006) was developed as a conceptual framework to allow communities and counties to examine their present criminal justice practices and consider alternatives at specific points in the process. As a conceptual tool, it does not have "empirical support" in the sense that investigators have conducted studies regarding its impact. It does appear, however, to enjoy growing support among those who provide consultation to counties and states regarding diversion and re-entry. For instance, the SIM is used by the Pennsylvania Mental Health and Justice Center of Excellence in "systems mappings" offered to Pennsylvania counties interested in diversion; during the first two years of operation, the Center expects to provide 15–18 such consultative mappings (www.pacenterofexcellence.pitt.edu).

Specialized Police Response

Police calls involving people with mental illnesses often differ from other calls: they tend to be longer in duration, more difficult to resolve, and may involve unusual behavior that is hard to interpret for an officer unfamiliar with the signs and symptoms of mental illness (Watson, Morabito, Draine, & Ottati, 2008). As the need for a specialized response to calls involving individuals with severe mental illness became clearer, police departments across the United States began to implement training in this area, focusing on specialized responding. The oldest and best known of the specialized police response models is CIT. The CIT training of officers, first developed in Memphis in 1988, involves 40 hours devoted to enhancing officers' awareness of the nature and symptoms of mental illness; the ways in which officers on the scene could respond without intensifying the agitation, fearfulness, or other problems experienced by the individual; and the alternatives to arrest. There were approximately 400

CIT programs in the United States as of 2006 (Watson et al., 2008). As such, CIT (sometimes called the "Memphis model") has been the most widely studied and emulated approach to specialized police responding (Compton, Bahora, Watson, & Oliva, 2008; Dupont & Cochran, 2002). Of course, simply making police officers more aware of the treatment needs of individuals with mental illness will not improve matters unless such treatment is actually available. Concretely, is there an agency, hospital, or program that will accept individuals who are dropped off by police officers following an encounter? To ensure that there is, communities must involve police, mental health, and legal professionals in reshaping policy and practice so that "treatment alternatives" for individuals are indeed a genuine alternative to arrest and prosecution (Tucker, Van Hasselt, & Russell, 2008).

Specialized CIT programs generally fall within three basic frameworks: police-based specialized police response, in which specially trained officers facilitate referrals to mental health services; police-based specialized mental health response, in which the police department hires mental health specialists; and mental health-based specialized mental health response, which may take the form of a mobile crisis unit (Deane, Steadman, Borum, Veysey, & Morrissey, 1999). As of 1996, a national survey indicated that 55% of U.S. cities with a population of 100,000 or more did not have specialized police responding (Deane et al., 1999). Although the percentage of cities that do have such specialized responding has undoubtedly risen during the last 15 years, this finding does underscore the reality that many cities do not have such specialized responding—and need it.

Specialized training in mental illness has been shown to increase the positive attitudes of police officers towards individuals with schizophrenia (Compton, Esterberg, McGee, Kotwicki, & Oliva, 2006). Similarly, beliefs about the causes of schizophrenia were changed in police officers who completed CIT. Officers were more likely to accurately perceive the substantial biological basis of schizophrenia, rather than attributing this illness primarily to personal or environmental factors, following training (Demir et al., 2009).

Problem-Solving Courts

Specialized problem-solving courts are new enough that the formal endorsement of such by a body of judges only occurred in the last five years (in 2006; Petrila & Redlich, 2007), but the "problems" that such courts are designed to correct have been recognized for much longer. When they are confined, for example, individuals with severe mental illness are much more likely to be incarcerated in jail or prison than to be hospitalized. The movement within the law to address such problems arose from an approach known as therapeutic jurisprudence, which (as the name implies) broadly seeks favorable outcomes through the law's greater emphasis on rehabilitation and lesser emphasis on punishment (Wexler & Winick, 1996). Over time, these specialty courts would take several forms, such as mental health courts, drug courts, or veterans' courts, but underlying these differences would be the unifying foundation of therapeutic jurisprudence.

Research involving these courts reflects largely positive results for participants, although researchers differ on the magnitude and particular measures of the results obtained. One study found that individuals participating in a jail diversion program experienced fewer arrests and days spent in jail in the 12 months following enrollment in the program than in the 12 months prior to enrollment, thus indicating a decrease in documented criminal activity across all participating individuals (Case, Steadman, Dupuis, & Morris, 2009).

An examination of arrest records after leaving a mental health court program reflected lower arrest rates for those who had been enrolled in the program. The largest positive change was observed for those who had completed the program (Hiday & Ray, 2010). A comparison of results for individuals who participated in a mental health court program versus a traditional court program found that those participating in the mental health court program had fewer re-arrests and days spent in jail than those who had come out of a traditional program (Steadman, Redlich, Callahan, Robbins, & Vesselinov, 2011). Other researchers have obtained similar results (McNiel & Binder, 2007).

Some researchers have suggested that mental health courts have evolved substantially since their introduction in 1997, with "second-generation mental health courts" having specific qualities that distinguish them from earlier mental health courts. Such distinguishing qualities include acceptance of more felony cases, use of post-plea adjudication, utilizing jail as a sanction, and having more intensive supervision (Redlich, Steadman, Petrila, Monahan, & Griffin, 2005).

To our knowledge, the specialized drug court first appeared in 1989 in Dade County, Florida. The model was quickly adopted in other jurisdictions, and the number of drug courts grew rapidly. As of 2005, there were approximately 1,300 drug courts in existence in the United States (Wilson et al., 2006). Studies of the results from drug courts have gone into some depth, trying to determine what specific aspects of such courts might be effective. One study (Goldkamp et al., 2001) found that numerous contacts with the judge, a regular program of drug testing, attendance in appropriate treatment services, and positive incentives, among other things, were useful in distinguishing drug courts with better records and individuals who were more successful under the jurisdiction of drug courts. This finding is generally consistent with other research, which has indicated that drug courts are effective and that there are particular factors that distinguish the more-effective from the less-effective courts.

The newest iteration of problem-solving courts, veterans' courts, is built on the drug court model. There are fewer veterans' courts than there are drug or mental health courts, which is not surprising in light of the relatively recent implementation of veterans' courts. Such veterans' courts have gained particular prominence in some U.S. cities, such as Anchorage and Buffalo (Hawkins, 2010; Pinals, 2010; Russell, 2009).

IMPLICATIONS FOR PRACTICE

Sequential Intercept Model

The five intercepts in the SIM lend themselves well to assessment of needs and the development of services at the different points of interception. Communities that have less well-formed linkages between mental health systems and criminal justice systems may have more individuals with mental illness moving through the system at later points of interception; as communities develop more programs and tighter linkages, more individuals with mental illness can be diverted from standard prosecution and referred to services at earlier points of contact (Munetz & Griffin, 2006; Munetz & Teller, 2004). The GAINS Center publication *Practical Advice on Jail Diversion* (2007) provides concrete advice on how to build new programs at the community level.

There are three specific implications for practice associated with the SIM. First, it is a very useful conceptual tool that can be applied toward "mapping" multiple systems in a single jurisdiction. By assembling representatives from the judiciary, law enforcement, mental health, jail, parole and probation, and other relevant systems and agencies, the facilitator can focus on current practices, particular problems, and unrealized opportunities for more effective or efficient practice at that particular intercept. Following a lengthy training (1–2 days) and a detailed report from the facilitator, a jurisdiction is well-positioned to make a series of informed decisions regarding changes in practice that would incorporate multiple systems and promote meaningful change.

The second practice implication involves the application of the SIM in less depth. The kind of "technical assistance" that a jurisdiction might seek prior to deciding to engage in a full-scale systems mapping can be facilitated by applying the SIM. For example, a jurisdiction might have a general sense that cost-effectiveness and public safety are important, as is reducing the number of individuals who are incarcerated as a result of acts directly attributable to a mental illness (and for which the risk would be considerably reduced through treatment). By using the SIM, the individual providing technical assistance to that jurisdiction could encourage the identification of particular points of emphasis—perhaps the implementation of effective practice across systems at some intercept points might be relatively straightforward, requiring reorganization and better communication, while others might by much more labor- and resource-intensive, and hence less feasible in the immediate future.

Finally, the SIM has been adopted for use by two state-level centers of excellence devoted to diversion (Ohio Criminal Justice Coordinating Center of Excellence; see www.neomed.edu/cjccoe/, and the Pennsylvania Mental Health and Justice Center of Excellence; see www.pacenterofexcellence.pitt.edu). Before either of these centers existed, however, the National GAINS Center (now the SAMHSA National GAINS Center; see http://gainscenter.samhsa.gov/html/) was providing education, technical assistance, and systems mappings to local jurisdictions. Operating since 1995, the GAINS Center has been led by Henry Steadman, a widely respected researcher in mental health policy, and his colleagues at Policy Research Associates in Delmar, NY. The GAINS Center uses the SIM in much of the education, technical assistance, and systems mapping that it does.

Specialized Police Response

There are also three practice implications of the specialized police response material that we have discussed in this chapter. The first, quite simply, is that specialized police response is an idea whose time has come. It has been estimated that as many as 10% of the calls received by police involve at least one individual with severe mental illness. Traditional policing responses to such individuals have been shown to be less effective, with commensurately higher risk of harm to the individual being arrested or the police officers involved. Additional training in this area is not a luxury. It can be a vitally effective tool for officers when dealing with individuals who are agitated, disorganized, irrationally frightened, and experiencing perceptual disturbances—all symptoms or by-products of the acute phases of different kinds of severe mental illness. The first implication for practice, therefore, is that implementing training in specialized police responding and coordinating efforts between police and mental health agencies are likely to result in safer, more effective police response to individuals with mental illness. Related to this, when there is a tragedy—when a mentally ill individual is seriously injured or killed in an encounter with police—there will be questions raised about whether such training was provided to the police officers in that jurisdiction. Whether the goal is to provide better police responding or to manage the risk of serious harm to citizens, the implementation of specialized training is a sensible part of the solution.

The second implication concerns the nature of the specialized police response training. CIT is the most widely recognized and best-researched model of specialized training and response in this area. It features a national organization (CIT International), which holds an annual conference and promotes an established approach to training (see www.citinternational.org/). There is considerable support of various kinds, in other words, for adopting CIT as the model for specialized police responding. It may be that a jurisdiction develops its own form of training and system interaction to address similar goals, but this is something that should be done only when there is considerable expertise in this area already available.

Like any significant change in practice, the adoption of CIT or another form of specialized police responding should be evaluated for effectiveness. This leads to the third implication for practice. Jurisdictions that implement this kind of change should collect and annually review relevant statistics in areas such as number of officers trained, number of encounters with individuals who are (or might have been) mentally ill, the nature of the intervention, and the resolution of the encounter. It may be, for instance, that comparing these statistics for CIT-trained versus non-CIT-trained officers can provide a concrete illustration of the impact of implementing a model such as CIT.

Problem-Solving Courts

The absence of adequate and appropriate services for people with mental illness—whether treatment services, housing, employment, or in other domains—can result in behavior that is disruptive, appears threatening to public safety, and may thus require the kind of police response discussed in the previous section. For some individuals, however, diversion at intercept one (police contact) is insufficient. Problem-solving courts were designed to address the rehabilitative needs of individuals whose problems (mental health, substance abuse, and/or others) are directly and strongly linked to their risk of offending. Offering a solution that includes structure, careful monitoring, and coordinated service delivery tracked through the court, the problem-solving courts discussed in this chapter are associated with three implications for practice.

The first practice implication includes philosophical and political components, as well as practice elements. Is the diversion of certain classes of individual from standard prosecution something that will be reasonably well supported within the community? There will always be those who argue that individuals should reap the consequences of their behavior, that those who "do the crime" should "do the time." When it becomes clear that problem-solving courts are not proposed as a universal solution, there may be more common ground for discussion.

The second implication involves the need for careful assessment. It is one thing to observe that the rate of serious mental illness in jails and prisons is higher than in the general population; that does not mean, necessarily, that all (or even most) individuals with severe mental illness

69

who are incarcerated would be good candidates for diversion to a problem-solving court. The relevant question is this: approximately how many individuals are incarcerated for offenses that are clearly manifestations of their illness (e.g., public intoxication; resisting arrest while acutely psychotic) and would be at low risk for reoffending if they were involved in appropriate treatment? By answering this question before implementing a specialized problem-solving court, a jurisdiction can determine the extent of the need and the likely volume of cases that could be handled through the specialized court. This information will relate directly to other decisions, such as those involving the level of resources needed to run the court (with associated services) effectively.

The third practice implication relates to both the establishment and the operation of problem-solving courts. Certainly drug courts and mental health courts are sufficiently well established and empirically supported that a community may justifiably conclude that the idea to establish one (or both) is sound. But the other advantage to the relative maturity of both kinds of problem-solving court is the existence of a large number of benchmarks, allowing the community to select several examples of problem-solving courts that operate in comparable jurisdictions— and to learn from their experience prior to formal implementation of their own court(s). As well, there are certain well-generalized conclusions that may be drawn from relevant research. Inter-agency collaboration is very important (Hartford, 2007); incentives that consistently include such outcomes as reducing or expunging charges upon successful completion are more effective than inconsistent incentives (Wilson et al., 2006); and a minimum "dosage" of drug treatment (e.g., 10 days) significantly lowers recidivism rates in drug courts (Gottfredson et al., 2003). To facilitate generalizability of outcome findings, it has been suggested that the evaluation of specialty courts be conducted by scoring the program on a high–low scale on measures of leverage, population severity, program intensity, predictability, and rehabilitation emphasis (Longshore et al., 2001). This would allow more systematic comparison within and across jurisdictions, and might eliminate some of the narrative quality of much specialty court research.

IMPLICATIONS FOR POLICY

Sequential Intercept Model

The SIM addresses alternatives to incarceration for people with mental illness. The first policy-relevant implication of the SIM, then, is that it is best applied toward the development or modification of policy regarding diversion.

Effective use of the SIM requires strong linkages and coordination of services between the courts, law enforcement, and mental health agencies. Such linkage and cross-system coordination are part of the second policy implication: developing policy that explicitly incorporates representation from different relevant systems (law, mental health, corrections, parole and probation, and others) is vital. Likewise, such policy could usefully incorporate other suggestions, such as regular communications or meetings between stakeholders, a no-refusal drop-off center for police referral cases, and the employment of a "boundary spanner," a liaison who could facilitate activities between the organizations (Hartford, Carey, & Mendonca, 2006).

Developing well-informed policy is best informed by data. The third policy implication of the SIM concerns how it might be applied in gathering relevant data. Organizations such as the GAINS Center and the centers of excellence discussed earlier in this chapter (or other groups, for that matter) can use the SIM in providing two kinds of data. First, they can offer a national perspective regarding the relevant scientific studies that have been published in peer-reviewed journals. Second, they can provide jurisdiction-specific information through technical assistance or systems mapping, applying the SIM to gather a great deal of information from representatives of different systems that can then be transformed into a series of jurisdiction-specific recommendations.

Specialized Police Response

There are three policy implications to the literature on, and development of, specialized police responding that has been discussed in this chapter. The first concerns the training that is appropriate for individual police officers. For a variety of reasons, it is unlikely that every police officer on every police force will volunteer for CIT training and the added level of specialization that it implies; one of the most important reasons is that CIT is voluntary training that would fail to change the practice of some officers if it were mandatory. However, having a policy that allows interested officers to receive this training and having specialized response-trained officers handle calls involving mentally ill individuals whenever possible are likely to improve the performance of those officers with respect to individuals with mental illness and lower the risk of harm to such individuals and the involved officers.

However, specialized police response training can also be regarded as a system-level intervention. The policy implications for such an intervention are considerable. Primarily, though, they involve the development or modification of policy that will promote diversion from standard prosecution, improve the performance of a police department with respect to citizens with mental illness, and reduce the risk of harm to officers and the individuals they encounter. Cases in which there are tragic outcomes will involve questions about the absence of such policy that, if present, would likely have reduced the risk of such tragic outcomes—at least under some circumstances.

When specialized police responding is viewed in the larger context of the SIM, it may be seen as the first, most defensible, and most cost-effective way of transforming the nature of a large number of encounters between police officers and mentally ill citizens. For jurisdictions that seek to promote diversion and treatment alternatives to prosecution within the larger context of public safety, the first step in revising applicable policy involves focusing on the police interactions with citizens—and how it may be altered through implementing a program of specialized police responding.

Problem-Solving Courts

Finally, there are also three policy implications stemming from the present discussion of problem-solving courts. First, the development of such courts seems, in many instances, to be a matter of the interest and initiative of a few individuals. It is both commendable and useful to have a judge or mayor, for instance, strongly advocating the development of a specialized court. Yet there comes a time during development (and certainly during operation) when the involvement of multiple systems—the judiciary, mental health, corrections, and parole/probation are typically all necessary—is required for effective operation. The work of the "boundary spanner" (a term originally coined by Steadman (1992) to describe an individual who can operate across multiple systems, when those systems are all involved in a distinct project such as a problem-solving court) is important. But this does not detract from the first policy implication: policy relevant to the effective operation of the specialized problem-solving court will explicitly incorporate multiple systems and require that the operation of the court not be overly dependent upon a single individual.

The second policy implication involves resources. If the problem-solving court is part of a process of diverting individuals who otherwise would have been incarcerated in a state prison, then there may be cost-shifting (from state to community) involved. This should appropriately be addressed as part of developing the specialized court. It may be that some costs can be shared, and other costs can be reduced through greater efficiency in services. But this should be considered, resolved, and addressed in policy as part of the court's development.

The third implication concerns the applicable law itself. Problem-solving courts are an interesting hybrid of criminal court and social work agency. As such, they may raise legal questions relevant for both the prosecution (e.g., how "successful" must a participant be in order to complete the program "successfully" and have charges expunged?) and the defense (e.g., how "voluntary" must "voluntary participation" be?). So the third implication concerns relevant legal policy, which needs to be established through participation of both the defense bar and the local prosecutor and revised as necessary as the court moves from development to full implementation.

CONCLUSION

Diversion from prosecution for individuals with mental illness, substance abuse, and other mental health-relevant problems has been a major and growing theme in community corrections and forensic mental health for the last two decades. It has incorporated two of the most important advances during this time: specialized policy responding and specialized problem-solving courts. Both have been conceptualized as represented by points of interception on the SIM, which has been applied toward the promotion of diversion and other community-based services during the last decade. The SIM should be used collaboratively and incorporate input from representatives of multiple systems. Applied when rehabilitation may be an effective alternative to incarceration for certain kinds of criminal offending, the SIM facilitates important cross-system communication vital to the development and operation of specialized police responding, problem-solving courts, and other community alternatives to incarceration.

DISCUSSION QUESTIONS

1. This chapter presents the *Sequential Intercept Model,* which is a conceptual framework for describing how people with mental illness become involved with the criminal justice system. Discuss the main components of the model.

2. How can communities involve police, mental health, and legal professionals in reshaping policy and practice so that "treatment alternatives" exist?

3. Do you agree with treatment alternatives for people with mental illness who are charged with a crime? Discuss.

LEARNING ASSIGNMENT

Role-Play

This role-play is designed to examine issues related to problem-solving courts. Assign three or four students to enact a community board that is charged with examining whether or not to develop a mental health court. The remaining students will be divided into two groups: half will present pro arguments that support the development of a mental health court, and the other half will present the con or opposing arguments to the board. After the debate, the class should consider their positions and identify what factors might lead to consensus and common ground.

SUGGESTED READING

DeMatteo, D., & Heilbrun, K. (2012). Introduction to the Special Issue on Diversion from Standard Prosecution. *Criminal Justice and Behavior, 39,* 349–350.

Greene, E., & Heilbrun, K. (2011). *Wrightsman's psychology and the legal system* (7th edition). Belmont, CA: Wadsworth.

Heilbrun, K., DeMatteo, D., Brooks Holliday, S., Shah, S., King, C., Bingham, A., & Hamilton, D. (in press). Community-based alternatives for justice-involved individuals with severe mental illness: Review of the relevant research. *Criminal Justice and Behavior.*

INTERNET RESOURCES

Center for Law and Social Policy: www.clasp.org

The Legal Aid Society: www.legal-aid.org

National Commission on Correctional Healthcare: ncchc.org

REFERENCES

Case, B., Steadman, H., Dupuis, S., & Morris, L. (2009). Who succeeds in jail diversion programs for persons with mental illness? A multi-site study. *Behavioral Sciences and the Law, 27,* 661–674.

CMHS National GAINS Center (2007). *Practical advice on jail diversion: Ten years of learnings on jail diversion from the CMHS National GAINS Center.* Delmar, NY: Author.

Compton, M., Bahora, M., Watson, A., & Oliva, J. (2008). A comprehensive review of extant research on crisis intervention (CIT) programs. *Journal of the American Academy of Psychiatry and the Law Online, 36,* 47–55.

Compton, M., Esterberg, M., McGee, R., Kotwicki, R., & Oliva, J. (2006). Crisis intervention team training: Changes in knowledge, attitudes, and stigma related to schizophrenia. *Psychiatric Services, 57*, 1199–1202.

Deane, M., Steadman, H., Borum, R., Veysey, B., & Morrissey, J. (1999). Emerging partnerships between mental health and law enforcement. *Psychiatric Services, 50*, 99–101.

Demir, B., Broussard, B., Goulding, S., & Compton, M. (2009). Beliefs about causes of schizophrenia among police officers before and after crisis intervention team training. *Community Mental Health Journal, 45*, 385–392.

Dupont, R., & Cochran, C.S. (2002). The Memphis CIT model. In G. Landsberg, M. Rock, L. Berg, & A. Smiley (Eds.), *Serving mentally ill offenders: Challenges and opportunities for mental health professionals* (pp. 59–69). New York: Springer.

Goldkamp, J., White, M., & Robinson, J. (2001). Do drug courts work? Getting inside the drug court black box. *Journal of Drug Issues, 31*, 27–72.

Gottfredson, D., Najaka, S., & Kearley, B. (2003). Effectiveness of drug treatment courts: Evidence from a randomized trial. *Drug Treatment Courts, 2*, 171–196.

Hartford, K. (2007). Diversion for people with concurrent disorders. *Research Insights of the Regional Mental Health Care, 4*, 1–57.

Hartford, K., Carey, R., & Mendonca, J. (2006). Pre-arrest diversion of people with mental illness: Literature review and international survey. *Behavioral Sciences and the Law, 24*, 845–856.

Hawkins, M. (2010). Coming home: Accommodating the special needs of military veterans to the criminal justice system. *Ohio State Journal of Criminal Law, 7*, 563–573.

Hiday, V., & Ray, B. (2010). Arrests two years after exiting a well-established mental health court. *Psychiatric Services, 61*, 463–468.

Longshore, D., Turner, S., Wenzel, S., Morral, A., Harrell, A., McBride, D., Deschenes, E., & Iguchi, M. (2001). Drug courts: A conceptual framework. *Journal of Drug Issues, 31*, 7–26.

McNiel, D., & Binder, R. (2007). Effectiveness of a mental health court in reducing criminal recidivism and violence. *The American Journal of Psychiatry, 164*, 1395–1404.

Munetz, M., & Griffin, P. (2006). Use of the sequential intercept model as an approach to decriminalization of people with serious mental illness. *Psychiatric Services, 57*, 544–549.

Munetz, M.R., & Teller, J.L.S. (2004). The challenges of cross-disciplinary collaborations: Bridging the mental health and criminal justice systems. *Capital University Law Review, 32*, 935–950.

Petrila, J., & Redlich, A. (2007). Mental illness and the courts: Some reflections on judges as innovators. *Court Review, 43*, 164–176.

Pinals, D.A. (2010). Veterans and the justice system: the next forensic frontier. *Journal of American Academy of Psychiatry and the Law, 38*, 163–167.

Redlich, A., Steadman, H., Petrila, J., Monahan, J., & Griffin, P. (2005). The second generation of mental health courts. *Psychology, Public Policy and Law, 11*, 527–538.

Russell, R. (2009). Veterans' treatment court: A proactive approach. *New England Journal on Criminal and Civil Confinement, 35*, 357–372.

SAMHSA's GAINS Center for Behavioral Health and Justice Transformation (2007). Practical advice on jail diversion. Retrieved July 12, 2012 from http://gainscenter.samhsa.gov/pdfs/jail_diversion/PracticalAdvice OnJailDiversion.pdfSteadman, H. (1992). Boundary spanners: A key component for the effective interactions of the justice and mental health systems. *Law and Human Behavior, 16*, 75–87.

Steadman, H.J., Redlich, A., Callahan, L., Robbins, P.C., & Vesselinov, R. (2010). Effect of mental health courts on arrests and jail days: A multisite study. *Archives of General Psychiatry, 68*, 167–172.

Tucker, A., Van Hasselt, V., & Russell, S. (2008). Law enforcement response to the mentally ill: An evaluative review. *Brief Treatment and Crisis Intervention, 8*, 236–250.

Watson, A., Morabito, M., Draine, J., & Ottati, V. (2008). Improving police response to persons with mental illnesses: A multi-level conceptualization of CIT. *International Journal of Law and Psychiatry, 31*, 359–368.

Wexler, D., & Winick, B. (Eds.) (1996). *Law in a therapeutic key: Developments in therapeutic jurisprudence*. Durham, NC: Carolina Academic Press.

Wilson, D., Mitchell, O., & Mackenzie, D. (2006). A systematic review of drug court effects on recidivism. *Journal of Experimental Criminology, 2*, 459–487.

Part Three

Community Mental Health Across the Life Cycle

Chapter 6

Community Mental Health with Children and Youth

Kathryn Krase

INTRODUCTION

Although widespread concern for the mental health of children often occurs after national traumas such as 9/11, Columbine, and Hurricane Katrina (Hacker & Darcy, 2006), children's mental health is too often overlooked as an ongoing matter. However, there currently exists a crisis in children's mental health in the United States (Hacker & Darcy, 2006). At least 10% of American children suffer from a mental illness that impairs their functioning (Burns et al., 1995; Shaffer et al., 1996a; United States Department of Health and Human Services, 1999; United States Department of Health and Human Services, Health Resources and Services Administration–Maternal and Child Health Bureau [USDHHS–MCHB], 2010). In some urban school districts, more than 50% of students manifest significant learning, behavior, and emotional problems (Center for Mental Health in Schools, 2003).

Children with mental disorders are more likely to experience other difficulties throughout childhood and adulthood. Children with mental health disorders are more likely than their counterparts to commit criminal offenses (Grisso, 2007). They have more school interruptions (including suspensions and expulsions) and are less likely to graduate from high school than their counterparts (Kapphahn, Morreale, Rickert, & Walker, 2006). As a result, they enter adulthood underprepared.

Further complicating this already alarming crisis, more than 40% of children diagnosed with mental illness *do not* receive treatment (USDHHS–MCHB, 2010). There are a multitude of reasons so many children are not given access to appropriate services. These reasons include lack of appropriate services in the community, unaffordable services, and fear of stigma. Even when children enter the mental health-care system, waiting lists for needed services undermine care for all children, regardless of race, class, or insurance status (Waxman, 2006).

The means through which our society addresses the mental health of children reflect the larger patterns of response to the mental health needs of society as a whole. The past 30 years have seen increasing emphasis on responding to children's mental health needs through community-based practice models, and keeping institutionalization of children as a last resort.

The goal of this chapter is to enlighten practitioners, administrators, and policymakers as to the realities of children's mental health. This chapter provides overview and context, paying special attention to current issues in the field, so that policy and practice can be better designed to meet the mental health needs of children and adolescents.

PREVALENCE OF MENTAL HEALTH DISORDERS IN CHILDREN AND YOUTH

There is no singular diagnosis for childhood mental illness. Children are diagnosed with numerous types of psychiatric disorder. More than half of children diagnosed with a psychiatric disorder are diagnosed with Attention Deficit Disorder or Attention Deficit/Hyperactivity Disorder (ADHD); more than 25% are diagnosed with an anxiety disorder; and more than 15% are diagnosed with depression (USDHHS-MCHB, 2010). Although children can be diagnosed with a psychiatric disorder throughout childhood, as children enter adolescence the likelihood of being diagnosed with a mental illness rapidly increases (Satcher, 1999; USDHHS-MCHB, 2010). Research shows that half of all lifetime cases of diagnosable mental illness begin by age 14 (Kessler et al., 2005).

Attention Deficit/Hyperactivity Disorder

ADHD is the most commonly diagnosed behavioral disorder of childhood (Satcher, 1999; USDHHS-MCHB, 2010). ADHD is often characterized by a combination of inattention and hyperactivity and/or impulsivity, as its name implies (Satcher, 1999). However, children can also be diagnosed as having ADHD while only exhibiting inattention *or* only hyperactivity/ impulsivity, and not necessarily both (American Psychiatric Association, 1994). Children suffering from ADHD have difficulty concentrating on tasks, are easily distracted, and are prone to disorganization (Satcher, 1999). As a result, children with ADHD often have difficulty in educational settings and in social interactions.

Between 3 and 6% of school-age children are given the ADHD diagnosis (Anderson, Williams, McGee, & Silva, 1987; Esser, Schmidt, & Woerner, 1990; Pelham, Gnagy, Greenslade, & Milich,1992; Shaffer et al., 1996a; USDHHS-MCHB, 2010; Wolraich, Hannah, Pinnock, Baumgaertel, & Brown, 1996). Boys are four times more likely to be diagnosed as ADHD than girls are (Ross & Ross, 1982; USDHHS-MCHB, 2010). Although ADHD affects children from all races and ethnicities, the rate of prevalence differs by group (CDC-MMWR, 2010; Satcher, 1999).

ADHD is often treated through the use of prescription psycho-stimulants (Satcher, 1999; National Institute of Mental Health [NIMH], 2008). Psycho-stimulants seem to benefit 70–90% of children with ADHD (Satcher, 1999). The growing use of these drugs to treat ADHD concerns parents and other advocates for children, who fear the use is too widespread and without proper oversight.

Pharmacological treatments are not the only type available for use with children with ADHD. Psychosocial treatments, including behavioral approaches, CBT, and psychoeducation are all non-pharmaceutical treatment options for children with ADHD (NIMH, 2008; Satcher, 1999). Psychosocial treatment for ADHD most often is provided through community-based social service agencies, outpatient clinics and schools.

Depression

Children suffering from depression are vulnerable and need immediate intervention. Depressed children often present as sad, but, in lieu of sadness, may present as irritable (American Psychiatric Association, 1994). They may no longer be interested in activities they used to enjoy. They may be self-critical and feel that others criticize them. They are often pessimistic and may feel hopeless about the future. They may have problems concentrating, or lack energy and motivation to complete tasks. They may neglect their physical appearance and hygiene. Often, depressed children have disturbed sleep patterns (American Psychiatric Association, 1994).

Although depression in children is diagnosed similarly to depression in adults, there are some potential differences to be aware of. Complicating the diagnosis of depression in youth is the fact that symptom expression may vary by developmental stage (Bhatia & Bhatia, 2007). For instance, children and adolescents of certain ages and abilities may not effectively describe their mood status (Bhatia & Bhatia, 2007).

In 2008, 8% of children between the ages of 12 and 17 experienced a major depressive episode (Substance Abuse and Mental Health Services Administration [SAMHSA], Office of Applied Studies, 2009). A major depressive episode is defined as the existence of five or more symptoms that amount to depressed mood and/or loss of interest or pleasure in daily activities consistently over a two-week period (*DSM-IV*). The risk of having a major depressive episode increases as a child ages (Shaffer et al., 1996b). Girls are three times more likely than boys to have a major depressive episode (Shaffer et al., 1996b; Waller et al., 2006).

Children with a history of a major depressive episode are at increased risk of suicide (SAMHSA, Office of Applied Studies, 2007). Suicide is the third leading cause of death for youth between 10 and 24 years old (Centers for Disease Control, 2010). The risk of suicide reaches its peak in the mid-adolescent years (Satcher, 1999). Almost 7 out of every 100,000 youth aged 15–19 commit suicide. For young adults between 20 and 24 years old, that rate increases to almost 13 out of every 100,000 (Centers for Disease Control, 2010). Girls are more likely than boys to report a suicide attempt (Lewinsohn, Rohde, Seeley, & Baldwin, 2001), but boys are four times more likely than girls to actually commit suicide (Satcher, 1999).

Childhood depression is often treated through psychosocial intervention. Research on interpersonal therapy and family therapy supports their use to address childhood depression. Use of CBT with depressed youth is strongly supported by research. These psychosocial interventions are offered in communities through social service agencies, outpatient clinics and schools.

The efficacy of a community-based, group format, CBT program for adolescents, "Coping with Depression," is supported by ongoing research. Coping with Depression is a group program for actively depressed adolescents. The program is usually provided through social service agencies, outpatient clinics, and schools. The program includes 16 two-hour sessions over an eight-week period. Adolescents are taught relaxation, conflict resolution, and communication skills. A component for parents informs parents of the information being presented to their children (California Evidence-Based Clearinghouse for Child Welfare, 2010).

When psychosocial intervention is not effective, or the child's depression is severe, treatment through the use of antidepressants may be warranted. Selective seratonin uptake inhibitors (SSRIs) are most often used to treat children and adolescent depression. Research

79

supports the efficacy of SSRIs in treating depression in youth. However, there are concerns regarding the safety of using antidepressants for children and adolescents. Research finds that children and adolescents who are taking SSRIs are four times more likely to have suicidal thoughts or ideations than depressed youth taking a placebo. In 2004, the United States Food and Drug Administration issued a "black box" warning, the strongest warning they issue, for the use of SSRIs in children and adolescents. The warning cautions that these drugs may increase suicidal thoughts and behavior among children and adolescents (NIMH, 2010).

Owing to the potential social and physical consequences of depression for children and adolescents, it is imperative that youth be screened and that services be available in communities. Coordination between parents, social services agencies, mental health clinics, and schools can best address the needs of depressed youth.

RISK FACTORS FOR CHILDHOOD MENTAL ILLNESS

The mental health of children is greatly impacted by biology, exposure to poverty, violence, and maltreatment (Hacker & Darcy, 2006). This is not to say that these factors *cause* the mental illness; the existence of the risk factors only increases the likelihood that a child will have a mental illness (Satcher, 1999).

Biological Risk Factors

Biological risk factors may be inherited through genetics and/or physiological, based on biological abnormalities unrelated to genetics. Research suggests that schizophrenia, ADHD, bipolar disorder, and autism all have genetic components. Non-genetic abnormalities can be caused through environmental influences such as injury, infection, poor nutrition, or exposure to toxins. It is important to note that research suggests genetic and environmental risk factors interact to affect onset of childhood mental illness.

Community-based efforts to address childhood mental illness should not ignore addressing biological risk factors. Community-based education about risk and prevention, as well as screening efforts, would benefit children affected by these risk factors by providing the means for early intervention.

Poverty

Research consistently finds that children living in poverty are at increased risk for mental health disorders. Poor children are almost twice as likely as non-poor children to be diagnosed with a mental health disorder (Howell, 2004). Poor children with mental health issues are further disadvantaged owing to inferior access to appropriate services. Poor children are more likely to live in communities that lack appropriate mental health services (Chow, Jaffee, & Snowden, 2003). Further complicating this community deficiency, poor children often lack transportation to access services outside their communities (Gamm, Stone, & Pittman, 2010; Pumariega, Glover, Holzer, & Nguyen, 1998).

Researchers and policymakers are puzzled by the conundrum: does poverty cause mental illness, or does mental illness cause poverty? Research does not provide a conclusive answer. There is also concern that poor children may be unjustly labeled as "mentally ill" because of professional judgment based on their family's situation (Wilson, 2009). As a result of the many unresolved questions, efforts to address the connection between childhood mental illness and poverty should be targeted both at anti-poverty initiatives, as well as improved access and quality of mental health services for low-income communities.

Exposure to Violence

Childhood exposure to violence negatively impacts childhood mental health. Children need not be direct victims of physical violence to be significantly affected by violence. Violence that takes place in the child's school (Flannery, Wester, & Singer, 2004), the larger community (Ceballo, Ramirez, Hearn, & Maltese, 2003), or in their own home among family members (Wolfe, Crooks, Lee, McIntyre-Smith, & Jaffe, 2003) can all impact childhood mental health. Violence exposure in children negatively impacts cognitive development, leads to regression in skills, and can result in PTSD (Stover & Berkowitz, 2005).

Domestic violence (also described as domestic abuse, spousal abuse, and intimate partner violence) includes a pattern of abusive behaviors by one or both partners in an intimate relationship. The violence may include physical, psychological, and emotional forms of abuse. In the United States, more than 15 million children live in families where domestic violence occurred at least once in the past year, and 7 million children live in families in which severe partner violence occurred (McDonald, Jouriles, Ramisetty-Mikler, Caetano, & Green, 2006).

Programs to prevent and respond to domestic violence have proliferated in recent years, largely supported by federal grants funded through the Violence Against Women Act of 1994 (United States Department of Justice, Office on Violence Against Women, 2010). Psychoeducational programs in schools, domestic violence shelters, and treatment programs for batterers are among the community-based initiatives to provide for safety within the home. Although physical safety is always the primary goal of these initiatives, the psychological and emotional needs of victims, including children in these homes, should not be ignored.

Child Abuse and Neglect

Children who are abused or neglected are more likely than other children to be diagnosed with a mental disorder. Child abuse and neglect involves the

> act or failure to act on the part of a parent or caretaker, which results in death, serious physical or emotional harm, sexual abuse, or exploitation, or an act or failure to act which presents an imminent risk of serious harm.
>
> (Child Abuse Prevention and Treatment Act, 2003)

Over 900,000 children were the victims of child abuse or neglect in the United States in 2008 (USDHHS–MCHB, 2010). Although the physical consequences of abuse and neglect may be obvious, the emotional and psychological consequences are more often not.

Children who are the victims of child abuse or neglect are at increased risk of mental or emotional health problems, as well as cognitive and social difficulties (Child Welfare Information Gateway, 2008). Almost 80% of young adults who were abused as children meet the diagnostic criteria for at least one psychiatric disorder by age 21. Childhood victims of abuse are more likely to suffer from depression, anxiety, eating disorders, panic disorder, dissociative disorders, ADHD, anger, PTSD, and reactive attachment disorder (De Bellis & Thomas, 2003; Silverman, Reinherz, & Giaconia, 1996; Springer, Sheridan, Kuo, & Carnes, 2007; Teicher, 2000). They are also more likely to attempt suicide. Parental neglect is also associated with borderline personality disorders and violent behavior in children (Schore, 2003).

Children who have been abused and neglected are at least 25% more likely to experience problems such as juvenile delinquent behavior, adult criminal behavior, sexual risk-taking, teen pregnancy, and low academic achievement (English, Widom, & Brandford, 2004; Johnson, Rew, & Sternglanz, 2006; Kelley, Thornberry, & Smith, 1997; Zolotor et al., 1999). Substance abuse is also linked to childhood victimization (Dube et al., 2001). As many as two-thirds of people in drug treatment programs report having been abused as children (Swan, 1998).

Community-based programs designed to prevent child abuse and neglect, as well as programs designed to address these risks, are common throughout the United States, although they are often underfunded. Increased commitment to these programs and their proliferation are needed to prevent and respond to the disastrous consequences of child abuse and neglect on the mental health of America's children.

SOCIETY'S RESPONSE TO MENTAL ILLNESS IN CHILDREN

Until the past 30–40 years, the response to the mental health needs of children and youth focused on residential care. Behaviorally disruptive children would be removed from their families and institutionalized. These children would be treated in residential treatment centers and state psychiatric hospitals (Dore, 2005). The child's home environment was thought to be the main cause of their behavioral problems, and thus such removal had a therapeutic goal.

Since the 1970s, there has been a shift away from institutional care, with an emphasis toward serving children while they remained in their homes, in the care of their families. Theoretical developments in the 1960s focused on the functioning of the whole family as a system. Therefore, treating a child separately from the family would not address the systemic issues (Dore, 2005).

A series of exposés in the late 1960s and early 1970s focused attention on the inadequate care children received in many institutions. A series of court decisions, followed by responsive federal and state statutory law, require children to be treated in the least restrictive setting. As a result, institutional settings downsized or closed their doors. Families with children needing mental health services looked to community-based services, through schools, social service agencies, and mental health clinics, to respond (Dore, 2005).

In 1982, the federal Child and Adolescent Services Program (CAASP) initiative incorporated a set of principles to influence the development of a "system of care" for children's mental health services within their home communities. These principles include attention to individual needs, use of strengths-based perspective, involving families in the care of children, coordination between service delivery providers, and the use of the least restrictive service setting that is clinically appropriate (New York State Council on Children and Families, 2010).

In 1987, the Education for All Handicapped Children Act (P.L. 94–142) became federal law. This law required that children with special education needs, including mental health disorders, be served in their community schools and mainstreamed into regular classes whenever possible. The Individuals with Disabilities Education Act (IDEA) of 1990 replaced P.L. 94–142, but retained many of its provisions.

The Substance Abuse and Mental Health Services Administration (SAMHSA) provides grants under the federal Child Mental Health Services Act to cities, counties, and states. Recipient communities must create and support a "system of care" for children with severe mental illness, involving key agencies, health-care providers, and private partners (Waxman, 2006). Almost 100 cities, counties, and states obtained $106 million in grants through this program in 2005. Despite evidence demonstrating effectiveness and substantial need across the country, the vast majority of communities do not receive this federal support (Waxman, 2006).

Even with almost 30 years of significant government focus on the needs of children and youth to receive mental health services in their communities, too many children continue without access to appropriate services. Hundreds of children are locked in psychiatric facilities for days after they have been cleared to leave, simply because other, less-restrictive settings of care are unavailable (Goldberg, 2005). One child was stuck in a hospital for nearly a year (Knox, 2000). Youth with mental illness are often "warehoused" in juvenile and criminal detention owing to a lack of mental health services in their community. In 2003, 14,603 youth were incarcerated unnecessarily because community mental health treatment was not available (United States House of Representatives, Committee on Government Reform, 2004). Data from 19 states in 2001 found that 12,700 youth were signed over to the child welfare or juvenile justice systems by their parents in order to obtain mental health care (United States Government Accountability Office, 2003). More needs to be done to meet the mental health needs of children and adolescents in their communities.

COMMUNITY MENTAL HEALTH SERVICES FOR CHILDREN AND YOUTH

Some children still receive care as residents in private and government institutions, but most children receive mental health services within their own communities. Community-based partnerships toward improving childhood mental health include schools, juvenile justice systems, youth development programs, and, most importantly, parents and families (Hacker & Darcy, 2006). Like parents of children with other forms of illness, parents of children with mental illness need support and guidance. Caring for a mentally ill child is challenging, frustrating, and sometimes isolating. Serving as a caretaker to a mentally ill child comes with its own stresses. It is important that the entire family is included in service planning to address the child's mental illness.

The responsibility to provide mental health services to children and youth has been divided among an array of agencies. Similar to the provision of community-based services for adults, children receive mental health services through social service agencies, mental health agencies, and private practitioners in their community. Unlike adults, children also receive mental health services through school-based services. There are many different forms of intervention utilized in community-based mental health services, specifically designed to address child mental health.

Play Therapy

Play therapy, or therapeutic play, is a form of psychotherapeutic intervention that uses play as a form of communication between the child client and the therapist. Play therapy is often used with younger children without the verbal or cognitive ability to verbally report or process their thoughts and feelings. Play therapy is commonly used with children who have been traumatized or abused.

Research suggests that play therapy can be effective in evaluating and treating traumatized or abused children. However, designing a quantitative evaluation of play therapy is difficult, and as a result there is no comprehensive review of the modality to provide clear conclusions on its efficacy.

School-Based Mental Health Services

School-based mental health services respond to children's mental health needs as they impact the child's educational attainment and classroom behavior. Schools are often responsible for identification and evaluation of childhood mental health issues. Owing to the almost universal provision of education services through schools, schools are also well suited for psycho-educational prevention and intervention programs.

Under IDEA, school districts must develop an "individualized education program" that meets the physical and mental needs of children with disabilities. Often times, these services include "special education" services, including smaller class size, smaller student-to-teacher ratios, physical, occupation, and speech therapies, as well as specialized instruction.

Family Therapy

Family therapy has been widely used over the past 30 years as an intervention to address child and adolescent mental health. Seeing the child as a part of a larger system, the family, family therapy works with the family unit instead of the individual.

Research supports the effectiveness of family therapy to address some childhood mental disorders, including ADHD, depression, and conduct disorders (Carr, 2009). Family therapy was found to be more effective at treating adolescent drug use than individual and group-based programs, as well as twelve-step programs for adolescents (Carr, 2009). The use of family therapy is often more effective when used in conjunction with other forms of psychotherapeutic intervention.

Multi-Systemic Therapy

Multi-systemic therapy (MST) was developed to respond to the needs of families with adolescents at risk for delinquent behavior (Berry, 2005). MST is a home- and family-based treatment aimed at changing troubled youth behavior in the youth's own environment (Berry, 2005). MST combines family therapy, individual therapy, and individual-skills training (Carr, 2009). In MST, a diverse and highly trained team of caregivers modifies treatment and therapy for the family based on the day-to-day condition of the child (Borduin, 1999). Within the youth's family, friends, school, and neighborhood systems, the highly trained MST therapists work to reduce negative relationships and encourage problem solving and positive behavior (Berry, 2005). Research has shown that MST reduces out-of-home placement, criminal behavior, substance abuse, school failure, and other behavioral problems in teenagers previously diagnosed with serious mental and emotional disorders (Ogden & Halliday-Boykins, 2004; Schaeffer & Borduinn, 2005). Unlike many other services for at-risk youth, the founders of MST at the University of South Carolina are dedicated to monitoring and insuring treatment fidelity by measuring therapists' adherence to the model (Berry, 2005).

PRACTICE ISSUES: LABELING OF CHILDREN WITH MENTAL DISORDERS

An increasing number of children manifesting emotional upset, misbehavior, and learning problems are being assigned psychiatric labels that denote internal disorders (Adelman & Taylor, 2006). These labels, including ADHD, depression, and learning disabled, suggest that the child's problem is rooted in internal pathology and not impacted by environmental circumstances (Adelman & Taylor, 2006). Research actually suggests the primary causes for most children's emotional, behavior, and learning problems are external factors related to neighborhood, family, school, and/or peer factors (Adelman & Taylor, 2006).

There are many significant results of this trend, including the use of inappropriate and expensive treatments (Adelman & Taylor, 2006). Additionally, parents avoid seeking evaluation and treatment for their children for fear that their children will be labeled.

Case Example: Bernard

Bernard was a busy toddler. His mother, Stacy, always said that he had "ants in his pants." When Bernard entered kindergarten at the local public school, his teachers expressed concern that he could not follow the instruction in the classroom. By the middle of first grade, his teacher suspected that Bernard had a learning disability or ADHD. The teacher believed that Bernard might benefit from special education services and suggested that Bernard be evaluated by the school psychologist. Stacy was resistant and refused to consent to the evaluation. Stacy had a cousin who was in "special ed," and he never graduated from high school.

■ What resources in the community can the family turn to for information and support?

PRACTICE ISSUES: PRESCRIBING PSYCHOTROPIC MEDICATIONS FOR CHILDREN

Mentally ill children are increasingly medicated with psychotropic medications (Olfson, Marcus, Weissman, & Jensen, 2002) and at earlier ages (NIMH, 2009). Psychotropic medications are prescription drugs that affect brain chemicals related to mood and behavior (NIMH, 2009).

85

Psychotropic medications include antidepressants, antipsychotics, anti-anxiety medications, and mood stabilizers. Psychotropic medications affect children's brains differently than adults (NIMH, 2009). Children's brains are still developing and highly sensitive to medication (NIMH, 2009). Dosing of psychotropic drugs for children depends on the child's weight and age. Research on the risk and benefits of using psychotropic medication in children suggests that the decision to use such medication for treatment should be carefully considered.

The possible physical and emotional consequences of medicating children are not quite clear (NIMH, 2009). Many psychotropic drugs have not been tested on children and adolescents. Mental illness was not always acknowledged in children, and as result studies on early psychotropic drugs did not involve children. More recently, children were excluded from clinical studies of psychotropic drugs owing to ethical concerns. Drug companies fear the possibility of damaging the physical and/or mental health of children during these clinical trials. However, the costs of not completing this research arguably overshadow the benefits of uninformed use. Therefore, federal policy encourages pharmaceutical companies to extend clinical studies of psychotropic drugs to children as young as preschool age, so that parents and professionals can make better-informed decisions (NIMH, 2009). As previously discussed, adolescent use of certain antidepressants has been linked to increased suicidal ideations through recent research (NIMH, 2009, 2010).

The NIMH recommend that the use of psychotropic drugs with children be limited to situations where the benefits of the treatment clearly outweigh the risks (2009). For instance, children whose condition can be managed through other types of treatment, such as psychotherapy, should avoid the use of psychotropic drugs (NIMH, 2009). However, the use of psychotropic medication is still recommended for children with severe problems who might suffer serious or dangerous consequences without psychotropic medication (NIMH, 2009). The NIMH recommend that the use of psychotropic medication for children *always* be used in combination with another form of treatment, such as individual or family therapy, behavior management strategies, and family support services (2009).

Poor children are more likely to be medicated with psychotropic drugs than non-poor children (Wilson, 2009). One of the reasons suspected for this disparity relates to health insurance coverage. Poor children are less likely to have access to behavioral health coverage that would pay for psychotherapeutic treatment, and so medication may be the more accessible and cheaper option to treat mental illness in children (Wilson, 2009).

Case Example: Alice

Alice was never considered outgoing or particularly social, but her parents grew more concerned during her freshman year of high school. Alice would come straight home every day afterschool and seemed sad. She did not get involved in school groups, or hang out with friends on weekends. At an annual physical examination for school, Alice's mom, Terry, mentioned her concerns to the pediatrician, who prescribed an antidepressant. Alice is not keen on taking the drug. Alice's father, Charles, recently watched a television news program that highlighted the dangers of the use of antidepressants by teens. No one in their family has ever sought assistance for mental health concerns before. The family feels isolated and increasingly stressed.

■ What resources in the community can the family turn to for information and support?

PRACTICE ISSUES: BULLYING

The suicides of adolescents who had been victims of bullying have made recent headlines. Fifteen-year-old Pheobe Prince was repeatedly called names and tormented by nine classmates and other area youth for months, by phone, text, email, and in person. They called her a "whore." In the middle of a crowded lunchroom, someone pointed at her and told her to "stay away from other people's men." After months of ongoing harassment, she hung herself (Bennett, 2010).

Tyler Clemente, a Rutgers University freshman, jumped off the George Washington Bridge to his death in September 2010. Tyler's death highlighted the increasing number of LGTB youth who commit suicide. Most suffered as bully victims due to their sexual orientation, or even just suspicion of their sexual orientation (McKinley, 2010).

Bullying among children involves intentional aggressive behavior that involves an imbalance of power or strength. Bullying can be physical, verbal, or emotional and includes a technological form of bullying called "cyberbullying." Cyberbullying involves aggression using electronic means. Cyberbullying generally includes harassing, threatening, humiliating, or hassling someone through text messages, email messages, webpages, and social networking sites (Hinduja & Patchin, 2010). Increasing research on this aspect of youth aggression has found 20–40% of youth in various studies reporting that they have been bullied through electronic means in their lifetimes (Hinduja & Patchin, 2010).

Individual, family, peer, school, and community factors all influence the risk for bullying (United States Department of Health and Human Services, Human Resources and Services Administration [USDHHS, HRSA], 2010). Children who bully, as well as those children who are bullied, are at increased risk of mental health disorders, though not of the same type. Bullies are more likely to have antisocial personality disorders than their peers, whereas those who are bullied are more likely to suffer from anxiety disorders. Children who bully *and* are bullied are at highest risk of mental health disorders (Sourander et al., 2007).

Widespread acknowledgment that bullying is a serious problem has resulted in the government, schools, and community services providers developing psychoeducational prevention programs, support programs for victims, and intervention/treatment programs for bullies (USDHHS, HRSA, 2010). In 2011, the state of New Jersey passed a law generally considered the toughest anti-bullying law in the country (Hu, 2011). This law requires schools to provide extensive training about bullying and to set in place strict procedures to prevent bullying and to respond to bullying allegations aggressively in an effort to prevent tragedies such as the deaths of Phoebe Prince and Tyler Clemente (Hu, 2011).

Case Example: Jonah

Jonah was a quiet seventh grader. His mother, Patti, was very proud. He made good grades and was respectful to teachers and his family. When Jonah refused to go to school one morning, Patti was shocked to learn that one of his classmates was threatening to beat him up after school that day. Jonah showed Patti a string of emails from this other student harassing Jonah for being a "wuss" and worse.

■ What resources in the community can the family turn to for information and support?

87

SUMMARY

As members of families, without the cognitive or legal capacity to attend to their own mental health needs, children are in a unique position. The primary responsibility for safeguarding children's mental health lies with parents, but communities need to develop systems of care to support parents and children toward this task. Research consistently finds that community-based mental health services are effective at addressing childhood mental illness. Unfortunately, millions of children, most often those with the greatest need, cannot access services owing to lack of availability or cost. Efforts should be targeted at expanding children's access to community-based mental health services.

DISCUSSION QUESTIONS

1. Why is it important for the mental health needs of children to be met through community-based programs wherever possible?

2. How are the mental health needs of children treated differently than those of adults?

3. What societal factors make meeting the mental health needs of children different from those of adults?

4. What current policy initiatives at the state and federal levels address children's mental health?

LEARNING ASSIGNMENT

As a class, design a system of care to meet the needs of mentally ill children. What components would you include?

SUGGESTED READINGS

Journal of Child and Adolescent Mental Health, published for the Association of Child and Adolescent Mental Health.

Child and Adolescent Psychiatry and Mental Health, online journal, www.capmh.com

Journal of Clinical Child & Adolescent Psychology, published by the Society of Clinical Child & Adolescent Psychology.

Clinical Child and Family Psychology Review

Child Abuse and Neglect: The International Journal, official publication of the International Society for Prevention of Child Abuse and Neglect.

INTERNET RESOURCES

National Institute of Mental Health, Child and Adolescent Mental Health: www.nimh.nih.gov/health/topics/child-and-adolescent-mental-health/index.shtml

National Institutes of Health, MedLine Plus, Child Mental Health: www.nlm.nih.gov/medlineplus/childmentalhealth.html

Substance Abuse and Mental Health Services Administration: www.samhsa.gov

National Center for Children in Poverty: www.nccp.org

American Academy of Child & Adolescent Psychiatry: www.aacap.org

REFERENCES

Adelman, H., & Taylor, T. (2006). Mental health in school and public health. Public Health Reports. May/June 2006, 294–298.

American Psychiatric Association. (1994). *Diagnostic and statistical manual of mental disorders* (4th ed.). Washington, DC: Author.

Anderson, J.C., Williams, S.C., McGee, R., & Silva, P.A. (1987). DSM-III disorders in preadolescent children: Prevalence in a large sample from the general population. *Archives of General Psychiatry, 44*, 69–76.

Bennett, J. (2010). From lockers to lockup: School bullying in the digital age can have tragic consequences. But should it be a crime? *Newsweek*, October 4, 2010. Retrieved from: www.newsweek.com/2010/10/04/phoebe-prince-should-bullying-be-a-crime.html

Berry, M. (2005). Overview of family preservation. In G.P. Mallon & P.M. Hess (Eds.), *Child welfare for the 21st century: A handbook for practices, policies and programs*. New York: Columbia Press.

Bhatia, S.K., & Bhatia, S.C. (2007). Childhood and adolescent depression. *American Family Physician*, Jan. 1, *75*, 73–80.

Borduin, C.M. (1999) Multisystemic treatment of criminality and violence in adolescents. *Journal of the American Academy of Child and Adolescent Psychiatry, 38*, 242–249.

Burns, B.J., Costello, E.J., Angold, A., Tweed, D., Stangl, D., Farmer, E.M.Z., & Erkanli, A. (1995). DataWatch: Children's mental health service use across service sectors. *Health Affair, 14*(3), 147–159.

California Evidence-Based Clearinghouse for Child Welfare (2010). Coping with depression for adolescents. Retrieved from: www.cebc4cw.org/program/127

Carr, A. (2009). The effectiveness of family therapy and systemic interventions for child-focused problems. *Journal of Family Therapy, 31*, 3–45.

Ceballo, R., Ramirez, C., Hearn, K., & Maltese, K. (2003). Community violence and children's psychological well-being: Does parental monitoring matter? *Journal of Clinical Child & Adolescent Psychology, 32*(4), 586–592.

Centers for Disease Control (2010). Youth suicide. Retrieved from: www.cdc.gov/ncipc/dvp/suicide/youthsuicide.htm

Center for Mental Health in Schools (2003). Youngsters' mental health and psychosocial problems: What are the data? Retrieved from: www.eric.ed.gov:80/ERICWebPortal/search/detailmini.jsp?_nfpb=true&_&ERICExtSearch_SearchValue_0=ED490009&ERICExtSearch_SearchType_0=no&accno=ED490009

Child Abuse Prevention and Treatment Act (2003) 42 U.S.C.A. § 5106g(2).

Child Welfare Information Gateway (2008). Long-term consequences of child abuse and neglect. Retrieved from: www.childwelfare.gov/pubs/factsheets/long_term_consequences.cfm

Chow, J.C., Jaffee, K., & Snowden, L. (2003). Racial/ethnic disparities in the use of mental health services in poverty areas. *American Journal of Public Health, 93*(5), 792–797.

De Bellis, M., & Thomas, L. (2003). Biologic findings of post-traumatic stress disorder and child maltreatment. *Current Psychiatry Reports, 5*, 108–117.

Dore, M.A. (2005). Child and adolescent mental health. In G.P. Mallon & P.M. Hess (Eds.), *Child welfare for the 21st century: A handbook for practices, policies and programs*. New York: Columbia Press.

Dube, S.R., Anda, R.F., Felitti, V.J., Chapman, D., Williamson, D.F., & Giles, W.H. (2001). Childhood abuse, household dysfunction and the risk of attempted suicide throughout the life span: Findings from the Adverse Childhood Experiences Study. *Journal of the American Medical Association, 286*, 3089–3096.

English, D.J., Widom, C.S., & Brandford, C. (2004). Another look at the effects of child abuse. *NIJ Journal, 251*, 23–24.

Esser, G., Schmidt, M.H., & Woerner, W. (1990). Epidemiology and course of psychiatric disorders in school-age children—results of a longitudinal study. *Journal of Child Psychology and Psychiatry, 31*, 243–263.

Flannery, D.J., Wester, K.L., & Singer, M.I. (2004). Impact of exposure to violence in school on child and adolescent mental health and behavior. *Journal of Community Psychology, 32*(5), 559–573.

Gamm, L., Stone, S., & Pittman, S. (2010). Mental health and mental disorders: A rural challenge. Rural Healthy People 2010 Project.

Goldberg, G. (2005). Outcry of "stuck kids" goes to court. *Boston Globe*, Apr. 25; Sect. A1.

Grisso, T. (2007). Do childhood mental disorders cause adult crime? *American Journal of Psychiatry, 164*, 1625–1627.

Hacker, K., & Darcy, K. (2006). Putting "child mental health" in public health. Public Health Reports. May/June 2006, 292–293.

Hinduja, S., & Patchin, J. (2010). Cyberbullying fact sheet: Identification, prevention, and response. Cyberbullying Research Center. Retrieved April 26, 2012, from: www.cyberbullying.us/Cyberbullying_Identification_Prevention_Response_Fact_Sheet.pdf

Howell, E. (2004). Access to children's mental health services under Medicaid and SCHIP. Washington, DC: Urban Institute. Retrieved from: www.urban.org/uploadedPDF/311053_B-60.pdf

Hu, W. (2011). Bullying law puts New Jersey schools on spot. *New York Times*, August 30, 2011.

Johnson, R., Rew, L., & Sternglanz, R.W. (2006). The relationship between childhood sexual abuse and sexual health practices of homeless adolescents. *Adolescence, 41*(162), 221–234.

Kapphahn, C., Morreale, M., Rickert, V., & Walker, L. (2006). Financing mental health services for adolescents: A position paper of the Society for Adolescent Medicine. *Journal of Adolescent Health, 39*, 456–458.

Kelley, B.T., Thornberry, T.P., & Smith, C.A. (1997). In the wake of childhood maltreatment. Washington, DC: National Institute of Justice. Retrieved from www.ncjrs.gov/pdffiles1/165257.pdf

Kessler, R.C., Berglund, P., Demler, O., Jin, R., Merikangas, K.R., & Walters, E.E. (2005). Lifetime prevalence and age-of-onset distributions of DSM-IV disorders in the national comorbidity survey replication. *Archives of General Psychiatry, 62*, 593–602.

Knox, R. (2000). Trapped in mental ward. *Boston Globe*, June 4, A1.

Lewinsohn, P.M., Rohde, P., Seeley, J.R., & Baldwin, C.L. (2001). Gender differences in suicide attempts from adolescence to young adulthood. *Journal of the American Academy of Child & Adolescent Psychiatry, 40*(4), 427–434.

McDonald, R., Jouriles, E.N., Ramisetty-Mikler, S., Caetano, R., & Green, C.E. (2006) Estimating the number of American children living in partner-violent families, *Journal of Family Psychology, 20*(1), 137–142.

McKinley, J. (2010). Suicides put light on pressure of gay teens. *New York Times*, October 3. Retrieved from: www.nytimes.com/2010/10/04/us/04suicide.html

National Institute of Mental Health (2008). Attention deficit hyperactivity disorder. NIH Publication No. 08–3572. Retrieved from: www.nimh.nih.gov/health/publications/attention-deficit-hyperactivity-disorder/adhd_booklet.pdf

National Institute of Mental Health (2009). Treatment of children with mental illness. NIH Publication No. 09–4702, Revised 2009. Retrieved from: www.nimh.nih.gov/health/publications/treatment-of-children-with-mental-illness-fact-sheet/nimh-treatment-children-mental-illness-faq.pdf

National Institute of Mental Health (2010). Antidepressant medications for children and adolescents: Information for parents and caregivers. Retrieved from: www.nimh.nih.gov/health/topics/child-and-adolescent-mental-health/antidepressant-medications-for-children-and-adolescents-information-for-parents-and-caregivers.shtml

New York State Council on Children and Families (2010). Child and Adolescent Services Program. Retrieved from: www.ccf.state.ny.us/Initiatives/CCSIRelate/CCSIResources/CASSP.pdf

Ogden, T., & Halliday-Boykins, C.A. (2004). Multisystemic treatment of antisocial adolescents in Norway: replication of clinical outcomes outside of the US. *Child and Adolescent Mental Health, 9,* 77–83.

Olfson, M., Marcus, S.C., Weissman, M.M., & Jensen, P.S. (2002). National trends in the use of psychotropic medications by children. *Journal of the American Academy of Child and Adolescent Psychiatry, 41*(5), 514–521.

Pelham, W.E., Jr., Gnagy, E.M., Greenslade, K.E., & Milich, R. (1992). Teacher ratings of DSM-III-R symptoms for the disruptive behavior disorders. *Journal of the American Academy of Child and Adolescent Psychiatry, 31,* 210–218.

Pumariega, A.J., Glover, S., Holzer, C.E., & Nguyen, H. (1998). Utilization of mental health services in a tri-ethnic sample of adolescents. *Community Mental Health Journal, 34*(2), 145–156.

Ross, D.M., & Ross, S.A. (1982). *Hyperactivity: Current issues, research, and theory.* New York: Wiley.

Satcher, D. (1999). *Mental health: A report from the Surgeon General.* Rockville, MD: U.S. Department of Health and Human Services.

Schaeffer, C.M., & Borduin, C.M. (2005). Long-term follow-up to a randomized clinical trial of multisystemic therapy with serious and violent juvenile offenders. *Journal for Consulting Clinical Psychology, 73,* 445–453.

Schore, A.N. (2003). Early relational trauma, disorganized attachment, and the development of a predisposition to violence. In M.F. Solomon & D.J. Siegel (Eds.), *Healing trauma: Attachment, mind, body, and brain.* New York: Norton.

Shaffer, D., Fisher, P., Dulcan, M.K., Davies, M., Piacentini, J., Schwab-Stone, M.E., Lahey, B.B., Bourdon, K., Jensen, P.S., Bird, H.R., Canino, G., & Regier, D.A. (1996a). The NIMH Diagnostic Interview Schedule for Children Version 2.3 (DISC- 2.3): Description, acceptability, prevalence rates, and performance in the MECA Study. Methods for the Epidemiology of Child and Adolescent Mental Disorders Study. *Journal of the American Academy of Child and Adolescent Psychiatry, 35,* 865–877.

Shaffer, D., Gould, M.S., Fisher, P., Trautman, P., Moreau, D., Kleinman, M., & Flory, M. (1996b). Psychiatric diagnosis in child and adolescent suicide. *Archives of General Psychiatry, 53*(4), 339–348.

Silverman, A.B., Reinherz, H.Z., & Giaconia, R.M. (1996). The long-term sequelae of child and adolescent abuse: A longitudinal community study. *Child Abuse and Neglect, 20*(8), 709–723.

Sourander, A., Jensen, P., Ronning, J.A., Niemela, S., Helenius, H., Sillanmaki, L., Kumpulainen, K., Piha, J., Tamminen, T., Moilanen, I., & Almqvist, F. (2007). What is the early adulthood outcome of boys who bully or are bullied in childhood? The Finnish "From a boy to a man" study. *Pediatrics, 120*(2), 397–404.

Springer, K.W., Sheridan, J., Kuo, D., & Carnes, M. (2007). Long-term physical and mental health consequences of childhood physical abuse: Results from a large population-based sample of men and women. *Child Abuse & Neglect, 31,* 517–530.

Stover, C.S., & Berkowitz, S. (2005). Assessing violence exposure and trauma symptoms in young children: A critical review of measures. *Journal of Traumatic Stress, 18*(6), 707–717.

Substance Abuse and Mental Health Services Administration, Office of Applied Studies (2007). The NSDUH report: Depression and the initiation of cigarette, alcohol and other drug use among youths aged 12 to 17. Rockville, MD: Author. Retrieved from http://oas.samhsa.gov/2k7/newUserdepression/newUserdepression.pdf

91

Substance Abuse and Mental Health Services Administration, Office of Applied Studies (2009). State estimates of substance use from the 2007–2008 National Surveys on Drug Use and Health. Retrieved from: www.oas.samhsa.gov/2k8state/Ch6.htm

Swan, N. (1998). Exploring the role of child abuse on later drug abuse: Researchers face broad gaps in information. *NIDA Notes, 13*(2). Retrieved from: http://archives.drugabuse.gov/NIDA_Notes/NNVol13N2/exploring.html

Teicher, M.D. (2000). Wounds that time won't heal: The neurobiology of child abuse. *Cerebrum: The Dana Forum on Brain Science, 2*(4), 50–67.

United States Department of Health and Human Services (1999). *Mental health: A report of the Surgeon General.* Rockville, MD: Department of Health and Human Services, Substance Abuse and Mental Health Services Administration, Center for Mental Health Services, National Institutes of Health, National Institute of Mental Health.

United States Department of Health and Human Services, Human Resources and Services Administration (2010). Stop Bullying Now. Retrieved from: www.stopbullying.gov

United States Department of Health and Human Services, Health Resources and Services Administration, Maternal and Child Health Bureau (2007). The National Survey of Children's Health 2007. Rockville, MA: U.S. Department of Health and Human Services. Retrieved from: www.mchb.hrsa.gov/nsch/07emohealth/index.html

United States Department of Justice, Office on Violence Against Women (2010). Fact sheets. Retrieved from: www.ovw.usdoj.gov/docs/about-ovw-factsheet.pdf

United States Government Accountability Office (2003) Child welfare and juvenile justice. Washington: GAO. Retrieved from: www.gao.gov/new.items/d03397.pdf

United States House of Representatives, Committee on Government Reform (2004). Incarceration of youth who are waiting for community mental health services in the United States. Washington: Minority Staff, Committee on Government Reform.

Waller, M., Hallfors, D., Halpern, C., Iritani, B., Ford, C., & Guo, G. (2006). Gender differences in associations between depressive symptoms and patterns of substance use and risky sexual behavior among a nationally representative sample of U.S. adolescents. *Archives of Women's Mental Health, 9*(3), 139–150.

Waxman, H. (2006). Improving the care of children with mental illness: A challenge for public health and the federal government. *Public Health Record,* May/June 2006, 299–302.

Wilson, D. (2009). Poor children likelier to get antipsychotics. *New York Times,* December 11.

Wolfe, D.A., Crooks, C.V., Lee, V., McIntyre-Smith, A., & Jaffe, P.G. (2003). The effects of children's exposure to domestic violence: A meta-analysis and critique. *Clinical Child and Family Psychology Review, 6*(3), 171–187.

Wolraich, M.L., Hannah, J.N., Pinnock, T.Y., Baumgaertel, A., & Brown, J. (1996). Comparison of diagnostic criteria for attention-deficit hyperactivity disorder in a county-wide sample. *Journal of the American Academy of Child and Adolescent Psychiatry, 35,* 319–324.

Zolotor, A., Kotch, J., Dufort, V., Winsor, J., Catellier, D., & Bou-Saada, I. (1999). School performance in a longitudinal cohort of children at risk of maltreatment. *Maternal and Child Health Journal, 3*(1), 19–27.

Chapter 7

Family Psychoeducation in the Treatment of Mental Illness

Historical Context, Current Practice, and Future Directions

Sarah P. Lynch, Nelma A. Mason, and William R. McFarlane

INTRODUCTION

The onset and long-term effects of mental illness impact the entire family. Additionally, the family can play a critical role in the course of illness. Today, we understand mental illness in a biopsychosocial context, with "interactive roles of genetic vulnerability, biological predispositions, family or life events stress, and psychological vulnerability" (Miklowitz, 2007). Because of the individual's biological sensitivity to symptoms, the family environment has a greater impact in either protecting against or exacerbating the illness. Despite advances in brain science and treatment of mental illness, stigma continues to be a barrier to accurate information reaching families, who play a key role in an individual's recovery.

In this chapter, we will focus on the family's experience of mental illness (MI), the history of the family's role in the treatment of MI, family psychoeducation as an evidence-based intervention, an overview of the psychoeducational multifamily group model, and current research focus on earlier identification and family-based treatment with risk factors for MI.

FAMILY'S EXPERIENCE

Severe mental illnesses such as schizophrenia and other psychotic disorders are disabling conditions marked by loss of touch with reality, cognitive decline and disorganization, impairment in social and role functioning, and disturbance in mood and behavior. The impact of these illnesses extends from the individual to the family and the community.

Approximately 70–80% of people with psychotic-spectrum illnesses have ongoing contact with their families, whether or not they reside with them (Brent & Guiliano, 2007). Family members are often the ones who help initiate the treatment for their loved one. It is common for a family to misattribute symptoms of psychosis to depression, character flaws, lack of motivation, adolescent developmental changes, or relationship stress. They may not get help until symptoms are more overt and disruptive (Compton, 2010).

Early on in illness onset, the family may experience worry, confusion, misattribution, and denial; over time, families experience an increase in "burden." Family burden is defined as both subjective and objective. Subjective burden includes psychological responses of family members, including grief, symbolic loss, sorrow, anger, resentment, and empathic pain. Objective burden includes caregiving responsibilities, financial strain, navigating services and systems, and family disruption and stress (Marsh & Johnson, 1997; Wong et al., 2008).

"Family burden increases the risk that other important dimensions of the family experience may be ignored, including the family's potential for a resilient response to this devastating event" (Marsh & Johnson, 1997). As family burden worsens over time, offering families earlier intervention in the course of illness onset may promote resiliency.

PARADIGM SHIFT IN FAMILY TREATMENT

Historically, schizophrenia was thought to be caused entirely by bad parenting or, more specifically, bad mothering. The "schizophrenogenic mother," labeled in the 1940s, described the rejecting, hostile, and overbearing mother as the cause of the illness (Neill, 1990). Conjoint family therapy, developed at the Mental Research Institute in Palo Alto around 1960, attempted to correct family communication patterns so that the "schizophrenic symptoms no longer had a function, and were supposed to disappear" (Bertrando, 2006). The treatment was ethically flawed, as it was based on no empirical data and led to "a guilt inducing practice, where non-psychotic family members were blamed for literally (and sometimes deliberately) causing schizophrenia" (Bertrando, 2006). Although this formulation was later rejected, the stigma and blame experienced by the family have been longstanding consequences.

Deinstitutionalization of psychiatric patients from hospitals into the community in the 1960s and 1970s led to families taking in their loved one and becoming the primary caregivers. Brown, Birley, and Wing (1972) conducted several studies examining the effect of family interactions on the course of illness. Brown found that "many schizophrenic patients remain[ed] very highly sensitive to their social environment, even when there [were] no apparent symptoms" (Brown et al., 1972). Brown discovered that emotional expression by both marital partners and parents caused symptom relapse, suggesting that the illness was exacerbated by highly charged interactions (Brown et al., 1972).

Expressed emotion (EE) in the family environment and its relationship to symptoms of mental illness have been studied extensively over the last three decades. EE is defined by the family members' level of criticism, hostility, and/or emotional overinvolvement (Miklowitz, 2007). High EE has been proven to be an environmental predictor of relapse in schizophrenia and mood disorders (Butzlaff & Hooley, 1998; Miklowitz, 2007). The finding that high EE in families exacerbates symptoms has led to family treatment focused on lowering EE in the environment.

Over the past decade, the evidence has been increasingly clear that there are susceptibility genes for major mental illnesses and demonstrated brain changes in neuroimaging (Lieberman et al., 2008). The brain basis of mental illness has led to less stigmatizing and blaming of families. Research studies began to look at the interaction between genetic risk and environment in the onset of major mental illness. A Finnish longitudinal adoption study over 21 years compared adoptees with and without first-degree biological risk for schizophrenia adopted into high- and low-EE families. The study showed that the adoptees with both genetic risk and a measure of high EE were at high risk for developing schizophrenia, whereas those with genetic risk and a measure of low EE were at no greater risk of developing schizophrenia than those with no genetic risk (Tienari et al., 2004). The family environment can protect against illness onset or exacerbate symptoms given a genetic risk.

Additionally, several studies have found that EE is higher in families of adults with chronic major mental illness than in families with recent onset of symptoms, suggesting that families develop high EE with the stress of the illness. Parents of young people in the early stages of psychosis show warmth and low levels of rejection and protectiveness (McFarlane & Cook, 2007). This finding suggests that earlier intervention in the course of illness may protect families against developing high EE.

Lack of information about the illness, along with uncertainty about its long-term impact, contributes to high EE in family members (Miklowitz, 2007). A number of trials of family-based treatment have led to a reduction in EE, family conflict, and relapse rates suggesting that families can alter their behaviors and positively affect the course of illness (Butzlaff & Hooley, 1998; Lieberman at al, 2008).

FAMILY PSYCHOEDUCATION

Family psychoeducation (FPE) is a family-based recovery model that incorporates both brain biology and environment. FPE is a departure from traditional family therapy, which focuses on addressing family dysfunction as the root cause of a family member's symptoms. FPE assumes that the family is functioning normally until proven otherwise, and that the family will need education and strategies to support recovery for their family member (McFarlane, 2002). Hogarty, one of the original developers of FPE along with Carol Anderson in the late 1970s, described:

> a then unfamiliar "alliance" with the family, the teaching of day to day survival skills, and a collaborative stepwise plan for reintegrating the patient into family and community life. The family's common emotional responses to schizophrenia were addressed (denial, fear, guilt, frustration, anger and hopelessness) along with attempts to improve communication and problem solving skills.
>
> (Hogarty, 2003)

FPE acknowledges the family's grief and burden and responds with a family-integrated treatment approach.

Today, FPE is an evidence-based practice for major mental illness based on decades of research illustrating its impact in reducing hospitalizations and relapse rates while improving symptom levels, and social and vocational functioning (Falloon, 2003; McFarlane et al., 2003; Murray-Swank & Dixon, 2004; Pitschel-Walsz, Leucht, Bäuml, Kissling, & Engel, 2001). A meta-analysis of studies on FPE shows a 15% relapse rate for patients in FPE groups with their families and taking medication, whereas those in individual therapy and taking medication, or taking medication alone experienced a relapse rate of 30–40% (McFarlane et al., 2002). In one meta-analysis of 25 studies, longer-term interventions (9–24 months) with families were found more effective than short-term ones (Pitschel-Walsz et al., 2001). FPE research results include improved family-member well-being, increased employment rates for consumers, and reduced costs of care (McFarlane et al., 2002). Hazel et al. found that caregivers of a client who received psychoeducational multiple family group (PMFG) intervention experienced substantially lower distress than clients in outpatient treatment whose families were not offered this intervention (Hazel et al., 2004).

In 1998, the Schizophrenia Patient Outcomes Research Team recommended family psychosocial interventions, including "education about the illness, family support, crisis intervention, and training in problem solving skills" (Dixon et al., 1999). SAMHSA offers a Family Psychoeducation Toolkit for practitioners as part of an evidence-based practice toolkit including other psychosocial interventions, such as Assertive Community Treatment and Supported Employment (www.samhsa.gov).

Family psychoeducation models can differ in format, structure, and setting, but a consensus was reached about key elements of the model at the World Schizophrenia Fellowship in 1998 by founders of the model, including Leff, Falloon, and McFarlane. The overarching goal established was a partnership between clients, families, and professionals in achieving the best outcome for the client, while also addressing the family's distress and burden through support, education, and collaborative problem solving (McFarlane et al., 2002).

FPEs are typically diagnosis specific. Over time, FPE models have been more broadly tested with other diagnoses. Although initially evidence-based in the treatment of schizophrenia, FPE has been proven effective in bipolar disorder, major depression, and dual diagnosis, PTSD, obsessive–compulsive disorder, anorexia nervosa, and borderline personality disorder (McFarlane, 2011).

PSYCHOEDUCATIONAL MULTIPLE FAMILY GROUPS

In this chapter, we will offer a detailed overview of the PMFG model, which is based on the principles of FPE, behavioral family management, and multifamily approaches. The first multifamily group was started by Laqueur back in the 1960s in an inpatient setting. Patients wanted to join groups held for their family members, and, when they did, Laqueur saw an improvement in their social functioning on the ward (McFarlane, 2002). The PMFG model combines current understanding of the psychobiology of the illness with validated components from previous models. McFarlane states the following goals for the client and family: an alliance with knowledgeable and empathic professionals; information about schizophrenia (or other disorders); guidelines for managing the illness; practice in solving problems created by the illness; and social support from others experiencing similar distress (McFarlane, 2002).

The PMFG offers a structured, multiple family intervention involving both the clients and their families. PMFGs are unique in bringing together multiple families, including the clients, and are co-facilitated by two professional clinicians. Family education groups (through NAMI's family-to-family program) or treatment groups for clients only are far more common than groups involving both client and family. PMFGs promote improved intra-family communication through inter-family reciprocal learning.

The structured group format is critical to the therapeutic process, as it slows down the communication process and levels the playing field among family members, as the group is as likely to problem solve for a parent or sibling as it is for the client themselves. Families are often able to hear suggestions from other families that may be too emotionally charged in their own family. In the group context, clients may be better able to communicate their needs and the family better able to communicate their worry or distress.

96

People with mental illness and their families are often more isolated than their peers. One community survey of caregivers and clients with schizophrenia indicated that the top three reported negative impacts of the illness were: a decline in family social activities, an increase in disagreements and fights among family members, and depression in other family members (Awad & Voruganti, 2008). Supportive social networks help to alleviate family burden and negativity (Magliano et al., 2003). The family's social network increases in the multifamily group, with other families offering diversity of "age, sex, personality, ethnicity, and class, yet they share a vital common experience and concern: mental illness in one member of the family" (McFarlane, 2002).

Table 7.1 offers an overview of the stages of treatment in PMFG. Following the table is a description of each phase of treatment.

Joining Phase

"Joining" is the method clinicians use to partner and engage with clients and their families. Developed as part of FPE and first introduced by Anderson, Reiss, and Hogarty (1986), joining means collecting and sharing information while supporting the client and family. Although joining is considered the first step in treatment, joining continues throughout the course of the intervention. The therapeutic alliance between the clinician and the family is a critical component of PMFG, as the trust formed helps families feel safe in coming to the larger workshop and ongoing groups.

Joining sessions with family members and the client may happen separately in the first few sessions, and then jointly at the third session. Joining may begin during an acute crisis or hospitalization, where the clinician's empathy and guidance toward ongoing care are critical for the family. The clinician will offer the family support while introducing the group as a hopeful intervention.

Initially, families are seen separately from the individual, so that they can share their perspective with the clinician without concern for their loved one's vulnerability. Families typically value an opportunity to disclose their own emotional experience and to express their concerns and grief. Both client and family are asked to describe their own reactions to the onset of symptoms and the impact it has had on each of their lives. Early warning signs, specific stressors, supports and functional status are assessed by the clinician through the input from

Table 7.1 *Stages of PMFG Intervention—Timeline*

Initial contact	1 week	2 weeks	3 weeks	4 weeks	6 weeks	8 weeks	Every other week . . . 1–2 years
Client & family outreach	Joining session 1	Joining session 2	Joining session 3	Family education workshop	1st PMFG	2nd PMFG	PMFG problem solving

97

all members of the family. The clinician determines family strengths, challenges, and strategies already in place for coping with illness.

The clinician will also share information about the illness and about the stepwise education that PMFG offers over time, which can diminish stigma, reduce blame, and emphasize recovery and hope. By providing some initial psychoeducation about the biology of the illness, clinicians reduce confusion experienced by families. The focus on brain function as primary and causative can minimize criticism and labeling of symptoms as laziness, stupidity, or willful behavior. The clinician stresses that, as with any newly diagnosed illness or condition, recovery can take time.

Family Education Workshop

Following the initial contacts with the client and family, the clinician invites the family to a multi-family psychoeducation workshop. Each co-facilitator, or clinician, has joined with half of the families entering the group. The workshop is set up in a classroom format, and the clinicians, or group co-facilitators, act as hosts, welcoming new families and introducing them to other families for the first time. Food, snacks, and breaks are provided.

The workshop includes information about the brain and psychobiology, medication, and the role of the family in supporting recovery. Psychotic disorders and other mental illnesses are presented as treatable medical conditions. The workshop also includes information about the research data supporting PMFG as a successful treatment intervention. A family who has participated in a PMFG shares their experience and provides hope to clients and families as they begin the process of recovery.

A doctor or nurse practitioner on the clinical team presents the psychobiology information, including areas of the brain impacted in psychosis. "The key concept is that the midbrain is impaired in its ability to adjust the activation of the brain and nervous system in ways that are normal or appropriate to the situation at hand" (McFarlane, 2002). Every person needs a certain amount of activation in order to pay attention. In psychosis, the brain is much more sensitive to inputs, and a person can become easily overloaded. Families are given an illustration of the breakdown in the filtering system in the brain and the role of medications in rebuilding those filters. It follows that families can also help recovery by creating a low-stimulation environment.

Families are asked to provide a supportive and structured environment so that recovery may occur. As families begin to understand that vulnerability to a psychotic disorder is biologically based, like diabetes, there can be a paradigm shift away from blame and despair to strategies for recovery. Families are taught interventions designed to address the functional deficits experienced by their loved ones. For instance, when people are having difficulty filtering and processing information, it is important to limit the amount of information shared to only that which is necessary to understand and respond to a particular situation.

Family Guidelines

Guidelines for recovery are offered to families by the clinicians. These guidelines help families create a protective environment through strategies designed to accommodate difficulties in information processing. Most significantly, families are told they have the power to affect the outcome.

The family guidelines listed below, according to Anderson et al. (1986) and McFarlane (2002), seem basic, but are more complex than they first appear. The guidelines are based in neuropsychology. The descriptions below each guideline offer more detail and direction to families and are written as clinicians would explain them in a workshop setting.

1. Go slow.

Things will get better in their own time. Healing takes time. Just as a runner with an injury needs to allow muscles to heal before returning to regular exercise, the brain needs time before it is challenged. The recovery process cannot be rushed without risking relapse. Pace yourself. Slow down. Successful management of stress will minimize the exacerbation of symptoms. As recovery occurs, it becomes easier to tolerate and manage stress.

2. Keep it cool.

Family members are asked to lower expressed emotion and compensate for an individual's difficulty in regulating arousal and activation. While enthusiasm is normal and natural, tone it down. "Keep it cool" also means decreasing stress and protecting against sensory overload (like Christmas shopping at the mall) or confrontational conversation (like loud arguments about chores). The brain in this vulnerable young person is having difficulty filtering and sorting through sensory input and information as well as with emotional regulation. Strive for neutral. Both enthusiasm and disagreement are normal in families. Try to experience both with less expressed emotion.

3. Give each other space.

It may be protective to allow the person experiencing symptoms to withdraw or retreat. He may need to keep the door closed while in his room or eat separately from the rest of the family in order to avoid overstimulation. Families can continue to invite their family member to participate when ready. Taking time out is a possible strategy for everyone in the family. Everybody experiences those times when they need to take a deep breath, get some fresh air, and clear their heads. Giving space may allow for emotional regulation. Try not to nag and accept refusals.

4. Keep it simple.

Remember that a vulnerable brain with difficulty processing information and sensory input needs information to be kept simple. Cognitive and coping capacities can be overwhelmed by complex environments and the stress of life events. Keep conversations brief, simple, and focused on the routine and mundane. Avoid excessive details and abstract theories. Also avoid topics such as religion, politics, philosophy or any subject in a family where there could be a highly charged, emotional response.

Break tasks down to their most simple steps. Allow the young person time to process information and incoming stimulation before expecting a response. Processing delays may lead to delays in response time. Don't speak for the client; avoid the appearance of mind reading. Be clear, calm and positive.

99

5. Ignore what you can't change.

It is hard to let some things slide, but there are things that should be ignored. Sometimes behavior is driven by delusional or disordered thinking; you cannot argue with delusions. It's better to try to change the subject or to focus on less stressful subjects. Never ignore violence or concerns about self-harm or suicide.

6. Follow doctor's orders.

Medications may help reduce vulnerability to stress and protect the brain. Keeping a log of medications and responses is helpful. There is a risk/benefit ratio with each medication and there can be negative side effects. Work with the clinical team to manage side effects, which could mean stopping one medication and trying another. Sometimes it takes a while to find the right medication, the right amount of medication or the right combination of medications.

Avoid street drugs and alcohol as well as nicotine and caffeine. All of these substances affect mood, emotion, and attention. Remember that emotional regulation is an issue at this time. Do not take any medication that is not prescribed for you. Just like antibiotics, do not stop taking your medication just because you feel better.

7. Set limits.

Every family has simple rules and expectations. As long as the limits are reasonable, family members should not be afraid to set them. A few good rules keep things clear and provide a less stressful and more predictable environment. Set limits clearly and without detailed discussion. This is especially true if the limit is related to safety, which is not a negotiation. Expect limits to be tested but do not overreact. Anger undermines the low stress, low expressed emotion environment. When in doubt about whether to set a limit, ask the clinical team.

8. Carry on business as usual.

Family members in a caregiver role must take care of themselves first. Try to create a normal routine and family environment. Stay in touch with family and friends. Social contacts can provide support and recreation. These same contacts may be the people you turn to in times of crisis, and it is important to maintain your connection with them. Establish and maintain regular schedules around sleep, eating and exercise.

9. No street drugs or alcohol.

Symptoms may worsen with the use of alcohol and/or street drugs. Many people think marijuana is a "harmless" drug. Researchers have found that use of marijuana may actually precipitate a psychotic episode in people with a particular vulnerability. Avoid nicotine and caffeine, as these are stimulants. As mentioned earlier, these substances affect mood, emotion and attention.

10. Pick up on early signs.

Consult your clinician and learn to identify the early warning signs and/or symptoms. The early warning signs specific to a particular person tend to reemerge when stressors occur. If symptoms reappear, contemplate what might be stressful and try to modify, slow down, and simplify the environment. For example, a family reunion might be more stimulating than the client can tolerate, but he might be able to attend a planned dinner.

11. Solve problems step-by-step.

No one can change everything at once. Consider the advantages and disadvantages when deciding on a solution to a problem. Maybe a student is having trouble getting up for his morning class. Instead of dropping the class, is it possible to take the class at another time during the day? Explore which strategies might work. Bring problems to PMFG so that the group can offer suggestions and help break it down into manageable steps.

12. Lower expectations temporarily.

With illness, the body requires rest, limited activity, and adequate sleep. A runner who breaks a leg does not immediately return to running marathons. He initially stays off the leg, then begins slow rehabilitation, then reconditions with limited walking and ultimately running again. Encourage everyone in recovery to use a personal yardstick, which means comparing progress from this month to last month instead of measuring oneself by other people's standards. While experiencing symptoms, a person may have more difficulty academically and be unable to cognitively match his former level of functioning. As cognitive processes improve, academic achievement will return.

PMFG Groups 1 and 2

Within the few weeks following the psychoeducational workshop, families meet for their first PMFG. The clinicians again act as hosts welcoming families. The group is set up in a horseshoe around a chalkboard. The structure of the group and the family guidelines are posted on the wall so that the co-facilitators may refer to them.

The first two groups are different from the ongoing format, but are still guided by the group facilitators. The first group is dedicated to getting to know one another. The goal is to begin the process of socialization and establishing connections with one another as unique people. These connections, based on interests and commonalities, are the basis for the socializing that occurs at the beginning and end of every group going forward.

In the first group, families are asked to introduce themselves and are encouraged to share information that is unrelated to symptoms or illness. One of the group facilitators begins the "check in" by modeling sharing information about him- or herself. Examples of information shared might include where you live, where you grew up, hobbies, your favorite movies and/or music, a dream vacation, or the name of your pet. Confidentiality and other group guidelines are reviewed.

In the second group, families are asked to share how illness and symptoms have affected them individually and as a member of the family. This may be the first time members of the family hear what the client has been experiencing in more detail. Facilitators expect families to talk about the pain and suffering, the lack of clarity about the future, and unsuccessful strategies tried thus far.

Prior to this meeting, the clinician has joined with families for three sessions in single-family format and given the family ample opportunity to say some things that they may not repeat in this group, with their family member present. People are asked to speak for themselves and express their own feelings, with sensitivity toward other family members. Group 2 is the only time that the group goes back into the history of what brings them to PMFG. The group going forward will focus on the present and next stages of recovery.

The role of the clinician in PMFGs is different from in traditional psychotherapy groups, in that clinicians are encouraged to share some information about themselves and experiences they've had with psychotic disorders, either professionally or personally, when they are asking families to do the same. This group, although emotionally challenging, should end with a message of hope. There is an agreement that families are all looking for the same result, a positive outcome for their loved one.

PMFG Format Ongoing (1–2 Years)

The PMFG is a structured process that begins and ends with socialization. The group is 90 minutes long and meets twice per month.

Co-facilitators role model appropriate social behavior and help families continue to get to know each other during the initial 15 minutes of socialization and snacks. As the more formal part of group starts, each member is asked to share some things that have gone well over the last two weeks and some things that could be better. One of the clinicians leads the "check in" at the board, while the other sits in the group circle. Each family member is asked to speak only for him- or herself. Clinicians may need to probe for more information, while paying attention to symptom exacerbation or situational stressors. Clinicians share biological information or refer to the guidelines when relevant.

Once the "check in" has been completed, the group facilitators will choose a problem or issue from the "what could be better" list, based on immediacy, risk for relapse, or next steps in recovery. The client or family member is asked permission to focus on his or her problem, being offered the option to decline. The facilitators keep track of ensuring that there is a rotation and balance among family problem solving. The formal, structured process enhances client and family emotional regulation. The clients and families know what to expect.

The issue is then presented in the form of a question stated in behavioral terms (e.g., "What can X do in the next two weeks to prepare for going back to school?"). Group members are then asked for possible solutions or suggestions. Any and all possible solutions are considered, no matter how unlikely they may sound. Group facilitators can add solutions, but should elicit the majority from the group. Group members are then asked to present the advantages and disadvantages of each suggestion, a collective exercise in seeing both sides of each option. The value of this process is that everyone gets to share his or her opinion; it broadens the scope of options and offers a new perspective on certain solutions.

The person who is the focus of the problem solving is encouraged to select a few of the proposed solutions within the parameter of what he is willing to try. The facilitators assist the person in developing a more specific plan to carry out the chosen solutions. The action plan should detail specific steps that can be taken before the group meets again in two weeks. For example, one of the suggestions is that the person will enroll in driver's education. The action plan might look like this: Tomorrow, X will check the Yellow Pages or the Internet for schools within a 5-mile radius. X will select three different schools of instruction. X will find out if the class meets the State's defined curriculum.

The plan is reviewed at the next meeting of the group. If successful, the client and clinician can build on this success by discussing the positive attributes. If the plan was unsuccessful, the clinician should engage with the client and family to assist with defining a different plan. The group ends with a few more minutes of socialization. This process of socialization, check-in, problem solving, action plan, and socialization is the format of every group.

Family guidelines have been developed as touchstones for families. The guidelines are a way for families to develop strategies and modify behavior and environment. The goal is to create a supportive environment with the best balance of stimulation and expectations. Group facilitators should reference the guidelines as they come up in the problem-solving process. As families become more familiar with the guidelines, they will recognize that they are using them to develop their suggestions. For example, if the parent talks about "just needing some time out of the house and away from the chaos," facilitators, or even other group members, can point out the use of the family guideline of "give each other space." The stress and strain of living with a family member with a potentially severe illness can be disabling. It is important to emphasize the need for family members to engage in good self-care. It is almost impossible for a family member to take care of a loved one when the member is not taking care of him- or herself. One method of self-care is to be involved in PMFG and treatment; to be educated about the actual and possible manifestation of the disorder; and to recognize one's potential to affect the outcome.

SOCIAL SUPPORT NETWORK

Over time, the multifamily group begins to act as a social support system, where people share experiences both positive and negative. For example, a young man had experienced a marked increase in anxiety when his parents were away overnight for the first time in years. One of the group members passed around a sheet of paper, and other members shared their phone numbers so that he might call one of them in the future. Using the crisis line is always an option, but this suggestion offered additional supports. Social supports within the group develop over time and are invaluable to the group members.

Case Example

Alex is a 22-year-old man with no previous psychiatric history. While visiting a group of friends in California, he became disorganized, paranoid, and grandiose. He is a college graduate who had been working in an entry-level position for an agency providing temporary staffing. He had planned to look for a career in media arts, his college major. This last temporary position had involved working overnights and lots of overtime hours. He left that agency, with a plan to vacation with friends in California.

During his stay in California, he reported special powers and abilities to communicate without speaking. He was talking about plans to take over as CEO at Facebook. He began posting a lot of his ideas on the Internet, but they were disorganized and hard to follow. He asked people to sign agreements with him, because he kept accusing his friends of stealing his ideas. He was not eating well and had gone several days without sleep. His friends became alarmed and called his family, who arranged for him to fly home.

At the airport, he was intrusive with other passengers and loudly proclaimed that God had blessed him with an important mission. He was escorted off the plane and taken to a local hospital, evaluated and assessed, and admitted to a psychiatric inpatient unit. He was there for a brief time and was treated with medications. He flew back home, where he was admitted to a program that offered PMFG. His initial symptoms were grandiosity, suspiciousness, disorganized communication with racing thoughts, and mood instability with euphoria.

Alex and his parents came in for the initial joining sessions. Alex was described as active, athletic, insightful, and educated. His family was very supportive, but shocked at the events that led to his psychotic episode. He wanted to continue with his plans to move to California, but his clinician talked with him and his parents about the family guidelines, especially going slow. He was treated with a combination of individual and family counseling, medications, and PMFG. Alex and his family were provided with extensive information about early symptoms of psychosis at the workshop and in the joining sessions. They were conscientious about keeping appointments and attending PMFG.

As symptoms remitted, Alex worked with the education/employment specialist. He started out doing volunteer work and, after six months of treatment, had a part-time paid job and was living in an apartment with a friend as a roommate. Throughout the course of treatment, he described his mood as stable, though sometimes on the low side. After seven months of treatment with medication, Alex requested a trial of no medications. This trial occurred over a period of about two months.

His parents were extremely worried about Alex stopping his medications. They brought their concern to PMFG and agreed to a problem solving.

Problem question: What can Alex's parents do to support Alex as he titrates off his medication? Possible solutions generated by the group:

1. Make a list of early warning symptoms and check in with Alex every few days.
2. Ask Alex if he would share his plan with his roommate in order to help him monitor his mood and behavior.
3. Create a safety plan in case symptoms return.
4. Meet with Alex's clinician together with Alex.
5. Ask Alex not to stop his medication.
6. Ask Alex to stay at your home as he goes off his medications.
7. Suggest that Alex keep a journal to help monitor mood and behavior.

The advantages and disadvantages were discussed by the whole group. After brainstorming, the family (including Alex) agreed to a joint meeting with Alex's clinician to review early warning symptoms and a plan in case of recurrence. His parents chose to ask Alex to share this plan with his roommate and to suggest that Alex keep a journal to help monitor his mood and behavior. During this transition, insomnia occurred, but Alex reported it and took medication as needed.

After a year of treatment, Alex was discharged from the program. His plan was to travel by car and train to California. He planned to do this slowly, with stops along the way to ensure adequate rest and to visit with friends and family. At this time, approximately 15 months after his first episode, he continues to be symptom-free, except for occasional insomnia. As sleep disturbance was one of his earliest symptoms, he responds quickly and uses medication and relaxation techniques. He is living close to his sister and currently looking for a job that will allow him to use his skills as a media artist, possibly in the music industry.

EARLY INTERVENTION IN MENTAL ILLNESS: FUTURE DIRECTIONS IN FAMILY INTERVENTION

Until the last decade, we did not think it was possible to identify warning signs of major mental illness early enough to make a difference in its course and possibly prevent its onset. Based on the premise that, "if you can catch cancer at the earliest stage, you can save a life," researchers have begun to look at identifying young people at risk for developing a psychotic illness to prevent an episode from progressing to full-blown psychosis. Since we know that the duration of untreated psychosis and the number of psychotic episodes delays or restricts remission, researchers hypothesize that the earlier the intervention begins, the better the long-term clinical outcomes.

Worldwide, public information campaigns and community outreach efforts have demonstrated effectiveness in identifying youth at risk for psychosis through educating the community at large, parents, and school, medical, and mental health professionals about early warning symptoms. Early data results from four clinical trials indicate that the onset of psychosis occurred at less than half of the expected rate with interventions of family psychoeducation, assertive community treatment, and medication (McFarlane et al., 2010).

A few larger-scale studies in the United States are currently researching the impact of identification and interventions in the prodromal, or early warning phase, of psychosis: North American Prodromal Longitudinal Study (NAPLS) and Early Detection and Intervention for the Prevention of Psychosis Program (EDIPPP). The EDIPPP study is a multisite study that incorporates PMFG groups for family members of young people in the early stages of psychosis. The research study is testing whether the PMFG model (as evidence-based for chronic mental illness) is as effective in early intervention.

IMPLICATIONS FOR POLICY AND PRACTICE

In the United States, 10% of people with severe mental illness have access to psychosocial rehabilitation programs, including FPE (Hogarty, 2003). Despite the evidence basis for family psychoeducation, family treatments are often difficult to access, unavailable, or not reimbursable.

> The omission of family-based treatment- in particular in the early course of illness of psychotic spectrum illnesses—may unintentionally increase the family's burden and its sense of stigmatization, making it more difficult to implement family interventions later in the course of treatment.
>
> (Brent & Guiliano, 2007)

105

Providers have a strong impact on a consumer's decision to involve family members in treatment. In a nationwide survey of NAMI members, it was found that consumers' attitude toward family involvement was most associated with providers' encouragement of family involvement. Family members' satisfaction with services was correlated with information received from providers (Marshall & Solomon, 2000). Family members do not always believe that they have the knowledge or power to change the outcome for their loved one. The effectiveness of family-based treatments demonstrates how critical the partnership between families, clients, and providers is to successful recovery.

DISCUSSION QUESTIONS

1. The authors note that, historically, mental illness was blamed on bad mothering. Why is this point of view so destructive for families? How does family psychoeducation conceptualize the family's role in treating mental illness?

2. Discuss and define expressed emotion (EE). How is it manifested in the family environment?

3. What are the benefits of family psychoeduation in treating serious mental illness?

LEARNING ASSIGNMENT

Research your community and develop a resource list of family psychoeducation services.

SUGGESTED READINGS

Anderson, C.M., Reiss, D.J., & Hogarty, G.E. (1986). *Schizophrenia and the Family*. New York: Guilford Press.

McFarlane, W.R. (2002). *Multifamily Groups in the Treatment of Severe Psychiatric Disorders*. New York: Guilford Press.

INTERNET RESOURCES

The Substance Abuse & Mental Health Services Administration (SAMHSA): www.samhsa.gov

National Institute of Mental Health: www.nimh.nih.gov

National Alliance on Mental Illness: www.nami.org

Prevent Mental Illness: www.preventmentalillness.org

Early Detection and Intervention for the Prevention of Psychosis Program (EDIPPP): www.changemymind.org

REFERENCES

Anderson, C.M., Reiss, D.J., & Hogarty, G.E. (1986). *Schizophrenia and the Family*. New York: Guilford Press.

Awad, A.G. & Voruganti, L.N.P. (2008). The burden of schizophrenia on caregivers. *Pharmacoeconomics, 26*(2), 149–162.

Bertrando, P. (2006). The evolution of family interventions for schizophrenia. A tribute to Gianfranco Cecchin. *Journal of Family Therapy, 28*, 4–22.

Brent, B.K. & Guiliano, A.J. (2007). Psychotic-spectrum illness and family-based treatments: a case-based illustration of the underuse of family interventions. *Harvard Review of Psychiatry, 15*(4), 161–168.

Brown, G.W., Birley, J.L.T., & Wing, J.K. (1972). Influence of family life on the course of schizophrenic disorders: a replication. *British Journal of Psychiatry, 121*, 241–258.

Butzlaff, A.M. & Hooley, D.P. (1998). Expressed emotion and psychiatric relapse: a meta-analysis. *Archives of General Psychiatry, 55*, 547–552.

Compton, M. (2010). The family's role in psychosis care. Retrieved March 24, 2010 from www.medscape.com

Dixon, L., Lyles, A., Scott, J., et al. (1999). Services to families of adults with schizophrenia: from treatment recommendations to dissemination. *Psychiatric Services, 50*(2), 233–238.

Falloon, I.R.H. (2003). Family interventions for mental disorders: efficacy and effectiveness. *World Psychiatry, 2*(1), 20–28.

Hazel, N.A., McDonell, M.G., Short, R.A., Berry, C.M., Voss, W.D., Rodgers, M.L., & Dyck, D.G. (2004). Impact of multifamily groups for outpatients with schizophrenia on caregivers' distress and resources. *Psychiatric Services, 55*(1), 35–41.

Hogarty, G.E. (2003). Does family psychoeducation have a future? *World Psychiatry, 2*(1), 29–30.

Lieberman, J.A., Drake, R.E., Sederer, L.I., Belger, A., Keefe, R., Perkins, D., & Stroup, S. (2008). Science and recovery in schizophrenia. *Psychiatric Services, 59*(5), 487–496.

Magliano, L., Fiorillo, A., Malangone, C., Marasco, C. Guarneri, M., & Maj, M. (2003). The effect of social network on burden and pessimism in relatives of patients with schizophrenia. *American Journal of Orthopsychiatry, 73*(3), 302–309.

Marsh, D.T. & Johnson, D.L. (1997). The family experience of mental illness: Implications for intervention. *Professional Psychology: Research and Practice. 28*, 229–237.

Marshall, T.B. & Solomon, P. (2000). Releasing information to families of persons with severe mental illness: A survey of NAMI members. *Psychiatric Services, 51*, 1006–1011.

McFarlane, W.R. (2002). *Multifamily Groups in the Treatment of Severe Psychiatric Disorders*. New York: Guilford Press.

McFarlane, W.R. (2011). Integrating the family in the treatment of psychotic disorders. *CBT for Psychosis*, 193–209.

McFarlane, W.R. & Cook, W.L. (2007). Family expressed emotion prior to onset of psychosis. *Family Process, 46*(2).

McFarlane, W.R., Cook, W.L., Downing, D., Verdi, M.B., Woodberry, K.A., & Ruff, A. (2010). Portland identification and early referral: A community-based system for identifying and treating youths at high risk of psychosis. *Psychiatric Services, 61*(5), 1–4.

McFarlane, W.R., Dixon, L., Lukens, E., & Lucksted, A. (2002). Severe mental illness. In D.H.Sprenkle (Ed.), *Effectiveness Research in Marriage and Family Therapy* (pp. 255–288). Alexandria: The American Association for Marriage and Family Therapy.

McFarlane, W.R., et al. (2003). Family psychoeducation and schizophrenia: A review of the literature. *Journal of Marital & Family Therapy, 29*, 223–245.

107

Miklowitz, D.J. (2007). The role of the family in the course and treatment of Bipolar Disorder. *Current Directions in Psychological Science, 16*(4), 192–196.

Murray-Swank, A.B. & Dixon, L. (2004). Family psychoeducation as an evidence-based practice. *CNS Spectrums, 9*(12), 905–912.

Neill, J. (1990). Whatever became of the schizophrenogenic mother? *American Journal of Psychotherap, 44*(4), 499–505.

Pitschel-Walsz, G., Leucht, S., Bäuml, J., Kissling, W., & Engel, R.R. (2001). The effect of family interventions on relapse and rehospitalization in schizophrenia—a meta-analysis. *Schizophrenia Bulletin, 27*(1): 73–92.

Tienari, P.A., Wynne, L.C., Sorri, A., Lahti, I., et al. (2004). Genotype-environment interaction in schizophrenia-spectrum disorder. *British Journal of Psychiatry, 184*, 216–222.

Wong, C., Davidson, L., McGlashan, T., Gerson, R., Malaspina, D., & Corcoran, C. (2008). Comparable family burden in families of clinical high-risk and recent-onset psychosis patients. *Early Intervention in Psychiatry, 2*(4), 256–261.

Chapter 8

Meeting the Mental Health Challenges of the Elder Boom

Michael B. Friedman, Kimberly A. Williams, Emily Kidder, and Lisa Furst

America is aging. The baby boom generation has become the elder boom generation, and the number of older adults in the United States will more than double between 2010 and 2050 and increase from 13% of the population to 20% (Grayson & Velkoff, 2010). This has fueled great concern about the viability of the social security system, about the sustainability of Medicare, and about the availability of a workforce to provide health and social services to people of all ages.

There is also widespread concern about the physical health of older adults and about Alzheimer's Disease. But, for the most part, other mental health needs are overlooked. This is unfortunate for five basic reasons.

First, contrary to the underlying agist assumptions of our culture, people can live well in old age, but one cannot live well without mental health. Mental health promotion and the prevention of mental illness, therefore, are critical to successful aging.

Second, mental illness has a terrible impact on physical health. People with mental disorders are more likely to have physical disorders, and people with co-occurring physical and mental and/or substance use disorders are at higher risk for disability and premature death and have far higher medical costs than those with physical disorders alone (Husaini et al., 2000; Katon & Ciechanowski, 2002; Kilbourne et al., 2005).

Third, mental health needs are prevalent in older adults, as approximately 20% of older adults have diagnosable mental and/or substance use disorders, including dementia (U.S. Department of Health and Human Services, 1999). This increases to over 50% of older adults by age 85 (Byers, Yaffe, Covinsky, Friedman, & Bruce, 2010). Over time, the most common mental disorder is dementia—the prevalence of which doubles every five years, beginning at age 60 (Cummings, & Jeste, 1999; U.S. Department of Health and Human Services, 1999). However, the range of behavioral health problems also includes:

- anxiety and mood disorders, which often co-occur with dementia in its early and middle stages;
- psychotic conditions such as schizophrenia and severe mood disorders;
- substance use disorders.

Some of these mental and substance use disorders begin early in life; some become more severe later in life, and others emerge in old age.

Fourth, untreated mental and/or substance use disorders contribute to avoidable placements in institutions, such as nursing homes, probably driving up the costs of long-term care (Friedman, 2009).

Fifth, all older adults face emotional, developmental challenges, including social and occupational role changes, diminished—but not lost—physical and mental abilities, losses of family and friends, and the inevitability of death. Untreated mental and/or substance use disorders also contribute to social isolation and high suicide rates among older adults (Centers for Disease Control and Prevention. National Center for Injury Prevention and Control, 2007).

In order to achieve the major goal of community mental health, which is to help people with psychiatric disorders avoid institutionalization and live where they prefer in the community, a number of key changes are needed in the systems of care for older adults. These include:

1. support for family caregivers, who provide 80% of the care (Spillman & Pezzin, 2000) for adults with disabilities;
2. housing alternatives to institutions for those who cannot remain at home without extensive support;
3. home-based services for those who are able to live in the community but are physically or psychologically homebound;
4. improved access to mental health and substance abuse services in community settings;
5. improved quality of services in community-based and institutional settings;
6. increased integration of physical and mental health care;
7. increased collaboration with the aging services system;
8. enhanced outreach and mental health education in the community;
9. a larger and more clinically and culturally competent workforce;
10. increased and restructured mental health financing, and more.

This chapter focuses on the behavioral health challenges of old age. The first section provides a brief overview of the critical demographic shifts and discusses the major mental and substance use disorders of old age and useful interventions. The second seciton addresses the failure of mental health policy in the United States to anticipate the elder boom and identifies key policy changes needed to meet its mental health challenges.

MENTAL AND SUBSTANCE USE DISORDERS IN OLD AGE

The March of Demography

Over the first half of the 21st century, the number of adults 65 and older in the United States will more than double, from 35 million in 2000 to 88.5 million in 2050. The greatest growth will take place between 2010 and 2030, when the population of older adults will increase from 40 million to 72 million (Grayson & Velkoff, 2010).

More important than the growth in numbers is the growth of older adults as a proportion of the population, from 13% to 20% (Grayson & Velkoff, 2010). Because the working age population will decline by 5% as a proportion of the population (Grayson & Velkoff, 2010), there are great concerns about the viability of social security pensions and Medicare. There are also concerns about whether there will be enough workers in the helping professions to provide the care that disabled older adults will need.

In addition, during the first half of the 21st century, there will be a vast increase in both the number and proportion of minorities. The Census Bureau projects that, by 2042, minorities will outnumber whites in the United States. For older adults, the Census Bureau projects that the minority proportion of the older population will grow from about 15% in 2000, to 20% in 2010, to nearly 30% in 2030, and 42% in 2050 (Grayson & Velkoff, 2010). Although the Asian population will grow at the fastest pace, Latinos will be by far the largest portion of the minority population.

This demographic change makes issues of "cultural competence" increasingly important. Can the systems of care for older adults in the United States, which currently are not adequately responsive to the needs of minorities, develop the capacity to meet the needs of an ever-larger population?

Psychiatric and Substance Use Disorders Among Older Adults

Approximately 20% of older adults have one or more diagnosable mental and/or substance use disorders in any given year (U.S. Department of Health and Human Services, 1999). This does not include people with minor depressions, emotional distress that does not meet the criteria for a diagnosis as a mental illness, or substance *misuse* that does not meet the criteria for *abuse*. For example, 17% of the population of older adults drink excessively (U.S. Department of Health and Human Services, 2009), but fewer than 2% have a diagnosable alcohol or drug use disorder (U.S. Department of Health and Human Services, 2009).

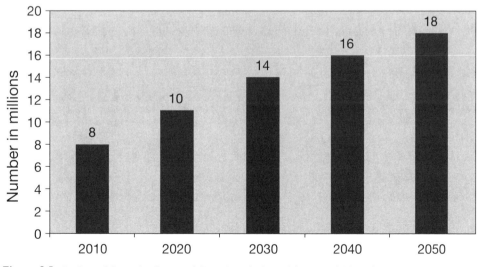

Figure 8.1 *Projected Growth of 65 and Over Population with Mental Disorders: 2010–2050*

Assuming that the prevalence of mental and substance use disorders among older adults remains constant, the number of older adults with diagnosable mental illnesses in the United States will more than double, from 7 million in 2000 to 14 million in 2030, to 18 million in 2050 (Grayson & Velkoff, 2010; Kessler & Wang, 2008).

Given the shortage of geriatric mental health services now, it is doubtful that so much growth can be handled without higher than proportional growth of mental health professionals, as well as restructuring of provider roles so as to get the most possible from paraprofessionals and volunteers.

A Heterogeneous Population

Older adults with mental disorders are a heterogeneous population, and most of them live, and want to remain, in the community. They include:

- people with long-term psychiatric disabilities who are aging;
- people with psychotic conditions that develop in late life;
- people with dementia, most commonly Alzheimer's Disease;
- people with mild to severe mood and/or anxiety disorders;
- people with substance use problems, primarily alcohol and prescription drug misuse, but also some abuse of illegal substances and some people with lifelong addictions;
- people whose behavior is challenging to their caregivers;
- people with emotional problems adjusting to old age.

Although the overall prevalence of mental disorders is roughly the same among older and younger populations, the mix of disorders varies significantly. Perhaps most surprising is the decline in major mood disorders as people age.

Lifelong and Late-Life Disorders

It is common and often useful to distinguish older adults with lifelong mental and/or substance use disorders from those with late-life disorders. However, with the exception of dementia,

Table 8.1 Prevalence of Mental Disorders Among Younger and Older Adults (U.S. Department of Health and Human Services, 1999)

Type of disorder	Ages 18–54	Ages 55+
Any disorder	21%	19.8%
Any anxiety disorder	16.4%	11.4%
Any major mood disorder	7.1%	4.4%
Schizophrenia	1.3%	0.6%
Severe cognitive impairment (mostly dementia)	1.2%	6.6%
Anti-social personality	2.1%	—

most people with mental illness in old age have had mental illness earlier in life as well (Kessler et al., 2005). Often, it has not been severe enough to be a major problem. Typically, something happens in later life that exacerbates the disorder, such as death of a spouse, job loss, or serious physical illness or injury. Therefore, it is often more useful to distinguish among people with long-term psychiatric disabilities, people with long-term mental disorders exacerbated in old age, and people with late-life disorders.

People With Long-Term Psychiatric Disabilities who Are Aging

Mr. C., who just turned 75, has suffered from severe mental illness since his early 20s. He lived in a state hospital for many years, moved to a single room occupancy hotel (SRO) during deinstitutionalization, became homeless when SROs were converted to luxury housing, but eventually was housed in an apartment where case managers check in as needed. In the beginning, his parents provided extra supports and advocated on his behalf, but they died ten years ago, and his siblings do not live nearby. As he has aged, he has become increasingly obese. Now he has diabetes and arthritis and the beginnings of dementia. His case manager has been unable to arrange good medical care or to find appropriate housing in the community. He has begun to consider referring him to a nursing home. Mr. C.'s fate will become increasingly common as more people with serious and persistent mental illness become elderly.

The population of older adults with serious long-term psychiatric disabilities is a very small portion of the general population—about 1% (McAlpine, 2003). But these are the people who have been the traditional, primary responsibility of the public mental health system. They include people with schizophrenia and people with severe mood disorders, such as bipolar disorder, that are "treatment refractory," i.e., do not respond to treatment. Many—if not most—of this population have had (or currently have) co-occurring substance use disorders. Most people with severe, persistent mental disorders experience functional limitations (disabilities) related to their illnesses. Over time, a significant number of people with long-term psychiatric disabilities "recover" (Anthony, 1993). Some become asymptomatic, while others may continue to experience symptoms of schizophrenia or a major mood disorder, but become more able to function independently and develop lives that they find satisfying and meaningful. Some "consumers," as they are often called, have become important leaders in the field of mental health.

One of the reasons that the prevalence of serious and persistent mental illness declines with age is that the life expectancy of people with serious mental illness is considerably lower than that of the general population. Reports range from 6 to 32 years (Colton & Manderscheid, 2006; Dembling, Chen, & Vachon, 1999; Piatt, Munetz, & Ritter, 2010). A major reason for lower life expectancy is poor health. People with serious mental illness are at high risk for obesity (related in part to their antipsychotic medications; Tiihonen et al., 2009), hypertension, diabetes, heart disease, pulmonary conditions (many are heavy smokers), and communicable

113

diseases, particularly hepatitis and HIV/AIDS, that are related to histories of drug abuse, of hard and dangerous periods of homelessness, and of being victims of crime. They are also at high risk for suicide and for accidental deaths, especially overdoses of their medications, as well as falls.

The greatest need of people with long-term psychiatric disorders is support to live in the community, especially stable housing, as well as cash and in-kind public assistance. Parents provide housing, financial assistance, and other supports for many younger adults with long-term psychiatric disabilities, but, as the parents age, become disabled, and ultimately die, they can no longer provide for their now aged children. Supplemental needs trusts can help, but usually to a limited extent, and, unless a sibling is willing and able to take over from the parents, older adults with continuing psychiatric disabilities will need supports to remain in their homes or alternative supportive housing arrangements to avoid institutionalization.

A broad range of mental health services organized into a comprehensive system is also necessary for this population. This includes psychiatric rehabilitation (especially employment opportunities, activity, and social interaction); outpatient treatment in clinics and day programs; inpatient treatment (preferably in local general hospitals); specialized crisis services (mobile crisis teams, as well as emergency rooms); outreach programs such "assertive community treatment"; and case management.

A "recovery" orientation is as essential to work with older adults as it is with younger populations. Often, however, recovery goals for older adults should not emphasize employment, because, for many (but not all) older people, employment is no longer a personal goal. Older adults with psychiatric disabilities do, however, have other important goals, such as serving as volunteers, enhanced socialization, improved relationships with their families, enhanced connections with houses of worship, improved management of their physical health conditions, and stable housing in the community that addresses declines in physical and cognitive capacity. The critical point is that older adults with long-term psychiatric disabilities can lead lives that they find satisfying and meaningful, and services should be organized in ways that help them do so.

Antipsychotic medications are useful for most people with long-term serious mental illness, even those in "recovery." However, the side effects of these medications can be particularly dangerous for older adults—especially for those who also develop dementia. Because this population is somewhat more likely to develop depression, antidepressant medications may also be helpful.

Typically, older adults react differently to medications than younger adults. For this reason, doses of psychiatric medications for older adults must be monitored very carefully and adjusted (usually down) as reactions to them change.

As they age, people with psychiatric disabilities are even more likely than other older adults to develop serious, chronic physical conditions for which routine treatment is necessary. Eventually, many develop physical disabilities and/or dementia, which will result in their needing additional care—especially home-based care—to be able to live in community settings. In general, housing designed for adults with long-term psychiatric disabilities does not build in the capacity to deal with serious, chronic physical conditions. As a result, many older adults with psychiatric disabilities end up in long-term health-care programs not designed to meet their mental health needs, including adult medical day centers, assisted living, and nursing homes.

114

Late-Life Psychotic Conditions

Ms. F. had lived with her mother all her life and never had a significant love relationship, but she had had a responsible job and many friends, despite occasional periods of major depression. She became depressed more frequently after she was forced to retire, but continued to have an active social life and took good care of her mother, who was in her 90s and increasingly disabled. When Ms. F. was 70, her mother died. Shortly after that, she became acutely psychotic, experiencing both hallucinations and delusions. After a brief stay in the psychiatric unit of a local general hospital, she recovered and returned home. Over subsequent years, she had similar psychotic breaks from time to time. She had good home health aides, but they were not prepared to deal with her mental condition, and the nephew who took responsibility for her care simply burned out after too many crises in the middle of the night. Ultimately, she could not manage in her home and was placed in a nursing home, where she lived, mostly unhappily, until she died about 5 years later.

People of any age, including older adults, can develop psychotic conditions, i.e., extreme disruptions of mental functioning that usually make people incapable of carrying on life as they ordinarily do. Hallucinations, delusions, loss of a sense of reality, and irrational thinking processes are all characteristic of psychotic episodes.

Psychotic conditions can be (1) transient, a one-time event that never recurs; (2) recurrent, characterized by relatively short periods of psychosis and normal functioning in between; or (3) chronic, shifting between acute phases and phases of poor functioning.

Older people who experience transient or recurrent psychotic episodes need the same sort of treatment that younger people do, including crisis management and outpatient and inpatient services. Transitional services such as partial hospitalization and a stay in a community residence may also be helpful, although it is generally best for people to return to their homes as rapidly as possible and for supports to be provided there. This is easier said than done, because of the shortage of in-home workers with competence regarding mental illness. Often, family members must be caregivers during the process of recovery, creating considerable family burden. Support for these caregivers is often key to avoiding institutionalization.

Older people for whom late-onset psychotic conditions become chronic are virtually indistinguishable from people with long-term psychiatric disabilities and, like them, need integrated physical and behavioral health services. They also can often benefit from the kinds of rehabilitation program that serve those with lifelong conditions. Unfortunately, eligibility rules for these programs often exclude people who have not had a long history in the mental health system. This is one reason why it is not uncommon for older adults who develop long-term psychotic conditions to be treated in the long-term health-care system, often rapidly ending up in nursing homes.

Psychotropic medications are generally used during a psychotic episode and are sometimes continued in the hope of preventing relapse. For older adults, special care must be taken with regard to dosage, especially for those who also have dementia, for whom antipsychotic medications can be lethal.

115

Dementia

Mr. V. began to experience confusion when he was 80, but he was able to hide it from his family and friends. He loved woodwork and made almost daily trips to the hardware store. Once, he forgot where he was going, got lost, and became very frightened. It happened again. He began to make excuses for not going out at all. Over time, he found it impossible to do crossword puzzles and began to display angry frustration. The family doctor diagnosed him as being in the early stages of dementia. In fact, Mr. V. was also depressed, as are approximately 25% of people with dementia. With treatment for the depression, he might have overcome some of his cognitive impairment and recovered a better quality of life.

Dementia, of which Alzheimer's disease is the most common form, is the most feared of all the possible mental disorders of old age, in part because it is increasingly common as people age, in part because it takes such a terrible toll on people's lives, and in part because there is no recovery. There are medications that can slow the process of deterioration, but, so far, that process is inexorable. The greatest hope for the moment is that deterioration can be slowed enough so that older people die of other conditions before they reach the end stage of dementia.

During the early and mid stages of dementia, when normal functioning is possible, though to a decreasing extent, it is not unusual for people to develop depression and/or anxiety disorders. Fortunately, both depression and anxiety are treatable in people suffering from dementia (Draper, 1999; Kraus et al., 2008; Snowden, Sato, & Roy-Byrne, 2003), and, as both depression and anxiety produce cognitive decline, successful treatment will improve the functioning of the person with dementia. It will not cure or stop the decline due to dementia, but it will help people to lead far better lives in the time they have.

Many people with dementia exhibit "behavior problems," such as refusal to follow through on treatment, wandering, verbal abuse toward caregivers, dangerous forgetfulness, and more. (We discuss behavior problems later in the chapter.) In general, non-pharmacological interventions based on a sense of the humanity of the person with dementia can be helpful and are preferable, because of the risks of psychiatric medications for this population. Unfortunately, there is considerable evidence that antipsychotic medications are overused to control behavior (Gill et al., 2007), and this should be monitored carefully wherever people with dementia get care. When psychiatric medications must be used for the treatment of psychotic, mood, or anxiety disorders, medication monitoring to ensure appropriate dosage is critical.

In addition, it is important to understand that the dread of dementia is, in part, in the mind of the beholder. There are those who find people with dementia to be more emotionally open and more willing to take interesting, creative risks (Zeisel, 2009; Zeisel & Raia, 2000). People with this perspective about those with dementia can help them make different, but meaningful, lives for themselves.

Finally, it is important to keep in mind that family members are the primary caregivers of older adults with dementia, and they are at high risk for mood and anxiety disorders, as well as for physical illnesses. They frequently "burn out" because of the stress, and, as a result, a significant number of older adults go to nursing homes who could remain in the community, if their families were given appropriate supports—including individual counseling at convenient times and places, crisis intervention, family counseling, access to caregiver support groups, and respite care. Studies indicate that providing this kind of support for family caregivers can defer placement in nursing homes 18 months or longer (Mittelman, Haley, Clay, & Roth, 2006).

Depression

Mrs. S. was 81 when she stopped playing bridge and going to the theater with her friends. It just wasn't fun anymore. She became more and more withdrawn and did not take much interest in her children or her grandchildren. Her daughter persuaded her to go to a psychiatrist, whom she told that she did not have the energy she used to have, and that she had trouble concentrating. She said that she did not think she was useful to anyone, and that "it's all downhill from here." With antidepressants and cognitive therapy, she soon resumed cards and theater and other pleasurable activities. She was lucky. Many older adults refuse to seek psychiatric help because they are embarrassed, because of their lack of knowledge about mental illness, or because they cannot find good treatment owing to shortages of geriatric mental health professionals, cost, travel, and other obstacles.

It is widely believed that depression is common in old age. In fact, however, a majority of older adults probably never experience depression, and epidemiological studies consistently show a decline of major depressive disorders in old age (Blazer, 2009; Byers et al., 2010).[1] It may or may not be that older adults are more likely to experience sadness, but sadness and major depression are not the same. A diagnosis of major depression requires the presence, for a period of at least two weeks, of one of two cardinal symptoms and a total of five symptoms altogether. The cardinal symptoms are (1) profound sadness with a sense of hopelessness and (2) a lack of interest or pleasure in people or activities that have been a source of interest or pleasure in the past. Although persistently sad mood is the symptom most commonly associated with depression, there can be depression without sadness, in which the predominant symptom experienced is the loss of the capacity to experience interest or pleasure in activities formerly enjoyed (Gallo & Rabins, 1999). Additional symptoms of depression include: disturbances of activity, eating, or sleep; rumination or inability to concentrate; irritability; and others. The most dangerous symptom is recurrent thoughts of death and/or suicide. Older adults are far more likely to complete suicide than younger people.

Fewer than 5% of older adults have a major depressive disorder in any given year (Blazer, 2009). Minor depression is more common, affecting 8–20% of older adults each year (U.S. Department of Health and Human Services, 1999). The likelihood of having major depressive disorder is greater among those with chronic physical conditions, still greater among those needing home health care (Hybels & Blazer, 2003), and greater still among those in institutions such as nursing homes (Blazer, 2009).

Although not as prevalent as widely believed, depression is dangerous. It has a negative impact on physical health, is correlated with premature disability and death, contributes to social isolation (see the end of the section on anxiety), and also contributes to the high rates of suicide among older adults (see next section).

Depression appears to be highly treatable. An extensive evidence base indicates that the use of medications and psychotherapy together is most effective, but that the use of medications or psychotherapy alone can also be effective. Psychotherapies with research support include cognitive therapy, CBT, problem-solving therapy, and interpersonal therapy.

Many people with mild or moderate major depression get treatment from primary care physicians, who—unfortunately—provide minimally adequate care for less than 15% of the people they treat (Wang et al., 2005). However, there are a number of evidence-based approaches to providing effective treatment of depression in older adults in primary care practices, including Improving Mood: Promoting Access to Collaborative Treatment (IMPACT) (Unützer et al., 2002) and Primary Care Research in Substance Abuse and Mental Health for the Elderly (PRISM-E) (Bartels et al., 2004), among others (Oxman, Dietrich, & Schulberg, 2005). All of these approaches provide a care manager to follow up with the patient, to be sure they are adhering to treatment and, in some cases, to provide brief counseling, such as problem-solving therapy, as well.

Of course, for those with severe or psychotic mood disorders, inpatient care, partial hospitalization, crisis intervention, and other services will be necessary.

Non-professional interventions are also helpful for older adults with major depression. Being active and involved with other people can make a big difference. Physical exercise also seems to be helpful. And, for many people, depression is linked to concrete or psychosocial problems, such as lack of adequate income, isolation, and loss of a loved one. Addressing these external "causes" of depression can also be enormously helpful.

Suicide

> Mr. A., who was 86, completed suicide shortly after his wife died and he was diagnosed with cancer. He had seen a doctor days before, but the physician did not notice that he was depressed, let alone recognize that he was at risk for suicide. It is a sadly common story. Older people complete suicide 50% more often than younger people, a rate that rises to nearly 500% higher in white men over the age of 85 (Centers for Disease Control and Prevention. National Center for Injury Prevention and Control, 2007), and most have seen primary care physicians shortly before they commit suicide (Schmutte, O'Connell, Weiland, Lawless, & Davidson, 2009).

Depression contributes to the high rate of suicide among older adults, who complete suicides 50% more than the general population or even teenagers and young adults (Centers for Disease Control and Prevention. National Center for Injury Prevention and Control, 2007). Suicide among older adults is primarily a white-male phenomenon, and it increases with age. White men 85 and older complete suicide nearly five times as often as the general population.

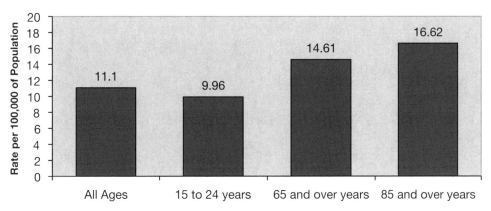

Figure 8.2 *Suicide Rates per 100,000 by Age (2002–2007)*

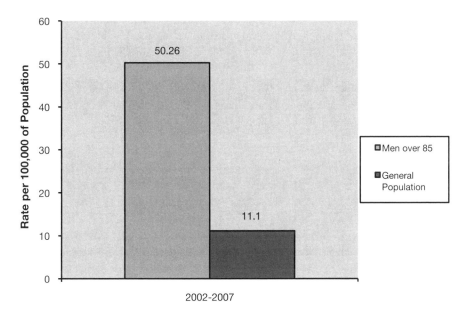

Figure 8.3 *Suicide Rates Among Male 85 and Over Population vs. General Population per 100,000*

Although depression is probably the most common cause of suicide, there are older people who chose to take their own lives who do not meet diagnostic criteria for major depression (Conwell et al., 1999). In fact, Oregon's assisted-suicide law is in part based on this fact (Chin, Hedberg, Higginson, & Fleming, 1999). There, people who want assistance taking their own lives have to be examined by a psychiatrist and found not to be mentally ill and to be able to make rational decisions before the assisted suicide can proceed legally.

In addition to depression, other risk factors for suicide among older adults include comorbid medical conditions, particularly those that cause pain and decline in physical, social, and/or occupational functioning, social dependency or isolation, family discord or losses, inflexible personality or rigid coping styles, and access to firearms. Those who have a history of suicide

119

attempts are at particularly high risk, especially if their suicide attempt has been planned rather than impulsive (Conwell, 2001).

Suicide prevention efforts should include improved identification of risk by primary care physicians and others who come in contact with older adults seeking help for one reason or another. This is not easy, because people with depression are often very skilled at hiding their emotions. The use of effective screening tools for depression—such as the PHQ-2 or -9[2]—is preferable to relying on a physician's perception alone. Providing treatment for those who are depressed can be helpful as a measure to prevent suicide. Additional effective prevention efforts to target high-risk groups include optimizing functioning and minimizing physical pain in primary care and home health, as well as decreasing social isolation and increasing social supports.

Crisis call centers can play an important role in efforts to prevent suicide (De Leo, Buono, & Dwyer, 2002; Gould, Kalafat, Munfakh, & Kleinman, 2007; Mishara et al., 2007). The National Suicide Prevention Lifeline (NSPL) provides a single telephone number that connects to about 150 call centers around the country. It should be well publicized everywhere— 1-800-273-TALK. NSPL has also introduced a number of online tools, using the power of social networks to reach people considering suicide. They probably do not reach many older adults now, but the new generation of older adults will undoubtedly be more computer-savvy than the current generation.

Mass public-education campaigns (Conwell, 2001) and accompanying toolkits, such as the Suicide Prevention Education and Awareness Kit (SPEAK) in New York State, can also be useful in improving awareness and reducing shame about seeking help.

Anxiety

Mrs. P. is 76 years old. She has been a "worry wart" all her life, but since her husband died she has become so anxious that it is difficult for her to manage the basic routines of her life. She can't concentrate or make day-to-day decisions. She feels restless almost all the time. She has trouble sleeping because her mind fills with worries. She goes to her doctor frequently with complaints about headaches and stomach problems. There is no physical explanation for her symptoms, and she spends much of her time with the doctor talking about her many worries. These include her feeling that no one will enjoy her company, that she's just not fun. She doesn't want to burden people with her presence and so has become increasingly socially isolated. Left alone with her thoughts, she becomes even more worried. This form of "generalized anxiety" is not uncommon among older people.

Anxiety disorders are the most prevalent mental illnesses among older (and younger) adults, affecting over 10% of those 65 and older (Byers et al., 2010). There are a number of different types of anxiety disorder, including generalized anxiety, social anxiety, phobias, obsessive–compulsive disorder, and PTSD. Many anxiety disorders are treatable in much the same way

Mrs. C. lived alone in the apartment in which she and her husband had raised their children. She had always been a bit distrustful. The butcher put his thumb on the scale. A teacher had it in for a daughter who wasn't doing well in school. After her husband died, her suspiciousness grew into paranoia. (Many serious mental disorders in old age are exacerbations of an underlying character trait or minor mental illness that are triggered by an adverse event, such as the death of a spouse, or poor health.) Mrs. C. came to distrust even her daughter, accusing her, for example, of stealing her diamond ring, which she had simply misplaced. Her daughter was tolerant to a point, but eventually arranged for help in the home, in part so she didn't have to face her mother's abuse every day. "You say my daughter sent you," the mother yelled through the door. "I know you're from the CIA." She did not open the door. Eventually, Mrs. C. had to go to the hospital for treatment of pneumonia. Her daughter and the social worker agreed that, given her growing physical disabilities and the difficulties she presented at home, she should be in a nursing home. Mrs. C. never went home again, a not uncommon fate for people who cannot accept help in the home.

that depression is treated, including psychotherapy, supportive interventions, and psychotropic medications.

Although anxiety disorders can be relatively mild and cause limited disruption in an older person's life, too often they are major causes of social isolation and unnecessary institutionalization. This is particularly true when anxiety takes the form of paranoia, which can range from suspiciousness to paranoid delusions, such as the belief that a neighbor is a spy. Such paranoid ideation can lead to a rejection of help, increasing the likelihood of institutionalization.

Social Isolation

Severe anxiety and depression, which frequently co-occur, often contribute to social isolation. In research studies and policy reports, living alone is frequently a proxy for social isolation, but that is a mistake. Social isolation does not mean living alone; it means being largely cut off from the outside world. People who are socially isolated have generally lost their relationships with family and friends, do almost nothing that gives them pleasure, and may not leave their homes except for doctors' visits or perhaps to buy groceries. Of course, some people are isolated because of physical problems, but many people are isolated because they are too depressed to rouse themselves or too frightened to leave their home. Frequently, they are caught in a vicious cycle. Contact with people and activity would lift their spirits and calm their fears, but they are too depressed or anxious to do what would help them most. And they become increasingly depressed and/or anxious because of their isolation. Breaking the cycle of isolation is exceedingly difficult. Often, it requires persistent outreach and great patience (Brennan, Vega, Garcia, Abad, & Friedman, 2005), and this is made all the more difficult because outreach services of this kind are usually not funded.

Substance Use Problems

ALCOHOL AND MEDICATION MISUSE AND ABUSE

Mrs. J. is 75 years old. She has lived alone since her husband died. At first, she kept up the relationships she and her husband had had together, but over time she began to feel like a third wheel and stayed alone more and more. She began to drink in the evenings to comfort herself and to help her fall asleep. One night, she fell and broke her hip.

Mr. L. retired with nothing to do and barely enough money to live on. Travel and other retirement activities were not financially possible for him. He began hanging out with his friends at the local bar. Over time, a couple of beers sipped slowly became a pitcher or two. He got drunk often and became a hazard to the highway when he drove home from the bar. His relationship with his wife became more and more troubled.

Mrs. S. had arthritis and was in constant pain. It was intolerable, and she would do anything to make the pain go away. She went to different doctors and got different prescriptions for painkillers. She bought whatever she could over the counter. She became addicted to opioids and damaged her stomach with excessive doses of aspirin, Tylenol, and ibuprofen.

Stories like this are sadly common. In fact, alcohol and prescription drug misuse affects over 15% of older adults. Few substance abuse programs are geared to meet their needs.

LIFELONG ADDICTION

Mr. R. had been a hard-core drug addict most of his life. He had robbed people to support his habit, been in and out of prison several times, and had been on the verge of death more than once from injuries and illnesses that are a typical part of a life on the street. But, somehow, he survived. When he turned 65, he looked back on his life with horror. He saw lost opportunities to have a meaningful life, as well as lost relationships with his parents, siblings, and his own children. He wanted to redeem himself; he wanted to resurrect long-lost relationships. Some people like Mr. R. manage to revive relationships with their family and to begin a different way of life. Some burned their bridges long ago.

Misuse and abuse of alcohol are the major substance use problems among older adults. The misuse or abuse of prescription and over-the-counter medications is also a significant problem. Both are more common than misuse or abuse of illegal substances. According to the study most often used in policy reports, 17% of older adults consume more alcohol than recommended by the U.S. National Institute on Alcohol Abuse and Alcoholism (NIAAA) and/or misuse medications (Blow, 1998). SAMHSA reported that, in 2002, "12.2% of older adults reported binge alcohol use and 3.2% reported heavy alcohol use." This report also noted,

"Among older adults, 1.4 million (1.8%) used an illicit drug during the past month. Marijuana was the most commonly used illicit drug (used by 1.1% older adults)" (Substance Abuse and Mental Health Services Administration [SAMHSA], 2005).

Although illegal drugs have not been used much by the current generation of older adults, it is widely expected that, when the baby boomers (the generation of "drugs, sex, and rock and roll") become the elder boomers, there will be increasing use of illegal substances among the elderly. And, because physical changes in the body as one ages reduce tolerance for alcohol and other substances that are used recreationally, the potential growth of older people who have been recreational drug users is a matter of concern.

Many older adults who misuse or abuse substances are people who under or over-utilize medications. Some people can't afford medication, so they take less of it. Some people can't remember to take their medication and end up under- or overdosing. Some people just don't like to take medications. Some people cannot tolerate incessant pain or other physical suffering and medicate themselves with anything they can get their hands on that seems to help, often creating significant iatrogenic health and mental health problems for themselves.

Among older adults, the onset and course of substance misuse or abuse varies. Some older adults began abusing substances earlier in life and have been using most of their lives. Some early-onset abusers are hard-core substance abusers who survive into old age, curtailing their addictions as they age. This includes people in methadone programs who are aging, and it also includes survivors who find new hope as they age and who want to make restitution and to build new lives for themselves. Few older adults are late-onset substance abusers. Rather, most are intermittent abusers who misused a substance when they were younger and are now returning to that substance in their later years, perhaps to cope with developmental challenges. In addition, there are older adults who were recreational users when they were younger, and the "use" of alcohol and/or drugs becomes misuse/abuse in later life, owing to age-related physical changes.

A number of different types of service are useful for people who misuse or abuse substances. Brief interventions, including counseling and public education (especially regarding reduced tolerance for alcohol, medications, and illegal drugs), particularly in primary care have shown to be effective. An evidence-based approach called "Screening, Brief Intervention, Referral, and Treatment" (S-BIRT) is fundable through Medicaid. It can be used in emergency rooms and primary care practices, as well as in mental health and substance abuse clinics.

Motivational interviewing is an important component of S-BIRT. It is also useful for primary care providers who identify substance use issues and want to help their patients change their behavior or lifestyle.

Other types of useful service include outpatient treatment, outpatient and residential detoxification, outpatient and residential rehabilitation, and mutual aid/self-help groups, such as Alcoholics Anonymous. Integrated treatment for those with co-occurring mental and substance use disorders and for those with co-occurring physical and/or behavioral disorders is especially important, but not widely available.

There are a number of medications for addiction that appear to be helpful.

Substance abuse programs need to be tailored for older adults, but, although age-specific treatments, including peer self-help groups, appear to be particularly helpful for older adults, they should be given a choice of being in programs only for people of their age or with younger people as well.

Whether confrontation-style interventions work for older adults is a matter of controversy. And whether the goal of treatment is abstinence or harm reduction is extremely controversial.

Behavioral Problems

> Mrs. S. was a "hoarder." Her apartment was beyond cluttered. Old newspapers, old clothes, mementos of her 81 years were everywhere. It was so crowded that she, a very small, thin woman, could barely walk from bedroom to bathroom to living room to kitchen. All the rooms were filled. She stopped cleaning, stopped washing dishes. Cockroaches took over the apartment, and a stench developed that was so bad that her neighbors called the police, who called the Health Department, which ordered her to clean up. When she didn't, Mrs. S. was referred to Adult Protective Services (APS). The worker tried to persuade her to clean up and threatened to have it done for her. She did nothing. A cleaning service came in and took away the stuff of Mrs. S.'s life. She became emotionally distraught. Mrs. S. was lucky a good worker from a mental health organization got involved and helped her weather what she experienced as an assault on her life. Often, people like Mrs. S. get moved to nursing homes, because APS workers have no other resources.

Older adults with dementia or other forms of mental illness often have "behavior problems." These include refusal to accept, resistance to, or inability to follow, treatment regimens; verbal, or occasionally physical, abuse of family and/or paid caregivers; sexually inappropriate behavior; wandering; dangerous behaviors such as smoking in bed or not turning the stove off; and maddeningly annoying behaviors such as constant complaining, asking the same question over and over again, or refusing to bathe.

Older adults with such problems frequently become socially isolated and alienate caregivers. Many end up in nursing homes because home-based care becomes impossible. And, in institutions, the people most difficult to the staff are often restrained chemically or physically, because appropriate non-pharmacological interventions are not available.

Understanding that behavior problems are not in the person said to have the problem, but in the relationship between the person and his/her caregivers, is key to being able to help them. Sometimes, finding a good match is all that is needed, but special training for both formal and informal caregivers is very important. This should include information about mental disorders, behavior management techniques, and practical methods of humane intervention based on appreciation of the individuality of each person whose behavior is troublesome to caregivers.

Emotional Problems Adjusting to Old Age

Dr. A. had been the Chairman of the Department of Cardiac Surgery at a major medical school. He believed that he should not continue to operate after the age of 60 and that, if he did not practice, he could not be an effective chairman, so he retired at 63. He had consulting work that kept him busy. He had very close family and friends, but he missed day-to-day contact with colleagues and ultimately he realized, as he put it, "I'm not a star anymore." He wanted the admiration and respect of others. He became depressed. Over time, Dr. A. found a role as a mentor to students at a nearby community college who were interested in careers in health care. This helped him to weather the often-painful transition to retirement. Increasingly, "civic engagement" is being recognized as a way to support the mental health of older adults and to provide help to younger and older people that otherwise would not be available.

Mr. F. had lost many family members and friends by the time he was 67. He had other people in his life and did not become isolated, but he found that people popped up in his mind like ghosts when he passed a restaurant where they used to meet for dinner, or on the tennis court where they used to play, or on the highway when he passed a town he used to go to for family get-togethers. The ghosts were bittersweet. He felt happy to be in their presence again but sad that they were just figments of his own imagination. Sometimes he felt called to join them, and more and more he thought that he too would soon be dead. It always made him a little tearful, though the tears were as invisible to others as his ghosts. Sometimes he worked at being ready to die; usually, however, he was so involved in real life that the idea of death surprised him. He, like all older adults, needed to come to terms with the fact of mortality. Some do it through their religious or spiritual experiences. Others do it without religion. It is often not an easy process.

Old age is a stage of life that, like all stages, has its emotionally difficult developmental challenges. People with or without mental illness have to face these challenges. Most people make the emotional transition with some pain, but without developing a diagnosable mental disorder; others develop diagnosable disorders or live in an unsettled state between an earlier phase of life and old age.

The major developmental challenges of old age are: major role changes such as retirement; loss of status (common in Western cultures, but not in some others where elders are revered for their wisdom); reduction (but usually not complete loss) of physical and mental capacities; the development of chronic health problems; loss of family and friends; and coming to terms with death.

125

Many people react to this list with the sense that getting old must be depressing. Not so. Most older people find a new meaning in their lives, new sources of satisfaction, ways to cope with physical and mental decline, and ways to handle mortality without denial.

Weathering the transition to old age successfully depends on good retirement planning; keeping active and involved with others; having access to good health care and to recreation, among other things. For many, a connection with a religious group is important. In addition, during this time of life, group and individual counseling is useful to many people.

The range of what is needed to promote "positive aging" has led to a number of different models for "age-friendly" or "livable" communities, efforts to make neighborhoods/towns/ villages better places for older people to live. Unfortunately, attention to mental health and substance use issues is rarely included in these models. The Geriatric Mental Health Alliance of New York has developed a guide to help community planners to include mental health promotion and treatment (Williams & Friedman, 2010).

NEEDED POLICY CHANGES

American society is poorly prepared to respond to the social needs that will emerge owing to the vast growth of the population of older adults over the next two decades. It is even more poorly prepared to meet the mental health challenges of the elder boom. Changes are needed in the size and structure of the mental health and substance abuse systems, in both the public and the private sectors. Changes are also needed in the health system—in primary care, specialty care, and long-term care. The aging services system also needs to pay considerably more attention to issues of mental illness and substance misuse among older adults, as well as to take advantage of opportunities to promote good mental health in old age.

What follows is the 12-Point Agenda for Change developed by the Geriatric Mental Health Alliance of New York. There are other advocacy agendas related to geriatric mental health that are available as well.[3]

CONCLUSION

In the first half of the 21st century, the population of older adults (65 and over) in the United States will more than double. Overall, about 20% of this population has a diagnosable mental or substance use disorder, and this rises to over 50% by age 85, largely because of the significant increase in dementia as people age. Thus, increasing longevity will result in disproportionately large increases in the numbers of older adults with mental health and/or substance use problems, creating an alarming challenge to the community mental health system, which is not prepared to meet this challenge, if only because the current and projected workforce is much too small and is not adequately educated or trained in geriatric mental health and/or substance use problems.

This chapter has provided an overview of the demography and epidemiology of the elder boom, as well as an overview of the mental and substance use disorders of old age and of helpful interventions. In addition, it has provided a brief overview of the shortcomings of current public policy with regard to geriatric mental health and a call to action built on a 12-Point Agenda for Change.

A 12-POINT AGENDA FOR IMPROVED GERIATRIC MENTAL HEALTH POLICY

1. **PROMOTE MENTAL HEALTH:** Pursue opportunities to promote mental health and to prevent the development or exacerbation of mental and substance use disorders in old age. It is particularly important to build this goal into the health care delivery system and into the efforts to modernize the aging services system and to develop "age-friendly" communities.

2. **SUPPORT AGING IN THE COMMUNITY:** Provide supports to enable older adults with mental disorders to live where they choose—usually in the community. It is particularly important to provide housing alternatives to institutions for older adults with co-occurring serious physical and mental disorders, including supportive housing and in-home care.

3. **PROVIDE FAMILY SUPPORT:** Provide support for family caregivers, including those who care for aging spouses or parents with mental disorders, older adults who care for grown children with mental disabilities, and grandparents raising grandchildren. This should include tax benefits as well as services such as counseling, psychoeducation, support groups, and respite.

4. **IMPROVE ACCESS TO MENTAL HEALTH AND SUBSTANCE ABUSE SERVICES:** To improve access to these services, it will be necessary (a) to increase the amount of service available in both the public and private sectors. In addition, (b) it will be very important to make services more affordable, mobile, and available in home and community settings such as senior centers, senior housing, naturally occurring retirement communities (NORCs), and houses of worship.

5. **IMPROVE QUALITY:** The quality of mental health and substance abuse services for older adults needs vast improvement in both community and institutional settings and in both the public and the private sectors. This must include improved identification and treatment of mental health and substance use problems by health and aging services providers as well as mental health and substance abuse providers.

6. **INTEGRATE MENTAL HEALTH, PHYSICAL HEALTH, AND AGING SERVICES:** (a) It is important to integrate screening for and treatment of mental and substance use disorders into primary and specialty health care if only because those with these disorders are likely to also have chronic physical health conditions and to be reluctant to go to specialty behavioral health settings. The emphasis on the development of comprehensive "medical homes" and "accountable care organizations" in federal health care reform creates an opportunity to focus on real integration of meaningful behavioral health services in primary care. (b) It is particularly important to improve identification and treatment of mental, substance use, and behavioral disorders in long-term care, i.e., in home health care, adult medical day care, assisted living, and nursing homes. (c) Aging services settings such as senior centers, senior housing, NORCs, meals-on-wheels, case management, etc. are should routinely engage in screening for

and treatment of mental and substance use disorders in partnership with mental health, substance abuse, or health care organizations. They should also emphasize mental health promotion.

7. **PROMOTE CULTURAL COMPETENCE:** Minority elders will increase from 15 to 25% of the older population over the next two decades. Services need to be adapted in response to cultural differences. It is particularly important for services to be provided in their native languages.

8. **PROVIDE PUBLIC EDUCATION:** (a) More extensive efforts are needed to combat stigma, which causes reluctance to acknowledge or get help with mental or substance use disorders. (b) Education is also needed about mental illness, the effectiveness of treatment, and where treatment is available. Expanded information and referral services specifically related to older adults would be of great value. (c) It is particularly important to combat agism, which results in the expectation that depression and other mental disorders are unavoidable among older adults, and ignorance about mental illness and its treatment.

9. **ADDRESS SOCIAL/ECONOMIC ISSUES:** Older adults with mental or substance use disorders often face social and economic problems such as social isolation, inadequate income, and poor housing. It is important to help them address these kinds of problems as well as to provide treatment for their mental and physical disorders.

10. **WORKFORCE DEVELOPMENT:** The current shortage of clinically and culturally competent providers will almost certainly get worse as the elder boom takes place. There are two distinct issues to address—size and quality. (a) To build a bigger workforce there need to be new incentives to attract new workers. (b) There should also be more initiatives to develop both paid and volunteer helping roles for older adults themselves. (c) Enhanced professional and paraprofessional education and training are also critical to building the workforce of the future.

11. **DESIGN NEW FINANCE MODELS:** Currently (a) there is not enough funding for geriatric mental health services in both the public and the private sectors. In addition, (b) financing models need to be restructured so as to support services in home and community settings, support integrated service delivery, encourage the use of state-of-the-art practices and service innovation, go beyond the medical model, broaden Medicare coverage to include essential services such as case management, and facilitate pooling funding across service systems.

12. **PROMOTE PUBLIC AND PRIVATE SECTOR READINESS:** (a) Neither plans nor structures have been created in government agencies to prepare for the mental health and substance abuse challenges of the elder boom. Planning and the clarification of responsibility for developing needed services should happen immediately. (b) The workplace can play an important role through programs to promote mental health among older workers and those who are about to retire and through efforts to support workers who are responsible for the care of older adult family members.

Time has run out for our nation's service systems to prepare in advance for the elder boom. Now we will have to confront the challenges of this vast demographic change while it is underway. We hope that our nation—which, as we write this, is under enormous economic stress—is up to the task.

DISCUSSION QUESTIONS

1. What is the "elder boom," and why is this important to community mental health services?

2. Explore ways in which our society is agist. Give some examples from the media and from personal experience. Think of ways you can reduce agist thinking in your personal life.

3. Identify community supports that could be helpful for family caregivers of older adults with mental health needs.

LEARNING ASSIGNMENT

As a class, create a design for an age-friendly community (housing complex or village) that is supportive to older people and is responsive to mental health and substance abuse issues. What components does your village/community have that support aging?

SUGGESTED READINGS

Blazer, D.G. (2009). Depression in late life: Review and commentary. *Focus: The Journal of Lifelong Learning in Psychiatry, 7*(1), 118–136.

Dembling, B., Chen, D., & Vachon, L. (1999). Life expectancy and causes of death in a population treated for serious mental illness. *Psychiatric Services, 50*(8), 1036–1042.

Kessler, R., & Wang, P. (2008). *The Descriptive Epidemiology of Commonly Occurring Mental Disorders in the United States. Annual Review of Public Health*, Vol. 29, pp. 115–129. Retrieved from: www.annual reviews.org/doi/abs/10.1146/annurev.publhealth.29.020907.090847?journalCode=publhealth

INTERNET RESOURCES

Ageworks: www.ageworks.com

American Association of Retired Persons: www.aarp.org

American Society on Aging: www.asaging.org

National Council of Senior Citizens: www.ncscinc.org

National Council on the Aging: www.ncoa.org

National Institute on Aging: www.nia.nih.gov

NOTES

1   There are three major theories about the apparent decline in major depression. One is that there isn't really a decline. The apparent decline is due to inappropriate diagnostic standards for older adults or reflects the fact that epidemiological studies are done only with people who live in the community and don't include institutionalized populations. A second theory is that the prevalence of depression varies from generation to generation. The current generation of very old people has weathered very tough times—the Depression, World War II, and more. Will the next generation of older adults have as much resilience as the current generation? A third theory to explain the apparent decline of major depression as people get older is that people with serious health conditions who are also depressed are at higher risk for disability and/or premature death than those who are not depressed. A significant number of people with depression just don't live to be old or are in institutions.

2   The most common screening instrument for depression is the "Patient Health Questionaire" (PHQ), which is available in two forms—the PHQ-2 and the PHQ-9. The PHQ-2 asks whether the person filling out the questionnaire is experiencing either or both of the two cardinal symptoms of depression. If the answer is no, it is not necessary to ask further questions. If the answer is yes, the PHQ-9 should then be administered. Some medical practices prefer to start with the PHQ-2; others start with the PHQ-9.

3   (1) The American Association for Geriatric Psychiatry: www.aagponline.org/; (2) The Older Women's League: www.mentalhealthweek.org/Policy_Recommendations.html; (3) Alzheimer's Association: www.alz.org/join_the_cause_advocacy.asp

REFERENCES

Anthony, W.A. (1993). Recovery from mental illness: The guiding vision of the mental health service system in the 1990's. *Psychosocial Rehabilitation Journal, 16*(4), 12–23.

Bartels, S.J., Coakley, E.H., Zubritsky, C., Ware, J.H., Miles, K.M., Arean, P.A., et al. (2004). Improving access to geriatric mental health services: A randomized trial comparing treatment engagement with integrated versus enhanced referral care for depression, anxiety, and at-risk alcohol use. *American Journal of Psychiatry, 161*, 1455–1462.

Blazer, D.G. (2009). Depression in late life: Review and commentary. *Focus: The Journal of Lifelong Learning in Psychiatry, 7*(1), 118–136.

Blow, F.C. (1998). *Substance abuse among older adults treatment improvement protocol.* DHHS Publication No. (SMA) 98–3179. Retrieved from www.ncbi.nlm.nih.gov/books/NBK14467/

Brennan, M., Vega, M., Garcia, I., Abad, A., & Friedman, M. (2005). Meeting the mental health needs of elderly Latinos affected by depression: Implications for outreach and service provision. *Care Management Journals, 6*(2), 98–106.

Byers, A., Yaffe, K., Covinsky, K.E., Friedman, M.B., & Bruce, M.L. (2010). High occurrence of mood and anxiety disorders among older adults: The National Comorbidity Survey replication. *Archives of General Psychiatry, 67*(5), 489–496.

Centers for Disease Control and Prevention. National Center for Injury Prevention and Control (2007). *WISQARS injury mortality reports, 1999–2007.* Retrieved from www.cdc.gov/ncipc/wisqars/

Chin, E., Hedberg, K., Higginson, G.K., & Fleming, D.W. (1999). Special report legalized physician-assisted suicide in Oregon—The first year's experience. *New England Journal of Medicine, 340,* 577–583.

Colton, C., & Manderscheid, R. (2006). Congruencies in increased mortality rates, years of potential life lost, and causes of death among public mental health clients in eight states. *Preventing Chronic Disease, 3*(2), A42.

Conwell, Y. (2001). Suicide in later life: A review and recommendations for prevention. *Suicide & Life—Threatening Behavior:* National Suicide Prevention Conference Background Papers, 31, 32–47. Retrieved December 14, 2010, from Research Library (document ID: 72665323).

Conwell, Y., Duberstein, P.R., Cox, C., Herrmann, J.H., Forbes, N.T., & Caine, E.D. (1999). Relationships of age and axis I diagnoses in victims of completed suicide: A psychological autopsy study. *American Journal of Psychiatry, 153,* 1001–1008.

Cummings, J.L., & Jeste, D.V. (1999). Alzheimer's Disease and its management in the year 2010. *Psychiatric Services, 50*(9), 1173–1177.

De Leo, D., Buono, M.D., & Dwyer, J. (2002). Suicide among the elderly: The long-term impact of a telephone support and assessment intervention in northern Italy. *British Journal of Psychiatry, 181,* 226–229.

Dembling, B., Chen, D., & Vachon, L. (1999). Life expectancy and causes of death in a population treated for serious mental illness. *Psychiatric Services, 50*(8), 1036–1042.

Draper, B. (1999). Practical geriatrics: The diagnosis and treatment of depression in dementia. *Psychiatric Services, 50,* 1151–1153.

Friedman, M. (2009). *Behavioral health is key to long-term care reform* [PowerPoint slides]. Retrieved from http://michaelbfriedman.com/mbf/images/stories/mental_health_policy/Finance_and_Managed_Care/BH_and_LTC_UHFWeb.pdf

Gallo, J., & Rabins, P. (1999). Depression without sadness: Alternative presentations of depression in late life. *American Family Physician, 60*(3), 820–826.

Gill, S.S., Bronskill, S.E., Normand, S.T., Anderson, G.M., Sykora, K., Lam, K., & Rochon, P.A. (2007). Antipsychotic drug use and mortality in older adults with dementia. *Annals of Internal Medicine, 146*(11), 775–W180. Retrieved from EBSCO*host.*

Gould, M., Kalafat, J., Munfakh, J., & Kleinman, M. (2007). An evaluation of crisis hotline outcomes: Part 2: Suicidal callers. *Suicide & Life—Threatening Behavior, 37*(3), 338–352. Retrieved December 21, 2010, from Research Library.

Grayson, V., & Velkoff, V. (2010). *The next four decades, the older population in the United States: 2010 to 2050, current population reports, P25–1138.* Washington, DC: U.S. Census Bureau. Retrieved from: www.census.gov/prod/2010pubs/p25-1138.pdf

Husaini, B.A., et. al. (2000). Prevalence and cost of treating mental disorders among elderly recipients of Medicare services. *Psychiatric Services, 51,* 1245–1247.

Hybels, C., & Blazer, D. (2003). Epidemiology of late-life mental disorders .*Clinics in Geriatric Medicine, 19*(4): DOI: 10.1016/S0749-0690%2803%2900042-9.

Katon, W., & Ciechanowski, P. (2002). Impact of major depression on chronic medical illness. *Journal of Psychosomatic Research, 53,* 859–863.

Kessler, R.C., Berglund, P., Demler, O., Jin, R., Merikangas, K.R., & Walters, E.E. (2005). Lifetime prevalence and age-of-onset distributions of DSM-IV disorders in the national comorbidity survey replication, *Archives of General Psychiatry, 62*(6), 593–602.

Kessler, R., & Wang, P. (2008). The descriptive epidemiology of commonly occurring mental disorders in the United States. *Annual Review of Public Health,* Vol. 29, pp. 115–129. Retrieved from: www.annualreviews.org/doi/abs/10.1146/annurev.publhealth.29.020907.090847?journalCode=publhealth

Kilbourne, A.M., Cornelius, J.R., Han, X., Hass, G.L., Salloum, I., Conigliaro, J., & Pinous, H.A. (2005). General-medical conditions in older patients with serious mental illness. *American Journal of Geriatric Psychiatry, 13*(3), 250–254.

Kraus, C., et al. (2008). Cognitive-behavioral treatment for anxiety in patients with dementia: Two case studies. *Journal of Psychiatric Practice, 14*(3), 186–192.

McAlpine, D. (2003). Patterns of care for persons 65 years and older with schizophrenia. In C. Cohen (Ed.), *Schizophrenia into later life* (pp. 3–17), Washington, DC: American Psychiatric Publishing.

Mishara, B.L., Chagnon, F., Daigle, M., Balan, B., Raymong, S., Marcoux, I., Bardon, C., Campbell, J., & Berman, A. (2007). Which helper behaviors and intervention styles are related to better short-term outcomes in telephone crisis intervention? Results from a silent monitoring study of calls to the U.S. 1–800-SUICIDE network. *Suicide and Life Threatening Behavior, 37*, 308–321.

Mittelman, M.S., Haley, W.E., Clay, O., & Roth, D.L. (2006). Improving caregiver well-being delays nursing home placement of patients with Alzheimer disease. *Neurology, 67*, 1592–1599.

Oxman, T.E., Dietrich, A., & Schulberg, H.C., (2005). Evidence-based models of integrated management of depression in primary care. *Psychiatric Clinics of North America, 28*, 1061–1077.

Piatt, E., Munetz, M., & Ritter, C. (2010). An examination of premature mortality among decedents with serious mental illness and those in the general population. *Psychiatric Services, 61*(7), 663–668.

Schmutte, T., O'Connell, M., Weiland, M., Lawless, S., & Davidson, L. (2009). Stemming the tide of suicide in older white men: A call to action, *American Journal of Men's Health, 3*, 189–200, DOI: 10.1177/ 1557988308316555.

Snowden, M., Sato, K., & Roy-Byrne, P. (2003). Assessment and treatment of nursing home residents with depression or behavioral symptoms associated with dementia: A review of the literature. *Journal of the American Geriatrics Society, 51*(9), 1305–1317. DOI: 10.1046/j.1532–5415.2003.51417.x.

Spillman, B., & Pezzin, L. (2000). Potential and actual family caregivers: Changing networks and the "sandwich generation." *Milbank Quarterly, 78*(3), 347–374.

Substance Abuse and Mental Health Services Administration (2005). *The NSDUH report: Substance use among older adults: 2002 and 2003 update.* Retrieved from www.oas.samhsa.gov/2k5/olderadults/olderadults.htm

Tiihonen, J., Lönnqvist, J., Wahlbeck, K., Klaukka, T., Niskanen, L., Tanskanen, A., et al. (2009). 11-year follow-up of mortality in patients with schizophrenia: A population-based cohort study (FIN11 study). *The Lancet, 374*(9690), 620–627. Retrieved from www.scopus.com

Unützer, J., Katon, W., Callahan, C.M., Williams, J.W. Jr, Hunkeler, E., Harpole, L., et al. (2002). Collaborative care management of late-life depression in the primary care setting: A randomized controlled trial. *Journal of the American Medical Association, 288*(22), 2836–2845. DOI: 10.1001/jama.288.22.2836.

U.S. Department of Health and Human Services (1999). *Mental health: A report of the Surgeon General.* Washington, DC: Author.

U.S. Department of Health and Human Services (2009). *Results from the 2008 National Survey on Drug Use and Health: National findings* (Office of Applied Studies, NSDUH Series H-36, HHS Publication No. SMA 09-4434). Rockville, MD: Author.

Wang, P.S., Lane, M., Olfson, M., Pincus, H.A., Wells, K.B., & Kessler, R.C. (2005). Twelve-month use of mental health services in the United States: Results from the national comorbidity survey replication. *Archives of General Psychiatry, 62*(6), 629–640.

Williams, K.A., & Friedman, M.B. (2010). Addressing the mental health needs of older adults in "Age-Friendly Communities"—A guide for planners. *Geriatric Mental Health Alliance Publication*, Mental Health Association of New York City. Retrieved from: www.mha-nyc.org/media/1251/agefriendly.pdf

Zeisel, J. (2009). *I'm still here: A breakthrough approach to understanding someone living with Alzheimer's.* New York: Penguin.

Zeisel, J., & Raia, P. (2000). Nonpharmacological treatment for Alzheimer's disease: A mind–brain approach. *American Journal of Alzheimer's Disease and Other Dementias, 15*, 331–340. DOI: 10.1177/ 153331750001500603.

Part Four

Diversity and Community Mental Health

Chapter 9

African–Americans, Racism, and Mental Health

Alma J. Carten

INTRODUCTION

Prior to the 2008 presidential election, the emotional mood of the country was one of marked foreboding. The economic recession, home foreclosures, increasing unemployment, loss of retirement assets, fear of terrorist threats, and the continuing involvement in the war in Iraq all contributed to the depressive mood that consumed virtually every segment of the American populace. As the election results came in, this national malaise was replaced by a euphoria that was virtually palpable as blacks and whites danced in the street, embraced, and cried unashamedly in public. A clinical interpretation of these scenes in response to the election of the country's first African–American president may well have been that this was a reflection of the catharsis that came with the purging of the collective psychological burden of guilt, paranoia, denial, splitting, and cognitive dissonance required to maintain a system of structured racism in a country founded on democratic ideals.

Following the election, it was widely believed that America had at long last overcome the crippling legacy of racism and had been catapulted into a post-racial society. It was to be, however, a short-lived euphoria, for it was not long after the new president, who in his very demeanor, intellect, and presence, dispelled every stereotype about African–Americans that had been carefully and systematically constructed since slavery, had settled into the Oval Office and took on the symbolic mantle of power associated with the office, that it quickly became apparent that race and racism continued to be defining factors in American society. Not even the most powerful office of the Western world was beyond the reach of their virulent effects.

Despite strong roots in social justice, advocacy, and traditions of client empowerment and consumerism, community mental health agencies and the professionals who staff them are not immune from the virulent effects of racist ideologies that pervade American institutional structures and shape socialization experiences of the individual over the entire life cycle. There is a compelling body of empirical evidence that racism occurring at the institutional and interpersonal levels plays a central role in contributing to striking racial disparities in mental health outcomes for Americans. Given the severity of the consequences of racism for the psychological well-being of consumers and practitioners, eradicating racism in its various forms must be given the highest priority by mental health providers.

PURPOSE

This chapter builds upon content on African–Americans and mental health that appeared in the first edition of this publication. Key themes addressed in the first edition chapter provided a review of the historical foundation of mental health services in the United States and the continuing effects of scientific racism in shaping mental health services for African–Americans; research developments in the 19th century that offered beginning empirically based insights for understanding etiology, risk, protective factors, and help-seeking behaviors of African–Americans; and new commitments at the federal level that seemed promising for correcting flawed practices of the past and improving mental health outcomes for African–Americans. The discussion in this chapter takes a closer look at the influence of institutional and interpersonal racism on mental health. While recognizing that African–Americans are overburdened by the consequences of racism, the discussion argues that greater attention should be given to the implications of racism for contributing to psychological distress experienced by whites, and encourages the use of an anti-racist model for addressing race and its residual effects in the mental health system.

AFRICAN–AMERICANS AND MENTAL HEALTH SERVICES: THE OVERVIEW

Racism and discrimination are dominating themes of the historical experiences of African–Americans in the nation's mental health system. Early in the history of the country, the doctrine of white supremacy served as the underlying belief system shaping the nation's developing economic, political, and social structures during the colonial period. In mental health, beliefs about the inherent racial superiority of whites resulted in the entrenchment of empirically unfounded racist assumptions about the behavior and mental capabilities of blacks, and served as the theoretical basis for scientific racism that continued to inform U.S. mental health policy and practice well into the 20th century (Carten, 2006).

During the colonial period, the non-conforming behaviors of rebellious runaway slaves were diagnosed as "draptomania" or "flight from home madness." Those who accepted their state of servitude were viewed as exhibiting normal behavior and described as "happy-go-lucky" and "faithful" (Thomas & Sillen, 1972). A 1904 publication authored by G. Stanly Hall, founder of the American Psychological Association, described African–Americans, along with Indians, Chinese, and Mexicans, as members of "adolescent races" and offered a biological explanation for understanding their incomplete development that placed them on the lower rung of the evolutionary ladder, which rendered them unable ever to catch up with whites. And throughout the 1950s and 1970s, professional journals were continuing to publish articles stating that African–Americans were not of sufficient mental sophistication or development to be susceptible to mental illnesses, nor capable of making effective use of insight therapy or the psychotherapies (Thomas & Sillen, 1972).

The long-term effects of racist practices are reflected in findings of the Supplement to the Surgeon General's *Report on mental health* (U.S. Department of Health and Human Services [USDHHS], 2001), which identifies striking racial disparities relative to access, utilization, availability, quality of care, and treatment outcomes. In addition to barriers of cost, service fragmentation, and stigma, the report asserts that these disparities are attributable in part to past and current racism and discrimination, which have also slowed adequate mental health theory development necessary for informing evidence-based practice with African–Americans.

Community mental health conceptualizes mental illness and wellness as resulting from a complex interaction among biological, psychological, social, and cultural factors. African–Americans have historically interacted within economic, political, and social environments characterized by pervasive inequalities. Consequently, African–Americans are at increased risk for poverty and other social problems found to have measurable effects of on the rates of mental illness (USDHHS, 2001). A number of protective factors have been identified that mitigate the adverse effects of racism on the psychological well-being, coping, and adaptive behaviors of African–Americans (Billingsley, 1968; Hill, 1971; Taylor & Chatters, 1991). Nonetheless, African–Americans experience greater persistence and severity of mental illness and are disproportionately represented among the homeless, mentally ill populations, those living in shelters, and those with co-occurring problems of chemical dependency.

Although the prevalence of mental health among African–Americans is similar to that of other ethnic groups, African–Americans are found to have higher rates of psychiatric-hospital admissions than whites and other ethnic groups (USDHHS, 2001; Williams et al., 2007). Early findings (Grier & Cobbs, 1968) indicating that clinicians often were unable to differentiate behavioral symptoms of paranoia associated with racial discrimination and prejudice from psychopathology remain a continuing theme of more recent research (Neighbors, Jackson, Campbell, & Williams, 1989; Snowden, 2001). There is also a significant body of evidence in the research literature that African–Americans are assigned more severe psychiatric diagnoses, are over-diagnosed for schizophrenia, and are underdiagnosed for the affective disorders (Neighbors et al., 1989; Trierweiler et al., 2000). Moreover, despite the high need for services, research findings indicate that mistrust of formal mental health systems, reinforced by clinician stereotyping and bias, is a significant deterrent to seeking treatment and service retention (Whaley, 2001). Included among the explanations offered for understanding these occurrences are bias present in standardized psychological tests, the interview situation, personal bias and predisposition of the individual clinician, and institutional racism (Snowden, 2001; USDHHS, 2001).

Since the pioneering publication of Grier and Cobbs (1968), there has been a significant rise in the research literature examining the implication of racism for the field of mental health (Snowden, 2001; USDHHS, 2001). These studies offer new insights for understanding the range of variables contributing to systemic barriers and influencing etiology and prevalence, and for diagnosing and treating mental disorders with African–Americans. This scholarship also examines more closely the confluence of clinical, cultural, organizational, and financial reasons influencing help-seeking and service-utilization behaviors of African–Americans, and encourages the use of culturally competent treatment interventions that incorporate an understanding of the histories, traditions, beliefs, and value systems of African–Americans (Davis & Ford, 2004; Neighbors, 1985; Neighbors & Jackson, 1984; Snowden & Cheung, 1990).

A HOLISTIC VIEW OF MENTAL HEALTH AND WELLNESS

Mental health and mental illness are viewed as existing along a continuum of severity, ranging from behaviors and personality traits that have little impact on the individual's ability to carry out primary life roles and tasks, to those that are severely incapacitating and disrupt thought processes, resulting in an inability to distinguish between the boundaries of reality and the individual's inner world. The World Health Organization defines mental health as, "a state of well-being in which the individual realizes his or her own abilities, can cope with the normal stresses of life, can work productively and fruitfully, and is able to make a contribution to his or her community." Similarly, the report to the Surgeon General on mental health takes a "wide-angle lens" that gives consideration to both mental illness and wellness and encourages the use of a public health model for the development of mental health policy. The public health model is concerned about the health of the population in its entirety and acknowledges the link between health and the physical and psychosocial environment. A public health model focuses on traditional areas of diagnosis, treatment, and etiology, as well as on epidemiologic surveillance of the health of the population at large, health promotion, and disease prevention (USDHHS, 1999, 2000).

A wellness model, as conceptualized by Myers, Sweeney, and Witmer (2000), provides a practical example of a holistic view of mental well-being. The model identifies the following as characteristic of healthy functioning: essence or spirituality, work and leisure, friendship, love, and self-direction. Subtasks included in the model include: sense of worth, sense of control, realistic beliefs, emotional awareness and coping, problem solving and creativity, sense of humor, nutrition, exercise, self-care, stress management, gender identity, and cultural identity. A holistic approach to mental health and wellness and the public health model logically lead to the consideration of the implications of racism in its many forms for mental health well-being.

INSTITUTIONAL, INTERNALIZED, AND INDIVIDUAL RACISM

Manifestations of racism in the United States have transformed from blatant forms of discrimination, as evidenced in "separate but equal" policies that legalized segregation in all public facilities throughout the country, to more subtle forms, of which there is no single or identifiable perpetrator, but which are no less harmful in their effects.

Racism is generally recognized as taking the form of institutionalized racism, internalized racism, and individual personal bigotry. Institutional racism, also referred to as systemic or structural racism, is the differential access and distribution of the resources, goods, services and opportunities, and power of society to the benefit of dominant racial groups, based on empirically unfounded assumptions of racial superiority. Sanctioned in both custom and law, despite the absence of empirical evidence, the notion of white supremacy has been a prevailing ideology of great staying power in American society since its founding. White supremacy has resulted in the unequal treatment of several groups identified as "the other" at various periods in the nation's history. Relative to African–Americans, white supremacy provided the rationale that justified and sustained the institution of slavery, Jim Crow laws developed during Reconstruction, practices of legal segregation that remained the "law of the land" until stuck down by the landmark 1954 Supreme Court decision, and various forms of institutional racism that are commonplace in contemporary American society. Further, underlying assumptions of white supremacy racist ideology have been integral to the socialization experiences shaping the worldview of Americans, their belief systems, and how they view themselves in relationship to others.

138

These assumptions have a great influence on mental health policy and practice, because they favor a deficit model for the understanding and treatment of the mental health needs of African–Americans. Further, this approach often pathologizes normative behaviors and makes flawed inferences about the capacity of African–Americans for positive psychological growth and their ability to make effective use of psychotherapy. Socialization experiences occurring in all institutions influence individual belief systems, worldviews, and the lens through which people view themselves and the behaviors of others. These socialization experiences provide the context for understanding the origins and dynamics of internalized racism, which may be manifested as internalized inferiority and oppression or an internalized belief in one's superiority and privilege.

Persistent racial stereotyping via blatant as well as subliminal messages and images contributes to internalized racism, which is defined as the acceptance among individuals who are members of racially stigmatized groups of negative perceptions about their own abilities and intrinsic worth. This, in turn, impacts feelings of self-esteem and self-worth for the individuals and others in his/her racial group. Internalized racism is expressed in behaviors that embrace attributes of "whiteness" as being more desirable and a devaluing of attributes associated with the racial group of identification. For whites, this result in an assumption of innate superiority based on skin color, and the internalization of feelings of privilege and entitlement that are taken for granted.

CONSEQUENCES OF RACISM FOR AFRICAN–AMERICANS AND WHITES

There is extensive reporting in the empirical literature on the consequences of white racism on the mental health and identity development of blacks (Allport, 1954; Chestang, 1973; Feagin, 1991; Franklin-Jackson & Carter, 2007; Pettigrew, 1973; Whaley, 2001). More recent reporting in the literature, acknowledging the changing presentations of racism in the United States, not only suggests that blacks suffer from the effects of traditional forms of both institutionalized and internalized racism, but also identifies the pernicious impact of more subtle forms of individual white bias and bigotry that are described as microaggressions (Sue, 2010). An understanding of these subtle forms of racism is based on the assumption that it is highly likely that anyone who is born and reared in the United States will internalize customs and beliefs that contribute to racial bias and race-based prejudicial assumptions. Microaggressions are conceptualized as the invisible forms of racial bias that operate at an unconscious level in well-intentioned whites, who see themselves as moral, fair-minded people, free of racial bias and prejudices.

African–Americans are subject to microaggressions on a fairly consistent basis, the cumulative effects of which make it more likely for them to perceive prejudice in their interactions within larger systems and to think about their race on a fairly consistent basis. Whites, on the other hand, are seldom required to consider their skin color and are more likely to believe that they live in a "color-blind" society and that racial prejudice is not a significant factor in American society. Lacking the protective shield of skin color, African–Americans are more likely to experience contextual stress emanating from perceived and actual race-related discrimination and prejudice. These experiences may contribute to feelings of anxiety, paranoia, anger,

139

resentment, helplessness, hopelessness, and fear, as well as increase risk for the psychomatizations of problems. These feelings are compounded when placed in a historical context of injustice and unequal treatment that has persisted over time and has yet to be addressed.

Although these data indicate that African–Americans are overburdened by the costs of racism, the underreporting in the literature on the impact of racism on whites is also a reflection of traditional views that white racism is largely a problem for African–Americans. Although emergent, with limited findings, more recent research that has been undertaken in an examination of the psychological consequences of racism for whites (Harvey & Oswald, 2000; Iyer, Leach, & Crosby, 2003; Pettigrew, 1973; Skillings & Dobbins, 1991; Spanierman, Poteat, Beer, & Armstrong, 2006; Sue, 2003) reveals that whites experience psychological distress related to white racism. For example, whites have reported experiencing anxiety, frustration, guilt, and shame when confronted with issues related to their own racism or to societal racism in general (Bowser & Hunt, 1996; Harvey & Oswald, 2000; Pettigrew, 1973). Furthermore, whites who consider themselves to be egalitarian, while simultaneously holding that some forms of discrimination against blacks are justified, have been found to experience emotional and psychological discomfort regarding discrimination. Findings from a study examining causal relationships between anxiety, racism, and self-esteem in a sample of white graduate and undergraduate students indicated that the level of respondent anxiety had a direct effect on anti-black attitudes, which, in turn, had a direct effect on respondent feelings of self-esteem (Utsey, McCarthy, Eubanks, & Adrian, 2002). Findings from a study replication with a national sample of white adults in various workplace settings recommended additional areas of research to gain insight for improving cross-cultural clinical counseling (Poteat & Spanierman, 2008). These findings suggest that whites must confront the psychological dissonance and denial required to accept without question the inherent contractions of white privilege in a democratic society based in the ideals of a meritocracy.

IDENTITY DEVELOPMENT

Social scientists have also used a stage or developmental model for understanding the influence of racism on the dynamics and process of identity development for both blacks and whites (Cross, 1995; Helms, 1995). Accordingly, it is posited that, for blacks, a central task is to achieve a positive sense of racial identity in the context of a society that devalues the racial group in which they hold membership. For whites, a successful resolution would result in the individual's acceptance of the contradictions of white privilege in a democratic society and willingness to relinquish the personal benefits accrued from white privilege.

Cross (1995) uses a five-stage model for describing the feelings and thought processes of African–Americans, set forth as his Nigresence Theory or the process of becoming black. At each stage, identified as pre-encounter, encounter, immersion/emersion, internalization, and internalization/commitment, the individual is called upon to resolve certain tasks as s/he deconstructs an internalized white worldview. Accordingly, the first stage is characterized by the belief that race does not matter. Subsequently, the individual moves through a process that results in the internalization of a positive racial identity and deintensification of feelings of animosity toward whites. The final stage is evident when a positive race identity is internalized into the individual's self-concept. Concurrent with the internalization of a positive black racial identity is the individual's commitment to activism that seeks to promote social justice and the civil rights of African–Americans, as well as other oppressed and marginalized groups.

More recently, researchers have examined the role of white racial identity attitudes in understanding the dynamics of white racism (Helms, 1990, 1995; Ponterotto, 1991). Helms (1995) sets forth a stage model for understanding white racial identity development conceptualized as: contact, disintegration, reintegration, and pseudo-independence. The first three of these, contact, disintegration, and reintegration, describe the struggle of whites to abandon racist belief systems. The successful resolution of the latter three, pseudo-independence, immersion–emersion, and autonomy, are characteristic of whites who are moving toward adopting a non-racist white identity, which requires them to accept their "whiteness" and acknowledge the ways in which they collude and benefit from racism. As for blacks, this resolution increases awareness of the many forms of social injustice and promotes a commitment to social activism.

Although these models are widely cited in the literature, it is also recognized that there is much inter-group diversity in the experiences of African–Americans and whites that influences and shapes the process of racial identity formation. Racial identity may also be viewed as a process that continues to evolve over the entire life cycle, influenced by context, time, and place. This need not be a linear process, but rather one that occurs concurrently with other internal processes required for the consolidation of an integrated sense of self, such as gender and sexual orientation.

Importantly, the experience of African–Americans is unique, because of the slave experiences and the long and egregious history of racism and discrimination in the United States. However, African–Americans comprise but one segment of the nation's black populations, making a "one size fits all" inappropriate for understanding the process of racial identity development for individuals who identify as being of African descent. Population and immigration trends are increasing the within-group diversity of blacks of African descent. A large share of people of African descent are immigrating from the anglophone Caribbean countries, Haiti, Central, Latin, and South American and African countries, as well as from Canada, France, and England. Although all people of African descent may be equally disadvantaged by discrimination based on race and skin color that has dominated patterns of racism in the United States, there is also a good deal of diversity among people of African descent as to their experiences with white racism. Some may have enjoyed relationships of equality with their white counterparts, or are from countries that have never experienced colonization, or from those in which blacks comprise the dominant racial group holding political power. These are but some of the additional contextual factors to take into consideration in determining where individuals of African descent are in the process of formulating a racial identity.

There continue to be considerable debate and disagreement about the existence and prevalence of race-based discrimination and prejudice in American society. However, extant research findings suggest that a shared task for both African–Americans and whites, in achieving a healthy racial identity in a society in which race continues to play a significant role, is the recognition that, on matters of race, "the personal is political." Concomitant to this is a willingness, in the Quaker tradition, to "speak truth to power," or evidence the courage to take necessary risks involved with promoting dialogues around institutional and interpersonal racism, in the face of resistances that can result in personal marginalization and devaluation. Psychological transformations necessary for achieving these tasks are manifested in the

141

internalization of a feeling of comfort and authenticity with one's personal racial heritage and commitment to advancing a social justice, human rights agenda for many marginalized groups. This new awareness comes from the recognition of the intersection of racism and other social forms of oppression—based on socioeconomic class, gender, sexual orientation, and citizenship or immigration status. Individuals who have evolved to this level of thinking also recognize that inequalities contribute to high levels of social problems, including mental illness, and undermine the quality of life in the society. Therefore, it is in the interest of every individual to promote social justice.

THE ANTI-RACIST MODEL—A PROMISING PRACTICE FOR SYSTEMIC CHANGE

An anti-racism model is emerging as a promising practice for addressing structural racism and uncovering the more subtle forms of institutional racism and personal bias that contribute to persistent racial disparities in many fields of practice in the health and human services, including the field of mental health.

A fundamental premise of the anti-racist work is that racism has been consciously and systematically constructed in the United States since the country's founding. Therefore, it is the responsibility of every individual to engage in planned and sustained actions in an effort to dismantle the legacy of racism and white supremacy that pervades all institutional and organizational structures in American society and is deeply embedded in the American psyche.

Over the last several years, New York City has experienced considerable success in bringing together an alliance of health and human services organizations to collaborate in the implementation of a coordinated anti-racist strategy for "undoing the effects" of racism as it is manifested in all levels of operations of health and human service agencies. The primary goal of the initiative is to raise awareness about the insidious and often invisible forms of institutional racism that nonetheless have very real effects on client access and retention in services and contribute to persistent racial disparities in outcomes across virtually all sectors of the health and human services. In support of these efforts, a recent edition of a publication (Mental Health News, 2011) with national distribution and a wide readership, which includes consumers and mental health professionals from many professional disciplines, was dedicated to an examination of a range of topics relevant to the impact of race on consumers, practitioners, organizations, and delivery systems.

The following are narratives of contributing authors describing their experiences as executives, administrators, and educators in participating in anti-racist work in an effort to transform organizational structures, an essential first step for creating an environment of sustainability for anti-racist work.

Where does the not-for-profit sector start in transforming organizational and administrative structures to address race and racism? My experience, as a senior administrator and executive of a large not-for-profit, is you start with the organization's mission. This means starting as close to practice as possible. For mental health organizations, that means the therapeutic relationship, which is built on honesty, trust and mutual respect between helper and client.

142

At the end of the (Undoing Racism) workshop, staff rated our organization against the continuum of becoming an anti-racist and multi-cultural institution. We were in for a rude awakening when there was general consensus that at best we were at stage 3, or symbolic change in the range of tolerance of racial and cultural differences. After the initial shock and denial, the training began to sink in, we were able to expose those structural areas where racism could indeed exist and begin to constructively look for ways to move the continuum needle.

In 1982, a group of social work students petitioned the faculty to have a required course for all students on "cultural diversity." They failed. Over the years, four other student groups made the same request, with the same results. Twenty-six years later, in 2008, yet another group met with the faculty and this time succeeded. The outcome of their efforts was the School's adoption of an anti-oppression and restorative social work lens for the year-long required foundational "Practice Lab" for all incoming students. Today, the course has moved from an exploratory pilot, to a requirement for all students.

CONCLUSIONS

Racism and discrimination have left an indelible mark on the nation's mental health system and play a central role in racial disparities in mental health outcomes. Although the largest share of the literature examining the implications of racism in the field of mental health has focused on its detrimental effects on African–Americans, the discussion encourages more research to support an expanded empirical knowledge base for understanding the effects and dynamics of racism across racial groups. This information can increase understanding of the dynamics of race and racism in cross-counseling relationships, structural barriers contributing to racial disparities in mental health outcomes.

Implicit in the discussion is that building inclusive mental health delivery systems that are free from the effects of racism and discrimination serves the interests of consumers, clinicians, provider agencies, and society. Further, core values of community mental health of consumerism and client empowerment, combined with the strong roots of these agencies in the community, place community mental health providers in an advantageous position to promote the use of anti-racist approaches for removing systemic barriers that contribute to poor mental health outcomes for African–Americans and other people of color.

DISCUSSION QUESTIONS

1. What is institutional racism and how does it impact mental health treatment for African–Americans?

2. Discuss the term microaggressions. In what ways do you see this subtle form of racism manifested in everyday life?

3. How does the chapter describe the impact of racism on the mental health of white Americans?

LEARNING ASSIGNMENT

Hold an in-class debate on the following statement: The mental health system in America is inherently racist: Yes/No.

SUGGESTED READINGS

Sue, Derald Wing (2010). *Microaggressions in Everyday Life: Race, Gender, and Sexual Orientation*. Hoboken, NJ: Wiley.

U.S. Department of Health and Human Services (2001) *Mental health: Culture, race and ethnicity a supplement to the mental health: A report to the Surgeon General*. Rockville, MD. Author.

INTERNET RESOURCES

The Office of Minority Health (OMH): minorityhealth.hhs.gov

Black Women and Mental Health: www.blackwomenshealth.com/blog/black-women-and-mental-health

Black Mental Health Alliance: www.blackmentalhealth.com

National Organization of People of Color against Suicide (NOPCAS): www.nopcas.org

REFERENCES

Allport, G.W. (1954). *The nature of prejudice*. Cambridge, MA: Perseus Books.

Billingsley, A. (1968). *Black families in white America*. Englewood Cliffs, NJ: Prentice Hall.

Bowser, B.P. & Hunt, R.G. (1996). *Impacts of racism on White Americans* (2nd ed.). Beverly Hills, CA: Sage.

Carten, A.J. (2006). African–Americans and mental health. In J. Rosenberg and S.J. Rosenberg (Eds.), *Community Mental Health: Direction for the 21st Century* (pp. 125–139). Routledge.

Chestang, L. (1973). Character development in a hostile environment. Occasional Paper #3. University of Chicago, School of Social Service Administration.

Cross, W.E. (1995). The psychology of niegrescence: Revisiting the Cross Model. In J. Pointerotto, J.M. Casas, L.A. Suzuki, & C.M. Alexander (Eds.), *Handbook of Multicultural Counseling* (pp. 93–122). Thousand Oaks, CA: Sage.

Davis, S. & Ford, M. (2004). A conceptual model of barriers to mental health services among African–Americans. *American Research Perspectives, 10*(1), 44–55.

Feagin, J.R. (1991). The continuing significance of race: Anti-black discrimination in public places. *American Sociological Review, 56*, 101–116.

Franklin-Jackson, D. & Carter, R.T. (2007). The relationship between race related stress, racial identity and mental health for Black Americans. *Journal of Black Psychology, 33*, 5–26.

Grier, W.H. & Cobbs, P.M. (1968). *Black rage*. New York: Basic Books.

Harvey, R.D. & Oswald, D.L. (2000). Collective guilt and shame as motivation for White support of Black programs. *Journal of Applied Social Psychology, 30,* 1790–1811.

Helms, J.E. (1990). Toward a model of White racial identity development. In J.E. Helms (Ed.), *Black and White racial identity: Theory, research and practice* (pp. 49–66). Westport, CT: Greenwood.

Helms, J.E. (1995). An update of Helm's white and people of color racial identity models. In J. Pointerotto, J.M. Casas, L.A. Suzuki, & C.M. Alexander (Eds.), *Handbook of multicultural counseling* (pp. 93–122). Thousand Oaks, CA: Sage.

Hill, R.B. (1971). *The strengths of black families.* New York: National Urban League.

Iyer, A., Leach, C.W., & Crosby, F.J. (2003). White guilt and racial compensation: The benefits and limits of self-focus. *Personality and Social Psychology Bulletin, 29,* 117–129.

Mental Health News (2011). www.mhnews.org. Winter.

Myers, J.E., Sweeney, T.J., & Witmer, J.M. (2000). The wheel of wellness counseling for wellness: A holistic model for treatment planning. *Journal of Counseling and Development, 78*(3), 251–266.

Neighbors, H.W. (1985). Seeking professional help for personal problems: Black Americans use of health and mental health service. *Community Mental Health Journal, 21*(3).

Neighbors, H.W. & Jackson, J.S. (1984). The use of informal and formal help: Four patterns of illness behavior in the black community. *American Journal of Community Psychiatry, 12*(6), 629–644.

Neighbors, H.W. & Jackson. J.S. (1996). *Mental health in Black America.* Thousand Oaks, CA: Sage.

Neighbors, H.W., Jackson, J.S., Campbell, L., & Williams, D. (1989). The influence of racial factors on psychiatric diagnosis: A review and suggestions for research. *Community Mental Health Journal, 25*(4).

Pettigrew, T.F. (1973). Racism and the mental health of White Americans. In C.V. Willie, B.M. Kramer, & B.S. Brown (Eds.), *Racism and mental health.* Pittsburgh, PA: University of Pittsburgh Press.

Ponterotto, J.G. (1991). The nature of prejudice revisited: Imnplications for counseling intervention. *Journal of Counseling and Development, 70,* 216–224.

Poteat, V.P. & Spanierman, L.B. (2008). Further validation of the psychosocial costs of racism to Whites scale among employed adults. *The Counseling Psychologist, 36,* 871–894.

Skillings, J.H. & Dobbins, J.E. (1991). Racism as a disease: Etiology and treatment implications. *Journal of Counseling and Development, 70,* 206–212.

Snowden, L.R. (2001). Barriers to effective mental health services for African–Americans. *Mental Health Services Research, 3*(4), 181–187.

Snowden, L.R. & Cheung, F.K. (1990). Use of inpatient mental health services by members of ethnic minority groups. *American Psychologist, 45*(3).

Snowden, L.R. & Pingitore, D. (2002). Frequency and scope of mental health service delivery to African–Americans in primary care. *Mental Health Services Research, 4,* 123–130.

Spanierman, L.B., Poteat, V.P., Beer, A.M., & Armstrong, P.I. (2006). Psychological costs of racism to Whites: Identifying profiles with cluster analysis. *Journal of Counseling Psychology, 53,* 434–441.

Sue, D.W. (2003). What is white privilege? In *Overcoming our racism: The journey to liberation* (pp. 23–44). San Francisco: John Wiley.

Sue, D.W. (2010). *Microaggressions in everyday life: Race, gender, and sexual orientation.* Hoboken, NJ: Wiley.

Taylor, R.J. & Chatters, L.M. (1991). Religious life. In J.S. Jackson (Ed.), *Life in Black America.* Newbury Park, CA: Sage.

Thomas, A. & Sillen, S. (1972). *Racism and psychiatry.* New York: Brunner/Mazel.

Trierweiler, S.J., Neighbors, H.W., Munday, C., Thompson, S.E., Binion, V.J., & Gomez, J.P. (2000). Clinician attributions associated with diagnosis of schizophrenia in African–American and non-African–American patients. *Journal of Consulting and Clinical Psychology, 68,* 171–175.

U.S. Department of Health and Human Services (1999) *Mental health: A report to the Surgeon General.* Rockville, MD: Author.

145

U.S. Department of Health and Human Services (2000). *Healthy people 2010*. Rockville, MD: Author.

U.S. Department of Health and Human Services (2001) *Mental health: Culture, race and ethnicity a supplement to the mental health: A report to the Surgeon General*. Rockville, MD: Author.

Utsey, S.O., McCarthy, E., Eubanks, R., & Adrian, G. (2002). White racism and suboptimal psychological functioning among White Americans: Implications for counseling and prejudice prevention. *Journal of Multicultural Counseling and Development, 30*, 61–95.

Whaley, A.L. (2001). Cultural mistrust: An important psychological construct for diagnosis and treatment of African–Americans. *Professional Psychology: Research and Practice, 32*, 555–562.

Williams, D.R., Gonzales, H.H., Neighbors, H., et al. (2007). Prevalence and distribution of major depressive disorder in African–Americans, Caribbean Blacks, and non-Hispanic whites. *Archives of General Psychiatry, 64*, 305–315.

Chapter 10

Community Mental Health Services to Asian–Americans

Russell F. Lim, Hendry Ton, and Francis G. Lu

INTRODUCTION

Asian–Americans and Pacific Islanders (AAPIs) with mental health issues have traditionally been seen in community mental health centers, because many of the AAPIs seeking services have been recent immigrants or refugees from foreign wars, and have been of lower socioeconomic status or without insurance. However, AAPIs relatively low utilization of mental health services has been well documented (U.S. Department of Health and Human Services, 2001). The chapter will detail the prevalence of mental illness in the AAPI community, discuss the utilization of mental health services by AAPIs, describe the barriers to services that AAPIs face, and suggest ways to improve mental health services to AAPIs, on the clinical, policy, and research levels.

DEMOGRAPHICS

Asian–Americans represent 5% of the U.S. population, or about 15.2 million people. They have had the fastest rate of growth of all major ethnic groups over the last 30 years, and represent 43 distinct ethnic groups and languages spoken (U.S. Census Bureau, 2010). Over one-third of all AAPI families speak a language other than English at home, which constitutes a significant barrier to mental health-care services owing to limited English proficiency (LEP), with Chinese, Tagalog, Vietnamese, and Korean being spoken in order of highest representation. Although the per capita income for Asian–Americans is $27,643, higher than the national average at $26,974, it is lower for some Asian–American groups, such as Laotians at $13,914, with a 13% poverty rate, Cambodians at $13,624, with a 21% poverty rate, and Hmong, $8,470, with a 31.7% poverty rate (Ponce et al., 2009). The overall Asian–American poverty rate is 11.8%, which may explain why 17.8% of Asian–Americans lack health insurance. Despite the stereotype of the model minority, many AAPIs do not receive adequate mental health care owing to the realities of poverty and lack of insurance, in addition to other factors that will be discussed in detail later on in this chapter, such as LEP, stigma, somatization leading to misdiagnosis, and other cultural issues.

PREVALENCE OF MENTAL HEALTH DIAGNOSES IN AAPIS

AAPI men have a lifetime risk of major depression of 7–12%, compared with 20–25% in women. The rate of depression in AAPIs varies, depending on the specific ethnicity and locale. Takeuchi et al. (1998) found that, in Los Angeles County in California, the lifetime rate of major depression in Chinese Americans is 6.9%, whereas the rate for dysthymia is 5.2%. These estimates may be an underestimate owing to the stigma of mental health and the fact that these patients are often not reported in studies (Chen, Chen, & Chung, 2002). Elderly AAPIs can be at risk for depression owing to declining health, limited resources, and inter-generational conflicts. Mui (1996) administered a culturally appropriate translated and back-translated 30-item Geriatric Depression Scale to 50 elderly Chinese residents (aged 62–91 years) in a U.S. metropolitan city and found that 12% of women were mildly depressed and 4% were moderately to severely depressed, which may explain the high rate of suicide seen in this age group. In addition, 20% of men in the study were mildly depressed, and none was severely depressed. Although the sample size of this study was small, the results suggest that elderly AAPI women should be screened for depression as a preventive measure to reduce the high rate of suicide in their age group.

Mental health providers who are not attentive to the physical experiences of distress of some AAPIs run the risk of missing the diagnosis of depression or bipolar disorder. A mis-diagnosis in young Asian–American women aged 15–24 years could have severe consequences, as they have the highest rates of completed suicide of any ethnic group among that age range (Office of Minority Health, 2007).

Most Americans with depression receive treatment from their primary care provider; however, for Asian–Americans, more than 30% do not have a primary care physician (Harris, 2005). Of those AAPIs who receive mental health services, 17% receive services at a later or more severe stage of illness than Caucasian patients (U.S. Department of Health and Human Services, 2001). Furthermore, studies indicate that AAPI individuals who are undergoing treatment for mental health services receive a lower quality of services. Simpson et al. (2007) found that Asian–Americans diagnosed with depression tended to be prescribed antidepressants less often than their Caucasian counterparts and were less likely to receive outpatient mental treatment after hospitalization. These disparities may be affected both by cultural and linguistic differences between the patient and provider, as well as system and provider biases, leading to disparities in services provided.

MENTAL HEALTH DISPARITIES IN AAPIS

According to recent statistics, only 17% of Asian–Americans in the United States sought some form of assistance for psychological problems, and fewer than 6% sought help from a mental health provider (U.S. Department of Health and Human Services, 2001). Abe-Kim et al. (2007) found that, in a 12-month period, 8.6% of Asian–Americans sought help from any service, with 4.3% using their primary care provider, and 3.1% using specialty mental health services. There were important differences in service use between immigrants and United States-born individuals, in that United States-born individuals used any services at a rate of 19.8%. For example, use of services differed according to nativity status, such that United States-born

148

individuals used mental health services at higher rates than Asians who immigrated to the United States. Also, second-generation individuals (children of immigrants) were more similar to immigrants in their use of services, when compared with third-generation individuals. These findings support a generational rather than ethno-racial approach to classification of respondents. Abe-Kim and her colleagues also found that United States-born Asian–Americans, particularly third-generation or later, gave higher ratings than first- and second-generation Asian–Americans on helpfulness and level of satisfaction with any form of service utilization for formal psychological and medical services. Specifically, more than 90% of Filipinos reported higher rates of satisfaction as a result of seeking professional psychological help at post-treatment than other ethnic groups in the study (Chinese = 72.1%; Vietnamese = 74.9%; other Asian = 88.1%), which could be due to increased acculturation in the third-generation group.

Barretto and Segal (2005) found that East Asians used more services than Southeast Asians, Filipinos, and other Asians, even when severity of illness was taken into account. They suggested that Southeast Asians had different service needs that should be addressed separately, and that Asians should not be aggregated in a single group, as that obscures the true needs of the AAPI population.

In a study by Le Meyer and others (Le Meyer et al., 2009), 28% of Asian–Americans diagnosed with psychological problems chose to receive Western-style mental health treatment, compared with 54% of the general population, and 23% of Asian immigrants with mental health issues obtained help from a professional. Of those who do seek mental health help, many do not receive the appropriate treatment or do not complete the therapy, according to the *Sacramento Bee*. Thus, Asian–Americans use mental health services less than the general population (Naurt, 2008).

BARRIERS FOR AAPIS TO MENTAL HEALTH UTILIZATION

There are many barriers for AAPIs to access mental health care, including LEP, socioeconomic status, cultural beliefs about mental illness, shame, stigma, and the tendency to describe their symptoms in somatic terms.

LANGUAGE

Snowden, Masland, Peng, Wei-Mien, and Wallace (2011) studied the effect of mandating language services for LEP patients by comparing newly identified threshold languages and associated utilization rates in selected California counties with the utilization rates prior to being identified. According to the California Cultural Competence Plan (California Department of Mental Health, 1997), counties must count the number of individuals speaking different languages, and when their number is equal to 3,000, or 5% of the Medi-Cal (California's version of Medicaid) population, then the language is designated as a threshold language, and the following services must be provided: (1) a 24-hour, toll-free phone line with linguistic capability; (2) the translation of written materials that assist beneficiaries in accessing medically necessary specialty mental health services, including personal correspondence; (3) linguistically capable staff or interpreters at key points of contact; and (4) information to ethnic consumers and communities about available language assistance services. Other counties implemented additional changes, such as (1) training staff in cultural competency; (2) provision of bilingual clinicians (service providers), and (3) provision of Asian language-specific clinics or service programs (ethnic-specific services (ESS)). Counties were also assessed for the presence of an Asian-language clinic. Their results showed that providing the language-specific services resulted in an increase in utilization by patients speaking that language, rising from 13% to 24%, or a factor of 1.87. Even when controlling for extra cultural-competence training and the presence of ESS, there still was a net increase of 14.5% in utilization. Failure to address linguistic differences in mental health service provision risks unnecessarily adding to the disease burden imposed by untreated mental illness. Language barriers likely prevent individuals with limited proficiency in the host country's language from using available mental health services.

POVERTY

Chow, Jaffee, and Snowden (2003) examined racial/ethnic disparities in mental health service access and use for those living in neighborhoods at different poverty levels in New York City. They compared demographic, clinical characteristics, and service use patterns of whites, blacks, Hispanics, and Asians living in low-poverty and high-poverty areas. Patterns of mental health service use of minority racial/ethnic groups were compared with those of whites in different poverty areas. They found that residence in a poverty neighborhood moderates the relationship between race/ethnicity and mental health service access and use. Higher utilization of emergency and inpatient services and having coercive referrals versus outpatient mental health care were more evident in low-poverty than in high-poverty areas. They concluded that neighborhood poverty and lack of community resources were key to understanding racial/ethnic disparities in the use of mental health services. For AAPIs living in high-poverty neighborhoods compared with whites, 18–20 year olds were 14 times more likely to use outpatient mental health services than 18–20-year-old whites, and AAPIs were twice as likely to use emergency services, had less likelihood to have had prior mental health service use, and had three times more likelihood of being diagnosed with schizophrenia. Furthermore, as compared with whites, they were less likely to have been referred by any recognized referral sources, including self-referral, family, friends, social service agencies, and the criminal justice system.

The pattern of utilization confirmed previous observations that AAPIs tend to wait until problems are very severe, before seeking mental health services as a last resort. The cultural factors of stigmatization and shame are the likely cause of Asian clients to have limited access and few contacts with the mental health service system. The authors suggested community outreach and public education to reduce the stigma of getting outpatient mental health treatment, as well as making communities aware of services available to them. ESS can act as an important cultural bridge to provide culturally appropriate services and referrals.

STIGMA

For AAPIs, stigma can manifest itself in the following ways: clients refuse treatment; show concerns about confidentiality; insist on paying cash instead of using insurance; question the clinician's qualifications; have poor attendance and adherence to medication regimens; lack support from family members; and the desire to have a white therapist. Some AAPIs, such as Chinese Americans, believe in Confucianism, which entails a group orientation and respect for elders; value stoicism; hold holistic health beliefs; have concern about their family's reputation, including loss of face and marriage prospects; and have shame, guilt, and embarrassment about mental health issues. AAPIs tend to seek help from family members; trusted friends outside agencies, such as family associations; herbalists; or hospital emergency rooms.

Golberstein, Eisenberg, and Gollust (2008) surveyed undergraduate and graduate students about their perceived need for mental health services and their willingness to seek help for these problems. They found that perceived stigma was highest among men, older students, AAPIs, international students, and students with lower SES.

Abe-Kim et al. (2007) suggested that stigma or loss of face may act as constraints on service use. Lin, Tardiff, Donetz, and Goresky (1978) found that Chinese Americans delayed referrals to a community mental health agency because of the stigma associated with admittance of personal problems, seen as flaws for which individuals need to seek mental health services. In Hawaii, Takeuchi, Leaf, and Kuo (1988) carried out a survey to assess perceived barriers to seeking mental health treatment and found that persons of Filipino, Japanese, and Native Hawaiian ethnicity felt that there were more barriers than Caucasian respondents did. In fact, the shame of admitting and seeking mental health treatment for alcohol and emotional issues was a major barrier to seeking mental health treatment for the Asian groups.

The Office of the U.S. Surgeon General has highlighted the deleterious effect of stigma on mental health service utilization (U.S. Department of Health and Human Services, 1999). Stigma associated with the field of mental health service was described as a "formidable obstacle" in preventing the use of the mental health services for all potential clients. Moreover, the stigma of mental illness and negative public attitudes about mental illness may be even more powerful for racial and ethnic minorities (U.S. Department of Health and Human Services, 2001). Specifically, AAPIs' tendency to avoid help seeking may be inhibited by individual stigmatization as well as the possibility of shaming one's family (Uba, 1994). Ting and Hwang (2009) address the "dual stigma" experience of Asian–Americans by polling a sample of Asian–American college students. They found that stigma tolerance might be a more direct measure of the degree to which an individual subscribes to the cultural attitudes regarding mental health problems and service use. The students' help-seeking behavior suggests that health service utilization is determined by the combination of environmental factors (e.g., location of services and types of service available) and population characteristics (i.e., characteristics specific to each individual). Low stigma tolerance was strongly correlated with more positive help-seeking attitudes (Ting & Hwang, 2009), because these individuals needed to get better to eliminate the stigma. These findings support Uba's (1994) stating that an individual's behaviors (both positive and negative) reflect upon his or her entire family in a collectivistic society. Thus, for AAPIs, it may be particularly difficult to tolerate being stigmatized, because their personal stigma affects the reputation and status of their family members as well.

MISDIAGNOSIS DUE TO SOMATIZATION

Many Asian–Americans express their illness in somatic terms, some to avoid the stigma of mental illness, others because they lack the words in their language to express their depression or distress. In the Chinese Classification of Diseases, 10th Edition (CCD-10), there is a diagnosis of neurasthenia ("*shenjing shuairuo*" in Mandarin Chinese), which is described as fatigue, lack of motivation, and anergia that can be thought of as the physical symptoms of depression. Neurasthenia was removed from *DSM-II*, but is accepted as a physical illness in China, removing some of the stigma of having a mental illness.

CULTURAL HEALTH BELIEFS

AAPIs have many different health beliefs that do not fit into the Western model of illness, the separation of mind and body, and the emphasis on pharmacology. Instead, many AAPIs have a more holistic view of health and causation of illness. For example, they may believe that their illness is caused by an imbalance of hot or cold, which might be corrected by a change in diet or the taking of herbs. They may feel that their *Chi*, or vital energy, needs to be redirected throughout the body by the use of needles or cupping. They may feel that they have forgotten to do some ritual, or that their misdeeds are causing their illness, and they may consult a shaman for the appropriate ritual, or go to the temple for advice from the monks on how to make up for their misdeed (Du, 2006). Fang and Schinke (2007) found that 82% of a sample of Chinese American patients at a community mental health center said that they used complementary strategies. Less than half (47%) used megavitamin therapy, 43% used herbal medications, and 25% used massage, acupuncture, and spiritual healing.

Once AAPIs have decided that Eastern methods are ineffective, they may attempt Western medicines, but, in their experience, Western medicines are "too strong." Research in ethno-psychopharmacology identifies a biological mechanism for this clinical observation, because many AAPIs are poor metabolizers of some psychopharmacological agents, and they experience intolerable side effects owing to polymorphisms in their CYP450 enzymes that make them less effective in breaking down psychotropic medications (Smith, 2006).

OVERCOMING BARRIERS TO MENTAL HEALTH SERVICE UTILIZATION BY AAPIS

Clinical Interventions

The APA added a focus on culture and its effects in developing the 4th edition of the *Diagnostic and Statistical Manual* (*DSM-IV*) (American Psychiatric Association, 1994), and its subsequent revision, *DSM-IV-TR* (Text Revision) (American Psychiatric Association, 2000). The *DSM-IV* and *DSM-IV-TR* include the Outline for Cultural Formulation (OCF) in Appendix I, as well as a Glossary of Culture Bound Syndromes. The OCF provides a framework for the delineation and the incorporation of the patient's cultural identity, health beliefs, supports and stressors, and the effect of culture on the patient–clinician relationship into a case formulation. The *DSM-IV-TR* also identifies culturally specific diagnoses, such as acculturation problem or spiritual crisis. Finally, there are sections in the narrative introductions to each of the major diagnostic categories for age, gender, and culture that will guide the clinician to properly assess persons with a different or unfamiliar ethnic background. In addition to the *DSM-IV-TR*, there are many

152

THE *DSM-IV-TR* OUTLINE FOR CULTURAL FORMULATION

A: Cultural identity of the individual

An individual's cultural identity includes the individual's cultural reference group(s), languages spoken, cultural factors in development, etc.

B: Cultural explanations of the illness

The cultural explanations of the illness refer to predominant idioms of distress and local illness categories. Also includes meaning and severity of symptoms in relation to cultural norms, as well as perceived causes and explanatory models, and help-seeking experiences and plans.

C: Cultural factors related to psychosocial environment and levels of functioning

These include social stressors and supports such as family or religious groups, as well as levels of functioning and disability.

D: Cultural elements of the clinician–patient relationship

This includes ethno-cultural transference and counter-transference, as well as the use of an interpreter, and psychological testing.

E: Overall cultural assessment

The overall cultural assessment is a summary of all of the above factors, and how they affect the treatment plan.

Source: Adapted from Manson, 1996

excellent books and articles on assessing the culturally different, such as the *Clinical Manual of Cultural Psychiatry* (Lim, 2006). Culturally appropriate assessment is critical to an accurate diagnosis and a culturally appropriate treatment plan.

Service Design

Chen, Kramer, and Chen, in New York City (2003), reported on collaboration between the primary care clinic and the mental health clinic in the Charles B. Wang Community Health Center, in which primary care doctors referred patients with mental illnesses to the mental health clinic in the same building and noticed an increase in utilization of the mental health clinic. The project was known as the Bridge Project, and it proved to be replicable at other sites. Yeung and colleagues (2004) implemented a similar model at South Cove Community Health Center in Boston and wanted to know if integrating psychiatry and primary health care improved referral to, and treatment acceptability of, mental health services among Chinese Americans. The project consisted of conducting training seminars for primary care physicians to improve recognition of common mental disorders, using a primary care nurse as the "bridge" to facilitate referrals to the Behavioral Health Department of the same facility, and co-locating

153

a psychiatrist in the primary care clinic to provide onsite evaluation and treatment. The rate of mental health service referrals and successful treatment engagement before and during the project were compared. During the 12-month period of the Bridge Project, primary care physicians referred 64 patients (1.05% of all clinic patients) to mental health services, a 60% increase in the percentage of clinic patients referred in the previous year. Eighty-eight percent of patients referred to mental health services during the project showed up for psychiatric evaluation, compared with 53% in the previous year. Integrating psychiatry and primary care was shown to be effective in improving access to mental health services and in increasing treatment engagement among low-income immigrant Chinese Americans in Boston and New York.

Culturally Appropriate Services and Treatments

There are many examples of culturally appropriate services in Portland, Boston, Seattle, Los Angeles, and Sacramento, among others. Portland, Oregon, has the Intercultural Clinic, which specializes in providing services for Southeast Asian patients (Boehnlein, Leung, and Kinzie, 2008). The clinic provides language support and cultural brokerage by bicultural and bilingual case managers and group leaders, as well as culturally based supervision from the clinical director.

An example of a culturally appropriate treatment modality for PTSD in Southeast Asian refugees was described by J. David Kinzie (2001) when he wrote about "The Therapist Variable," in which he described the trauma experienced by Southeast Asian patients, and that they have four primary needs, safety, both physical and emotional, predictable and stable relationships, reduction of symptoms, and the re-establishment of social relationships. According to Kinzie, the therapist must be able to listen to a person's trauma without interruption, and be present as a dependable and stable relationship. The therapist must believe that healing is possible, despite the evil that humankind has done to fellow human, and should also be prepared to receive gifts of modest value from traumatized Southeast Asians, such as prayers, seasonal dishes, or social invitations, despite training not to accept gifts of any kind, as it is therapeutic for them and represents a culturally appropriate way for a person to honor the therapist–patient relationship.

In Boston, Massachusetts, Hinton and Otto (2006) described a way of modifying CBT for the treatment of PTSD in Cambodians, who conceived of their illness as being caused by bad "wind," muscle tension or dizziness, which may have been caused by forced labor, chronic starvation, and sleep deprivation experienced in the killing fields. *Wind* is conceived as a source of energy flowing through the body, and a loss of wind, signified by tension in a joint, would lead to bad health outcomes, such as the death of the limb away from the tension owing to the lack of blood flow, and the dangerous ascent of wind and blood in the body, into the trunk of the body. The catastrophic cognition would be that this wind could cause a heart attack or the person's breathing to stop, or rupture of the blood vessels in the neck or into the head, leading to fainting, blindness, or death. Treatment for the bad wind would be "cupping," or causing redness on the skin by applying negative pressure thorough a heated glass bulb applied to the skin, or coining, using coins to rub the skin. In the adapted CBT protocol, the therapist introduces the "Limbic Kid" to explain the automatic responses and thoughts associated with

154

the catastrophic cognitions (Otto and Hinton, 2006). The therapist then induces dizziness by having the person play a childhood game called "hung," where s/he holds his or her breath while running to retrieve a stick, experiencing dizziness, but no other ill effects, and allowing a disconnection of the physical sensation from catastrophic cognitions. Finally, the therapist incorporates a Buddhist ritual, the three bows, with three statements. Thus, the first bow acknowledges the pain. The second is the acceptance that it has lingering effects, and the third is returning a focus to the present, planning to have a good life now.

Another example is a Vietnamese support group in Sacramento that used principles of wellness and adaptation to the host culture by serving tea, doing relaxation exercises, and teaching English to the members (Truong and Gutierrez, 2009). The group leaders, third-year psychiatry residents who were ethnically Vietnamese, found that the people were willing to share in a group format, despite predictions found in the literature that Asians would not feel comfortable in groups owing to cultural prohibitions against sharing private matters (Tsui, 1985), showing again that one cannot predict the behavior of all AAPIs with generalizations about an entire ethnic group that is very heterogeneous.

Finally, in Sacramento, California, Cameron et al. (2008) describe the founding of an ESS agency to address the needs of the AAPI community. Funded by the Mental Health Services Act, a proposition passed by California voters in 2004 to tax state personal income over $1 million by 1% for mental health services, the Transcultural Wellness Center (TWC) was designed to serve 13 different Asian cultural groups. As of 2008, TWC has 9 of 13 languages represented by bilingual or bicultural mental health staff. The TWC has also been able to incorporate traditional healing practices, such as acupuncture, tai chi, yoga, and shamanic healing rituals, into their treatment plans. Other billable services offered include transportation, medical care, education, employment training, automobile repair, clothing, groceries, and utilities.

POLICY INTERVENTIONS

Cultural and Linguistic Appropriate Services (CLAS) Standards

In 1998, the U.S. Department of Health and Human Services Office of Minority Health requested a review and comparison of existing cultural and linguistic competence standards and measures on a national level, and then proposed national standards language. An analytical review of standards, regulations, key legislation, and contracts currently in use by federal and state agencies and other national organizations was conducted. Proposed standards were then developed, with input from a national advisory committee of health-care providers, policy administrators, and health services researchers. Fourteen standards were created, defining culturally competent care, how to provide services in the appropriate languages for the client, and supporting cultural competence in the organization (Office of Minority Health, 2001). Applying these standards to a mental health clinic could improve that agency's ability to outreach and educate AAPIs so that they use available services. The CLAS standards are presented in Box 10.2.

NATIONAL STANDARDS FOR CULTURALLY AND LINGUISTICALLY APPROPRIATE SERVICES CULTURALLY COMPETENT CARE

Culturally competent care:

1. Health-care organizations should ensure that patients/consumers receive from all staff members effective, understandable, and respectful care that is provided in a manner compatible with their cultural health beliefs and practices and preferred language.

2. Health-care organizations should implement strategies to recruit, retain, and promote at all levels of the organization a diverse staff and leadership who are representative of the demographic characteristics of the service area.

3. Health-care organizations should ensure that staff at all levels and across all disciplines receive ongoing education and training in culturally and linguistically appropriate service delivery.

Language access services:

4. Health-care organizations must offer and provide language assistance services, including bilingual staff and interpreter services, at no cost, to each patient/consumer with limited English proficiency at all points of contact, in a timely manner, during all hours of operation.

5. Health-care organizations must provide to patients/consumers in their preferred language both verbal offers and written notices informing them of their right to receive language assistance services.

6. Health-care organizations must assure the competence of language assistance provided to limited English proficient patients/consumers by interpreters and bilingual staff. Family and friends should not be used to provide interpretation services (except on request by the patient/consumer).

7. Health-care organizations must make available easily understood patient-related materials and post signage in the languages of the commonly encountered groups and/or groups represented in the service area.

Organizational supports for cultural competence:

8. Health-care organizations should develop, implement, and promote a written strategic plan that outlines clear goals, policies, operational plans, and management accountability/oversight mechanisms to provide culturally and linguistically appropriate services.

9. Health-care organizations should conduct initial and ongoing organizational self-assessments of CLAS-related activities and are encouraged to integrate cultural and linguistic competence-related measures into their internal audits, performance improvement programs, patient satisfaction assessments, and outcomes-based evaluations.

10. Health-care organizations should ensure that data on the individual patient's/consumer's race, ethnicity, and spoken and written language are collected in health records, integrated into the organization's management information systems, and periodically updated.

11. Health-care organizations should maintain a current demographic, cultural, and epidemiological profile of the community, as well as a needs assessment to accurately plan for and implement services that respond to the cultural and linguistic characteristics of the service area.

12. Health-care organizations should develop participatory, collaborative partnerships with communities and utilize a variety of formal and informal mechanisms to facilitate community and patient/consumer involvement in designing and implementing CLAS-related activities.

13. Health-care organizations should ensure that conflict and grievance resolution processes are culturally and linguistically sensitive and capable of identifying, preventing, and resolving cross-cultural conflicts or complaints by patients/consumers.

14. Health-care organizations are encouraged to regularly make available to the public information about their progress and successful innovations in implementing the CLAS standards and to provide public notice in their communities about the availability of this information.

Source: Office of Minority Health, 2001

Research Agenda

In an article on a national health agenda for AAPIs, Ghosh recommends the following: (1) One organization to oversee the entire agenda, to allow consensus, promote oversight, and provide direction, and to help prevent conflicting messages. The contributions of many organizations, community members, researchers, clinicians, and policymakers should be gathered under a central umbrella. (2) Collect and analyze subpopulation data, which will produce useful data to implement culturally competent medical interventions, as subgroups have different needs. The largest and most rapidly increasing subgroups and health issues should be prioritized. (3) Use local organizations that have already invested in, and are trusted by, AAPI communities. Partnering will allow for data gathering and more effective dissemination of improved medical practices. (4) Advocate that all levels of government should be advised about the agenda and kept informed about policies that could help improve the health of AAPIs. (5) Disseminate by publishing an annual health status report and sponsor national health meetings. The report would include updates on the most current AAPI health research and data, thriving health practices, and summaries of national AAPI health conference proceedings. That would bring together the various sectors invested in the improvement of health for AAPIs to present successful strategies and exchange ideas annually or bi-annually. (6) Disseminate community-based participatory research methods, because most national studies cannot register AAPI health status owing to small AAPI sample sizes. Community-based participatory research can serve as a strong alternative while engendering effective collaboration between academia and communities. (7) Partner with AAPI- serving institutions. There are about 40 academic institutions of higher education with AAPI student populations of greater than 10% that are recognized by the federal government as AAPI-serving institutions. Create curricula focused on AAPI health needs to inspire future researchers and clinicians. (8) Interact with health professional training institutions. As the Association of American Medical Colleges' definition of underrepresented minority has changed to allow health profession institutions to define it individually, based on community need, members of some AAPI subgroups can now be included. Also, the inclusion of health equity concepts in curricula should be promoted. (9) Work towards Healthy People 2020 goals. Developed by the U.S. DHHS, Healthy People 2020 maps strategies and goals for health in the United States over the next decade. The AAPI agenda should align with Healthy People 2020 to harness the resources that accompany it (Ghosh, 2010).

Finally, the Supplement to the Surgeon General's *Report on Mental Health: Culture, Race, and Ethnicity*, ends with "A vision for the future," in which recommendations are grouped in six areas: (1) continue to expand the science base; (2) improve access to treatment; (3) reduce barriers to treatment; (4) improve quality of care; (5) support capacity development; and (6) promote mental health (U.S. Department of Health and Human Services, 2001).

CONCLUSIONS

AAPIs have a higher than expected population growth, a prevalence of mental disorders that contradicts the "model minority" stereotype, and a lower than expected utilization of mental health services. The disparities can be explained by the heterogeneity of the AAPI population. Reducing disparities can be accomplished by reducing barriers to mental health treatment by providing appropriate interpretation for AAPIs who are non-English speaking, and by decreasing the double stigma of being a minority and a person with a mental illness by outreaching to the community and providing public education. The use of the *DSM-IV-TR* OCF and awareness of idioms of distress, such as somatization, or of different explanatory models will improve diagnoses and the therapeutic alliance. Innovative programs such as the Bridge Program, which links primary care with mental health, and specifically tailored treatment plans, such as seen in Portland and Boston, or ESS, such as seen in Los Angeles and Sacramento, increase the likelihood that AAPIs will engage with the mental health system in an effective manner. Applying the CLAS standards will increase the retention rates of such programs.

DISCUSSION QUESTIONS

1. Discuss how neighborhood poverty and lack of community resources are linked to racial/ethnic disparities in the use of mental health services.

2. Based on the reading, identify cultural health beliefs that are associated Asian–Americans and Pacific Islanders.

3. What are the essential components of a mental health service or program that is culturally competent?

LEARNING ASSIGNMENT

As a group project, review the National Standards for Cultural and Linguistic Appropriate Services (CLAS) (see Box 10.2). Assess your school's counseling center and determine how well it meets these standards. Discuss your findings in class.

SUGGESTED RESOURCES

Lee, E. (Ed.) (2000). *Working with Asian–Americans—A Clinical Guide*, New York: Guilford Press.

Leong, F.T., Juang, L., Qin, D.B., & Fitzgerald, H.E. (2011). *Asian–American and Pacific Islander Children and Mental Health*, Santa Barbera: ABC-Clio.

Uba, L. (2003). *Asian–Americans: Personality Patterns, Identity, and Mental Health*, New York: Guilford Press.

INTERNET RESOURCES

National Asian–American Pacific Islander Mental Health Association: naapimha.org

Asian–American Health Office of Minority Health: minorityhealth.hhs.gov

Association of Asian Pacific Community Health Organizations: www.aapcho.org

REFERENCES

Abe-Kim, J., Takeuchi, D.T., Hong, S., Zane, N., Sue, S., Spencer, M.S., & Alegria, M. (2007). Use of mental health-related services among immigrant and US-born Asian–Americans: Results from the national Latino and Asian–American study. *American Journal of Public Health, 97*(1), 91–98.

American Psychiatric Association (1994). *Diagnostic and Statistical Manual, Fourth Edition (DSM-IV)*, Washington, DC: APPI.

American Psychiatric Association (2000). *Diagnostic and Statistical Manual, Fourth Edition, Text Revision (DSM-IV-TR)*, Washington, DC: APPI.

Barretto, R.M. & Segal, S.P. (2005). Use of mental health services by Asian–Americans. *Psychiatric Services, 56*(6), 746–748.

Boehnlein, J.K., Leung, P.K., & Kinzie, J.D. (2008). Cross-cultural psychiatric residency training: The Oregon experience. *Academic Psychiatry, 32*(4), 299–305.

California Department of Mental Health (1997). *Cultural Competence Plan Requirements: Addendum to the Implementation Plan for Phase II Consolidation of Medi-Cal Specialty Mental Health Services*. Sacramento, CA: California Department of Mental Health.

Cameron, R.P., Ton, H., Yang, C., Endriga, M.C., Lan, M.F., & Koike, A.K. (2008). The Transcultural Wellness Center: Rehabilitation and recovery in Asian and Pacific Islander mental health care. *Journal of Social Work in Disability & Rehabilitation, 73*(4), 284–314.

Chen, J.P., Chen, H., & Chung, H. (2002). Depressive disorders in Asian–American adults. *The Western Journal of Medicine, 176*, 239–244.

Chen, H., Kramer, E.J., & Chen, T. (2003). The Bridge Program: A model for reaching Asian–Americans. *Psychiatric Services, 54*(10), 1411–1412.

Chow, J.C., Jaffee, K., & Snowden, L. (2003). Racial/ethnic disparities in the use of mental health services in poverty areas. *American Journal of Public Health, 93*(5), 792–797.

Du, N. (2006). Asian–American patients. In Lim, R.F. (Ed.), *Clinical Manual of Cultural Psychiatry*. Arlington, VA: APPI, pp. 69–117.

Fang, L. & Schinke, S.P. (2007). Complementary alternative medicine use among Chinese Americans: Findings from a community mental health service population. *Psychiatric* Services, *58*(3), 402–404.

Ghosh, C. (2010). A national health agenda for Asian–Americans and Pacific Islanders. *Journal of the American Medical Association, 304*(12), 1381–1382.

Golberstein, E., Eisenberg, D., & Gollust, S.E. (2008). Perceived stigma and mental health care seeking. *Psychiatric* Services, *59*(4), 392–399.

Harris, P.A. (2005). The impact of age, gender, race and ethnicity on the diagnosis and treatment of depression. *Journal of Managed Care Pharmacy, 10*, S2–7.

Hinton, D.E. & Otto, M.W. (2006). Symptom presentation and symptom meaning among traumatized Cambodian refugees: Relevance to a somatically focused cognitive-behavior therapy. *Cognitive and Behavioral Practice, 13*(4), 249–260.

Kinzie, J.D. (2001). Psychotherapy for massively traumatized refugees: The therapist variable. *American Journal of Psychotherapy, 55*(4), 475–490.

Le Meyer, O., Zane, N., Cho, Y., & Takeuchi, D.T. (2009). Use of speciality mental health services by Asian Americans with psychiatric disorders. *Journal of Consulting and Clinical Psychology*, 77(5), 1000–1005.

Lim, R.F. (2006). *Clinical Manual of Cultural Psychiatry*. Arlington, VA: APPI.

Lin, T., Tardiff, K., Donetz, G., & Goresky, W. (1978). Ethnicity and patterns of help-seeking. *Culture, Medicine, & Psychiatry, 2*, 3–13.

Manson, S. (1996). The wounded spirit: A cultural formulation of post-traumatic stress disorder. *Culture, Medicine and Psychiatry, 20*(4), 489–498.

Mui, A.C. (1996). Depression among elderly Chinese immigrants: An exploratory study. *Social Work, 41*, 633–645.

Naurt, R. (2008). Asian–Americans shun mental health care, *Psych Central News*, http://psychcentral.com/news/2008/09/24/asian-americans-shun-mental-health-care-2/2998.html. September 9, 2008, accessed January 22, 2011.

Office of Minority Health (2001). Think cultural health—CLAS and the CLAS standards, www.thinkcultural health.hhs.gov/Content/clas.asp, accessed May 4, 2012.

Office of Minority Health (2007). Health Status of Asian–American and Pacific Islander Women, http://minorityhealth.hhs.gov/templates/content.aspx?ID=3721, accessed May 4, 2012.

Otto, M.W. & Hinton, D.E. (2006). Modifying exposure-based CBT for Cambodian refugees with Posttraumatic Stress Disorder. *Cognitive and Behavioral Practice, 13*(4), 261–270.

Ponce, N., Tseng, W., Ong, P., Shek, Y.L., Ortiz, S., Gatchell, M., et al. (2009). *The state of Asian–American, Native Hawaiian and Pacific Islander Health in California Report*. Sacramento, CA: California Asian Pacific Islander Joint Legislative Caucus.

Simpson, S.M., Krishnan, L.L., Kunik, M.E., et al. (2007). Racial disparities in diagnosis and treatment of depression: A literature review. *Psychiatric Quarterly, 78*, 3–14.

Smith, M. (2006.) Ethnopsychopharmacology. In Lim, R.F. (Ed.), *Clinical Manual of Cultural Psychiatry*. Arlington, VA: APPI.

Snowden, L.M., Masland, M.C., Peng, C.J., Wei-Mien Lou, C., & Wallace, N.T. (2011). Limited English proficient Asian–Americans: Threshold language policy and access to mental health treatment. *Social Science & Medicine, 72*(2), 230–237.

Takeuchi, D.T., Chung, R.C., Lin, K.M., et al. (1998). Lifetime and twelve-month prevalence rates of major depressive episodes and dysthymia among Chinese Americans in Los Angeles. *American Journal of Psychiatry*, *155*, 1407–1414.

Takeuchi, D.T., Leaf, P.J., & Kuo, H.S. (1988). Ethnic differences in the perception of barriers to help-seeking. *Social Psychiatry and Psychiatric Epidemiology*, *23*(4), 273–280.

Ting, J.Y. & Hwang, W.C. (2009). Cultural influence on help-seeking attitudes in Asian–American students. *American Journal of Orthopsychiatry*, *79*(1), 125–132.

Truong, K. & Gutierrez, E. (2009). *A Vietnamese Process Group*. UC Davis Department of Psychiatry Grand Rounds, June.

Tsui, A.M. (1985). Psychotherapeutic considerations in sexual counseling for Asian immigrants. *Psychotherapy*, *22*, 357–362.

Uba, L. (1994). *Asian–Americans: Personality Patterns, Identity, and Mental Health*. New York: Guilford Press.

U.S. Census Bureau (2010). *US Census Bureau Newsroom: Facts for Features; Special Editions: Facts for Features: Asian/Pacific American Heritage Month: May 2010*, www.census.gov/newsroom/releases/archives/facts_for_features_special_editions/cb10-ff07.html, accessed January 13, 2011.

U.S. Department of Health and Human Services (1999). *Mental Health: A Report of the Surgeon General*. Rockville, MD: Department of Health and Human Services, Substance Abuse and Mental Health Services Administration, Center for Mental Health Services, National Institutes of Health, National Institute of Mental Health.

U.S. Department of Health and Human Services (2001). Executive summary. In: *Mental Health: Culture, Race, and Ethnicity. A Supplement to Mental Health: A Report of the Surgeon General*. Rockville, MD: Department of Health and Human Services, Public Health Service, Office of the Surgeon General.

Yeung, A., Kung, W.W., Chung, H., Rubenstein, G., Roffi, P., Mischoulon, D., & Fava, M. (2004). Integrating psychiatry and primary care improves acceptability to mental health services among Chinese Americans. *General Hospital Psychiatry*, *26*(4), 256–260.

Chapter 11

Community Mental Health Services to Latinos

Leopoldo J. Cabassa

INTRODUCTION

Latinos are a growing and vibrant segment of the United States population that contribute to the social, economic, and political progress of this nation. According to the U.S. Census Bureau (2007), this diverse population is now the largest ethnic minority group in the United States, representing 14% of U.S. households. The diversity of the Latino population poses unique challenges for clinicians and policymakers to understand Latinos' mental health status and how to meet their needs for mental health services. This chapter begins with an overview of the sociodemographic diversity of the Latino population relevant to mental health care. It then presents a review of current epidemiological studies documenting the prevalence of mental health disorders in the Latino adult population, followed by a discussion of the disparities this population faces in mental health care. Next, examples of culturally competent mental health treatments are presented to illustrate current efforts to improve the access and quality of mental health care in this population. The chapter ends with recommendations for the delivery of community mental health services to Latino populations.

OVERVIEW OF THE U.S. LATINO POPULATION

There are approximately, 40.5 million Latinos in the United States (U.S. Census Bureau, 2007). Mexicans account for the largest proportion (64%) of the U.S. Latino population, followed by Puerto Ricans (9.6%), Central Americans (7.2%; e.g., Salvadorans, Hondurans, Guatemalans), and Cubans (3.6%). It is estimated that, by 2050, one in every four Americans will be of Latino descent (Passel & Cohn, 2008). This continuous growth is attributed in part to the large number of immigrants from Mexico, Central and South America and the Caribbean, the influx of migrants from Puerto Rico, and the high fertility rates of Latinas (Alarcón & Ruiz, 2010).

Latinos are a heterogeneous population on a range of factors, including mode of entry into the United States, length of time in the country, geographic location, levels of acculturation, degrees of contact and affiliation with their home country, cultural values, social norms, and political participation (Villarruel et al., 2009). There are also a wide range of sociodemographic factors among Latino groups that impact their mental health status and care. According to the U.S. Census Bureau's American Community study (2007), the median age of Latinos (26.9 years) is approximately 13 years younger than the median age of the non-Latino white population (40.1 years), with Mexicans having the lowest median age (25.3 years), and Cubans the highest (40.6 years). In terms of educational attainments, 60% of Latinos aged 25 and older are high-school graduates, compared with 89% of non-Latino whites. Yet, the proportions of high-school graduation vary by Latino subgroups, and the proportuin is highest among Colombians and Peruvians (85% or higher), followed by Puerto Ricans, Cubans, Ecuadorians, and Dominicans (60–80%), and lowest among Mexicans, Guatemalans, Hondurans, and Salvadorans (50% or lower). Latinos as a group are overrepresented among the poor, with 22% living below the poverty level, compared with 9% of non-Latino whites. Poverty rates, however, vary between Latino groups. Poverty rates are highest among Dominicans (28.1%), Puerto Ricans and Hondurans, (23.7%), and Mexicans (23.6%) and lowest among Colombians (10.6%), Cubans (15.2%), and Peruvians (13.6%). Language proficiency also varies among Latino groups. Among Latinos aged 5 and older, three-quarters speak a language other than English at home. In general, Puerto Ricans report being more English-proficient than Cubans and Mexicans, whereas Cubans report being more Spanish-proficient than other Latino groups (Guarnaccia et al., 2007). In sum, as this population continues to grow, it is critical to understand and take into consideration its diversity in order effectively to develop and implement culturally and linguistically appropriate community mental health services and policies that are responsive to their needs.

PREVALENCE OF COMMON PSYCHIATRIC DISORDERS AMONG LATINO ADULTS

Over the past decade, three national epidemiological studies—the National Comorbidity Survey-Replication (NCS-R; Kessler et al., 2004), National Epidemiologic Survey on Alcohol and Related Conditions (NESARC; Grant et al., 2004), and National Latino and Asian–American Study (NLAAS; Alegría, Canino et al., 2008) have documented the prevalence of psychiatric disorders among Latinos adults in the United States. This section summarizes the main results of these studies and provides an overview of the distribution of psychiatric disorders in this diverse population.

The NCS-R conducted between 2001 and 2003 examined the lifetime and last-year prevalence of common psychiatric disorders in a national U.S. sample of approximately 9,282 people, with 529 English-speaking Latino participants (Kessler & Merikangas, 2004). *DSM-IV* psychiatric disorders were ascertained with the World Mental Health Composite International Diagnostic Interview (WMH-CIDI; Kessler & Ustun, 2004), a fully structured lay-administered diagnostic interview. Compared with non-Latino whites, Latinos in the NCS-R reported significantly lower prevalence rates of any anxiety and depressive disorders and similar rates of substance use disorders (Kessler et al., 2005). These findings confirmed previous studies that Latinos in general report lower risk of common mental disorders than the non-Latino white population (Kessler et al., 1994; Ortega, Rosenheck, Alegría, & Desai, 2000). The NCS-R, however, provides an incomplete picture of the U.S. Latino population. A major limitation of this study is that it did not include Spanish-speaking Latinos, thus excluding less acculturated Latinos and recent immigrants, who tend to report lower rates of psychiatric disorders than their United States-born and English-speaking counterparts (Burnam et al., 1987; Ortega et al., 2000).

The NESARC conducted between 2000 and 2001 addressed NCS-R limitations by including a large national household sample of English- and Spanish-speaking Latinos (n = 4,558) that included large numbers of Mexican Americans, Cubans, and Puerto Ricans (Grant et al., 2004). In this national study, *DSM-IV* psychiatric disorders were ascertained with the Alcohol Use Disorder and Associated Disabilities Interview Schedule-IV (AUDADIS-IV), a structured diagnostic interview designed for use by lay interviewers in large-scale surveys (Grant, Dawson, & Hasin, 2001). This study showed that foreign nativity acts as a protective factor for most psychiatric disorders among Latinos, but its impact varies by Latino subgroups and types of disorder. For instance, foreign-born Mexican Americans reported significantly lower rates of any depressive, anxiety, or substance use disorders than their United States-born counterparts and United States-born non-Latino whites (Grant et al., 2004). In contrast, foreign nativity among Puerto Ricans and Cubans was only protective for substance use disorders (Alegría, Canino, Stinson, & Grant, 2006). These findings support the "immigrant paradox," in which foreign-born people report less psychiatric morbidity than their United States-born counterparts, despite the stressful experiences and poverty associated with immigration (Burnam et al., 1987). A common explanation for this paradox is that traditional Latino cultures may act as a protective buffer against psychiatric disorders, and this protection erodes as Latinos acculturate into the U.S. culture (Alegría & Woo, 2009; Grant et al., 2004).

To examine within-group differences in psychopathology in the Latino population, the NLAAS—a national household study conducted between 2000 and 2003—was specifically designed to examine the prevalence of mental disorders and mental health service use rates of Latinos and Asian–Americans living in the United States (Alegría, Canino et al., 2008). The NLAAS Latino respondents included: Mexicans (n = 868), Cubans (n = 577), Puerto Ricans (n = 495), and other Latinos (n = 614). Similar to the NCS-R methods, diagnoses of psychiatric disorders in the NLAAS were based on the WMH-CIDI, facilitating the comparison of findings between these two national studies.

Figure 11.1 presents the age- and gender-adjusted lifetime prevalence rates of common psychiatric disorders stratified by NCS-R non-Latino whites, total Latino NLAAS sample, and the main NLAAS Latino subgroups. This figure illustrates several important findings about the distribution of mental disorders in the adult Latino population. First, NLAAS findings corroborate that, in aggregate, Latinos consistently report lower rates of lifetime psychiatric disorders than non-Latino whites (Alegría, Canino et al., 2008). Second, when prevalence rates are disaggregated by Latino subgroups, significant differences exist. Compared with Mexicans and Cubans, Puerto Ricans report higher risks for any psychiatric, anxiety, or substance use disorders, yet no significant differences in the rates of depressive disorders are observed between these groups. In fact, the rates of psychiatric disorders among Puerto Ricans approach those of non-Latino whites (Alegría, Canino et al., 2008). The mechanisms that place Puerto Ricans at higher risk for psychiatric disorders are unknown but may be attributed to the continuous influence that U.S. culture and policies have on Puerto Rican culture, given that Puerto Rico has been a territory of the United States for over a century. Puerto Ricans are also more likely to be bilingual and English-proficient and to have adopted many of the

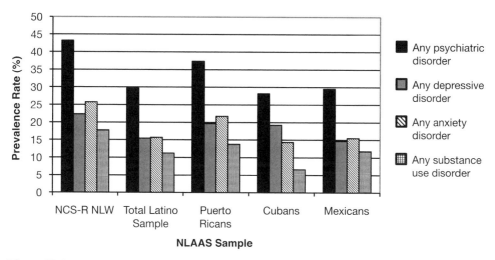

Figure 11.1 *Lifetime Prevalence Rates of Common Psychiatric Disorders for NCS-R Non-Latino Whites and NLAAS Latino Participants*

Note: NCS-R: National Comorbidity Survey-Replication; NLW: Non-Latino whites; NLAAS: National Latino and Asian–American Study. Rates are derived from Alegría et al., 2008. All prevalence rates are age- and gender-adjusted.

same lifestyle patterns of U.S. society (Guarnaccia et al., 2007). Lastly, Puerto Ricans in the NLAAS consistently reported higher rates of family cultural conflicts—a measure that captures familial cultural and intergenerational conflicts over values and goals—which is associated with increased psychopathology (Cook, Alegría, Lin, & Guo, 2009).

The NLAAS also provides an opportunity to conduct a fine-grained examination of the "immigrant paradox" in the Latino population. When Latinos were stratified by subgroups and nativity, a more heterogeneous picture of the "immigrant paradox" was found. Similar to the NESARC findings, the protective impact of foreign nativity was found for depressive and anxiety disorders among Mexicans, and, consistently for substance use disorders for Mexicans, Cubans, and other Latino groups, but not for Puerto Ricans (Alegría, Canino et al., 2008). Thus, the immigrant paradox holds true for some Latino groups but not others and varies by psychiatric disorder. Moreover, acculturation factors (e.g., generational status, time in the United States, context of entry) and cultural factors (e.g., perceived discrimination, family cultural conflict) also influence the risk of psychiatric disorders among Latinos. For example, the longer Latino immigrants remain in their country of origin, the lower their risk of psychiatric disorders, but, once in the United States, Latino immigrants experience similar risk of onset as United States-born Latinos of similar age (Alegría, Sribney, Woo, Torres, & Guarnaccia, 2007). Moreover, recent studies have found that several cultural factors may explain the pathways linking acculturation to the mental health status of Latinos. Cook and colleagues (2009) reported that perceived discrimination and family cultural conflict play a significant role in explaining the association between time spent in the United States and the likelihood of Latinos experiencing a psychiatric disorder.

In sum, findings from the NCS-R, NESARC, and NLAAS indicate that, compared with non-Latino whites, Latinos as a group report lower levels of psychiatric disorders. When Latinos

165

are disaggregated into subgroups, great variability exists in the rates of psychiatric disorders, with Puerto Ricans reporting significantly higher rates of common psychiatric disorders than any other Latino group. These studies also indicate that the "immigrant paradox" in mental disorders is not uniform across Latino groups, suggesting a differential risk of psychopathology in Latinos that varies by nativity, Latino subgroup, age of immigration, type of mental disorder, and differences in cultural factors. In all, these findings have important practice implications, as clinicians should not generalize the protective impact of foreign nativity for all Latino individuals, and should recognize that this protective effect varies, depending on the type of mental disorder and Latinos' experiences with their social and family environment (Alegría, Canino et al., 2008).

MENTAL HEALTH-CARE DISPARITIES IN THE LATINO ADULT POPULATION

Although the prevalence of mental disorders in the overall Latino population is similar to, or lower than, that for non-Latino whites, Latinos adults in need of mental health care are less likely than non-Latino whites to access mental health services, and, when they do receive care, it tends to be poor in quality (Institute of Medicine [IOM], 2003; U.S. Department of Health and Human Services [USDHHS], 2001). In this section, we describe these disparities in care and examine a series of factors that impact the access, engagement, and retention of Latinos in mental health services.

Latinos experience disparities throughout the entire continuum of mental health care. Compared with non-Latino whites with similar mental health needs, Latinos, particularly immigrants, non-English speaking, and those with low levels of acculturation, consistently underutilized specialty mental health services, even after adjusting for differences in age, educational levels, gender, health insurance, and socioeconomic status (Cabassa, Zayas, & Hansen, 2006; Sentell, Shumway, & Snowden, 2007). For instance, a recent national study of people with past-year depressive disorders found that 63.7% of Latinos, compared with 40.2% non-Latino whites, did not access any past-year mental health treatment in the general medical or specialty mental health sectors (Alegría, Chatterji et al., 2008). More alarming is that, despite advancements in the treatment of mental disorders, disparities in the receipt of mental health care for Latinos seem to be increasing, particularly in the number of overall mental health visits, visits that resulted in the prescription of psychotropic medications, and psychotherapy visits (Blanco et al., 2007).

Latinos who suffer from common mental disorders (e.g., depression, anxiety disorders) are also less likely than non-Latino whites to receive evidence-based treatments and are likely to discontinue mental health care prematurely. Olfson, Marcus, Tedeschi, and Wan (2006), using national data from the Medical Expenditure Panel Survey, found that, compared with non-Latino whites, Latinos are significantly more likely to discontinue antidepressant medication during the first 30 days of treatment (41.3% vs. 53.8%, respectively), a major risk for relapse. Moreover, nonadherence to common psychotropic medications (e.g., antipsychotics, antidepressants, mood stabilizers) is higher among Latinos compared with non-Hispanic whites, particularly among Latinos who are monolingual Spanish speakers, lack health insurance, and have a lower socioeconomic status (Lanouette, Folsom, Sciolla, & Jeste, 2009).

166

Lastly, Latinos who suffer from a mental disorder in the United States and Puerto Rico tend to rely more often on the general medical sector than on specialty mental health services and use a combination of professional and lay advisors to cope with their disorders (Cabassa et al., 2006). However, the delivery of mental health services in primary care remains suboptimal for many Latinos. Compared with non-Hispanics whites, Latinos in primary care are more likely to receive care from a physician who fails to detect an existing mental health problem (Borowsky et al., 2000) and are less likely to receive either a diagnosis of depression or antidepressant medications (Lewis-Fernández, Das, Alfonso, Weissman, & Olfson, 2005; Sclar, Robison, Skaer, & Galin, 1999). As a result of these inequalities in mental health care, Latinos experience a disproportionate and unnecessary burden of disability associated with mental disorders (USDHHS, 2001).

FACTORS ASSOCIATED WITH MENTAL HEALTH-CARE DISPARITIES IN THE LATINO POPULATION

The determinants of mental health-care disparities in the Latino population are complex and include a confluence of system-, provider-, and patient-level factors. Reducing these inequities in care will require multilevel public health interventions (Blanco et al., 2007) and involve efforts to improve access and quality of care in community mental health clinics, primary care settings, and social service agencies (Blanco et al., 2007). A series of factors that contribute to these disparities in care are discussed below. This is not an exhaustive list of all factors that impact disparities in mental health care, but gives examples of key issues that need to be considered by clinicians, researchers, and policymakers in order to improve the access and quality of mental health care for the Latino population.

Uninsurance

Lack of health insurance is a major barrier that prevents many Latinos from having a regular source of health care and from receiving adequate mental health care. Uninsurance rates are higher in Latinos (36.8%) than among non-Latino whites (14.3%), particularly among recent immigrants and those with limited English proficiency (Alegría, Cao et al., 2006; DeNavas-Walt, Proctor, & Lee, 2006). Similar to other sociodemographic indicators, marked variability in insurance rates exists between Latino groups. According to NLAAS results, Mexicans have the highest rates of uninsurance and lower rates of public insurance than Puerto Ricans and Cubans, whereas Puerto Ricans report the highest rates of public insurance than any other Latino group (Alegría, Cao et al., 2006). Increasing access to affordable health insurance is an essential step to help reduce mental health-care disparities in the Latino population.

Stigma

Stigma is a pervasive barrier that prevents many people from engaging in mental health care (USDHHS, 2001). Stigma refers to a set of negative attitudes and beliefs that motivate

167

individuals to fear, reject, avoid, and discriminate against people with mental illness (Corrigan & Penn, 1999). The internalization of these negative attributes and the desire to avoid being labeled with a mental illness are believed to contribute to individuals' apprehension in seeking and remaining in mental health treatments (Link, Phelan, Bresnahan, Stueve, & Pescosolido, 1999). Although few studies have examined stigma towards mental disorders and treatments in the Latino population, the existing evidence underscores how stigma acts as major barrier for this population. For instance, Whaley (1997), in one of the few studies comparing levels of stigma between racial and ethnic groups using a nationally representative sample, found that, after controlling for sociodemographic variables and level of contact with persons suffering from mental illness, Latinos perceived people with mental illness as more dangerous than whites did. Several studies have also found that Latinos from different groups (e.g., Cubans, Puerto Ricans, Mexicans) tend to view antidepressants as addictive and harmful and prefer psychotherapy over psychotropic medications (Cabassa, Hansen, Palinkas, & Ell, 2008; Cabassa, Lester, & Zayas, 2007; Cabassa & Zayas, 2007; Interian et al., 2010; Nadeem et al., 2007; Pincay & Guarnaccia, 2007). Latinos' apprehensions toward antidepressant medications seem to be tied to fears of dependency, loss of control, and physical harm, and beliefs that these medications make people numb, drugged, and unable to function (Cabassa et al., 2008; Pincay & Guarnaccia, 2007). Many Latinos also relate the use of antidepressant medications to social deficiencies, such as being viewed as *loco* (crazy), weak, or unable to cope with stressors (Cabassa et al., 2008; Interian, Martinez, Guarnaccia, Vega, & Escobar, 2007).

More recent studies have begun to link stigma to the receipt and outcomes of mental health care. Nadeem and colleagues (2007) reported that stigma-related concerns were common among immigrant women (including Latinas) and may account for their underutilization of mental health-care services. Interian, Ang, Gara, Rodriguez, and Vega (2011), in a longitudinal study of Latinos receiving depression care, found that stigma acted as a barrier for depressive-symptom remission. Similarly, Vega, Rodriguez, and Ang (2010) found that, among Latinos (mostly Spanish-speaking) receiving depression treatment in primary care, those who reported high levels of perceived stigma were less likely to be currently taking antidepressants and managing their depression symptoms, less likely to disclose their depression to family and friends, and more likely to have missed appointments. Taken together, the existing evidence indicates that stigma negatively impacts Latinos' use and engagement in mental health services and represents an important determinant of mental health-care disparities that requires future research and clinical attention.

Language Barrier

Effective communication between patients and clinicians is at the heart of mental health care. Limited English proficiency (LEP) is a serious barrier for many Latinos, as it disrupts their ability to communicate effectively in health and mental health-care settings, thus compromising their access and quality of care. It is estimated that more than one in four Latinos live in linguistically isolated households where no one over the age of 14 speaks English "very well" (IOM, 2004). This segment of the Latino population faces considerable barriers in locating basic health information, navigating the health-care system, and following clinicians' recommendations (Lewis-Fernández et al., 2005). People with LEP also report being less satisfied with the consumer–provider relationship, have more difficulty developing rapport with providers, and show less understanding of medical diagnoses. Despite federal requirements stipulated by Executive Order 13166, which requires health-care organizations that receive federal funds to ensure meaningful access to LEP patients in accordance with Title VI of the Civil Rights Act of 1964, disparities in access and quality of care for people with LEP persist (Snowden, Masland, & Guerrero, 2007). The limited availability of trained mental health interpreters and the dearth of bilingual mental health providers throughout the United States further compound this serious language barrier (USDDHS, 2001). Reducing language barriers through the use of professional interpreters and cultural brokers and increasing the number of bilingual mental health providers can help improve access and quality of care to this underserved population.

Poor Patient–Provider Interactions

Related to language barriers is the quality of patient–provider interactions during the medical encounter. Patients' and providers' cultures intersect during the medical encounter, creating a "local moral world," that is, a social space that illuminates cultural relational issues between consumers and providers (Katz & Alegría, 2009, p. 1242). Language, social norms, educational levels, trust, respect, power, and institutional rules shape how information is shared and understood in the medical encounter. Poor patient–provider interaction can result in misdiagnosis, mistreatment, and lack of treatment engagement (Snowden, 2003; Teal & Street, 2009). A major consequence of poor patient–provider interactions is minority patients feeling disrespected and discriminated against because of their race, ethnicity, and/or language abilities. In a nationwide survey, Latinos were more likely than whites to report that racism was a major problem in health care and felt more likely to be mistreated and to receive low-quality health care because of their race/ethnicity (Lillie-Blanton, Brodie, Rowland, Altman, & McIntosh, 2000). Efforts to empower both Latino patients and their providers to improve their communication are essential to improve the quality of care.

Limited Health Literacy

Lastly, health literacy is an important factor that influences the provision and quality of mental health care for Latinos, and yet it has received limited attention in the mental health field. Health literacy is "the degree to which individuals have the capacity to obtain, process, and understand basic health information and services needed to make appropriate health decisions" (IOM, 2004, p. 2). Health literacy levels are lower among older adults, racial and ethnic minorities, people with limited education, the poor, and those with LEP (IOM, 2004). Low health literacy is related to poor management of chronic diseases, lack of basic knowledge about medical conditions and treatments, less understanding and use of preventive services, worse health outcomes, and higher rates of hospitalization and emergency care use, thus resulting in higher medical costs (IOM, 2004). Limited health literacy impacts Latinos' use and engagement in mental health care in several ways. Patients with limited health literacy report major problems in accessing and navigating the medical system, completing medical forms, following medication instructions, and feeling misunderstood by their medical providers (Baker et al., 1996). Moreover, many mental health treatment modalities and patient education materials require high literacy levels, which prevents many people with limited health literacy from engaging and benefiting from these treatments and resources (Lincoln et al., 2008). In all, there is a great need to take into consideration patients' health literacy concerns and to provide written and verbal mental health information at appropriate literacy levels in order to reduce miscommunication and medical errors, while at the same time improving access to, and engagement with, mental health care.

PRACTICE ISSUES: EXAMPLES OF CULTURALLY GROUNDED MENTAL HEALTH TREATMENTS

In response to the persistent mental health-care disparities experienced by Latinos, a growing number of clinicians and researchers have begun to develop and test interventions to improve the mental health of Latinos. In this section, we describe two examples of promising interventions: a collaborative care management program for depression and a disease management intervention.

Culturally Grounded Collaborative Care Management for Depression

Kathleen Ell and colleagues developed the Multifaceted Depression and Diabetes Program (MDDP) for Hispanics to improve the receipt of depression care and depression and diabetes outcomes in low-income Latinos receiving care in safety-net public primary care clinics. MDDP provides an example of an intervention package that blends evidence-based depression treatments and sociocultural adaptations aimed at addressing Latinos' mental health-care disparities (Ell et al., 2009). The core elements of MDDP are based on evidence-based guidelines for treating depression in primary care using a 12-month stepped-care algorithm that includes: (a) antidepressant medication management by the treating physician; (b) problem-solving therapy (Nezu, Nezu, Felgoise, McClure, & Houts, 2003) delivered by bilingual master level social work diabetes depression clinical specialists (DDCSs); (c) monthly DDCS telephone follow-up symptom monitoring, treatment maintenance, and relapse prevention; and (d) service system navigation by an assistant patient navigator (PN).

A unique element of MDDP is that it integrates evidence-based depression treatment guidelines with specific sociocultural adaptations for low-income Hispanics patients to address structural-, provider-, and patient-level barriers to mental health care. Sociocultural adaptations included: use of bilingual DCCSs and PNs; initial psychoeducational sessions to dispel depression treatment misconceptions, reduce stigma, and enhance therapeutic alliance; delivery of patient education materials adapted for people with limited health literacy in both English and Spanish; patient choice of first-line treatment (PST or medication); family participation; flexible delivery of 8–12 weeks of PST, in person or via telephone and tailored for literacy and idiomatic content; linking PST to diabetes and depression self-management; coping with socioeconomic stress; and patient navigation assistance to facilitate access to depression and diabetes treatments and referrals to community resources.

170

MDDP was evaluated in an 18-month randomized controlled trial in two large public safety-net clinics in Los Angeles, California (Ell et al., 2010). Compared with enhanced usual care (e.g., depression screening, patient education), patients randomized to the MDDP treatment reported significant reductions of depressive symptoms, improvements in emotional and physical functional outcomes, and lower burden of diabetes symptoms and pain at 18 months. No significant differences between MDDP and EUC were found in A1C levels, diabetes complications, self-care management, or body mass index. MDDP provides initial evidence that a culturally adapted collaborative care depression management program is feasible and effective in improving the quality of depression care and depression and functional outcomes in low-income Latino populations in safety-net primary care clinics.

A Culturally Modified Disease Management Program

Dr. Alex Kopelowicz culturally modified the medication and symptoms management modules of the UCLA Social and Independent Living Skills Program for Latino patients with schizophrenia and their families (Kopelowicz, 1997; Liberman, 1994). This program is based on social-skills training that utilizes behavioral principles and techniques to enable people with schizophrenia and other serious mental disorders to acquire interpersonal disease management and independent living skills to improve their functioning in the community (Kopelowicz, Liberman, & Zarate, 2006).

The *medication management module* focuses on four skill areas: (1) obtaining information about medications; (2) recognizing side effects; (3) monitoring side effects; and (4) negotiating medication issues with physicians and caregivers. The *symptom management module* helps patients develop skills in the following four areas: (1) how to identify the warning signs of relapse; (2) how to intervene early to prevent relapse once these signs appear; (3) how to cope with persistent psychotic symptoms; and (4) how to avoid drugs and alcohol. Both modules are taught in 90-minute group sessions that meet four times a week for 3 months.

Several cultural modifications of the program were conducted. All training materials, checklists, and monitoring sheets were translated into elementary-school-level universal Spanish using established back-translation methods. Mexican American actors dubbed the translated video scripts over the audio portions of the education videos used throughout the program. Patients' relatives were included as participants to act as coaches and help patients enhance the generalization of skills in their everyday environments by participating in weekly generalization sessions. Ethnic and language match of skills trainers was implemented by using bilingual/bicultural staff indigenous to the outpatient community clinic. Trainers were also instructed to use an informal personal style with patients and relatives to encourage warm interactions and increase treatment retention.

In a 9-month randomized controlled trial of 92 Latino patients with schizophrenia, the family-assisted, culturally adapted social-skills training program outperformed usual outpatient care in several measures: positive- and negative-symptom improvements, skills acquisition and generalization, level of functioning, and decrease rates of rehospitalization (Kopelowicz, Zarate, Gonzalez Smith, Mintz, & Liberman, 2003). No significant differences between the two groups were found in quality of life and caregiver burden. This study shows that a culturally adapted skills training program for Latinos with schizophrenia is effective in improving disease management skills and can be delivered in a community mental health setting serving this population.

Overall, these two examples show how the systematic incorporation of key cultural adaptations into existing evidence-based practices can help improve the quality and outcome of mental health care among Latino adults with disabling psychiatric disorders. Common cultural adaptations used in both interventions included: using trained bilingual clinicians; providing culturally and linguistically appropriate supervision to all clinicians involved; incorporating patients' relatives into the treatment process; adapting materials in both English and Spanish for people with low literacy; delivering the intervention in a trusted community location; and involving Latino researchers and clinicians in the development, delivery, and evaluation of the interventions. Both teams worked closely with the original intervention developers as a way to ensure that the cultural adaptations did not dilute the core active elements of the original interventions. Future work in this area is needed to evaluate the cost-effectiveness of these interventions, and how to transport these promising treatments into real-world community settings.

POLICY ISSUES AND CONSIDERATIONS

In sum, the mental health needs of Latino adults in the United States are shaped by the social, economic, structural, and cultural diversity of this vibrant population. This chapter points to several recommendations to help address the mental health needs and disparities in this diverse population

First, future studies are needed to continue examining the epidemiology of mental disorders in the Latino population and the links between social, cultural, and biological factors, in order to expand our understanding of their mental health needs and inform mental health practice and policies. Longitudinal studies are greatly needed to understand the trajectory of mental disorders across the lifespan and help identify determinants at multiple ecological levels that shape the mental health of Latinos.

Second, state and national data systems are needed to track the persistent mental health care disparities experienced by Latinos in the United States. Departments of Health and Mental Health across the nation need to develop and implement common indicators of mental health-care disparities in both access and quality of care that can provide up-to-date information about at-risk communities. These data can be used to inform the public about inequities in mental health care, thus creating political pressure and support to improve care. They can also be used to inform and monitor system-wide interventions and quality improvement efforts at state and local levels to ameliorate inequities in care. A fundamental step stipulated the IOM (2009) is to standardize the collection of race, ethnicity, and language data across health systems. The collection of data by itself will not stimulate policy and practice changes, but it is a crucial step that sets the stage for subsequent progress in developing a more equitable mental health-care system.

Third, the expansion of affordable health insurance throughout the Latino population is a fundamental step to improve access to mental health care. At both state and local levels, community mental health agencies and advocacy organizations need to disseminate information throughout Latino communities about immigrants' rights to health care and work with local, state, and federal representatives to re-evaluate and reformulate existing policies that restrict immigrant populations' access to health insurance. The implementation of the Patient

Protection and Affordable Care Act provides an opportunity to examine how current reforms of the U.S. health-care system improve access to affordable health insurance in the Latino community and in turn helps address disparities in mental health care.

Fourth, stigma, low health literacy, and misconceptions about mental health treatments are important barriers that prevent many Latinos from accessing and engaging in mental health care. The development, testing, and dissemination of culturally and linguistically appropriate mental health literacy tools and educational campaigns throughout the Latino community are needed to help reduce stigma-related barriers. Current examples provide innovative approaches to address stigma in the Latino community. For instance, Cabassa, Molina, and Baron (2010) used two health behavior theories and the entertainment–education communication strategy (Singhal & Rogers, 1999), as well as findings from several depression studies, to develop a depression *fotonovela* composed of posed photographs and simple text-bubbles to portray a soap opera narrative aimed at increasing knowledge and recognition of depression, reducing stigma, and encouraging those in need to seek mental health care. Similarly, Lopez and colleagues (2009) developed *La CLAve* (The Clue), a 35-minute psychoeducational program for Spanish-speaking people to increase psychosis literacy using popular cultural icons derived from music, art, and videos. Future innovative efforts that use health communication theories and multiple media are needed to disseminate information about mental disorders and their treatments and help reduce stigma.

Lastly, more mental health treatments that link evidence-based practices with culturally and linguistically appropriate strategies are needed to improve the mental health of Latinos. Partnerships between researchers, clinicians, Latino patients and their families, policymakers, and local leaders can serve as an avenue to develop and test the effectiveness of culturally and linguistically appropriate mental health treatments and enhance the transportability and implementation of these treatments throughout Latino communities.

CONCLUSION

As the Latino population continues to grow in numbers and diversity, it is essential, for the health of the entire nation, to understand the mental health needs of this population and translate this knowledge to develop practices and policies aimed at creating a more equitable mental health-care system (Cabassa et al., 2006). To achieve this important goal, multidisciplinary collaborations and community engagement are needed to develop multilevel interventions and policy innovations aimed at reducing disparities in mental health care, decreasing the burden of mental disorders, and ultimately improving the quality of life of the Latino population.

DISCUSSION QUESTIONS

1. What is the immigrant paradox and how does it influence Latinos' mental health?

2. What are the mental health care disparities in the Latino population?

3. What factors impact the use and quality of mental health care in the Latino population?

LEARNING ASSIGNMENT

Role-Play

Assign student pairs to enact a patient–provider medical encounter. Have some pairs act out a *poor patient–provider interaction*. Next, have pairs of students enact *a good patient–provider interaction*. How do they differ? Pay special attention to issues of social norms, educational levels, language, trust, respect, power, and institutional rules that shape how information is shared and understood.

SUGGESTED READINGS

Alegría, M., Canino, G., Shrout, P.E., Woo, M., Duan, N., Vila, D., et al. (2008). Prevalence of mental illness in immigrant and non-immigrant U.S. Latino groups. *American Journal of Psychiatry, 165*(3), 359–369.

Cabassa, L.J., Zayas, L.H., & Hansen, M.C. (2006). Latino adults' access to mental health care: a review of epidemiological studies. *Administration and Policy in Mental Health, 33*(3), 316–330.

Institute of Medicine (2003). *Unequal Treatment: Confronting Racial and Ethnic Disparities in Healthcare.* Washington, DC: National Academies Press.

Lanouette, N.M., Folsom, D.P., Sciolla, A., & Jeste, D.V. (2009). Psychotropic medication nonadherence among United States Latinos: a comprehensive literature review. *Psychiatric Services, 60*(2), 157–174.

Kleinman, A. (1988). *Rethinking Psychiatry: From Cultural Category to Personal Experience.* New York: Free Press.

Lewis-Fernández, R., Das, A.K., Alfonso, C., Weissman, M.M., & Olfson, M. (2005). Depression in US Hispanics: diagnostic and management considerations in family practice. *Journal of the American Board of Family Practice, 18*(4), 282–296.

Lopez, S., & Guarnaccia, P.J. (2000). Cultural psychopathology: Uncovering the social world of mental illness. *Annual Review of Psychology, 51*, 571–598.

Miranda, J., Bernal, G., Lau, A., Kohn, L., Hwang, W., & LaFromboise, T. (2005). State of the science on psychosocial interventions for ethnic minorities. *Annual Review of Clinical Psychology, 1*, 113–142.

U.S. Department of Health and Human Services (2001). *Mental Health: Culture, Race, and Ethnicity: A Supplement to Mental Health: A Report of the Surgeon General.* Bethesda, MD: U.S. Department of Health and Human Services.

Villarruel, F.A., Carlo, G., Grau, J.M., Azmitia, M., Cabrera, N.J., & Chahin, T.J. (2009). *Handbook of U.S. Latino Psychology: Development and Community-Based Perspectives.* Thousand Oaks, CA: Sage.

INTERNET RESOURCES

U.S. Census Bureau: www.census.gov

Pew Hispanic Center: pewhispanic.org

National Council of La Raza: www.nclr.org

Office of the U.S. Surgeon General: www.surgeongeneral.gov

Institute of Medicine: www.iom.edu

National Institute of Mental Health: www.nimh.nih.gov

National Resource Center for Hispanic Mental Health: www.nrchmh.org

REFERENCES

Alarcón, R.D., & Ruiz, P. (2010). Hispanic Americans. In P. Ruiz & A. Primm (Eds.), *Disparities in Psychiatric Care: Clinical and Cross-Cultural Perspectives* (pp. 30–39). Baltimore: Lippincott Williams & Wilkins.

Alegría, M., Canino, G., Shrout, P.E., Woo, M., Duan, N., Vila, D., et al. (2008). Prevalence of mental illness in immigrant and non-immigrant U.S. Latino groups. *American Journal of Psychiatry, 165*(3), 359–369.

Alegría, M., Canino, G., Stinson, F.S., & Grant, B.F. (2006). Nativity and DSM-IV psychiatric disorders among Puerto Ricans, Cuban Americans, and non-Latino Whites in the United States: Results from the National Epidemiologic Survey on Alcohol and Related Conditions. *Journal of Clinical Psychiatry, 67*(1), 56–65.

Alegría, M., Cao, Z., McGuire, T.G., Ojeda, V.D., Sribney, B., Woo, M., et al. (2006). Health insurance coverage for vulnerable populations: Contrasting Asian–Americans and Latinos in the United States. *Inquiry, 43*(3), 231–254.

Alegría, M., Chatterji, P., Wells, K., Cao, Z., Chen, C.N., Takeuchi, D., et al. (2008). Disparity in depression treatment among racial and ethnic minority populations in the United States. *Psychiatric Services, 59*(11), 1264–1272.

Alegría, M., Sribney, W., Woo, M., Torres, M., & Guarnaccia, P. (2007). Looking beyond nativity: The relation of age of immigration, length of residence, and birth cohorts to the risk of onset of psychiatric disorders for Latinos. *Research in Human Development, 4*(1), 19–47.

Alegría, M., & Woo, M. (2009). Conceptual issues in Latino mental health. In F.A. Villarruel, G. Carlo, J.M. Grau, M. Azmitia, N.J. Cabrera, & T.J. Chahin (Eds.), *Handbook of U.S. Latino Psychology: Development and Community-Based Perspectives*. Thousand Oaks, CA: Sage.

Baker, D.W., Parker, R.M., Williams, M.V., Pitkin, K., Parikh, N.S., Coates, W., et al. (1996). The health care experience of patients with low literacy. *Archives of Family Medicine, 5*(6), 329–334.

Blanco, C., Patel, S.R., Liu, L., Jiang, H., Lewis-Fernández, R., Schmidt, A.B., et al. (2007). National trends in ethnic disparities in mental health care. *Medical Care, 45*(11), 1012–1019.

Borowsky, S.J., Rubenstein, L.V., Meredith, L.S., Camp, P., Jackson-Triche, M., & Wells, K.B. (2000). Who is at risk of nondetection of mental health problems in primary care? *Journal of General Internal Medicine, 15*(6), 381–388.

Burnam, M.A., Hough, R.L., Escobar, J.I., Karno, M., Timbers, D.M., Telles, C.A., et al. (1987). Six-month prevalence of specific psychiatric disorders among Mexican Americans and non-Hispanic whites in Los Angeles. *Archives of General Psychiatry, 44*(8), 687–694.

Cabassa, L.J., Hansen, M.C., Palinkas, L.A., & Ell, K. (2008). *Azúcar y nervios*: Explanatory models and treatment experiences of Hispanics with diabetes and depression. *Social Science & Medicine, 66*(12), 2413–2424.

Cabassa, L.J., Lester, R., & Zayas, L.H. (2007). "It's like being in a labyrinth:" Hispanic immigrants' perceptions of depression and attitudes toward treatments. *Journal of Immigrant and Minority Health, 9*, 1–16.

Cabassa, L.J., Molina, G.B., & Baron, M. (2010). Depression *Fotonovela*: Development of a depression literacy tool for Latinos with limited English proficiency. *Health Promotion Practice*.

Cabassa, L.J., & Zayas, L.H. (2007). Latino immigrants' intentions to seek depression care. *American Journal of Orthopsychiatry, 77*(2), 231–242.

Cabassa, L.J., Zayas, L.H., & Hansen, M.C. (2006). Latino adults' access to mental health care: A review of epidemiological studies. *Administration and Policy in Mental Health, 33*(3), 316–330.

Cook, B., Alegría, M., Lin, J.Y., & Guo, J. (2009). Pathways and correlates connecting Latinos' mental health with exposure to the United States. *American Journal of Public Health*, *99*(12), 2247–2254.

Corrigan, P.W., & Penn, D.L. (1999). Lessons from social psychology on discrediting psychiatric stigma. *American Psychology*, *54*(9), 765–776.

DeNavas-Walt, C., Proctor, B.D., & Lee, C.H. (2006). *Current Population Reports: Income, Poverty, and Health Insurance Coverage in the United States: 2005.* Washington, DC: U.S. Census Bureau.

Ell, K., Katon, W., Cabassa, L.J., Xie, B., Lee, P.J., Kapetanovic, S., et al. (2009). Depression and diabetes among low-income Hispanics: Design elements of a socioculturally adapted collaborative care model randomized controlled trial. *International Journal of Psychiatry Medicine*, *39*(2), 113–132.

Ell, K., Katon, W., Xie, B., Lee, P.J., Kapetanovic, S., Guterman, J., et al. (2010). Collaborative care management of major depression among low-income, predominantly Hispanic subjects with diabetes: A randomized controlled trial. *Diabetes Care*, *33*(4), 706–713.

Grant, B.F., Dawson, D.A., & Hasin, D.S. (2001). *The Alcohol Use Disorders and Associated Disabilities Interview Schedule — Version for DSM-IV (AUDADIS-IV).* Bethesda, MD: National Institute on Alcohol Abuse and Alcoholism.

Grant, B.F., Stinson, F.S., Hasin, D.S., Dawson, D.A., Chou, S.P., & Anderson, K. (2004). Immigration and lifetime prevalence of DSM-IV psychiatric disorders among Mexican Americans and non-Hispanic whites in the United States: Results from the National Epidemiologic Survey on Alcohol and Related Conditions. *Archives of General Psychiatry*, *61*(12), 1226–1233.

Guarnaccia, P.J., Martinez, I.E., Alegría, M., Shrout, P.E., Lewis-Fernández, R., & Canino, G. (2007). Assessing diversity among Latinos: Results from the NLAAS. *Hispanic Journal of Behavioral Sciences*, *29*(4), 510–534.

Institute of Medicine (2003). *Unequal Treatment: Confronting Racial and Ethnic Disparities in Healthcare.* Washington, DC. National Academies Press.

Institute of Medicine (2004). *Health Literacy: A Prescription to End Confusion.* Washington, DC. National Academies Press.

Institute of Medicine (2009). *Race, Ethnicity and Language Data: Standardization for Health Care Quality Improvement.* Washington, DC. National Academies Press.

Interian, A., Martinez, I.E., Guarnaccia, P.J., Vega, W.A., & Escobar, J.I. (2007). A qualitative analysis of the perception of stigma among Latinos receiving antidepressants. *Psychiatric Services*, *58*(12), 1591–1594.

Interian, A., Ang, A., Gara, M.A., Link, B.G., Rodriguez, M.A., & Vega, W.A. (2010). Stigma and depression treatment utilization among Latinos: Utility of four stigma measures. *Psychiatric Services*, *61*(4), 373–379.

Interian, A., Ang, A., Gara, M.A., Rodriguez, M.A., & Vega, W.A. (2011). The long-term trajectory of depression among Latinos in primary care and its relationship to depression care disparities. *General Hospital Psychiatry*, *33*(2).

Katz, A.M., & Alegría, M. (2009). The clinical encounter as local moral world: Shifts of assumptions and transformation in relational context. *Social Science and Medicine*, *68*(7), 1238–1246.

Kessler, R.C., & Merikangas, K.R. (2004). The National Comorbidity Survey Replication (NCS-R): Background and aims. *International Journal of Methods in Psychiatric Research*, *13*(2), 60–68.

Kessler, R.C., & Ustun, T.B. (2004). The World Mental Health (WMH) Survey Initiative Version of the World Health Organization (WHO) Composite International Diagnostic Interview (CIDI). *International Journal of Methods in Psychiatric Research*, *13*(2), 93–121.

Kessler, R.C., McGonagle, K.A., Zhao, S., Nelson, C.B., Hughes, M., Eshleman, S., et al. (1994). Lifetime and 12-month prevalence of DSM-III-R psychiatric disorders in the United States. Results from the National Comorbidity Survey. *Archives of General Psychiatry*, *51*(1), 8–19.

Kessler, R.C., Berglund, P., Chiu, W.T., Demler, O., Heeringa, S., Hiripi, E., et al. (2004). The U.S. National Comorbidity Survey Replication (NCS-R): Design and field procedures. *International Journal of Methods in Psychiatric Research*, *13*(2), 69–92.

Kessler, R.C., Berglund, P., Demler, O., Jin, R., Merikangas, K.R., & Walters, E.E. (2005). Lifetime prevalence and age-of-onset distributions of DSM-IV disorders in the National Comorbidity Survey Replication. *Archives of General Psychiatry, 62*(6), 593–602.

Kopelowicz, A. (1997). Social skills training: The moderating influence of culture in the treatment of Latinos with schizophrenia. *Journal of Pscyhopathology and Behavioral Assessment, 19*(2), 101–108.

Kopelowicz, A., Liberman, R.P., & Zarate, R. (2006). Recent advances in social skills training for schizophrenia. *Schizophrenia Bulletin, 32*(Suppl. 1), S12–23.

Kopelowicz, A., Zarate, R., Gonzalez Smith, V., Mintz, J., & Liberman, R.P. (2003). Disease management in Latinos with schizophrenia: A family-assisted, skills training approach. *Schizophrenia Bulletin, 29*(2), 211–227.

Lanouette, N.M., Folsom, D.P., Sciolla, A., & Jeste, D.V. (2009). Psychotropic medication nonadherence among United States Latinos: A comprehensive literature review. *Psychiatric Services, 60*(2), 157–174.

Lewis-Fernández, R., Das, A.K., Alfonso, C., Weissman, M.M., & Olfson, M. (2005). Depression in US Hispanics: Diagnostic and management considerations in family practice. *Journal of the American Board of Family Practice, 18*(4), 282–296.

Liberman, R.P. (1994). Psychosocial treatments for schizophrenia. *Psychiatry, 57*(2), 104–114.

Lillie-Blanton, M., Brodie, M., Rowland, D., Altman, D., & McIntosh, M. (2000). Race, ethnicity, and the health care system: Public perceptions and experiences. *Medical Care Research and Review, 57*(Suppl. 1), 218–235.

Lincoln, A., Espejo, D., Johnson, P., Paasche-Orlow, M., Speckman, J.L., Webber, T.L., et al. (2008). Limited literacy and psychiatric disorders among users of an urban safety-net hospital's mental health outpatient clinic. *Journal of Nervous and Mental Disease, 196*(9), 687–693.

Link, B.G., Phelan, J.C., Bresnahan, M., Stueve, A., & Pescosolido, B.A. (1999). Public conceptions of mental illness: Labels, causes, dangerousness, and social distance. *American Journal of Public Health, 89*(9), 1328–1333.

Lopez, S.R., Lara Mdel, C., Kopelowicz, A., Solano, S., Foncerrada, H., & Aguilera, A. (2009). La CLAve to increase psychosis literacy of Spanish-speaking community residents and family caregivers. *Journal of Consulting and Clinical Psychology, 77*(4), 763–774.

Nadeem, E., Lange, J.M., Edge, D., Fongwa, M., Belin, T., & Miranda, J. (2007). Does stigma keep poor young immigrant and U.S.-born black and Latina women from seeking mental health care? *Psychiatric Services, 58*(12), 1547–1554.

Nezu, A.M., Nezu, C.M., Felgoise, S.H., McClure, K.S., & Houts, P.S. (2003). Project Genesis: Assessing the efficacy of problem-solving therapy for distressed adult cancer patients. *Journal of Consulting and Clinical Psychology, 71*(6), 1036–1048.

Olfson, M., Marcus, S.C., Tedeschi, M., & Wan, G.J. (2006). Continuity of antidepressant treatment for adults with depression in the United States. *American Journal of Psychiatry, 163*(1), 101–108.

Ortega, A.N., Rosenheck, R., Alegría, M., & Desai, R.A. (2000). Acculturation and the lifetime risk of psychiatric and substance use disorders among Hispanics. *Journal of Nervous and Mental Disease, 188*(11), 728–735.

Passel, J.S., & Cohn, D. (2008). *U.S. Population Predictions: 2005–2050.* Washington, DC: Pew Research Center.

Pincay, I.E.M., & Guarnaccia, P.J. (2007). "Its's like going through an earthquake": Anthropological perspectives on depression among Latino immigrants. *Journal of Immigrant and Minority Health, 9*, 17–28.

Sclar, D.A., Robison, L.M., Skaer, T.L., & Galin, R.S. (1999). Ethnicity and the prescribing of antidepressant pharmacotherapy: 1992–1995. *Harvard Review of Psychiatry, 7*(1), 29–36.

Sentell, T., Shumway, M., & Snowden, L. (2007). Access to mental health treatment by English language proficiency and race/ethnicity. *Journal of General Internal Medicine, 22*(Suppl. 2), 289–293.

Singhal, A., & Rogers, E. (1999). *Entertainment-Education: A Communication Strategy for Social Change.* Mahwah, NJ: Lawrence Erlbaum.

177

Snowden, L.R. (2003). Bias in mental health assessment and intervention: Theory and evidence. *American Journal of Public Health, 93*(2), 239–243.

Snowden, L.R., Masland, M., & Guerrero, R. (2007). Federal civil rights policy and mental health treatment access for persons with limited English proficiency. *American Psychologist, 62*(2), 109–117.

Teal, C.R., & Street, R.L. (2009). Critical elements of culturally competent communication in the medical encounter: A review and model. *Social Science and Medicine, 68*(3), 533–543.

U.S. Department of Health and Human Services (2001). *Mental Health: Culture, Race, and Ethnicity: A Supplement to Mental Health: A Report of the Surgeon General.* Bethesda, MD: U.S. Department of Health and Human Services.

U.S. Census Bureau (2007). *The American Community: Hispanics: 2004.* Washington, DC: U.S. Department of Commerce.

Vega, W.A., Rodriguez, M.A., & Ang, A. (2010). Addressing stigma of depression in Latino primary care patients. *General Hospital Psychiatry, 32*(2), 182–191.

Villarruel, F.A., Carlo, G., Grau, J.M., Azmitia, M., Cabrera, N.J., & Chahin, T.J. (2009). *Handbook of U.S. Latino Psychology: Development and Community-Based Perspectives.* Thousand Oaks, CA: Sage.

Whaley, A.L. (1997). Ethnic and racial differences in perceptions of dangerousness of persons with mental illness. *Psychiatric Services, 48*(10), 1328–1330.

Chapter 12

Community Mental Health

Cross-Cultural Mental Health Response in Disasters

April Naturale

INTRODUCTION

Humanitarian, faith-based and social services aid organizations provide global responses to community mental health needs in the aftermath of disasters and traumatic events. Much of this work utilizes mental health interventions that are based on Western constructs of mental health problems, neglects to adapt services to the local culture (Betancourt et al., 2008), and points to the need for culturally appropriate assessment and treatment in disaster services (Bass, Bolton, & Murray, 2007). The current decade has brought growing attention to the issue of cross-cultural adaptation of community mental health interventions, with a focus on those affected by the trauma of war and disasters. An increasing body of evidence is now informing the field on community-based initiatives, training efforts, research, and outcomes in this area.

FIRST, DO NO HARM

In the aftermath of several large-scale disasters and subsequent incidents of mass violence in the past decade (for example, Hurricane Katrina in the United States and the tsunami in Southeastern Asia), the problem of inappropriate community mental health responses has been glaringly noted. Some international aid organizations and many well-meaning individuals provide emergency and disaster mental health interventions, yet lack the necessary understanding of how different cultures perceive, identify, and respond to mental health issues. Foreign mental health response workers often enter a post-disaster environment with little or no local-language skills. Many have no understanding of the culture in which they begin to apply Western-based assessment processes, crisis intervention, and other community mental health supports, nor understand how their lack of information may lead them actually to cause harm to those they are, instead, trying to help.

In a post-disaster setting, communities are highly vulnerable to foreign-based mental health workers' imposing their own values and ideas, especially regarding the needs of the community. In addition, those who are most affected tend to be historically underserved populations, living in poverty and lacking basic mental health services. Thus, interventions in post-disaster settings must address fundamental issues of social justice. This is exemplified by a post-earthquake situation in Haiti, where faith-based aid workers attempted to move over 33 children out of the country without the proper authority and, possibly, without informed consent of the parents (Pavia, 2010). Removing these children from their home in such a manner was inappropriate. Attempting placement in an orphanage away from their families, outside of their native country, did not address the real social issue, which was poverty. Although parental concern in the wake of the physical and economic devastation of the disaster may have moved some of these parents to allow their children to be taken away from them, inadequate assessment and hasty action by seemingly well-intentioned outsiders had the potential to cause irreparable harm.

RESILIENCY BUILDING, CAPACITY BUILDING, AND SUSTAINABILITY

The ecological perspective incorporates cross-cultural services as a means to inform community mental health interventions. This perspective includes the biological health, ethnic, social and familial (both historical and current), environmental, emotional functioning, spiritual and religious beliefs, financial and political structures, as well as other variables of those we aim to serve. Diagnosis and treatment applications that have been deemed the most appropriate because they are evidence based, yet lack any integration of the local community's cultural aspects or input, are ineffective (Sphere Project, 2004).

The overall goals of resiliency building, capacity building, and sustainability should be based on the local community members' perceptions of health, mental health, mental illness, and wellness. This is our challenge, not only in humanitarian aid work in general, but most especially in community mental health responses to natural disasters, armed conflict, and other emergencies.

Entering a disaster or emergency situation and providing various types of aid without comprehensive planning that involves local leaders and includes steps designed to enable the community to sustain the supports provided does not work (Sphere Project, 2004). This issue itself is indeed now at the heart of controversy over aid to Africa in general (Flintoff, 2007). There, governments and their people have continued to be dependent on outside aid, to the point where $1 trillion of support over the past 60 years has not increased the per capita income of most people on the continent, a place where twice the number of people now live on less money than they did in the 1970s (Dambisa & Ferguson, 2009).

OVERVIEW OF COMMUNITY MENTAL HEALTH ISSUES IN DISASTERS

There are an ever-increasing number of natural disasters and human-made, large-scale, traumatic events across the globe. The United Nations Under-Secretary-General for Humanitarian Affairs and Emergency Relief Coordinator, John Holmes, reported that this past decade has seen an increase in emergency situations worldwide (Holmes, 2008). These include not only natural events, such as earthquakes and resulting tsunamis, but flooding as a result of hurricanes and the effects of global warming. Conflicts between countries and cultures have existed as far back as can be recorded, and, although the occurrence of conflicts has not changed, there is an increase in the size and scope of injuries and damage due to the sophistication, as well as the expanded use, of arms. These events often require large-scale and long-term disaster response interventions that include not only addressing the physical damage and destruction, but also emotional distress, which is the second largest effect of traumatic events on both individuals and communities (Center for Mental Health Services, 2001). Mental health interventions for post-disaster communities are a necessary component of emergency response work and are generally integrated as part of the delivery of overall health and psychosocial support services.

In the early phases, psychosocial services to trauma-affected communities focus on the delivery of crisis intervention, monitoring and assessment (identifying those who may be suffering from more severe emotional reactions), psychoeducation, skills training, and case management. In the intermediate and longer-term response phases, services are primarily delivered in a group format to strengthen bonds and increase opportunities for community building. This approach empowers those affected and enhances the sustainability of activities that support recovery.

This chapter will briefly describe several international guides currently accepted as best practice in the delivery of community mental health psychosocial interventions in cross-cultural settings. These guides inform emergency mental health workers who are aiding those affected by emergencies and traumatic events by providing recommendations for the development of community-based programs, individual interventions, and key concepts for training. Best practice guides include the Sphere Project (Sphere Project, 2004), the Inter-Agency Standing Committee's (IASC) *Guidelines on Mental Health and Psychosocial Support in Emergency Settings* (Inter-Agency Standing Committee, 2007), the Psychological First Aid (PFA) *Field Operations Guide* (National Child Traumatic Stress Network & National Center for PTSD, 2005), and the International Society for Traumatic Stress Studies' (ISTSS) "Guidelines for International Training in Mental Health and Psychosocial Interventions for Trauma Exposed Populations in Clinical and Community Settings" (Weine et al., 2002). The purpose of these resources is to provide the best available guidance in the absence of empirical evidence. This is accomplished by incorporating information from related research, theory, and practice, as well as expert consensus to present an "evidence-informed" approach that may be helpful and above all, "does no harm" (Anderson, 1999; Figley, 1995; National Child Traumatic Stress Network & National Center for PTSD, 2005).

HISTORICAL BACKGROUND

Emergency mental health assistance has its roots in the agency most associated with the delivery of emergency assistance to communities affected by disasters and war: the Red Cross. The Red Cross began as the International Committee for Relief to the Wounded, in Geneva in 1863, founded by a small group of men intending to provide neutral humanitarian relief in the form of medical care, water, food, and other basic needs to prisoners of war and combatants. After World War I, the League of Red Cross Societies built a volunteer base of millions with a large body of expertise. They formed a cooperative group of agencies that continued to grow in number and in reach. As of 1991, these collective organizations are known as the

International Federation of Red Cross and Red Crescent Societies (International Federation of Red Cross and Red Cresent Societies, 2010).

In the United States, on May 21, 1881, Clara Barton and a circle of acquaintances founded the American Red Cross (ARC) in Washington, DC (American Red Cross, 2010). Since that time, the ARC has been the nation's premier emergency response organization. The ARC has expanded its services over the years, always with the aim of preventing and relieving suffering, as part of a worldwide movement that offers neutral humanitarian care to the victims of war. The American Red Cross further distinguishes itself by aiding victims of devastating natural disasters. In addition to providing medical aid, water, and safety, support and relief came in the form of what the ARC describes as a "compassionate presence" to those in need.

Disaster mental health services were not initially identified as such in the early development of emergency and disaster response programs. Over time, they have slowly become recognized as a distinctive service, but still usually fall under the parameters of "health services" in most emergency response programs. Disaster mental health service providers need to be aware of numerous challenges in service provision. These include the following:

- Most individuals and communities prefer to be self-reliant, and, as a result, most individuals will refuse help even when in need, although they are often eager to suggest a neighbor or friend who might benefit from assistance.
- Mental health services are still highly stigmatized. They are most often associated with serious and persistent mental illnesses such as schizophrenia and bipolar disorders, which many assume require long-term institutionalization and an ultimate rejection by the community. Stigma is pervasive in some professions such as the rescue/recovery industry and in the military, where acknowledging any level of emotional distress can result in loss of employment or assignment.
- Disaster mental health services are not often understood as a unique type of service, different from traditional mental health counseling.
- Most disaster and trauma survivors will recover naturally, utilizing the coping skills they have used in other stressful times and the support of family and friends.

In light of the above, why do we provide disaster community mental health services at all? The answer is because the psychological effect of traumatic events can be severe, and, despite difficulties in delivering services, we have an obligation to assess the scope and severity of the emotional toll of an event on survivors and communities. Disaster mental health interventions can assist those who may be experiencing mild or moderate distress to understand what is happening to them; to validate their experiences; to normalize what may feel like abnormal responses; to mitigate the development of more serious distress symptoms; and to move the recovery process forward (Norris, Friedman, & Watson, 2002). Additionally, Norris and Kaniasty (1996) tell us that people who receive support in times of emergency and trauma fare better than those who are isolated or feel marginalized or neglected.

CURRENT GUIDELINES

As mentioned earlier in this chapter, there are several informational documents that outline international emergency mental health response programs for individuals and communities.

These guidelines are described briefly here for the purposes of this chapter, but a thorough review of each is highly recommended.

The Sphere Project: The Humanitarian Charter and Minimum Standards in Disaster Response Handbook

The Sphere Project is the earliest program that defines standards for disaster response work incorporating community mental health concerns into the larger structure. This initiative was launched in 1997 by a group of humanitarian non-governmental organizations and the Red Cross and Red Crescent movement, who developed the Humanitarian Charter and identified Minimum Standards to be followed in disaster assistance programs. The Humanitarian Charter and the Minimum Standards create an operational framework for accountability in disaster assistance efforts and make up the Sphere handbook (2004). Within the five key areas (water supply and sanitation, nutrition, food aid, shelter, and health services), mental health falls under health services, referring to "direct" impacts such as injury and psychological trauma (p. 254). One of the primary goals of a humanitarian response to a disaster that addresses the psychological consequences is "the promotion of return to normalcy." Provision of basic needs such as safety, food, and water, along with mental health supports, can help to accomplish this goal.

The Charter identifies the core principles of humanitarian action, including the right of the population affected by a disaster (including armed conflict) to protection and assistance, reasserting the right of disaster-affected populations to life with dignity. This document stresses the need for a cultural adaptation process, describing as essential the participation of these communities in the design, implementation, monitoring, and evaluation of health services. It further recommends that health-care responders specifically seek women's views as a means of ensuring that services are equitable, appropriate, and accessible. Women contribute to an understanding of cultural factors and "should therefore actively participate in the planning and implementation of health care services from the outset" (p. 257). The Handbook indicates that "building local capacity together with affected populations is probably the most effective means of helping communities to recover from disasters and to prepare them for future disasters" (p. 29). Equally important is ensuring that local health facilities are supported and strengthened by responding agencies. Local health workers should be supported and integrated into health-service delivery, with the expectation that health services incorporate or adapt the existing national standards and guidelines of the disaster-affected or host country.

The Inter-Agency Standing Committee's *Guidelines on Mental Health and Psychosocial Support in Emergency Settings*

The IASC *Guidelines on Mental Health and Psychosocial Support in Emergency Settings* (2007) provide a framework for the coordination of mental health response agencies delivering services and identifies useful practices, as well as potentially harmful ones. The IASC Guidelines are an extraordinarily rich resource for all agency managers, policy developers, and coordinating councils involved in humanitarian response work, as well as individual mental health responders.

The key actions in the IASC Guidelines that apply to community mental health interventions are found in Section 5.1 and include detailed recommendations addressing six key areas:

- coordinating efforts to mobilize the community;
- assessing the political, social, and security environment at the earliest possible stage;
- talking with a variety of key informants through formal and informal groups, learning how local people are organizing and how different agencies can participate in the relief effort;
- facilitating the participation of those who are marginalized;
- establishing safe and sufficient spaces early on to support planning discussions; and
- sharing and disseminating information and promoting the community-mobilizing process.

These guidelines were developed for use in non-Western, low- and middle-income countries. However, the general approach and overall philosophy are also applicable to the low- and middle-income socioeconomic areas of most countries. Therefore, the focus on how to address key concepts for engaging local-community members using an appropriate, culturally sensitive, and empowering approach may be useful globally.

The *Psychological First Aid: Field Operations Guide*

The *Psychological First Aid* [PFA] *Field Operations Guide* (National Child Traumatic Stress Network & National Center for PTSD, 2005) is a consensus-driven and "evidence-informed" manual that provides a thorough description of those immediate response actions that are most likely to aid post-disaster survivors by reducing distress and, as importantly, "do no harm." This manual provides the response community with a consensus on best practices for the immediate-phase mental health response to disasters. The immediate phase is generally defined as the first 2–4 weeks post-incident. The core actions of the PFA are:

- contact and engagement;
- safety and comfort;
- stabilization;
- information gathering: current needs and concerns;
- practical assistance;
- connection with social supports;
- information on coping and linkage with collaborative services.

The PFA stresses the need to tailor one's approaches to the affected community in a culturally appropriate manner and is gaining international attention for use in cross-cultural settings.

Guidelines for International Training in Mental Health and Psychosocial Interventions for Trauma Exposed Populations in Clinical and Community Settings

The ISTSS convened a task force on international psychosocial training, drawing upon a core group of its membership with extensive field experience. As a result, it has presented the traumatic stress field with an evidence-informed, consensus document, "Guidelines for International Training in Mental Health and Psychosocial Interventions for Trauma Exposed Populations in Clinical and Community Settings" (Weine et al., 2002). These guidelines highlight the key areas to address in order to achieve practical, effective, and culturally competent psychosocial training internationally. The guidelines are broken into values, contextual challenges, core curriculum, and monitoring/evaluation.

COMPREHENSIVE AND INCLUSIVE PLANNING

Without inclusive, comprehensive preparation and planning, local community leaders may not recognize how any foreign-based interventions may be of assistance to their community. Despite high needs, the community may erroneously determine that the supports offered will not be effective and may hesitate or refuse to work with international assistance agencies in the current situation or in the future. Additionally, without comprehensive planning, those involved in the implementation of services may be unable to successfully carry out or support the community mental health response process. Such failure has the potential to cause harm, as it may create a false sense of incompetence or even decrease the confidence that the community had in their recovery potential prior to the arrival of aid organizations.

Comprehensive preparation and planning activities for community psychosocial mental health emergency response include the following:

- identification of those who may benefit from psychosocial services—a process of assessment as well as monitoring and surveillance of the community members involved in all activities;
- a strategy as to how to conduct successful outreach, identifying special populations in need and properly referring those with more extensive, or alternate, related needs;
- how properly to coordinate the delivery of services;
- how to organize and coordinate community group meetings, self-help groups, peer supervision groups, and training;
- knowledge and skills to manage group dynamics;
- knowledge and skills necessary to coordinate or conduct an evaluation.

The complexity of implementing comprehensive programs may discourage or limit culturally appropriate psychosocial work as part of overall community trauma response planning. These challenges must be addressed prior to starting the work (Young, Ruzek, Wong, Salzer, & Naturale, 2006).

PRACTICE CONSIDERATIONS

Uganda During a Long-Term, Post-Conflict Community Mental Health Response Effort

Background

The Republic of Uganda is 93,000 square miles, about the size of the state of Oregon in the United States. Like much of central Africa, Uganda was originally a land of farmers and cattle herders. About 70% of the country is woodlands and grassland. In the 1830s, slave traders invaded the area, and, by the 1860s, British explorers and abolitionists became interested in the region as they searched for the source of the Nile. In 1962, Uganda was granted independence from Britain. Although Uganda was a republic, tribally based local kingdoms retained a strong role in government.

In 1966, Uganda's Prime Minister Milton Obote assumed all governmental powers and abolished the traditional kingdoms. Idi Amin Dada overthrew Obote in 1971 and gave himself absolute power, beginning 8 years of social decline and massive human rights violations aimed primarily at the Acholi and Langi ethnic groups. Amin's henchmen murdered between 100,000 and 300,000 Ugandans. Uganda gained international attention in 1976, when Amin took Israeli hostages in Entebbe (Amnesty International, 1978; International Commission of Jurists, 1977).

The atrocities of Amin's reign were finally brought to light and, in 1979, he was forced out of the country. Disputes over the powers of the presidency continued, and, by May of 1980, Uganda was ruled by a military commission. Obote was returned to power as president. Human rights violations by the Obote's security forces were said to be the worst in the world during the next 5 years (United States Department of State, 2009). In 1985, Yowari Museveni's National Resistance Army took the capital, Kampala. From 1986 to 2003, more than 100,000 people of the Acholi region in northern Uganda were killed, an estimated 1.5 million were displaced, and over 20,000 children were abducted by armed rebel groups trying to destabilize the state (United States Department of State, 2009). After regaining control, President Museveni put an end to human rights abuses and is promoting economic reforms and increased freedoms. Most displaced Ugandans have returned. However, many difficulties exist in relation to reclaiming and resettling land, rebuilding homes, and reestablishing relationships with those who remained.

Although Westerners created the legal borders for the country, the inhabitants of the area consider many members of tribes from nearby Sudan, Kenya, and the Democratic Republic of the Congo as family and, thus, speak the many languages of their neighbors. It is not unusual to meet a Ugandan man or woman who speaks six to eight local languages. The country has a 70% literacy rate through primary school. Eighty-five percent of the people in Uganda are Christian, and 12% are Muslim. Traditional rituals and religious customs from a time prior to the conversion of so many Ugandans by Christian missionaries can be witnessed in most of the small villages throughout the countryside.

Uganda remains a primarily rural, agricultural society, growing coffee, tea, sugar cane, and flowers to sell, as well as bananas, corn, cassava, potatoes, and millet for consumption. The temperature is quite moderate owing to softly rolling hills. Rainfall is regular. Uganda has many natural resources, but continuous conflict has resulted in the country being one of the poorest and least developed in the world. In addition, many non-governmental organizations and other psychosocial service delivery agencies are working in Uganda to provide humanitarian assistance and education and to promote stronger links with other countries (United States Department of State, 2009).

A Community Mental Health Initiative

A large-scale community emergency response education and training mental health program is being conducted in the Tesso region of Uganda. Activities are structured by the International

Trauma Studies program at Columbia University, USA, and the Transcultural Psychosocial Organization (TPO) located in the Ugandan capital city of Kampala. This psychosocial training of trainers (TOT) designs and implements culturally adapted education and training sessions in small group settings in various villages throughout the region. The TOT provides a thorough integration of the IASC and ISTSS guidelines, with significant attention to culture.

The contextual challenges of cross-cultural training are addressed by the inclusion of local stakeholders at a meaningful level. Local leaders are involved in every aspect of the project. This allows for consultation and feedback to address concerns with a sense of mutuality. Village leaders promote individuals from within their community to participate in training exercises with the international mental health professionals, with the goal of becoming psychosocial workers themselves. Representatives from Western-based humanitarian aid organizations, mostly mental health professionals, are paired together, and the training responsibilities are equally shared.

While training activities are conducted, variations in the community norms are addressed by establishing rules in the group setting with mutual agreement. This type of group training allows for a natural integration of traditional rituals. The villagers ask questions, make comments, and talk openly about how they might apply the newly learned concepts to their daily lives.

The group training also encourages the members to speak among themselves and to help each other. Often during these times, thoughtful conversation emerges with regard to the relationship between traditional, ritual healings and modern or Western health-care practices. Western trainers remain observers, promoting "teaching moments" for the local leaders and others from within the community to establish themselves as the experts. In one circumstance, when an elderly "herbalist" healer announced that the traditional mix of herbs could heal fetal alcohol syndrome (FAS), his peers confronted him quite harshly. A local leader took control and he not only challenged the healer by asking if the traditional herbs cured AIDS, but he suggested the healer consider the new information that was being taught about FAS in the training.

Attending to the short- and long-term needs of the community is addressed by having local Ugandans become the new trainers. After initial training activities are completed, the TPO supervisors and new trainers from the Tesso region meet regularly with villagers. The Ugandan trainers continue to help these leaders in developing the process by which the most salient issues for the different villages are identified (Bolton & Tang, 2004). TPO provides group supervision and case conferencing for all the local trainers, instructing them on how to work with difficult group members and also how to refer people with serious emotional distress to appropriate resources. They also work with the program evaluators coordinating group meetings to determine the outcomes of the training activities. This model of training in community mental health emergency response exemplifies the community capacity building and sustainability that psychosocial training programs strive to achieve.

SUCCESSES IN CROSS-CULTURAL COMMUNITY MENTAL HEALTH INTERVENTIONS

The most successful aspect of community mental health interventions focuses on bringing together groups of community members to receive the same information and to process this information together, with international and local guidance. The imparting of psychoeducational material accomplishes the goals of:

- normalizing distress responses;
- decreasing stigma related to emotional distress in a post-trauma setting;
- increasing the local mental health providers' sense of competence, allowing them to apply information, as opposed to formal interventions, as a useful tool to address distress symptoms.

Involving local leaders in the development and implementation of trainings accomplishes the goals of:

- integrating culturally appropriate descriptions and local terms for emotional distress;
- increasing buy-in from the local community, which sees its leaders as the trusted sources of information and instruction, establishing these leaders as the experts;
- adapting examples, coping recommendations, and resources to a particular community;
- building capacity for the community to continue the mental health intervention, expanding the learning through the cascade effect, where those trained in providing interventions train others, provide supervision, or, at a minimum, continue to provide the trainings themselves;
- increasing the potential for sustainability when the community members recognize positive outcomes and develop ways to continue utilizing the interventions.

In settings where travel for community members is impossible, or in situations where cost is prohibitive, communities are more apt to accept responders coming to them directly and meeting informally. In unsafe situations, responders may need to meet with members of the community individually in homes, rather than in large groups in public places, etc.

CHALLENGES AND RECOMMENDATIONS IN IMPLEMENTING CROSS-CULTURAL TRAININGS

Assessing Needs

Organizations providing mental health support are not always prepared to conduct a thorough needs assessment, owing to a lack of time or resources. Therefore, consideration of partnering with another agency that can provide needs assessment data is essential. Such data are necessary in order to determine what type of information and support might help spur recovery, rather than foster unrealistic expectations or dependency.

Existing Infrastructure and Local Resources

Response efforts may fail when a community's needs are so basic that the targeted population would not benefit from anything other than survival supports, such as clothing, blankets, food, water, and medication. An example of this problem can be seen in post-conflict Sierra Leone, a country still trying to recover from a brutal war 10 years later. There, significant numbers of locals trained in psychosocial service delivery are without employment or any means to support their families. In addition, there are minimal community mental health services available to refer those with more serious mental health concerns, such as schizophrenia or chronic substance abuse.

A number of small, faith-based and other non-governmental organizations based there still rely on severe movement restriction, which they describe as a way of "protecting" the community from those with mental illness and substance abuse, rather than actively or effectively treating the symptoms of the patients. At several of these mental health service organizations, as well as the only government-run psychiatric hospital in the entire country, patients are literally chained to walls, floors, and bedposts for long periods of time. One patient cried to this writer during a visit, stating that he had not had any real food for two weeks. The attendant who was my guide indicated that the patient's statement was quite likely true, as the facility had run out of food several weeks earlier, and this patient had no family who lived close enough to bring him meals.

Several of the humanitarian aid organizations offering psychosocial services there have returned to the planning table in an effort to determine how to increase local capacity to assist those with substance abuse and serious mental illnesses. Additionally, these agencies are looking at how to assist in providing basic education, labor skills, and employment opportunities. All mental health planning efforts are focused on how these basic needs can be met, before comprehensive mental health services can even be designed.

Language and Translation Skills

Translation continues to be the primary challenge in developing and delivering cross-cultural training, regardless of the accessibility to local translators, liaisons, or language experts. The numerous and layered variations in the meaning of different words to identify the simplest of emotional and psychological concepts, delivered with a variety of facial expressions, hand motions, body positions, voice tone, and volume, ensure that errors will inevitably occur. A good example of this was seen in Yogyakarta, Indonesia, where this writer facilitated extensive translation services for training, only to find that, in the field, the young, local psychosocial workers utilize a very different language when speaking to the elderly than the general adult population. An entirely different translation was necessary, requiring extensive time and consultation, to properly speak with older adults in that community.

We have a tendency to underestimate the amount of time required to translate, not only exact words, but even more so, the meaning of concepts that have no distinct word or phrase in some languages. This is especially true when trying to identify a mental health disorder, a distress syndrome, or emotional issues in general. Responders need to allow adequate time to identify how a particular culture perceives health, mental health, and mental illness, as well as how to refer to them in a manner that is understandable to the local community. The process of freelisting, where open-ended conversation is used to identify the general life-challenging issues of the target population without assumption or use of Western terminology, has shown validity (Bass, Bolton, & Murray, 2007).

189

Self-Efficacy

The strength of a community resides in the ability of its members to care for themselves without external assistance, preserving dignity, pride, and opportunities for self-efficacy. Self-efficacy should be promoted and not diminished by the assumption that people are "better off" when given resources without an opportunity for reciprocity, even if it comes at a much later time in the response. This can be accomplished best by working with families and other natural groupings to strengthen their abilities to care for themselves and those within their immediate social circle (Gitterman, 2001).

POLICY ISSUES AND CONSIDERATIONS

Most humanitarian aid organizations have strict screening, credentialing, and training policies that ensure staff are capable as well as ethical in their interactions internationally. It is often professionals acting independently or with service providers unfamiliar with cross-cultural work who enter into the field in a manner that has the potential to cause harm, despite good intentions. In an effort to meet the moral obligations of providing culturally appropriate services and ensuring that no harm is done, the field needs to expand policies that protect international communities from well-meaning, but often inept, community mental health providers.

Mandating that mental health professionals adhere to the same practices and policies that are required in order to maintain their licensure or certification from their original credentialing agent may be one policy consideration. If the country that grants them these privileges requires that the same ethical and practice considerations are extended to any point of service delivery, then the quality of services may be improved, or at least the potential for causing harm mitigated. Properly adapted practices should be rigorously implemented, despite the lack of guidelines or regulations in the country receiving the services.

SUMMARY

The field of community mental health is becoming increasingly important internationally, as we learn more about implementing cross-cultural interventions for those affected by the trauma of disasters, terrorism, and armed conflict. We have a moral obligation to assist those in need during emergencies and to promote evaluation and research that will inform humanitarian and social aid professionals as to the types of community mental health intervention that ensure no harm and provide effective, positive outcomes for the communities they serve. The global efforts to improve and expand the quality of these programs have increased over the past decade. The community mental health field must continue to require the appropriate planning, preparation, training, and implementation of services to trauma-affected populations in cross-cultural situations.

DISCUSSION QUESTIONS

1. What do you think about the Western-based perspective of mental health and mental illness (e.g., diagnosis, treatment, and research)? Do you feel that the Western perspective is "right" or "best"? And, based on that perspective, what is the best way to assist other cultures that don't agree with that perspective to determine what are effective interventions?

2. Identify specific cultural beliefs, attitudes towards gender, cleansing and/or sexual rites/rituals, and other behaviors (e.g., genital mutilation) that you feel are against human rights. Discuss how to address such issues from a community mental health point of view.

3. Do these human rights issues (especially those that are clearly violations) present a responsibility for developed countries to intervene on a community mental health level, or do you consider such interventions an intrusion?

LEARNING ASSIGNMENT

Interview an immigrant family member, friend, or neighbor. Work with a small group to develop a list of questions in preparation for the interview. What questions would inform about the person's home culture in terms of their perception of health, mental health, mental illness, and treatment. What questions would help identify how they define "family" and "community."

SUGGESTED READINGS

Beah, I. (2007). *A Long Way Gone: Memoirs of a Boy Soldier*. New York: Farrar, Strasum and Groux.

Chaskin, R.J., Brown, P., Venkatesh, S., Vidal, A., and De Gruyter, A. (2001). *Building Community Capacity*.

Foa, E.B., Keane, T.M., and Friedman, M.J. (Eds.) (2000). *Effective Treatments for PTSD*. New York: The Guilford Press.

Danieli, Y., Brom, D., and Sills, J. (Eds.) (2005). *The Trauma of Terrorism*. New York: The Haworth Press.

Danieli, Y., and Dingman, R.L. (Eds.) (2005) *On the Ground after September 11: Mental Health Responses and Practical Knowledge Gained*. New York: The Haworth Press.

Meredith, M. (2005). *The Fate of Africa: A History of Fifty Years of Independence*. New York: Public Affairs.

Mitchell, J.T., and Resnik, H.L.P. (1981). *Emergency Response to Crisis*. Prentice Hall International.

Raphael, B. (1986). *When Disaster Strikes*. New York: Basic Books.

Raphael, B., and Wilson, J. (2000). *Psychological Debriefing*. Cambridge, UK: Cambridge University Press.

Ritchie, E.C., Watson, P., and Friedman, M.J. (Eds.) (2006). *Interventions Following Mass Violence and Disasters*. New York: The Guilford Press.

INTERNET RESOURCES

Inter Agency Standing Committee Guidelines: www.who.int/hac/network/interagency/news/iasc_guidelines_mental_health_psychososial_upd2008.pdf

International Humanitarian Aid activities: www.globalhumanitarianassistance.org/

Psychological First Aid Field Operations Guide: www.ptsd.va.gov/professional/manuals/psych-first-aid.asp

International Society For Traumatic Stress Studies: www.istss.org

The Sphere Project: www.sphereproject.org

National Center for Posttraumatic Stress Disorder: http://www.ptsd.va.gov/

International Red Cross: www.redcross.int

United Nations Office for the Coordination of Humanitarian Affairs: www.unocha.org/

REFERENCES

American Red Cross (2010). Retrieved July 20, 2006, from www.redcross.org

Amnesty International (1978). *Human Rights in Uganda: Report.* London: Amnesty International.

Anderson, M. (1999). *Do No Harm. How Aid Can Support Peace or War.* Boulder, CO: Lynne Rienner.

Bass, J.J.K., Bolton, P.A., & Murray, L.K. (2007). Do not forget culture when studying mental health. *The Lancet, 370*(September 15), 918–919.

Betancourt, T,. Borisova, I., Rubin-Smith, J., Gingerich, T., Williams, T., & Agnew-Blais, J. (2008). Psychosocial adjustment and social reintegration of children associated with armed forces and armed groups: The state of the field and future directions. Retrieved from: http://psychologybeyondborders.com/userfiles/file/RPCGA%20CAAFAG%20REPORT%20FINAL%20JULY%202008.pdf

Bolton, P., & Tang, M.T. (2004). Using ethnographic methods in the selection of post-disaster, mental-health interventions. *Prehospital and Disaster Medicine, 19*(1), 97–101.

Center for Mental Health Services (2001). *An Overview of the Crisis Counseling Assistance and Training Program* (CCP-PG-01). Rockville, MD: Center for Mental Health Services.

Dambisa, M., & Ferguson, N. (2009). *Dead Aid: Why Aid is Not Working and How There Is a Better Way for Africa.* New York: Farrar, Straus & Giroxu.

Figley, C.R. (1995). *Compassion Fatigue: Coping with Secondary Traumatic Stress Disorder in Those who Treat the Traumatized.* New York: Brunner/Mazel.

Flintoff, C. (2007). Is aid to Africa doing more harm than good? "Intelligence squared, US." Retrieved from: www.npr, December 12, 2007.

Gitterman, A. (2001). Vulnerability, resilience and social work with groups. In Kelly, T.B., Berman-Rossi, R., and Palombo, S. (Eds.), *Group Work: Strategies for Strengthening Resiliency* (pp. 19–26). New York: Haworth Press.

Holmes, J. (2008). More help now, please: How to tackle tomorrow's disasters. *The Economist,* Nov. 19, 2008, 110.

International Federation of Red Cross and Red Crescent Societies (2010). Retrieved from: www.ifrc.org, December 17, 2010.

Inter-Agency Standing Committee (2007). *IASC Guidelines on Mental Health and Psychosocial Support in Emergency Settings.* Geneva: IASC.

International Commission of Jurists. (1977). *Uganda and Human Rights: Report of the UN Commission on Human Rights*. Geneva: Author.

National Child Traumatic Stress Network and National Center for PTSD (2005). *Psychological First Aid: Field Operations Guide*, September 2005.

Norris, F.H., Friedman, M.J., & Watson, P.J. (2002). 60,000 disaster victims speak: Part II. Summary and implications of the disaster mental health research. *Psychiatry: Interpersonal and Biological Processes, 65*(3), 240–260.

Norris, F.H., & Kaniasty, K. (1996). Received and perceived social support in times of stress: A test of the social support deteriorations deterrence model. *Journal of Personality and Social Psychology, 71*(3), 498–511.

Pavia, W. (2010). Church group arrested in Haiti taking children across border. Retrieved from: www.thetimes.co.uk January 31, 2010.

Sphere Project (2004). *Humanitarian Charter and Minimum Standards in Disaster Response*. Retrieved from: www.shpereproject.org

United States Department of State (2009). Human Rights. Retrieved from: www.state.gov/g/drl/hr/ November 23, 2009.

Weine, S., Danieli, Y., Silove, D., van Ommeren, M., Fairbank, J., & Saul, J., for the International Society for Traumatic Stress Studies (2002). Guidelines for international training in mental health and psychosocial interventions for trauma exposed populations in clinical and community settings. *Psychiatry, 65*(2), 156–164.

Young, B.H., Ruzek, J.I., Wong, M., Salzer, M.S., & Naturale, A.J. (2006). Disaster mental health training: Guidelines, considerations and recommendations. In Ritchie, E.C., Watson, P.J., and Friedman, M.J. (Eds.), *Interventions Following Mass Violence and Disaster* (pp. 55–79). New York: The Guilford Press.

Part Five

Best Practices in Community Mental Health

Chapter 13

Assertive Community Treatment

An Evidence-Based Practice and Its Continuing Evolution[1]

John J. McLaughlin

INTRODUCTION

Assertive Community Treatment (ACT) is a widely recognized and effective evidence-based practice (EBP) for the treatment of "serious" mental illness (SMI). SMI is also known as "major" or "severe and persistent" mental illness. ACT, sometimes known as PACT (Program of Assertive Community Treatment), can simply be described as a combination of case management and psychiatric treatment delivered by a mobile team. It borrows from the old social work casework model in that it maintains "a dual focus on the client and the environment, working directly with and indirectly on behalf of individual clients and families in need" (National Association of Social Workers, 1992). As opposed to case management, the team does not broker (i.e., bring the consumer to) treatment services, but actually delivers them, including medication, assessment, advocacy, family counseling, and crisis intervention (Substance Abuse and Mental Health Services Administration [SAMHSA], 2008). Services are delivered to the consumers and their support network (families, friends, caregivers, residence staff) in the community, that is, in their home, place of work, and offices and stores in the neighborhood or town (Kopelowicz, Liberman, & Zarate, 2007). It is recognized as an EBP by the U.S. federal government (the Substance Abuse and Mental Health Services Administration (SAMHSA) and the Department of Veterans Affairs (VA)), the National Alliance on Mental Illness (NAMI), most U.S. states, several other nations, the National Association of State Mental Health Program Directors (NASMHPD), and the influential Dartmouth Psychiatric Research Center (DPRC; formerly the New Hampshire Dartmouth PR Center).

According to the NASMHPD's Research Institute (NRI), as of 2010, ACT programs were operating in 45 states; in fiscal year (FY) 2008, a total of at least 48,476 clients were served (32 states reported on numbers of both teams and clients, nine states reported on only one of these categories, and nine reported on neither). A total of at least 727 teams were reported; some states had many ACT programs, such as Michigan with 88, New York with 78, and Wisconsin with 76 (Lutterman, 2011). According to the NRI, North Carolina, through an initiative to increase the availability of ACT, has more than doubled its number of teams over a one-year period, from 45 in 2009 to 115 in 2010 (T. Lutterman, Director of Research Analysis, personal communication, January 25, 2011). In addition, the federal VA, as of

December 2010, operated 115 ACT programs called mental health intensive case management (MHICM) programs nationwide (MHICM, n.d.). In FY 2009, these MHICM programs had a census of 7,596 clients and served 8,426 clients over the course of the year (U.S. Department of Veterans Affairs [VA], Northeast Program Evaluation Center, 2010). Fourteen other nations have or are developing ACT programs, including Canada, Australia, Japan, the United Kingdom, and several others in Europe (C. Sixby, Executive Director, ACT Association, personal communication, August 21, 2010).

OVERVIEW

ACT began in 1972, in Wisconsin, as an attempt to assist adult patients with SMI maintain the gains that they had achieved on inpatient units when they were discharged back into the community (this had often not been the case). Researchers on an inpatient research unit hypothesized that an inpatient-like multidisciplinary team, stationed in the community to provide 24-hour, seven-days-a-week care (mimicking inpatient care), would help their consumers maintain these gains. This approach with clients still in need of hospital care (69% diagnosed with schizophrenia) seemed to be very successful and, over the long term, economical, as it reduced inpatient hospitalization days and emergency room visits (Marx, Test, & Stein, 1973). Subsequent research, which has been extensive, proved it to be so: results have consistently indicated that the introduction of ACT services that remain true to the model ("high-fidelity") result in fewer hospitalizations, increased housing stability, and higher client and family satisfaction with services. Also, ACT often promotes an improved quality of life, fewer symptoms, and increased social functioning (Morse & McKasson, 2005; Phillips et al., 2001; SAMHSA, 2008).

> ACT case management is currently one of the most effective systematic methods of organizing clinical and functional interventions in psychiatry. However, the ACT model was designed specifically for and works best with consumers with severe mental illness and the greatest functional impairments.
>
> (Rosen, Mueser, & Teesson, 2007, p. 821)

As will be explored later in this chapter, over the years the model has been extended to treat other diagnostic categories (borderline personality disorder, co-occurring mental illness and substance abuse, and dual-diagnosis mental illness and developmental disability) and special populations (the homeless, veterans, forensic consumers, and adolescents). It has been paired with other treatment models, such as integrated dual disorders treatment (IDDT) for co-occurring mental illness and substance abuse, supported employment (SE), family psychoeducation (PE), and illness management and recovery (IMR). This has caused a tension between the need for flexibility to address different treatment issues and fidelity to the ACT model. Also, the Great Recession and its lingering after-effects may cause financially strapped agencies and programs to increase caseloads and/or consider "step-downs" of ACT consumers to less intensive forms of care (e.g., standard clinic treatment with intensive case management (ICM)).

198

HISTORICAL BACKGROUND

The ACT model was developed in the late 1960s, based on research by Arnold Marx, MD, Leonard Stein, MD, and Mary Ann Test, Ph.D., on an inpatient research unit of Mendoza State Hospital in Madison, Wisconsin. The first ACT Team (the program was initially called Training in Community Living) was launched in 1972 in Madison, when the researchers moved inpatient hospital staff into the community to test their hypothesis (Stein & Santos, 1998). Thus the program is sometimes referred to as a "hospital without walls" (Burns, Swartz, & Harron, 1994; Morse & McKasson, 2005, p.317).

Interest in the model, now known as PACT, grew owing to the continuing deinstitutionalization policies and programs of the 1970s, 1980s, and 1990s. Deinstitutionalization, the discharge of people suffering from SMI from public hospitals (mostly run and funded by the states) to the community began in the 1950s owing to more effective medications and the need for reform of the state psychiatric hospitals. From 1955 to 1994, the patient population in U.S. public psychiatric hospitals decreased by 82.0%, from 558,239 to 71,619. However, if the increasing population of the United States over that period is taken into account, the effective deinstitutionalization rate is more akin to 91.3% (Torrey, 1997).

Also, there was a related emphasis on (and funding of) community mental health programs. The needed, and sometimes court-mandated, reforms to the state hospitals cost the states money, and they began to look more to the federal government for financial assistance in this area. The Community Mental Health Act (CMHA) of 1963 provided grants to the states for the creation and construction of community mental health centers (CMHCs) (Polgar, n.d.; Pratt & Gill, 2005). The federal Medicaid program, introduced in 1965, provided funding for treatment if it was provided in the community (but not in state psychiatric hospitals). This resulted in a dramatic increase in the rate of deinstitutionalization, which would continue over the next 10 years (Stein & Santos, 1998). However, many of the CMHCs were not focused on treating the SMI population but those with less severe disorders. In response, the federal government created the Community Support Program (CSP), in 1977, to provide grants to create community support systems (CSSs) for people with SMI (Johnson, 2010). Also, in 1972, the federal government created Supplemental Security Income (SSI), which provided federal financial assistance to disabled people (including those with SMI) with little or no work history. This further enhanced the ability of people with SMI to survive in the community (Johnson, 2010; Polgar, n.d.; Pratt & Gill, 2005).

As Johnson (2010) noted, with the passage of the CMHA of 1963 and the subsequent federal legislation and programs,

> the field of mental health had an official mandate to revolutionize care of individuals with mental illness and move patients from institutional care into decentralized, local community-based treatment programs. More importantly, in response to this mandate, various models of clinical interventions were developed.
>
> (p. 28)

PACT (later shortened to ACT) was one of these programs. ACT programs began to appear in Wisconsin and other Midwestern states. However, despite very positive research findings, a survey by Deci and associates in 1993 found that there were only 340 ACT programs in the

USA (not including the MHICM programs of the VA) in 34 states. Two states, Michigan and Wisconsin, had 153 of these programs. Some 303 programs responded to the survey, and, of these, only 100 had what the authors considered to be the six essential characteristics necessary for positive outcomes (Deci, Santos, Hiott, Schoenwald, & Dias, 1995). This limited dissemination of the ACT model was largely due to federal funding problems under Medicaid (Torrey, 1997).

The year 1998 was a watershed year for ACT. The Schizophrenia Patient Outcomes Research Team (PORT) of the NIMH issued a report that included ACT as a recommended treatment for schizophrenia, based on the existing scientific evidence, but noted that it was often not available to people who might benefit from it (Lehman et al. 1998). Also during that year, the Robert Wood Johnson Foundation convened a panel of experts who identified ACT and five other interventions as EBPs for the treatment of SMI; the other five were standardized pharmacological treatment, IMR skills, SE, PE, and IDDT. Based on these recommendations, NAMI announced a national initiative aimed at establishing ACT programs in every state (Johnson, 2010). As part of this initiative, Allness and Knoedler (2003) developed a manual for ACT implementation based on the national standards that they had developed earlier for SAMHSA (Allness and Knoedler, 1998).

In 1999, the Supreme Court issued the Olmstead Decision, which required states, when possible, to provide community-based services rather than institutional placements for people with disabilities. In response, the Bush administration's 2001 Freedom Initiative mandated federal agencies, including SAMHSA, further to promote community-based care. Towards this end, the Medicaid program worked with states to develop more flexible Medicaid reimbursement schemes via the use of waivers (Employment Support Institute, 2011). Also in 1999, *The Surgeon General's Report on Mental Health* noted the effectiveness of ACT for people with SMI and the federal Health Care Financing Administration (HCFA) clarified the use of Medicaid funds for ACT services. In 2002, SAMHSA chose the utilization of ACT as one of the three quality indicators of a state's mental health system and, picking-up on the Johnson Foundation's EBP recommendations, funded, with the Johnson Foundation, the National Implementing Evidence-Based Practices Project. This project developed programs to assist the states and the VA in implementing the six identified EBPs (Morse & McKasson, 2005).

In 2003, the President's New Freedom Commission on Mental Health published a report that made recommendations to "advance evidence-based practices using dissemination and demonstration projects" and to "improve and expand the workforce providing evidence-based mental health services and supports" (President's New Freedom Commission on Mental Health, 2003, p. 25). The Schizophrenia PORT updated its recommendations in 2003 and 2010 and continues to recommend ACT as a psychosocial treatment for schizophrenia (Dixon et al., 2010).

THE MODEL

A review of the literature indicates that there are 14 *core components* (also referred to as characteristics or principles) of the ACT model that are generally recognized. These can be divided into three broad and somewhat overlapping categories: structural, administrative, and clinical (Allness & Knoedler, 2003; Bond, 2002; Chandler, 2007; DeLuca, Moser, & Bond,

2008; Lewin Group, 2000; Morse & McKasson, 2005; Phillips et al., 2001; SAMHSA, 2008; Stein & Santos, 1998; Trawver, 2010):

I. Structural:
    1. A multidisciplinary team approach, including a team leader, a psychiatrist, a nurse, and specialists in substance abuse and employment. Some programs add housing, family, and peer specialists.
    2. Flexible service delivery—team members meet daily to assess client functioning and quickly adjust services, including intensity, to the need of the client.
    3. A shared caseload—team members share responsibility for consumers served by the team.
    4. A small caseload—a staff-to-consumer ratio of approximately 1:10.
    5. *In vivo* services: the majority of contacts are in community settings.
    6. Open-ended services—there are no arbitrary time limits regarding receiving services and discharge from the program.
    7. 24/7 availability—services are available 24 hours/day, seven days/week to provide what is needed, when it is needed, as often as it is needed.
    8. A fixed point of responsibility—team members "assertively" attempt to engage clients and directly provide individualized and comprehensive treatment, support, and rehabilitation services.
II. Administrative:
    9. A service-delivery model versus a pure case management one—treatment and services are both delivered directly and brokered by the ACT team.
    10. Services targeted to a specific group of individuals with SMI with the most persistent problems and who have benefitted least from other mental health services.
    11. Fidelity to the model, which increases the likelihood of positive client outcomes.
III. Clinical:
    12. Individualized services that are client-centered, that is, stress a therapeutic alliance with the client and incorporate client input and goals into the treatment plan.
    13. A primary goal of recovery through community treatment and habilitation utilizing community resources, including family, support systems (e.g., religious institutions/ groups, friends, landlords, neighbors), and other agencies.
    14. The team leader must be clinically and administratively strong and skilled, spend half of her/his time in direct client service, and meet with the team daily (as noted in component 2).

In 1995, Teague, Bond, and Drake at the New Hampshire DPRC developed the Dartmouth ACT Fidelity Scale (DACTS) to measure a program's "*fidelity*" (faithfulness) to the ACT model (Lewin Group, 2000; Stein & Santos, 1998). This scale has 28 components, covering structure and human resources, organizational boundaries, and the nature of services; each component has specific standards (Phillips et al., 2001; Teague, Bond, & Drake, 1998). The scale was adopted by SAMHSA for inclusion in its ACT EBP Toolkit (SAMHSA, 2008). Johnson (2010) notes that the scale emphasizes structural components that are measurable versus clinical ones "that may be important to the model's effectiveness but that are more difficult to measure" (p. 32).

The *clinical rationale* for the effectiveness of the model is that very symptomatic clients who have not had much success with other forms of treatment need a more intense and flexible form of outreach and comprehensive type of care. The team is encouraged to go to great lengths to connect with the consumer and gain his/her trust (and the trust of the consumer's support network—family, friends, landlords, neighbors, clergy, church/temple congregation, local police). The comprehensiveness of the services should increase that trust, and the consumer will gradually connect to the whole team (as against one clinician). This will broaden the consumer's social network and reduce his/her isolation, as well as allow the team members to play different roles with the consumer (confidant, enforcer, teacher, broker, etc.). It also allows the consumer to learn from the team members a broad array of skills and clinical knowledge—for example, medication management, cooking, symptom management, housekeeping, substance abuse coping skills, budgeting, employment skills, problem solving, and shopping (Phillips et al., 2001; Stein & Santos, 1998; SAMHSA, 2008).

Because it is a team approach, communication among the team members is key. A daily meeting led by a skilled team leader is the backbone of the model and harkens back to its inpatient roots. In the meeting, daily assignments are made, based on the current status and needs of the clients. All members of the team have input, with clinical leadership supplied by the psychiatrist. Assignments are often made based on staff members' clinical specialty (medication administration by a nurse, benefit advocacy by a social worker, the substance abuse specialist accompanying a client to an Alcoholics Anonymous meeting) or informal specialty (helping and teaching how to repair a broken door, a shopping trip for a new outfit for the holidays, a cooking lesson). The office manager/administrative assistant also plays a vital role in team communication, acting as a kind of "air traffic controller" who maintains a presence at the office, while the other team members are out "in the field" in the community. He/she must assist the team leader in coordinating and monitoring team members' whereabouts, while effectively dealing with calls from clients and orchestrating changes in plans necessitated by emergencies and other client needs (DeLuca et al., 2008; Morse & McKasson, 2005; Stein & Santos, 1998; Trawver, 2010). There is also an added benefit from the team approach in that it may decrease staff burnout and turnover (McGrew & Bond, 1997).

The ACT team must stand ready to deliver a broad array of *services*, or arrange for those services, as they are needed by its clients. The core ACT services can be summarized as follows:

■ crisis assessment and intervention, including hospitalization assistance;
■ comprehensive assessment;
■ illness management and recovery;
■ individual supportive therapy;
■ integrated substance abuse treatment;
■ employment-support services, including educational counseling;
■ social skills counseling and training, including recreational and leisure planning;
■ side-by-side assistance with activities of daily living (shopping, cooking, laundry, budgeting, home repairs, etc.);
■ intervention with support networks (family, friends, religious institutions/groups, landlords, counselors, neighbors, police, etc.);
■ support and advocacy services regarding medical care, benefits, housing, and transportation;

■ medication prescription, procurement, administration, and monitoring; and,
■ other case management (Morse & McKasson, 2005; Phillips et al., 2001; SAMHSA, 2008).

McGrew, Pescosolido, and Wright (2003) surveyed 73 ACT Teams as to the importance of 27 critical ingredients and the benefits of 16 clinical activities. The critical ingredients related to a team approach and medical aspects (most notably, having a full-time nurse) were rated highest; medication management was seen as the most beneficial clinical activity, followed by continuing assessment and regular home visits. The ingredients implemented least were, in order, a full-time (FT) vocational specialist, a FT housing specialist, a FT substance abuse specialist, and never discharging clients.

PRACTICE ISSUES AND CONSIDERATIONS

Diagnostic Categories

SAMHSA estimates that 11 million adults (≥ 18 years of age), or 4.8% of the adult population in the United States, suffered from SMI in 2009, and that 25.7% of these people also had a substance abuse disorder in the past year (SAMHSA, 2010). Trawver (2010) notes that ACT programs generally limit new clients to those with SMI who have been diagnosed with psychotic disorders (schizophrenia, schizoaffective, and bipolar disorder) on Axis I (clinical disorders) in the *DSM-IV-TR* system (American Psychiatric Association, 2000). Cuddeback, Morrissey, and Meyer estimated that 50% of people with SMI could benefit from ACT (2006), although some estimates are as low as 15–20% (DeLuca et al., 2008). Research has shown that the clients who derive the most benefit from ACT are clients with SMI who have the most functional problems and have not been able to utilize and/or benefit from other types of psychiatric treatment (DeLuca et al., 2008; Phillips et al., 2001; Rosen, Mueser, & Teeson, 2007).

The VA includes the diagnosis of PTSD in its criteria for admission to its MHICM programs (VA, Veterans Health Administration, 2006). As of 2010, about 12% of its MHICM client population carried a PTSD diagnosis (VA, Northeast Program Evaluation Center, 2010). No data are available on the effectiveness of this treatment.

A significant number of clients diagnosed with borderline personality disorder have been treated by ACT programs. Some programs have incorporated elements of dialectical behavior therapy, the psychosocial intervention usually used to treat borderline personality disorder in the United States. However, there is very limited research on the effectiveness of any of these ACT interventions (Horvitz-Lennon et al., 2009).

There have been three studies regarding the use of ACT with dually diagnosed clients with SMI and a developmental (intellectual) disability: two in the United Kingdom and one in Canada. The two UK studies found no significant differences between ACT outcomes versus standard treatment in terms of quality of life, unmet needs, functioning, and career burden. The Canadian study reported decreased hospital admissions and inpatient bed use when comparing clients' pre-ACT and post-ACT histories. In addition, a 2009 survey of Ontario (Canada) ACT programs found that 9.3% of current ACT clients and 10.8% of ACT waiting-list clients had an intellectual disability (Burge, 2009).

Although some earlier studies had found a connection between ACT and a lower level of substance use among clients with co-occurring disorders (CoDs) of SMI and substance abuse (McHugo, Drake, Teague, & Xie, 1999; Phillips et al., 2001), more recent studies found no such correlation (Dixon et al., 2010). The addition to the team of a substance abuse specialist who utilizes IDDT did somewhat increase positive outcomes in the area of substance abuse (Morrissey, Meyer, & Cuddeback, 2007).

Special Populations

Veterans

As previously noted, since 1987, the VA has operated the MHICM program, based on the ACT model, nationwide. By FY 2003, the VA was operating 74 MHICM teams, and 8 more were in development. Collected data indicated that the program was cost-effective, produced sustainable results, and could be implemented and monitored in VA settings. The target group was veterans with SMI who were high users of VA inpatient services. Outcomes included a significant reduction in psychiatric inpatient days, increased housing independence (14%), improvement of symptoms and quality of life, and higher client satisfaction ratings compared with standard VA mental health services (Neale et al., 2004).

MHICM teams must have at least four full-time-equivalent (FTE) clinical "on the street" staff (VA, Veterans Health Administration, 2006) and a ratio of 1 FTE staff for every 7–15 clients (VA, Veterans Health Administration, 2008). Fidelity is monitored, and outcomes are measured on an annual basis (VA, Northeast Program Evaluation Center 2010; VA, Veterans Health Administration, 2009).

The VA maintains a database that is reported on an annual basis. In FY 2009 (last report available), the average MHICM team caseload was 1 FTE staff to 11.96 clients; 89% of the clients were male, with a mean age of 51.0; 73% were unemployed owing to disability; and 22.3% had a history of combat exposure. Diagnostically, 89% had an Axis I psychotic disorder, and 18% were dual-diagnosis mentally ill with a substance abuse disorder. Twelve percent were diagnosed with PTSD. The mean number of years for clients participating in the MHICM program was 4.0 (VA, Northeast Program Evaluation Center, 2010).

According to Dr. Samala Mohammed, MD, of the VA's Northeast Program Evaluation Center, the VA has recently added smaller MHICM teams as part of the Rural Access Network for Growth Enhancement (RANGE) program, in an attempt to better serve the rural population. Standard RANGE teams have two clinical FTE staff, usually a nurse and a social worker. Enhanced RANGE teams, which do outreach to the homeless, have three clinical FTE staff (an additional social worker or nurse). These teams have a lower client maximum regarding the staff-to-client ratio: one FTE staff for every seven to ten clients. There are currently a total of 41 RANGE teams: 25 standard teams and 16 enhanced teams (personal communication, January 6, 2011).

The Homeless

Homelessness is a social problem that has a strong connection to the deinstitutionalization of the SMI population from asylums to the community, as does the reinstitutionalization of many

SMI clients to jails and prisons. Coldwell and Bender (2007) conducted a meta-analysis of 10 studies of ACT interventions with exclusively homeless clients that were published from 1992 to 2001. They found that ACT "offers significant advantages over standard case management models in reducing homelessness and symptom severity in homeless persons with severe mental illness" (p. 393).

On the other hand, although the use of the ACT model with *forensic clients*, often called forensic assertive community treatment (FACT) has proliferated, there have been few studies of it (Cuddeback, Morrissey, Cusack, & Meyer, 2009). Two studies in 2004 showed that ACT intervention produced a reduction in jail days, hospital days, and cost, but the evidence is limited and therefore weak. The FACT model needs to be better defined and researched (Cuddeback, Morrissey, & Cusack, 2008; Morrissey et al., 2007).

Marriage With Other Treatment Models

Combining ACT with some of the other five recognized EBPs has proven to be effective in improving some client outcomes (Morse & McKasson, 1995). Combining ACT with family PE increases employment outcomes (McFarlane, 1997); ACT teams with a supported employment component also have better employment outcomes (Rosen et al., 2007). As previously noted, ACT teams with a substance abuse specialist utilizing IDDT have better substance abuse outcomes (Morrissey et al., 2007). A recent study by Salyers et al. compared ACT teams with and without an IMR component utilizing peer specialists as IMR practitioners. Some implementation issues were noted, but the clients exposed to IMR showed a decrease in hospital use (Salyers et al., 2010).

Team Size and Composition

Stein and Santos (1998) recommend a team of 10–12 staff, not counting the psychiatrist and secretary/office manager, and the use of social workers as team members; they point out that social workers have clinical skills and are trained as "generalists" with a "broad perspective" (p.58). Morse and McKasson (2005) state that a team of 10–12 professionals, including the psychiatrist, is "typical" (p.321). The SAMHSA (2008) recommends a multidisciplinary team of 10–12 practitioners for a caseload of about 100 clients. McGrew and Bond (1995) reported that a panel of 20 experts did not agree on a recommended team size—one subgroup recommended a large multidisciplinary team with a caseload of 100 clients, and another subgroup a small generalist team serving 50. Regarding ideal staffing, these experts most frequently mentioned psychiatrists, nurses, and social workers.

In 1997, McGrew and Bond reported on a study of 19 ACT teams that indicated a correlation between smaller team size and fewer services to clients; the authors speculate that smaller teams may be less efficient. However, all of these considerations must take into account the context of the ACT team in the delivery system. A smaller team may be able to operate as efficiently as a large one, if it has agency back-up and resources, such as an emergency off-hours telephone service; an operational fleet of cars, vans, trucks, and ambulances; available and flexible medical services; emergency housing; emergency financial assistance; psychiatric coverage, etc. As noted above, the VA utilizes smaller teams, especially in rural settings, with good results.

Some ACT programs have begun to utilize nurse-practitioners as medication prescribers as a cost-saving measure. A nurse-practitioner, also known as an "advanced practice registered nurse" (APRN), is licensed to prescribe and administer medication under the supervision of a medical doctor. ACT teams have begun to employ them in this capacity in some rural states. Research needs to be done on the effect this practice has on ACT outcomes (Williams, Kukula, Bond, McKasson, & Salyers, 2009).

POLICY ISSUES AND CONSIDERATIONS

Cost

A number of studies have shown that high-fidelty ACT programs serving high-risk clients are cost-effective in that the relatively expensive care they provide (compared with standard outpatient treatment) is offset by the savings generated by reduced hospitalization rates and other superior outcomes (Allness & Knoedler, 1998; Morse & McKasson, 2005; Phillips et al., 2001; SAMHSA, 2008). This does not take in to account the long-term societal benefits that are generated by ACT clients' increased employment and housing stability (Rosen et al., 2007).

Increased Staff-to-Client Ratios

The DACTS calls for a staff-to-client ratio of 1:10 or fewer, but there has been much discussion in the literature over the years regarding the need for some flexibility in this area. Teams with more unstable and symptomatic clients (e.g., new teams absorbing recently hospitalized clients or teams serving the homeless or rural areas) may need to have smaller caseload ratios of fewer than 10 clients per FTE staff; older teams with more stable clientele may be able to handle up to 20 clients per FTE staff (DeLuca et al., 2008). Also, McGrew and Bond's study (1997) showed no correlation between staff-to-client ratio and service intensity (teams ranged from 1:7 to 1:15). As noted above, VA MHICM teams are allowed to have ratios as high as 1:15.

Discharge and "Step-Down" Programs

Early research re discharge of ACT clients indicated that clients arbitrarily discharged to standard care after 1 year of ACT treatment saw a steady deterioration of the gains that they had made (Stein & Santos, 1998). However, a study by Salyers, Masterton, Fekete, Picone, and Bond (1998) indicated that "stepping-down" a client to less-intensive treatment services without negative consequences was possible if done carefully and on an individualized basis. Allness and Knoedler (2003) suggest that a client be able to function independently with minimal ACT assistance for at least 2 years before being considered for discharge. A review of VA MHICM administrative data of 192 clients transitioned to lower-intensity services found that only 5.7% needed to be returned to a higher-intensity level of services (Rosenheck, Neale, & Mohamed, 2010).

ACT and Assisted Outpatient Treatment

ACT has sometimes been criticized for being "coercive," but this is not supported by research. One reason for the misconception may be ACT's core components of assertive (persistent) engagement, perhaps sometimes carried too far, and lifetime membership (Phillips et al., 2001; Rosen et al., 2007; SAMHSA, 2008). Another reason is that it is sometimes associated with assisted outpatient treatment (AOT), which is also known as outpatient commitment. AOT is court-ordered outpatient treatment (including medication) for individuals who have a history of treatment noncompliance. Forty-four states now have outpatient commitment laws on the books. Violation of the court-ordered conditions can result in the individual being hospitalized for further treatment (Treatment Advocacy Center, 2010). In some states, such as New York, clients can be mandated by the court, via AOT, to be treated by an ACT Team. In fact, in New York, all AOT orders mandate some form of case management (Office of Mental Health, 2005). One study of a New York ACT program compared AOT and voluntary clients: they had essentially the same outcomes, except that the AOT group had lower inpatient admissions and was less satisfied with treatment (Perese, Wu, & Raganathan, 2004).

Cultural, Ethnic, Racial, and International Issues

In the United States, ACT has been shown to be effective for many different ethnic, cultural, and age groups (Bond, 2002). As previously noted, ACT is now being practiced in 14 other countries—most recently, quite successfully in Japan (Ito, Oshima, Nishio, & Kuno, 2009). However, results of research on ACT programs in the United Kingdom and other European countries have been mixed (Chandler, 2007; Salyers & Bond, 2009).

CASE EXAMPLE

Below is a summary of an actual case from an ACT team that serves an urban and suburban area in northern New Jersey. The client's name and some other facts have been changed to protect her identity.

Elena is a 43-year-old, single, Puerto Rican and Italian–American Catholic woman referred to the county ACT team four and a half years ago by a local medical center psychiatric inpatient (IP) unit after hospitalization for suicidal ideation. During the previous six months, she had been to the emergency room (ER) 15 times. She was a frequent user of the medical center's inpatient unit, emergency room, and psychiatric mobile crisis team. A referral to an ICM program by Elena's former outpatient clinic failed because she would not cooperate with it. Elena was also uncooperative with her outpatient psychiatric and medical treatment, including keeping appointments and taking medications as prescribed.

Elena has carried many diagnoses over the years, including schizophrenia, schizoaffective disorder, bipolar disorder, major depression, and borderline personality disorder. She is a polysubstance abuser—she has tried and used many drugs in the past, but at the time of admittance to the ACT team was clean for almost a year. She has several medical problems, including asthma, obesity, hypertension, and diabetes. The team psychiatrist, after a careful review of her history, several meetings with the client, and discussion with the team, formulated a working diagnosis of schizoaffective disorder, PTSD, and rule out borderline personality disorder. He prescribed a mood stabilizer and an injectable antipsychotic.

Elena has had a very difficult life. Her father suffered from alcoholism, and her mother from SMI. She was raised in extreme poverty, was physically and sexually abused as a child, and was placed in foster care at age 6. At age 12, she was raped and soon thereafter began heavily using marijuana; she has also used, over the years, many other illegal and prescription drugs. She was in special education for a learning disability, finished high school, and worked at various jobs. At times, she has been homeless—she is very resourceful in her ability to survive. She has often been despondent regarding her social isolation and future and has attempted suicide at least 10 times. She is bisexual, has never been married, and has no children; many of her lovers have been abusive. She has not been able to work since age 33 and is dependent on SSI and Medicaid. She lives alone in a small apartment. Her parents are deceased, and, upon referral to the ACT team, she was estranged from her family (siblings), had few friends, and was socially isolated.

When the team met with Elena to formulate her treatment plan, she focused on her need to improve her physical health and stay clean and sober. She wanted to lose weight, stop smoking, and stay out of the medical center's psychiatric and medical IP units. The team agreed to these goals and to financially assist her in obtaining a gym membership. The team leader/medical nurse began to work with Elena on an IMR plan for both medical and psychiatric issues. The psychiatrist promised to work with the client regarding some of her objections to the psychotropic medications, if she would take them as prescribed, abstain from recreational drugs, and keep her medical appointments.

Shortly after this meeting, Elena was assaulted and robbed on the street near her home; she suffered a shoulder injury in the attack. The ACT team was very active in assisting her with the medical, legal, financial, and psychological issues that resulted from this traumatic event. Elena often called the office and the on-call staff during off-hours when she was having a panic attack, felt depressed and lonely, or experienced paranoid thinking. The team always responded with telephone counseling, unscheduled and/or increased home visits, and, if necessary, medication. The team's peer specialist accompanied Elena to many legal, medical, and "reviews of benefits" appointments to provide support and advocacy. Elena was very impressed with all of this and called the team "her family." Despite some suicidal ideation, which was handled by the team, she did not request to go to the ER. She has not visited the ER or been rehospitalized since. She had one brief period of cocaine use a few months after the mugging, but, with the assistance of the team's psychologist/substance abuse specialist, recovered from that episode.

Over the last three and a half years, Elena has made steady progress, with one minor setback. The setback occurred when her sister died, and, at the same time, she reinjured her shoulder. A medical doctor, against the advice of the ACT psychiatrist, prescribed pain medication for Elena to which she became addicted. This injured her self-esteem, as she took great pride in her hard-won abstinence from drugs. With the assistance of the psychologist/substance abuse specialist and Narcotics Anonymous groups, Elena weaned herself off the painkiller. Elena later said that she was very impressed with the team's non-judgmental attitude.

Owing to events beyond her control, Elena had to find a new apartment; with the assistance of the team's social worker/housing specialist, she quickly did so. The team helped her with the move, and the medication nurse, who is also the team's handyman (nickname: "Bob Vila"), helped her make some improvements and minor repairs on the apartment. Elena's IMR program was very effective: she exercised regularly, lost 70 lbs, stopped smoking, and improved her overall health. She became more compliant with her medical and psychiatric treatment, including eating a healthy diet, keeping appointments, and taking her medications as prescribed. She began to use the team's psychologist/family specialist to explore her feelings of loneliness and isolation; later, she reestablished contact with one of her brothers and now spends holidays (always a difficult time for Elena) with him and his family. She also used counseling by the team to explore and end a relationship with an abusive boyfriend, grieve the death of her sister, and return to attending church. Her spiritual life has blossomed, which is a great comfort to her, and she has begun to attend social events and make friends in her parish as well.

Elena has taken a few adult education courses and has begun to explore the possibility of part-time work or volunteer work with the team's nurse/employment specialist. An attempt to have her "step down" to an ICM program and a clinic, suggested by administration, ended when she protested and became more symptomatic.

SUMMARY

ACT, despite its reputation as bedrock EBP for the treatment of SMI, finds itself in 2011 facing a somewhat uncertain future. Its classic model for the treatment of clients with the most functional impairments and risks, including the homeless and veterans, is losing some of its financial sheen, as the number of hospital beds dwindles and comparative costs thereby increase. Adaptations of the model that pair it with other EBPs (e.g., IDDT) and best practices (e.g., dialectical behavior therapy) need more research, and its international dissemination has stalled somewhat in Europe.

Most notably, the lingering effects of the Great Recession are placing unprecedented strains on federal and state budgets, with deleterious effects on mental health services. Between 2008 and the beginning of 2011, 32 states and Washington, DC, cut $1.8 billion from their mental health budgets (Wyatt, 2011). One of the services hit hard was ACT (Honberg, Diehl, Kimball, Gruttadaro, & Fitzpatrick, 2011). Politicians think short term (namely, their term), and the temptation has been strong to cut funds for start-up costs and subsidies for programs such as ACT, which have long-term cost-saving effects (Canady, 2011). In late 2010, the EBP Implementation Project inexplicably vanished, almost completely, from the SAMHSA website. And the immediate future looks even more dire—with the expiration of enhanced federal Medicaid reimbursement rates (which were part of the American Recovery and Reinvestment Act of 2009) to the states on June 30, 2011, the state percentage of Medicaid spending is forecasted to increase by 18.6%. Therefore, states plan to cut Medicaid provider rates in 2012 (New York Association of Psychiatric Rehabilitation Services, 2011).

Evidence suggests that the ACT model will survive and eventually prosper, based on its sound principles rooted in empirical social science, social casework, and consumerism. When the economy improves, and the kinks in the marriage of the model to the other EBPs are worked out, a new wave of dissemination will be called for. It is imperative, though, that mental health professionals, consumers, and families continue to advocate for high-quality, evidence-based treatment for our mentally ill citizens. They have the right to be treated in their homes and communities as against long-term hospitals, shelters, jails, prisons, and the streets. And many studies show that, in the long term, it is more cost effective to do so (Harvard Medical School, 2011; SAMHSA, 2008).

DISCUSSION QUESTIONS

1. ACT is sometimes called "a hospital without walls." Explain what that means.

2. Some groups consider ACT too intrusive, especially if it is court-mandated, e.g., by AOT. Do you agree? What if the consumer has attempted suicide? Or homicide?

3. What do you think is the most effective component/principle of ACT? Why?

LEARNING ASSIGNMENTS

Group Project

Show the documentary *A Hospital Without Walls*. Then, plan and simulate a home visit by two ACT staff members to Elena, the consumer described in the Case Example. Have the rest of the class critique the visit.

SUGGESTED READINGS AND VIEWINGS

Allness, D.J., & Knoedler, W.H. (2003). *A Manual for ACT Start-Up: Based on the PACT Model of Community Treatment for Persons with Severe and Persistent Mental Illnesses*. Arlington, VA: The National Alliance for the Mentally Ill. (A solid resource for new programs.)

Burns, B.J. (Executive Producer), Swartz, M.S. (Executive Producer), & Harron, B. (Producer & Director) (1994). *Hospital Without Walls* [Motion picture]. Durham, NC: Division of Social and Community Psychiatry, Department of Psychiatry, Duke University Medical Center. (An excellent documentary about an ACT team in action, but it is difficult to find copies. A shortened version (DVD format) was part of the SAMHSA ACT EBP KIT, but as of this writing the SAMHSA store was out of stock.)

DeLuca, N.L., Moser, L.L., & Bond, G.R. (2008). Assertive community treatment. In K.T. Mueser & D.V. Jeste (Eds.), *Clinical Handbook of Schizophrenia* (pp. 329–338). New York: The Guilford Press. (Another good, brief overview with recommendations for practice.)

Harvard Medical School (2011). Assertive community treatment. *The Harvard Mental Health Letter, 27*(2), 4–5. (Retrieved from the Harvard Medical School publications website: http://www.health.harvard.edu; a good, concise description of the model and some related research.)

Morse, G., & McKasson, M. (2005). Assertive community treatment. In R.E. Drake, M.R. Merrens, & D.W. Lynde (Eds.), *Evidence-Based Mental Health Practice: A Textbook* (pp. 317–347). New York: W.W. Norton & Company. (A good, brief overview that clearly shows how ACT is an EBP.)

Stein, L.I., & Santos, A.B. (1998). *Assertive Community Treatment of Persons with Severe Mental Illness.* New York: W.W. Norton & Company. (Stein was one of the originators of the model.)

Trawver, K. (2010). Assertive community treatment. In A. Rubin, D.W. Springer, & K. Trawver (Eds.), *Psychosocial Treatment of Schizophrenia* (pp. 187–252). Hoboken, NJ: John Wiley and Sons. (A comprehensive and practical overview.)

INTERNET RESOURCES

The Assertive Community Treatment Association (ACTA): www.actassociation.org

The National Alliance on Mental Illness (NAMI): www.nami.org

The U.S. Department of Health and Human Services (DHH), Substance Abuse and Mental Health Services Administration (SAMHSA)—download the ACT EBP KIT at: store.samhsa.gov/product/Assertive-Community-Treatment-ACT-Evidence-Based-Practices-EBP-KIT/SMA08-4345

Many U.S. states, such as Wisconsin and New York, have websites, or parts of websites, on the subject of ACT or PACT.

For Wisconsin go to: www.dhs.wisconsin.gov/mh_mendota/programs/Outpatient/OUTPAT.HTM

For New York: bi.omh.ny.gov/act/index

NOTE

1 This chapter is dedicated to Gilean Kelly, RN, Team Leader, and the other members of the South Richmond ACT Team of South Beach Psychiatric Center, Staten Island, New York. The work they do is inspiring and heroic.

REFERENCES

Allness, D., & Knoedler, W. (1998). *National program standards for ACT teams.* Retrieved from the National Alliance on Mental Illness website: www.nami.org

Allness, D.J., & Knoedler, W.H. (2003). *The PACT model of community-based treatment for persons with severe and persistent mental illnesses: A manual for PACT start-up.* Arlington, VA: National Alliance for the Mentally Ill.

American Psychiatric Association (2000). *Diagnostic and statistical manual of mental disorders* (4th ed., text revision). Washington, DC: Author.

Bond, G.R. (2002). Assertive community treatment for people with severe mental illness. Retrieved from the Behavioral Health Management Project (funded by the Illinois Department of Human Services) website: www.bhrm.org/guidelines/ACTguide.pdf

Burge, P. (2009). Assertive community treatment teams and adults with intellectual disabilities. *Journal on Developmental Disabilities, 15*(3), 96–102.

Burns, B.J. (Executive Producer), Swartz, M.S. (Executive Producer), & Harron, B. (Producer & Director) (1994). *Hospital without walls* [Motion picture]. Durham, NC: Division of Social and Community Psychiatry, Department of Psychiatry, Duke University Medical Center.

Canady, V. (2011, February 14). State budget shortfalls continue to impact mental health systems. *Mental Health Weekly*. Retrieved from: www.mentalhealthweeklynews.com

Chandler, D. (2007). Implementing SAMHSA evidence-based practice toolkits: Assertive community treatment (ACT). Retrieved from the California Institute for Mental Health website: www.cimh.org

Coldwell, C.M., & Bender, W.S. (2007). The effectiveness of assertive community treatment for homeless populations with severe mental illness: A meta-analysis. *American Journal of Psychiatry, 164*, 393–399.

Cuddeback, G.S., Morrissey. J.P., & Cusack, K.J. (2008). How many forensic assertive community treatment teams do we need? *Psychiatric Services, 59*, 205–208.

Cuddeback, G.S., Morrissey, J.P., Cusack, K.J., & Meyer, P.S. (2009). Challenges to developing forensic assertive community treatment. *American Journal of Psychiatric Rehabilitation, 12*, 225–226.

Cuddeback, G.S., Morrissey, J.P., & Meyer, P.S. (2006) How many assertive community treatment teams do we need? *Psychiatric Services, 57*, 1803–1806.

Deci, P.A., Santos, A.B., Hiott, D.W., Schoenwald, S., & Dias, J.K. (1995). Dissemination of assertive community treatment programs. *Psychiatric Services, 46*, 676–678.

DeLuca, N.L., Moser, L.L., & Bond, G.R. (2008). Assertive community treatment. In K.T. Mueser & D.V. Jeste (Eds.), *Clinical handbook of schizophrenia* (pp. 329–338). New York: The Guilford Press.

Dixon, L., Dickerson, F., Bellack, A.S., Bennett, M., Dickinson, D., Goldberg, R.W., et al. (2010). The 2009 schizophrenia PORT psychosocial treatment recommendations and summary statements. *Schizophrenia Bulletin, 36*(1), 48–70.

Employment Support Institute (last updated 1/26/11). The Olmstead decision. Retrieved from the Virginia Commonwealth University's School of Business website: www.workworld.org/wwwebhelp/the_olmstead_decision.htm

Harvard Medical School (2011). Assertive community treatment. *The Harvard Mental Health Letter, 27*(2), 4–5. Retrieved from the Harvard Medical School publications website: www.health.harvard.edu

Honberg, R., Diehl, S., Kimball, A., Gruttadaro, D., & Fitzpatrick, M. (2011). State mental health cuts: A national crisis. Retrieved from the National Alliance on Mental Health website: www.nami.org/budgetcuts

Horvitz-Lennon, M., et al (2009). The role of assertive community treatment in the treatment of people with borderline personality disorder. *American Journal of Psychiatric Rehabilitation, 12*, 261–277.

Ito, J., Oshima, I., Nishio, M., & Kuno, E. (2009). Initiative to build a community-based mental health system including assertive community treatment for people with severe mental illness in Japan. *American Journal of Psychiatric Rehabilitation, 12*, 247–260.

Johnson, S.J. (2010). *Assertive community treatment: Evidence-based practice or managed recovery.* New Brunswick, NJ: Transaction Publishers.

Kopelowicz, A., Liberman, R.L., & Zarate, R. (2007). Psychosocial treatments for schizophrenia. In P.E. Nathan & J.M. Gorman (Eds.), *A guide to treatments that work* (pp. 243–269). New York: Oxford University Press.

Lehman, A.F., Steinwachs, D.M., and the Survey Co-Investigators of the PORT Project (1998). Patterns of usual care for schizophrenia: Initial results from the Schizoprenia Patient Outcomes Research Team (PORT) Client Survey. *Schizophrenia Bulletin, 24*(1), 11–20.

Lewin Group (2000, April 28). Assertive community treatment literature review: prepared for: Health Care and Financing Administration (HCFA) and Substance Abuse and Mental Health Services Administration (SAMHSA). Retrieved from the Minnesota Department of Human Services website: www.dhs.state.mn.us/main/groups/disabilities/documents/pub/dhs_id_027776.pdf

Lutterman, T. (2011). ACT programs 2010 (draft). The National Association of State Mental Health Program Directors Research Institute, Inc. (NRI), Alexandria, VA.

Marx, A.J., Test, M.A., & Stein, L.I. (1973). Extra-hospital management of severe mental illness. *Archives of General Psychiatry, 29,* 505–511.

McFarlane, W.R. (1997). FACT: Integrating family psychoeducation and assertive community treatment. *Administration and Policy in Mental Health, 25,* 191–198.

McGrew, J.H., & Bond, G.R. (1995). Critical ingredients of assertive community treatment: Judgements of the experts. *The Journal of Behavioral Health Services and Research, 22,* 113–125.

McGrew, J.H., & Bond, G.R. (1997). The association between program characteristics and service delivery in assertive community treatment. *Administration and Policy in Mental Health, 25,* 175–189.

McGrew, J.H., Pescosolido, B., & Wright, E. (2003). Case managers' perspectives on critical ingredients of assertive community treatment and on its implementation. *Psychiatric Services, 54,* 370–376.

McHugo, G.J., Drake, R.E., Teague, G.B., & Xie, H. (1999). Fidelity to assertive community treatment and client outcomes in the New Hampshire dual disorders study. *Psychiatric Services, 50,* 818–824.

MHICM (Mental health intensive case management) (n.d.). Retrieved January 6, 2011 from the Veterans Administration Errera Community Care Center, West Haven, CT, website: www.erreraccc.com/mihcm

Morrissey, J., Meyer, P., & Cuddeback, G. (2007). Extending assertive community treatment to criminal justice settings: Origins, current evidence, and future directions. *Community Mental Health Journal, 43,* 527–544.

Morse, G., & McKasson, M. (2005). Assertive community treatment. In R.E. Drake, M.R. Merrens, & D.W. Lynde (Eds.), *Evidence-based mental health practice: A textbook* (pp. 317–347). New York: W.W. Norton & Company.

National Association of Social Workers (1992). *National standards for social work case management.* Retrieved from the NASW website: www.naswdc.org/practice/standards/sw_case_mgmt.asp

Neale, M., Rosenheck, R., Castrodonatti, J., Martin, A., Morrissey, J., & Anderson, J. (2004). *Mental health intensive case management (MHICM) in the Department of Veterans Affairs: The Seventh National Performance Monitoring Report—FY 2003.* Report for the Department of Veterans Affairs, Northeast Program Evaluation Center. Retrieved from: http://consensusproject.org/downloads/ACT-MHICM.pdf

New York Association of Psychiatric Rehabilitation Services (NYAPRS). (2011, August 3). 33 states plan to cut Medicaid provider rates in 2012. Retrieved from NYAPRS website: www.nyaprs.org/e-news-bulletins

Office of Mental Health (OMH), State of New York (2005*). Kendra's Law: Final report on the status of assisted outpatient treatment.* Retrieved from the OMH website: www.omh.state.ny.us/omhweb/kendra_web/finalreport/

Perese, E.F., Wu, Y.-W.B., & Ranganathan, R. (2004). Effectiveness of assertive community treatment for patients referred under Kendra's Law: Proximal and distal outcomes. *International Journal of Psychosocial Rehabilitation, 9*(1), 5–9.

Phillips, S.D., Burns, B.J., Edgar, E.R., Mueser, K.T., Linkins, K.W, Rosenheck, R.A., et al. (2001). Moving assertive community treatment into standard practice. *Psychiatric Services, 52,* 771–779.

Polgar, M. (n.d.). Community mental health: definition. Retrieved January 9, 2011 from the *Encyclopedia of Mental Disorders*: www.minddisorders.com/Br-Del/Community-mental-health.html

Pratt, C.W., & Gill, K.J. (2005). What are community mental health services? In R.E. Drake, M.R. Merrens, & D.W. Lynde (Eds.), *Evidence-based mental health practice: A textbook* (pp. 21–41). New York: W.W. Norton & Company.

President's New Freedom Commission on Mental Health (2003). *Achieving the promise: Transforming mental health care in America.* Retrieved from the Substance Abuse and Mental Health Services Administration website: http://store.samhsa.gov/shin/content//SMA03-3831/SMA03-3831.pdf

Rosen, A., Mueser, K.T., & Teeson, M. (2007). Assertive community treatment—Issues from scientific and clinical literature with implications for practice. *Journal of Rehabilitation Research and Development, 44,* 813–826.

Rosenheck, R.A., Neale, M.S., & Mohammed, S. (2010). Transition to low intensity case management in a VA assertive community treatment model program. *Psychiatric Rehabilitation Journal, 33,* 288–296.

Salyers, M.P., & Bond, G.R. (2009). Innovations and adaptations of assertive community treatment. *American Journal of Psychiatric Rehabilitation, 12,* 185–190.

Salyers, M.P., Masterton, T.W., Fekete, D.M., Picone, J.J., & Bond, G.R. (1998). Transferring clients from intensive case management: Impact on client functioning. *American Orthopsychiatric Association, 68*, 233–245.

Salyers, M.P., McGuire, A.B., Rollins, A.L., Bond, G.R., Mueser, K.T., & Marcy, V.R. (2010). Integrating assertive community treatment and illness management and recovery for consumers with severe mental illness. *Community Mental Health Journal, 46*, 319–329.

Stein, L.I., & Santos, A.B. (1998). *Assertive community treatment of persons with severe mental illness.* New York: W.W. Norton and Company.

Substance Abuse and Mental Health Services Administration (2008). *Assertive community treatment: Evidence-based practice kit* (DHHS pub. id SMA08–4345). Rockville, MD: Author.

Substance Abuse and Mental Health Services Administration (2010). How many Americans experienced mental illness in the past year? *SAMHSA News, 18*(6), 10–11. Retrieved from the SAMHSA website: http://store.samhsa.gov/shin/content/SAM10-186/SAM10-186.pdf

Teague, G.B., Bond, G.R., & Drake, R.E. (1998). Program fidelity in assertive community treatment: Development of a measure. *American Journal of Orthopsychiatry, 68*(2), 216–232.

Torrey, E.F. (1997). *Out of the shadows: Confronting America's mental illness crisis.* New York: John Wiley & Sons.

Trawver, K. (2010). Assertive community treatment. In A. Rubin, D.W. Springer, & K. Trawver (Eds.), *Psychosocial treatment of schizophrenia* (pp. 187–252). Hoboken, NJ: John Wiley and Sons.

Treatment Advocacy Center (2010). Assisted outpatient treatment laws. Retrieved from the Treatment Advocacy website: www.treatmentadvocacycenter.org/index.php?option=com_content&task=view&id=39&Itemid=68

U.S. Department of Veterans Affairs, Northeast Program Evaluation Center (2010). *Mental health intensive case management (MHICM) in the Department of Veterans Affairs: The Thirteenth National Performance Monitoring Report FY 2009.* Retrieved from: http://vaww.nepec.mentalhealth.med.va.gov

U.S. Department of Veterans Affairs, Office of the Inspector General (April 6, 2009). *Healthcare inspection: Implementation of VHA's Uniform Mental Health Services Handbook.* Retrieved from: www.va.gov/oig/54/reports/VAOIG-08-02917-105.pdf

U.S. Department of Veterans Affairs, Veterans Health Administration (2006). *VHA mental health intensive case management (MHICM): VHA directive 2006–2004.* Retrieved from: www1.va.gov/vhapublications.

U.S. Department of Veterans Affairs, Veterans Health Administration (2008). Uniform mental health services in VA medical centers and clinics. In *Veteran Health Administration handbook.* 1160.01. Retrieved from: www1.va.gov/vhapublications

Williams, K., Kukula, M., Bond, G.R., McKasson, M., & Salyers, M.P. (2009). Can a nurse practitioner serve in the prescriber role on an assertive community treatment team? *American Journal of Psychiatric Rehabilitation, 12*, 205–224.

Wyatt, K. (2011). State budget cuts decimate mental health services. *Washington Post.* March 9. Retrieved from: www.washingtonpost.com

Evidence-Based Treatment for Adults with Co-Occurring Mental and Substance Use Disorders

Current Practice and Future Directions[1]

David E. Biegel, Lenore A. Kola, Robert J. Ronis, and Ric Kruszynski

Mental health and substance abuse providers, advocates, and policymakers across the country have become increasingly aware of the challenges related to the needs of clients with co-occurring mental and substance disorders. At the same time, there has been increasing attention concerning the importance of basing practice and service delivery on research-based evidence of effectiveness (evidence-based practice). This chapter discusses the characteristics and needs of adults with co-occurring mental and substance disorders; the need for integrated treatment and the problems with earlier treatment models; the components of an integrated treatment model and the research supporting its effectiveness; the application of integrated treatment to substance abuse service systems; barriers to implementation of this model and support mechanisms that can address these barriers; and the need to integrate behavioral health with primary care.

CHARACTERISTICS AND NEEDS OF ADULTS WITH CO-OCCURRING MENTAL AND SUBSTANCE DISORDERS

A clinical awareness of the problem of dual disorders began in the early 1980s (Caton, 1981; Pepper, Krishner, & Ryglewicz, 1981). The terms co-occurring disorders, dual disorders, and dual diagnosis, as used here, indicate the presence of both severe mental illness and a substance use disorder. Data in the last two decades have established the fact that dual disorders are common. The Epidemiological Catchment Area (ECA) study, based on data collected from 1980 to 1985, showed that the lifetime rate of substance disorder for persons with severe mental illness was approximately half, with 48% of persons with schizophrenia and 56% of persons with bipolar disorder affected (Regier et al., 1990). Findings from the more recent National Comorbidity Study (NCS), with data collected from 1990 to 1992 from a nationally representative sample, also document a high prevalence of co-occurring mental and addictive disorders. In the NCS, 41–65% of participants with a lifetime occurrence of addictive disorder also reported a lifetime occurrence of at least one mental disorder, and 51% of those with a lifetime occurrence of mental disorder reported a lifetime occurrence of at least one addictive disorder as well (Kessler et al., 1996). Studies have suggested that 25–35% of persons with a severe mental illness have an active or recent (within the last 6 months) substance disorder (Mueser, Bennett, & Kushner, 1995). Additionally, numerous studies report high rates of substance abuse among clients in treatment for severe psychiatric disorders (Mueser et al., 1990, 2000).

Dual diagnosis is associated with a variety of negative outcomes. These include higher rates of relapse (Swofford, Kasckow, Scheller-Gilkey, & Inderbitzin, 1996), hospitalization (Johnson, 2000), violence (Steadman et al., 1998; Walsh, Buchanan, & Fahy, 2002), incarceration (Abram & Teplin, 1991; De Leon, Sacks, & Wexler, 2002), homelessness (Caton et al., 1994), and serious infections such as HIV and hepatitis (Compton, Cottler, Ben-Abdallah, Cunningham-Williams, & Spitznagel, 2000; Rosenberg et al., 2001) than are found for persons with only one diagnosis. Drug abusers with comorbid mental disorders are more likely to engage in risky behaviors, such as unprotected sex and needle sharing, that jeopardize their health (Leshner, 1999). Dually diagnosed bipolar patients experience more mixed episodes and rapid cycling, longer recovery times, greater resistance to lithium, and earlier and more frequent hospitalizations (Albanese & Khantzian, 2001).

Co-occurring disorders also pose special challenges for clients' treatment (Horsfall, Cleary, Hunt, & Walter, 2009). There is strong evidence that substance abuse weakens the abilities of persons with a severe mental illness to develop and adhere to effective treatment plans and can shatter already fragile social networks. As a result, dually diagnosed individuals tend to use more psychiatric services than those with a single diagnosis, particularly such costly services as ER visits and inpatient hospitalizations (Dickey & Azeni, 1996). Similarly, substance abuse treatment seeking and adherence can be negatively impacted by symptoms and other effects of mental illness (Grant, 1997; Mueser, Drake, & Miles, 1997). For example, clinical depression may increase substance-abusing individuals' susceptibility to environmental influences that lead to relapse (Leshner, 1999).

THE NEED FOR INTEGRATED TREATMENT: THE PROBLEMS WITH EARLIER TREATMENT MODELS

Professionals working in the fields of mental health and addictions have increasingly recognized the simultaneous occurrence of mental and substance use disorders as presenting extensive problems. Individuals who suffer from this co-occurring disorder have problems in two areas: those arising within themselves as a result of their disorders, which result in clinical challenges and require multiple interventions and paradigm shifts in clinical services currently being offered, and those problems of external origin that derive from the conflicts, limitations, and clashing philosophies of the mental health and addiction treatment systems, which result in systemic challenges (Shollar, 1993).

Historically, services for individuals with co-occurring disorders have been either non-existent or fragmented, and therefore ineffective in demonstrating positive outcomes for the psychiatric or substance use disorder (Drake, Mueser, Clark, & Wallach, 1996; Torrey et al., 2001). Since the problem of dual disorders became more readily apparent in the early 1980s, researchers have demonstrated that parallel but separate mental health and substance abuse treatment systems, as well as sequential treatment, the most common model utilized, have not demonstrated effective outcomes (Drake, McHugo et al., 1998; Mangrum, Spence, & Lopez, 2006).

Persons with dual disorders often find it difficult to access these parallel but separate mental health and substance abuse treatment systems so common in the United States (Substance Abuse and Mental Health Services Administration [SAMHSA], 2002; Tracy & Biegel, 2006). For example, most severely mentally ill clients are unable to navigate between the separate systems, and their conflicting approaches to treatment often complicate or thwart their recovery (Ilgen, Hu, Moos, & McKellar, 2008). Individuals with co-occurring problems have typically responded poorly to traditional primary substance abuse treatment. Similarly, dually disordered individuals have not received maximum benefits from traditional psychiatric treatment programs, and their substance abuse often goes unrecognized, underdiagnosed, and untreated, thereby intensifying the negative consequences of their mental disorder (Singer, Kennedy, & Kola, 1998).

Clients' drug abuse may necessitate adjustments in psychopharmacological treatments for mental illness (Carey, 1995; Leshner, 1999). Historically, each system has insisted that symptoms of the "other" disorder abate before treatment can be considered; i.e., substance abuse professionals require remission or control of psychiatric symptoms, and mental health professionals require sobriety (Mangrum, Spence, & Lopez, 2006). Dually diagnosed clients may not have the wherewithal, perhaps owing to transient or long-term cognitive impairment, to be readily aware of their substance disorder and its negative impact on their mental illness, and therefore may not be motivated to seek treatment for it.

Researchers have studied the use of traditional substance abuse treatments, such as 12-step programs, in populations with serious mental disorders since the early 1980s, with disappointing results. However, a series of NIMH-funded demonstration projects in the late 1980s, incorporating assertive outreach and addictions interventions modified to meet the needs of mentally ill persons, began to show promise (Mercer-McFadden, Drake, Brown, & Fox, 1997). Programs began to incorporate motivational approaches and other comprehensive interventions in the context of multidisciplinary treatment teams in the 1990s, yielding initial positive outcomes, including remission of substance abuse, reductions in hospital utilization, and improved quality of life, as measured by uncontrolled studies (Drake, McHugo, & Noordsay, 1993). Later studies of comprehensive, integrated treatment programs indicated that extended participation (e.g., 18 months or longer) yielded several positive outcomes, including greater engagement, decreased substance abuse, and decreased hospitalization (Drake, Mercer-McFadden, Mueser, McHugo, & Bond, 1998; McCoy et al., 2003; Mueser, Noordsy, Drake, & Fox, 2003).

As a result of these early findings, and through the efforts of consensus panels, there has been an accelerated movement to develop, refine, and evaluate comprehensive, integrated dual disorders treatment (IDDT) programs that meet the variety of clinical and service delivery challenges of this population (Dixon et al., 2010; Drake, 2007; Drake, Morrissey, & Mueser, 2006; Mueser, Drake, & Noorsdy, 2004; Sacks, 2000; Ziedonis et al., 2005). The recent update to the Schizophrenia PORT Psychosocial treatment guidelines recommended that persons with schizophrenia and a co-occurring substance use disorder should be offered substance abuse treatment delivery in a model that integrates mental health and substance abuse treatment.

217

The key elements of that treatment should include motivational enhancement, behavioral strategies focused on engagement in treatment, and coping skills and relapse prevention training (Dixon et al., 2010).

However, although IDDT services are widely advocated, they remain largely unavailable to consumers, owing to innumerable policy, clinical program, and implementation barriers (Drake et al., 2001; Ducharme, Knudsen, & Roman, 2006: Office of Applied Studies, SAMHSA, 2002). Policy barriers include separation of state-level mental health and substance abuse administrative authorities, with separate funding streams, advocacy groups, enabling legislation, information systems, and credentialing criteria (Ridgely, Goldman, & Willenbring, 1990). Local program administrators have often lacked incentives, administrative guidelines, and service models to implement integrated care models (Mercer-McFadden, Drake, & Clark, 1998). Clinician biases based on training experiences with earlier models may create resistances to adopting change; similarly, consumers and family members may lack appropriate psycho-education on dual disorders, or, like other substance abusers, believe that drugs and alcohol are useful in alleviating distress (Mueser, Drake, & Wallach, 1998). Finally, even when appropriate training occurs, frequent turnover in staffing may impede agencies' abilities to sustain fidelity in implementation (Woltmann & Whitley, 2007).

THE NEW HAMPSHIRE-DARTMOUTH INTEGRATED DUAL DISORDERS TREATMENT MODEL

The IDDT model developed by Robert Drake and colleagues at Dartmouth College (Mueser et al., 2003) and recognized by the U.S. SAMHSA as an evidence-based practice involves cross-trained practitioners providing integrated, comprehensive services directed toward the two disorders simultaneously in the same venue, with the goal of recovery from both illnesses. It also assumes that treatment occurs in an orderly fashion geared to the motivation and readiness of the client and involves a long-term commitment on the part of both the practitioner and the client.

In order to develop effective treatment for clients with dual disorders, a cohesive, unitary system of care that is a seamless integration of psychiatric and substance abuse interventions is hypothesized as being necessary (Mueser et al., 2003). This integrated service model addresses many of the limitations of traditional approaches to intervening with these disorders. It combines philosophical, organizational, and treatment characteristics of both systems to provide coordinated interventions for individuals with co-occurring severe mental and substance use disorders. The model utilizes biopsychosocial treatments that combine pharmacological, psychological, educational, and social interventions that are directed to both clients and their families and friends. It promotes client and family involvement in service delivery, and stable housing and employment as necessary conditions for recovery. The focus of the model begins with the assertion that a core value is that of shared decision-making, i.e., developing a collaborative relationship between the service provider and the client (Mueser et al., 2003).

However, the most fundamental aspect of integrating services is that the burden of treating both problems is the responsibility of the treatment system and not that of the client, as it has been in both the historical parallel and sequential models of treatment. The interventions, regardless of their format, need to focus on this integration with a set of consistent and cohesive philosophies of treatment.

Components of the IDDT model that have emerged as an evidence-based practice for the dually disordered population include the following characteristics:

Integrated Treatment

Effective dual disorders treatment programs combine mental health and substance abuse interventions at the clinical level. In the integrated treatment model, the same clinician or clinical team provides both mental health and substance abuse interventions, with the objective of motivating the patient toward a process of recovery (Bellack & DiClemente, 1999; Mueser et al., 2003). From the vantage point of the consumer, a consistent philosophy and set of recommendations guide the treatment, rather than the confusion of receiving mixed messages from multiple providers and systems with differing priorities and perspectives. An integrative perspective informs each aspect of the treatment, from education about the disorders to counseling approaches and pharmacologic interventions.

Comprehensiveness

Effective programs recognize the need to integrate mental health and substance abuse treatment in all aspects of the service delivery system, and across all aspects of the client's living environment. Crisis intervention services, hospitalization and aftercare services, pharmacologic and psychotherapeutic treatments, physical health management, and housing and vocational services must be tailored to address the specific needs of the dual diagnosis patient. Additional interventions continue to be developed and tested and can be added to this arsenal of treatment interventions as the research in this area expands (Drake, 2007; Sacks, Chandler, and Gonzales, 2008). Healthy lifestyles are promoted through learning about diet and exercise, avoiding high-risk situations and behaviors, decreasing involvement in activities that adversely affect health and wellness, and developing friendships with people who do not abuse alcohol and drugs (Mueser et al., 2003).

Stage-Wise Treatment

Incorporating the stages of change model of Prochaska and DiClemente (1984) and the stages of treatment (Osher & Kofoed, 1989), interventions are directed to where the client is with respect to his or her mental illness and substance abuse. The stages of treatment include *engagement*—forming a trusting relationship between provider and consumer; *persuasion*—developing motivation to define objectives and engage in treatment; *active treatment*—a process of acquiring skills and supports to achieve treatment objectives; and *relapse prevention*—enhancing the skills necessary to maintaining stable recovery (Mueser et al., 1995).

Assertive Outreach and Engagement Strategies

Effective integrated treatment programs engage clients through outreach services such as intensive case management or assertive community treatment (Meisler, Blankertz, Santos, &

219

McKay, 1997; Mercer-McFadden et al., 1998). Case managers may find clients at their residence or on the streets and offer services, including assistance with housing and financial entitlements; linkages with general health-care and social services providers; and transportation to community services or meetings. Interventions aim at improving access to services and fostering a trusting relationship with the provider. Without such efforts, engagement and adherence to treatment tend to be low (Hellerstein, Rosenthal, & Miner, 1995).

Motivational Interventions

Interventions such as motivational interviewing are intended to assist clients in understanding the impacts of their illness and drugs and alcohol on their lives, as well as to alert them to the hopeful possibility of recovery (Miller & Rollnick, 2002). Motivational interventions exploit underlying ambivalence to help move the individual to a state of readiness for treatment. Techniques such as expressing empathy, avoiding argumentation, and rolling with resistance allow the therapist to help the client identify discrepancies between current behaviors and future goals, and to develop strategies to begin to achieve them. A review of a small number of studies of motivational interviewing has demonstrated that some people are helped to become engaged in treatment and others become abstinent (Mueser, Drake, & Wallach, 2005).

Counseling

Successful IDDT programs incorporate several kinds of counseling aimed at developing skills and supports to pursue and maintain recovery from both mental illness and substance abuse (Mueser et al., 1998; Roberts, Shaner, & Eckman, 1999). Counseling may include individual, group, and family approaches, and may involve teaching cognitive and behavioral skills that help consumers to identify internal cues that may precede relapse and to cope more effectively with negative mood states or symptoms that, in the past, might have been addressed by using substances.

Social Support

Social supports may be enhanced by group treatments in which consumers share strategies and experiences, by family interventions such as family psychoeducation (Lefley, 2009), and other techniques aimed at strengthening social networks (Tracy & Biegel, 2006). Self-help groups provide support and companionship for individuals motivated to achieve and maintain abstinence and include a range of options, from traditional groups such as Alcoholics Anonymous and Narcotics Anonymous, to groups tailored to special needs of individuals with severe mental illness and substance use disorders, such as Dual Recovery Anonymous (DRA) or Double Trouble. Each individual group has its own particular characteristics. Clinicians should assist consumers in selecting appropriate self-help groups as a means to enhance treatment and relapse prevention. Group treatments that conform to stages of recovery have been a mainstay of treatment for dually disordered clients in the IDDT model (Osher & Kofoed, 1989), but research indicates that group interventions can become even more effective if they are diagnosis-specific (Drake, 2007).

Long-Term Perspective

Research suggests that consumers with dual disorders may experience cycles of relapse and recovery throughout their lives and will achieve the highest quality of life when they have access to services at all times. Even in intensive treatment programs, people with co-occurring mental and substance use disorders rarely achieve stability and functional improvements quickly; rather, improvement occurs over months and years. Effective programs recognize the likelihood of relapse and provide time-unlimited services, including secondary interventions for treatment non-responders, and incorporate effective rehabilitation activities intended to enhance and maintain gains (Alverson, Alverson, & Drake, 2000).

In summary, the IDDT model incorporates a number of components, including integrated treatment, stage-wise interventions, assertive outreach and engagement, motivational interventions, counseling and social support services, and relapse prevention interventions, organized within a comprehensive system of care that takes a long-term perspective to treatment. This model thus addresses the clinical as well as programmatic challenges of professionals working with this population.

Because of the benefits of the IDDT model discussed above, there have begun to be adaptations of the model. On such adaptation, reported by Short et al. (2010), describes the adaptation and implementation of the IDDT outpatient model to a psychiatric inpatient program. The authors discuss the changes that occurred as a result within the hospital's organizational structure, and how the treatment culture was improved, resulting in a significant impact on the quality of services to patients. As discussed below, Kola and colleagues (Kola & Kruszynski, 2010) propose another adaptation of the IDDT model, the extension of IDDT model components into use with substance abuse agencies' clients with co-occurring substance use and mental disorders.

THE EXTENSION OF THE INTEGRATED TREATMENT MODEL INTO SUBSTANCE ABUSE TREATMENT SYSTEMS

The IDDT model discussed in this chapter was developed to meet the needs of persons with severe mental illness, such as schizophrenia or bipolar disorder, as well as a co-occurring substance use disorder. However, there has not been a significant, parallel development in the substance abuse literature on the development of evidence-based treatment models focusing on dual disorders among those with a substance use disorder and the "less severe" mental disorders of anxiety, depression, PTSD, and borderline disorders, in either adults or adolescents (Kola & Kruszynski, 2010; Kola & Singer, 2007; Straussner & Nemenzik, 2007).

According to the U.S. Department of Health and Human Services, an estimated 41–65% of persons with a lifetime substance use disorder have a lifetime history of one mental disorder, which represents a significant portion of individuals in the addiction system that may or may not be receiving assistance with their mental disorders. Models to assist substance abuse agencies in assessing their capacity to develop appropriate evidence-based practices for persons with co-occurring disorders have been developing and may, in the future, lessen the gap between empirical knowledge and practice wisdom (Gotham, Clause, Selig, & Homer, 2010; McGovern, Fox, Xie, & Drake, 2004; McGovern, Matzkin, & Giard, 2007; McGovern, Xie et al., 2007; Timko, Dixon, & Moos, 2005).

A number of components of the evidence-based IDDT model discussed above that have been utilized with individuals with substance use disorders and severe mental illness may present a challenge when attempting to implement them with this those who have a substance use disorder, but with a less severe mental illness (Mueser et al., 2003). This would require a paradigm shift from viewing substance use disorders as isolated from mental illness to developing best practices in the addiction field. The IDDT model may provide a conceptual model for such integration. Common components of the model do emerge and should be considered in adapting the model (Kola & Kruszynski, 2010).

As discussed above, IDDT is an effective model that combines both mental health and substance abuse interventions at the clinical level, with the same clinical team and in the same venue, with the objective of motivating the client toward a process of recovery (Bellack & DiClemente, 1999; Mueser et al., 2003). This integrative perspective provides a comprehensive array of services, all of which are tailored to meet the needs of clients with dual diagnoses (Mueser et al., 2003).

The various components include multidisciplinary teams that require cross-training in both mental health and substance abuse, and both psychiatrists and nurses are routinely included on the team so that appropriate pharmacological interventions can be used. This has not typically been the norm within the substance abuse agencies, which historically have not distinguished between non-addictive and potentially addictive psychotropic medications that assist in the recovery process (Minkoff, 1989).

Other components would include stage-wise interventions and motivational enhancement interventions. Stage-wise interventions focus on matching clients to effective interventions that are consistent with the client's readiness for treatment (Osher & Kofoed, 1989; Prochaska, DiClemente, & Norcross, 1992). The term motivational interventions describes the process by which clients are assisted in understanding the impact of their co-occurring disorders on their lives, as well as being alerted to the hopeful possibility of recovery (Miller & Rollnick, 2002). However, most substance abuse services are designed for the most motivated clients, despite the lack of readiness of many substance abuse clients to engage at that level of treatment.

Time-unlimited services and outreach programming are two other components that may be more difficult to implement in substance abuse services, as they have not been the norm for substance abuse treatment, because most programs conform to a fairly explicit program structure ranging from 7 to 28 days, with some extended programming lasting upwards of a year. Similarly, outreach programming presents a particular challenge, as treatment has historically been based on the belief that recovery is related to personal motivation. This belief makes the assumption that individuals who have a problem with substances have both the internal and external resources to secure necessary services for themselves.

Other components such as substance abuse counseling, family and group treatment, and self-help groups have been longstanding staples of the addiction treatment system, but have been less geared toward dual disorders. DRA or Double Trouble groups have not been developed within that system.

One aspect of the IDDT model that may be a flash point for addiction services, as it relates to the reduction of negative consequences, is the concept of harm reduction. This would include any attempt to protect the client from the direst consequences of his or her substance abuse. This component is directed toward those clients who do not endorse abstinence in the early stages of recovery. This would occur while simultaneously trying to develop a working relationship with the client through the process of stage-wise treatment (Mueser et al., 2003).

Other interventions to promote health, such as STD/HIV prevention, physical health care, nutrition, and other aspects of wellness, have been incorporated into substance abuse treatment. Also, there has recently been recognition that smoking is a major health problem and contributes to relapse (Smeltz, 2007; Williams & Zedonis, 2006). This recognition requires agencies to begin to address this addiction, despite some long-held beliefs that clients should not be asked to give up all addictive substances.

The field of behavioral health has grown more complex and requires that substance abuse agencies adopt models of practice that are more consistent with the complexity of their client population, who have co-occurring mental health and substance abuse problems, as well as transferring the extant technology that will assist these clients in their recovery (Kola & Kruszynski, 2010).

EFFECTIVENESS OF INTEGRATED TREATMENT MODELS: OUTCOME RESEARCH STUDIES

There have been a number of research studies that have evaluated specific components of the IDDT model. In a review of 26 controlled studies of psychosocial interventions for people with severe mental illness and co-occurring substance use disorders, reported or published since 1994, Drake and colleagues (Drake, Mueser, Brunette, & McHugo, 2004) identified 16 outpatient studies, including 12 experimental and 4 quasi-experimental designs. The experimental studies tended to focus on briefer clinical interventions, whereas comparisons of long-term interventions aimed at organizational aspects of care tended to utilize quasi-experimental designs. Seven studies (Barrowclough et al., 2001; Carmichael et al., 1998; Drake, McHugo et al., 1998; Drake, Yovetich, Bebout, Harris, & McHugo, 1997; Godley, Hoewing-Roberson, & Godley, 1994; Jerrell & Ridgely, 1995; Penn & Brooks, 2000) compared integrated versus nonintegrated treatments in longer-term studies with treatment duration varying from a few months to 3 years. Most of these studies included motivational counseling and some form of active substance abuse counseling for clients in active treatment. In some of these studies, the intervention was structural (i.e., mental health and substance abuse clinicians were combined on the same team), rather than clinical (i.e., integration of specific clinical interventions was not specified).

Nearly all of these studies found some evidence that the more integrated form of treatment was superior in terms of abstinence or reductions in severity of alcohol or drug use, overall symptom reduction, hospital utilization, and other general outcomes. Although some studies showed no differences, none favored the less-integrated programs. For example, Drake and colleagues (1997) showed better outcomes in terms of progress toward recovery, reduced hospitalization, and reductions in alcohol abuse, but similar outcomes with respect to drug use, psychiatric symptoms, and quality of life. Mixed findings within two studies were partly

223

explained by poor fidelity to implementing integrated treatment and to treatment drift (i.e., difficulties keeping the interventions separate for the purposes of study) (Drake, Mercer-McFadden, Mueser, McHugo, & Bond, 1998; Godley et al., 1994). Nevertheless, persons with dual disorders were more likely to achieve full remission on teams showing high fidelity to integrated treatment than on low-fidelity teams (43% vs. 15%) (McHugo, Drake, Teague, & Xie, 1999).

Studies focused on more limited integrated interventions, while generally supporting efficacy, were less robust, suggesting that successful integration may require the incorporation of multiple integrated elements. For example, Ho and colleagues (1999) found integrated day treatment plus assertive community treatment and skills training resulted in greater abstinence than integrated day treatment alone, while Hellerstein and colleagues (1985) found no differences between integrated and nonintegrated outpatient group treatment at 4 and 8 months. James et al. (2004) found that a 6-week group intervention, based on motivational interviewing and tailored to subjects' stages of change and reasons for drug use, showed greater reductions in psychopathology, alcohol and drug use, and hospitalization over usual care, while Burnam et al. (1995) found no group differences at 6- and 9-month follow-ups to a comparison of 3 months' intensive integrated day treatment versus nonintegrated outpatient services. Of three studies comparing the impact of a single motivational interview in hospital versus usual care, two studies showed that the intervention group was more likely to attend their first outpatient visits and had a greater reduction in alcohol consumption at 6 months, while one study found no difference (Baker et al., 2002; Hulse & Tait, 2002; Swanson, Pantalon, & Cohen, 1999). Other studies looked at short- and long-term residential treatments, comparing integrated residential treatments with nonintegrated residential care. Despite large rates of attrition from all groups, integrated residential treatment appeared superior in almost all studies to treatment as usual with respect to treatment retention, abstinence or reduced relapse, and criminal activity.

There have been a number of more recent reviews of treatment programs for adults with co-occurring mental and substance use disorders (e.g., Bride, MacMaster, & Webb-Robins, 2006; Dixon et al., 2010; Donald, Dower, & Kavanagh, 2005; Kavanagh & Mueser, 2007; Tiet & Mausbach, 2007). Donald and colleagues (2005) reviewed 10 randomized controlled trials that compared integrated and non-integrated treatment for persons with mental illness and substance abuse, while Tiet and Mausbach's (2007) review of 59 studies included 7 studies of non-specific mental illness and comorbid substance related disorders.

Both reviews were equivocal in terms of whether integrated treatments were superior to nonintegrated treatments for persons with dual disorders. Donald et al. (2005) found that three of seven studies in mental health agencies reported that integrated programs had significantly improved outcome measures for psychiatric symptomatology or reductions in substance abuse. However, neither of the two studies in substance abuse agencies reported significantly improved symptomatology outcomes. Other findings showed that higher treatment compliance was found for clients receiving integrated treatment in four studies, an important finding given the difficulties of treatment engagement and maintenance with this population. One study provided some evidence that integrated treatment might have a positive impact on long-term social adjustment. The Tiet and Mausbach (2007) review found no advantages of integrated treatment in terms of substance abuse or psychiatric outcomes in two studies, with greater improvement on some substance abuse outcomes in two other studies. Both literature reviews indicated that there were a number of methodological limitations in

224

the studies examined, discussed below, which need to be taken into consideration in considering these findings.

Kavanagh and Mueser (2007) reviewed 17 randomized controlled trials of interventions for persons with co-occurring disorders, with partial overlaps in studies reviewed by Donald et al. (2005) and Tiet and Mausbach (2007). Although findings from this review were also mixed, the authors concluded that integrated programs tended to have superior outcomes, although impacts on substance use outcomes tended to be modest or inconsistent.

As noted above, the studies examined in these reviews had a number of limitations, although there have been improvements in study methodology over time. Limitations include: combining diverse categories of dual diagnosis; problems in implementation of interventions, particularly related to the differences between the treatment conditions in the integrated and nonintegrated groups; small sample sizes; unrepresentative population samples; high attrition; lack of attention to racial/ethnic and cultural differences; and the failure to examine the effect of the total amount of services received on treatment outcomes. Additionally, differences in study design and implementation made comparison across studies difficult, resulting in a lack of replicated studies.

Tiet and Mausbach (2007) recommend that future studies of integrated treatment should examine the impact of moderating and mediating factors that would indicate which types of patient benefit from which specific dual diagnosis treatments. They also recommend examinations of how treatment, clinician, and environmental factors affect client outcomes. Such analyses could lead to a better understanding of ways to address barriers to program implementation. Kavanagh and Mueser (2007) also recommend studying the impact of different interventions that are provided at different stages of treatment.

IMPLEMENTING THE IDDT MODEL: NEED FOR SYSTEM CHANGE AND IMPLEMENTATION SUPPORT

There are significant systemic challenges that must be addressed to successfully implement and maintain the IDDT practice. Although many state mental health systems are attempting to implement integrated services for the dually disordered clients, barriers to the development of this integrated model are numerous. To address these barriers, changes are required at all levels of the mental health and substance abuse service delivery systems. These include changes that involve organization and financing at the policy level, both structural and functional agency changes to support innovative programming, training and supervision for clinicians at both the clinical and programmatic levels, and developing dissemination mechanisms to inform consumers so that they may advocate for the development of these programs (Drake et al., 2001; Mueser et al., 2003).

Equally pertinent are implications for state-level policy changes that accommodate the need for infrastructural, regulatory, reimbursement, and contracting mechanisms that align with EBP model principles. Many of the IDDT model principles do not consistently align with the prevailing acute-care model of treatment. Episodic versus time-unlimited care of two chronic illnesses, and a locus of care that emphasizes office-based versus community-based care are just a few examples of where there is potential for disconnect between policy and EBP (Finnerty et al., 2009; White, 2008). Many programs fail to meet all of these critical characteristics;

225

however, research consistently supports that programs demonstrating high fidelity to the model described here—those that incorporate more of the core elements—produce better clinical outcomes (Ho et al., 1999; Jerrell & Ridgely, 1999; McHugo et al., 1999).

It is now recognized that barriers to implementation of EBPs in the mental health and other fields cannot be overcome solely by traditional, time-limited disseminating strategies of training of professionals and provision of written materials. While these strategies may be a necessary component of bringing about program change, they are insufficient by themselves to bring about change in behavior (Torrey et al., 2001). How well a practice such as IDDT translates from research into practice has limited impact on the weight of the evidence regarding program outcomes. That is to say, although good clinical evidence can inform the organizational decision-making process regarding what services it may be preferable to provide, outcomes evidence contributes little or nothing that will assist that organization with effective implementation strategies to install the practice into their organizational culture, as well as the broader community. As Fixsen and colleagues note, "the challenges and complexities of implementation far outweigh the efforts of developing the practices and programs themselves" (Fixsen, Naoom, Blasé, Friedman, & Wallace, 2005).

In addition, successful implementation of EBPs is often greatly assisted by longer-term, on-site implementation support involving programmatic and clinical consultation by experts in the model to be implemented and the creation of communication and support networks among providers implementing EBPs. Such oversight can shape implementation with an organizational change framework that closely mirrors the stages of change principles and that can help address resistance to various aspects of organizational change being undertaken to effectively install the practice model (Kruszynski & Boyle, 2006; Lehman, Greener, & Simpson, 2002).

Many variables can positively or negatively impact successful implementation efforts. The need for inclusion of key community and systems stakeholder input from the inception of implementation can pave the way for monitoring and troubleshooting when necessary (Rapp et al., 2008). Other important variables that impact implementation include: practitioner and supervisor characteristics, staff selection, clinical leadership, professional attitudes, application of effective training strategies, and agency leadership strategies that include consensus for the vision and roll-out of the practice model (Brousselle, Lamothe, Sylvain, Foro, & Perreault, 2010; Fadden, 1997; Fixsen et al., 2005; Kruszynski & Boyle, 2006; Wieder and Kruszynski, 2007).

Over the past decade, there has been considerable attention on the national level paid to a comprehensive approach to this issue as part of the Implementing Evidence-Based Practices for Severe Mental Illness Project, which was funded by the MacArthur, Johnson & Johnson, and Robert Wood Johnson Foundations, the U.S. Substance Abuse and Mental Health Services Administration, the NAMI, and state and local mental health organizations. This project involved promoting change in the use of EBPs through three program elements: predisposing/disseminating strategies (educational materials and training), enabling methods (practice guidelines and decision support), and reinforcing strategies (practice feedback mechanisms) via an array of technical supports (McHugo et al., 2007; Rapp et al., 2008; Torrey et al., 2001).

In Ohio, the Ohio Departments of Mental Health (ODMH) and Alcohol and Drug Addiction Services (ODADAS) provided funding that facilitates the aforementioned technical support for EBP implementation in the form of a statewide coordinating center external to

226

both the mental health and substance abuse service delivery systems (Biegel et al., 2003). Thus, the Center for Evidence-Based Practices (CEBP) at Case Western Reserve University's Substance Abuse and Mental Illness Coordinating Center of Excellence (SAMI CCOE) was created to facilitate the implementation and maintenance of high fidelity to the IDDT EBP model in Ohio's mental health system. The SAMI CCOE is one of seven current coordinating centers in Ohio developed over the past several years and funded by ODMH, whose purpose is to promote the use and maintenance of a variety of high-quality evidence-based mental health treatment modalities.

The CEBP is focused on assisting programs to implement and maintain high fidelity to the IDDT and other EBP models in Ohio. The center accomplishes this purpose through the provision of training and technical assistance, dissemination, and research into mental health and substance abuse programs implementing this treatment model in Ohio, nationally, and internationally. The goals of the CEBP are to:

1. provide ongoing clinical training and direct clinical supervision for professional staff from mental health and substance abuse systems involved in the delivery of services and/or supervision and management of such services for persons with dual diagnosis;
2. provide administrative consultation on SAMI program design and implementation issues to administrators from mental health and substance abuse systems involved in the delivery, supervision, and/or management of such services for persons with a dual or co-occurring diagnosis;
3. disseminate evidence-based research about integrated treatment for persons with dual diagnosis and other related practice models, such as supported employment and motivational interviewing;
4. conduct research focused on the assessment of program fidelity model adaptations, and consumer, family, and systems performance outcomes for programs implementing the IDDT and other EBP models.

The SAMI CCOE supports fidelity to the IDDT model while appreciating the need for adaptations to the many service system and situational challenges existing in Ohio (Kruszynski, Kubek, Boyle, & Kola, 2006).

INTEGRATING BEHAVIORAL HEALTH WITH PRIMARY CARE

No current review of IDDT services should exclude consideration of the so-called "triple diagnoses" of medical illness and psychiatric and substance use disorders. Indeed, recent interest in better managing the complex interactions between psychiatric and medical illnesses has been demonstrated in such documents as the President's New Freedom Commission on Mental Health (2003), in a report of the Medical Directors Council of the National Association of State Mental Health Program Directors (Parks, Pollack, & Mauer, 2005), in SAMHSA initiatives promoting integrated behavioral and physical health care (e.g., Bella & Palmer-Barnette, 2010), and in the implications of the recently enacted health-care reform legislation, the Patient Protection and Affordability Care Act of 2010 (Public Law 111–118, 2010).

The link between primary care service availability and improved medical outcomes has long been demonstrated in the general population. Access to such services, however, may be particularly challenging for patients with mental illness and/or substance use disorders. Socioeconomic disadvantages, difficulties in obtaining health insurance, cognitive limitations, and misattribution of physical symptoms to psychopathology by treating physicians, all these play roles in limiting access to medical care for persons with mental illness. For those receiving psychiatric services in the public sector, specialty mental health clinics and emergency rooms may be the only points of contact with the health-care system (Druss, Rohrbaugh, Levinson, & Rosenheck, 2001).

At the same time, both psychiatric and substance use disorders have been consistently associated with excess medical morbidity and mortality. Schizophrenia, for example, has long been described as a "life-shortening disease" (Allebeck, 1989), with early studies demonstrating shortened life expectancies of 9–12 years compared with the general population (Brown, Inskip, & Barraclough, 2000; Goldman, 1999). A literature review in 1996 found that standardized mortality ratios of both natural and unnatural causes of death among psychiatric patients were more than twice those of the general population (Felker, Yazel, & Short, 1996). More recent studies of mortality and medical comorbidity among patients with serious mental illness in the public sector have shown a standardized mortality ratio for all causes of death of 3.2, with a mean of 32 years of potential life lost (Miller, Paschall, & Svendsen, 2006). Although intentional self-harm and accidents account for a portion of excess mortality, heart disease, obesity, hypertension, diabetes mellitus, and chronic obstructive pulmonary disease (COPD) are also common contributors. Similarly, medical comorbidities in patients with substance use disorders are well documented, including those with direct causal relationships to the substances of abuse, such as liver, heart, and GI disease related to alcohol, or pain-related diagnoses among those with narcotic addictions, but also such diseases as COPD, diabetes, and hypertension (Mertens, Yun, Parthasarathy, Moore, & Weisner, 2010; Zornberg & Weiss, 1997).

Few studies have looked specifically at the association of the combination of substance use disorders, mental illness, and medical disorders. Even the National Comorbidity Study (Kessler et al., 1994) included no information about comorbid medical disorders. One study considering health-care utilization patterns in individuals with depression, alcohol abuse, and medical problems found the likelihood of seeking treatment was lower when all three conditions were present (Jackson, Manning, & Wells, 1995). An observational study of adult Medicaid recipients with schizophrenia found no differences in age- and gender-adjusted rates of diabetes, hypertension, heart disease, asthma, and other conditions between those with and those without co-occurring substance use disorders (Dickey, Azeni, & Weiss, 2000), while another found that "the presence of a substance use disorder contributed to the prevalence of five of the (eight studied) medical disorders" (heart disease, asthma, GI disoders, skin infections, and acute respiratory disorders) among adults with mental illness (Dickey, Normand, Weiss, Drake, & Azeni, 2002).

Several factors directly associated with mental illness are known to increase the risk of medical illness, including use of medications that contribute to weight gain (associated with diabetes and hypertension), high prevalence of smoking (associated with asthma, heart disease, and lung cancer), poor personal hygiene (associated with skin infections), and reduced physical activity (associated with hypertension and heart disease) among others (Dickey et al., 2002). It is unclear whether these factors alone, or some unexplained variance, account for the higher risk of medical comorbidity in patients with co-occurring disorders. Certainly, however, there are implications for the design of services, and for challenging, in particular, the dominant practice of separating behavioral health services from medical care services in both the private and public sectors. Patients with psychiatric illness, especially younger adults with serious mental illness, are at high risk for not receiving medical services (Cradock-O'Leary, Young, Yano, Wang, & Lee, 2002). Most mental health professionals are neither trained nor qualified to diagnose and treat medical problems, and psychiatric symptoms such as depression and psychosis may interfere with the patients' abilities to communicate concerns to medical physicians when they are accessed (Holmberg, 1988). For many of these patients, provision of primary care services in the behavioral health setting may be optimal—if the expertise and resources can be made available.

Parks et al. (2005) have applied the Four Quadrant Clinical Integration Model, developed under the auspices of the National Council for Community Behavioral Healthcare (NCCBH) to determining the best locus of care for persons with co-occurring behavioral (both mental illness and substance use disorders) and medical disorders: Analogous to its application to dual diagnosis services, Quadrant I describes individuals with low behavioral and physical health risk/status, who might receive both primary care and basic behavioral health interventions in the primary care setting. Quadrant II, those with higher behavioral health risk but lower physical health, are best served in a specialty behavioral health system that provides basic primary care screening and coordinates care with primary care, which is optimally co-located in the behavioral health-care setting. Quadrant III describes those with relatively low behavioral health but high medical complexity/risk, best served in the primary/medical care sector, with access to behavioral health specialists on site. And Quadrant IV describes the "triply diagnosed," with both high behavioral health and high medical complexity/risk, who require both specialty and primary care services, and for whom both behavioral and medical care case managers must work to coordinate services collaboratively.

Clearly, however, "one size does not fit all." Other factors, such as age, socioeconomic status, acculturation, and expectation, may have a significant impact, as is demonstrated by findings that older patients are more likely to accept collaborative mental health treatment within primary care settings than in specialty clinics (Bartels et al., 2004). Regardless of the setting, future research studies are needed to evaluate whether integration of primary care/physical health services with IDDT demonstrates superior health outcomes and reduced morbidity/mortality for persons with co-occurring psychiatric and substance use disorders.

CONCLUSION

Policymakers, practitioners, consumers, and their families have reason to be optimistic about the future care of individuals with co-occurring substance and mental disorders, given advances in the development of EBPs for this population, which provide hope for recovery from dual disorders. However, as we have seen, to date, EBP for adults with co-occurring disorders is not the norm, with significant barriers to both clinical and organizational issues still significant issues. Ongoing state- and county-level collaborations are essential among currently parallel mental health, substance abuse, criminal justice, housing, and vocational rehabilitation systems, in order for EBPs to be successfully implemented and maximally sustained with high fidelity.

229

In addition, treatment strategies that allow substance abuse agencies to extend integrated treatment for clients with substance use problems and less severe mental illness need to be developed and tested, as do treatment models than integrate behavioral health care with primary care.

DISCUSSION QUESTIONS

1. The authors provide research that supports the efficacy of an integrated treatment model for clients with co-occurring disorders. Given that this model has been shown to be effective, why do so many barriers to implementation exist?

2. What does the term "triple diagnosis of medical illness, psychiatric, and substance use disorders" mean, and why is it an important concept in service design and delivery?

3. Discuss the benefits of the provision of primary care services in the behavioral health settings.

LEARNING ASSIGNMENT

Research your community and determine what, if any, integrated services for co-occurring disorders exist. Find out as much as you can about what treatment is provided, who it serves, etc. Present what you learn in class.

SUGGESTED READINGS

Drake, R.E., Mueser, K.T., Brunette, M.F., & McHugo, G.J. (2004). A review of treatments for people with severe mental illnesses and co-occurring substance use disorders. *Psychiatric Rehabilitation Journal, 27,* 360–374.

Kola, L.A. & Kruszysnki, R. (2010) Adapting the integrated dual-disorder treatment model for addiction services. *Alcoholism Treatment Quarterly, 28*(4), 437–450.

Mueser, K.T., Noorsdy, D.L., Drake, R.E., & Fox, L. (2003). *Integrated Treatment for Dual Disorders: A Guide to Effective Practice.* New York: Guilford Press.

INTERNET RESOURCES

Center for Evidence-Based Practices, Case Western Reserve University: www.centerforebp.case.edu

Co- Occurring Disorders Treatment Manual and Workbook published by the Louis de la Parte Florida Mental Health Research Institute, University of South Florida: mhlp.fmhi.usf.edu/research/rdetail.cfm?prid=121

Dartmouth Psychiatric Research Center: prc.dartmouth.edu

NOTE

1 Research for this chapter was supported by grants from the Ohio Departments of Mental Health and Alcohol and Drug Addiction Services.

REFERENCES

Abram, K.M. & Teplin, L.A. (1991). Co-occurring disorders among mentally ill jail detainees: Implications for public policy. *American Psychologist, 46,* 1036–1045.

Albanese, M. & Khantzian, E. (2001). The difficult-to-treat patient substance abuse. In M.J. Dewan (Ed.), *The difficult-to-treat psychiatric patient* (pp. 273–298). Washington, DC: APPI.

Allebeck, P. (1989). Schizophrenia: a life shortening disease. *Schizophrenia Bulletin, 15,* 81–89.

Alverson, H., Alverson, M., & Drake, R.E., (2000). An ethnographic study of the longitudinal course of substance abuse among people with severe mental illness. *Community Mental Health Journal, 36,* 557–569.

Baker, A., Lewin, T., Reichler, H., Clancy, R., Carr, V., Garrett, R., Sly, K., Devir, H., & Terry, M. (2002). Motivational interviewing among psychiatric in-patients with substance use disorders. *Acta Psychiatrica Scandinavica, 106,* 233–240.

Barrowclough, C., Haddock, G., Tarrier, N., Lewis, S.W., Moring, J., O'Brien, B., Schofield, N., & McGovern, J. (2001). Randomized controlled trial of motivational interviewing, cognitive behavior therapy, and family intervention for patients with comorbid schizophrenia and substance use disorders. *American Journal of Psychiatry, 158*(10), 1706–1713.

Bartels, S.J., Coakley, E.H., Zubritsky, C., Ware, J.H., Miles, K.M., et al. (2004). Improving access to geriatric mental health services: A randomized trial comparing treatment engagement with integrated versus enhanced referral care for depression, anxiety and at-risk alcohol use. *American Journal of Psychiatry 161*(8), 1455–1462.

Bella, M. & Palmer-Barnette, L. (2010). *Options for integrating care for dual eligibles: A center for healthcare strategies inc. Technical assistance brief.* Rockville, MD: Substance Abuse and Mental Health Services Administration.

Bellack, A.S. & DiClemente, C.C. (1999). Treating substance abuse among patients with schizophrenia. *Psychiatric Services, 50,* 75–80.

Biegel, D.E., Kola, L.A., Ronis, R.J., Boyle, P.E., Delos Reyes, C.M., Wieder, B., & Kubek, P. (2003). The Ohio Substance Abuse and Mental Illness Coordinating Center of Excellence: Implementation support for evidence-based practice. *Research in Social Work Practice, 13*(4), 531–545.

Bride, E., MacMaster, S.A., & Webb-Robins, L. (2006). Is integrated treatment of co-occurring disorders more effective than nonintegrated treatment? *Best Practices in Mental Health, 2*(2), 43–57.

Brousselle, A., Lamothe, L., Sylvain, C., Foro, A., & Perreault, M. (2010). Key enhancing factors for integrating services for patients with mental and substance use disorders. *Mental Health and Substance Use: Dual Diagnosis, 3*(3), 203–218.

Brown, S., Inskip, H., & Barraclough, B. (2000). Causes of the excess mortality of schizophrenia. *British Journal of Psychiatry, 177,* 212–217.

Burnam, M.A., Morton, S.C., McGlynn, E.A., Peterson, L.P., Stecher, B.M., Hayes, C., & Vaccaro, J. (1995). An experimental evaluation of residential and nonresidential treatment for dually diagnosed homeless adults. *Journal of Addictive Diseases, 14,* 111–134.

Carey, K. (1995). Treatment of substance use disorders and schizophrenia. In A.F. Lehman & L.B. Dixon (Eds.), *Double jeopardy: Chronic mental illness and substance use disorders* (pp. 85–108). Chur, Switzerland: Harwood Academic Publishers.

Carmichael, D., Tackett-Gibson, M., O'Dell, L., Menon, R., Jayasuriya, B., & Jordan, J. (1998). *Texas dual diagnosis project evaluation report, 1997–1998*. College Station, TX: Texas A&M University, Public Policy Research Institute.

Caton, C.L.M. (1981). The new chronic patient and the system of community care. *Hospital and Community Psychiatry, 32*, 475–478.

Caton, C.L.M., Shrout, P.E., Eagle, P.F., Opler, L.A., Felix, A., & Dominguez, B. (1994). Risk factors for homelessness among schizophrenic men: A case control study. *American Journal of Public Health, 84*, 265–270.

Compton, W.M., Cottler, L.B., Ben-Abdallah, A., Cunningham-Williams, R., & Spitznagel, E.L. (2000). The effects of psychiatric comorbidity on response to an HIV prevention intervention. *Drug and Alcohol Dependence, 58*(3), 247–257.

Cradock-O'Leary, J., Young, A.S., Yano, E.M., Wang, M., & Lee, M.I. (2002). Use of general medical services by VA patients with psychiatric disorders. *Psychiatric Services, 53*(7), 874–878.

De Leon, G., Sacks, S., & Wexler, H.K. (2002). Modified prison therapeutic communities for the dual- and multiple-diagnosed offender. In C.G. Leukefeld & F. Tims (Eds.), *Treatment of drug offenders: Policies and issues*. New York: Springer Publishing Company.

Dickey, B. & Azeni, H. (1996). Persons with dual diagnoses of substance abuse and major mental illness: Their excess costs of psychiatric care. *American Journal of Public Health, 87*(7), 973–977.

Dickey, B., Azeni, H., Weiss, R., et al. (2000). Schizophrenia, substance use disorders, and medical co-morbidity. *Journal of Mental Health Policy and Economics, 3*, 27–33.

Dickey, B., Normand, S.T., Weiss, R.D., Drake, R.E., & Azeni, H. (2002) Medical morbidity, mental illness and substance use disorders. *Psychiatric Services 53*(7), 861–867.

Dixon, L.B., Dickerson, F., Bellack, A.S., Bennett, M., Dickinson, D., Goldberg, R.W., et al. (2010). The 2009 Schizophrenia PORT psychosocial treatment recommendations and summary statements. *Schizophrenia Bulletin, 36*(1), 48–70.

Donald, M., Dower, J., & Kavanagh, D. (2005). Integrated versus non-integrated management and care for clients with co-occurring mental health and substance use disorders: A qualitative systematic review of randomized controlled trials. *Social Science & Medicine, 60*, 1371–1383.

Drake, R.E. (2007). Psychosocial intervention research on co-occurring disorders. *Journal of Dual Disorders, 3*(2), 85–93.

Drake, R.E., Essock, S.M., Shaner, A., Carey, K.B., Minkoff, K., Kola, L., Lynde, D., Osher, F.C., Clark, R.E., & Rickards, L. (2001). Implementing dual diagnosis services for clients with severe mental illness. *Psychiatric Services, 52*, 469–476.

Drake, R.E., McHugo, G.J., Clark, R.E., Teague, G.B., Xie, H., Miles, K., & Ackerson, T.H. (1998). Assertive community treatment for patients with co-occurring severe mental illness and substance use disorder: A clinical trial. *American Journal of Orthopsychiatry, 68*, 201–215.

Drake, R.E., McHugo, G., & Noordsay, D.L. (1993). Treatment of alcoholism among schizophrenic outpatients: Four year outcomes. *American Journal of Psychiatry, 150*, 328–329.

Drake, R.E., Mercer-McFadden, C., Mueser, K.T., McHugo, G.J., & Bond, R. (1998). Review of integrated health and substance abuse treatment for patients with dual disorders. *Schizophrenia Bulletin, 24*, 589–608.

Drake, R.E., Morrissey, J.P., & Mueser, K.T. (2006). The challenge of treating forensic dual diagnosis clients: Comment on "Integrated treatment for jail recidivists with co-occurring psychiatric and substance use disorders." *Community Mental Health Journal, 42*(4), 427–430.

Drake, R.E., Mueser, K.T., Brunette, M.F., & McHugo, G.J. (2004). A review of treatments for people with severe mental illnesses and co-occurring substance use disorders. *Psychiatric Rehabilitation Journal, 27*, 360–374.

Drake, R.E., Mueser, K.T., Clark, R.E., & Wallach, M.A. (1996). The course, treatment, and outcome of substance disorder in persons with severe mental illness. *American Journal of Orthopsychiatry, 66*, 42–51.

Drake, R.E., Yovetich, N.A., Bebout, R.R., Harris, M., & McHugo, G.J. (1997). Integrated treatment for dually diagnosed homeless adults. *Journal of Nervous and Mental Disease, 18*, 298–305.

Druss, B.G., Rohrbaugh, R.M., Levinson, C.M., & Rosenheck, R.A. (2001). Integrated medical care for patients with serious psychiatric illness. *Archives of General Psychiatry, 58*, 861–868.

Ducharme, L.J., Knudsen, H.K., & Roman, P.M. (2006). Availability of integrated care for co-occurring substance abuse and psychiatric conditions. *Community Mental Health Journal, 42*(4), 363–375.

Fadden, G. (1997). Implementation of family interventions in routine clinical practice following staff training programs: A major cause for concern. *Journal of Mental Health, 6*(6), 599–612.

Felker, B., Yazel, J.J., & Short, D. (1996). Mortality and medical comorbidity among psychiatric patients: A review. *Psychiatric Services 47*, 1356–1363.

Finnerty, M.F., Rapp, C.A., Bond, G.R., Lynde, D.W., Ganju, V., & Goldman, H.H. (2009). The State Health Authority Yardstick (SHAY). *Community Mental Health Journal, 45*, 228–236.

Fixsen, D., Naoom, S.F., Blasé, K.A., Friedman, R.M., & Wallace, F. (2005). *Implementation research: A synthesis of the literature*. Tampa, FL: University of South Florida, Louis de la Parte Florida Mental Health Institute, The National Implementation Research Network (FMHI Publication 231).

Godley, S.H., Hoewing-Roberson, R., & Godley, M.D. (1994). *Final MISA Report*. Bloomington Lighthouse Institute.

Goldman, L.S. (1999). Medical illness in patients with schizophrenia. *Journal of Clinical Psychiatry, 60*, 10–15.

Gotham, H.J., Clause, R.E., Selig, K., & Homer, A.L. (2010). Increasing program capability to provide treatment for co-occurring substance use and mental disorders: Organizational characteristics. *Journal of Substance Abuse Treatment, 38*, 160–169.

Grant, B. (1997). The influence of comorbid major depression and substance use disorders on alcohol and drug treatment: Results of a national survey. In L. Onken, J. Blaine, S. Genser, & A. Horton, Jr. (Eds.), *Treatment of drug-dependent individuals with comorbid mental disorders* (NIDA Research Monograph 172, Publication No. 97–4172, pp. 4–15). Rockville, MD: National Institutes of Health.

Hellerstein, D.J., Rosenthal, R.N., & Miner, C.R. (1995). A prospective study of integrated outpatient treatment for substance abusing schizophrenic patients. *American Journal on Addictions, 4*, 33–42.

Ho, A.P., Tsuang, J.W., Liberman, R.P., Wang, R., Wilkins, J.N., Eckman, T.A., & Shaner, A.L. (1999). Achieving effective treatment of patients with chronic psychotic illness and comorbid substance dependence. *American Journal of Psychiatry, 156*, 1765–1770.

Holmberg, S. (1988). Physical health problems of the psychiatric client. *Journal of Psychosocial Nursing and Mental Health Services, 26*, 35–39.

Horsfall, J., Cleary, M., Hunt, G.E., & Walter, G. (2009). Psychosocial treatments for people with co-occurring severe mental illness and substance use disorders (dual diagnosis): A review of empirical literature. *Harvard Review of Psychiatry, 17*(1), 24–34.

Hulse, G.K. & Tait, R.J. (2002). Six month outcomes associated with a brief alcohol intervention for adult in-patients with psychiatric disorders. *Drug and Alcohol Review, 21*, 105–112.

Ilgen, M.A., Hu, K.U., Moos, R.H., & McKellar, J. (2008). Continuing care after inpatient psychiatric treatment for patients with psychiatric and substance use disorders. *Psychiatric Services, 59*(9), 982–988.

Jackson, C.A., Manning, W.G., & Wells, K.B. (1995). Impact of prior and current alcohol use on use of services by patients with depression and chronic medical illnesses. *Health Services Research, 30*, 687–702.

James, W., Preston, N.J., Koh, G., Spencer, C., Kisely, S.R., & Castle, D.J. (2004) A group intervention which assists patients with dual diagnosis to reduce their drug use: A randomized controlled trial. *Psychological Medicine, 34*, 983–990.

Jerrell, J.M. & Ridgely, M.S. (1995). Comparative effectiveness of three approaches to serving people with severe mental illness and substance abuse disorders. *Journal of Nervous and Mental Disease, 18*, 566–576.

Jerrell, J.M. & Ridgely, M.S. (1999). Impact of robustness of program implementation on outcomes of clients in dual diagnosis programs. *Psychiatric Services, 50*, 109–112.

Johnson, J. (2000). Cost-effectiveness of mental health services for persons with a dual diagnosis: A literature review and the CCMHCP. The cost-effectiveness of community mental health health care for single and dually diagnosed project. *Journal of Substance Abuse Treatment, 18*(2), 119–127.

Kavanagh, D.J. & Mueser, K.T. (2007). Current evidence on integrated treatment for serious mental disorder and substance misuse. *Journal of the Norwegian Psychological Association, 44*, 618–637.

Kessler, R.C., McGonagle, K.A., Zhao, S., et al. (1994). Lifetime and 12 month prevalence of DSM-IIIR psychiatric disorders in the United States: Results from the National Comorbidity Survey. *Archives of General Psychiatry, 51*, 8–19.

Kessler, R.C., Nelson, C.B., McGonagle, K.A., Edlund, M.J., Frank, R.G., & Leaf, P.J. (1996). The epidemiology of co-occurring addictive and mental disorders: Implications for prevention and service utilization. *American Journal of Orthopsychiatry, 66*, 17–31.

Kola, L.A. & Kruszysnki, R. (2010). Adapting the integrated dual-disorder treatment model for addiction services. *Alcoholism Treatment Quarterly, 28*(4), 437–450.

Kola, L.A. & Singer, M.I. (Eds.) (2007). (Editorial) Dual disorders. *Special Issue of the Journal of Social Work Practice in the Addictions.*

Kruszynski, R. & Boyle, P. (2006). Implementation of the integrated dual disorders treatment model: Stage-wise strategies for service providers. *Journal of Dual Diagnosis, 2*(3), 147–155.

Kruszynski, R., Kubek, P., Boyle, P.E., & Kola, L.A. (2006). *Implementing IDDT: A step-by-step guide to stages of organizational change.* Cleveland, OH: Ohio SAMI CCOE, Case Western Reserve University.

Lefley, H. (2009). *Family psychoeducation for serious mental illness.* New York: Oxford University Press.

Lehman, W.E.K., Greener, J.M., & Simpson, D.D. (2002). Assessing organizational readiness for change. *Journal of Substance Abuse Treatment, 22*(4), 197–209.

Leshner, A. (1999). Drug abuse and mental disorders: Comorbidity is reality (Director's Column). *NIDA Notes, 14*(4), 1–3.

Mangrum, L.F., Spence, R.T., & Lopez, M.L. (2006). Integrated versus parallel treatment of co-occurring psychiatric and substance use disorders. *Journal of Substance Abuse Treatment, 30*, 79–84.

McCoy, M.D., Devitt, T., Clay, R., Davis, K.E., Dincin, J., Pavick, D., et al. (2003). Gaining insight: Who benefits from residential integrated treatment for people with dual diagnoses? *Psychiatric Rehabilitation Journal, 27*, 140–150.

McGovern, M.P., Fox, T.S., Xie, H., & Drake, R.E. (2004). A survey of clinical practices and readiness to adopt evidence-based practices: Dissemination research in an addiction treatment system. *Journal of Substance Abuse Treatment, 26*, 305–312.

McGovern, M.P., Matzkin, A.L., & Giard, J.A. (2007). Assessing the dual diagnosis capability of addiction treatment services: The Dual Diagnosis Capability in Addiction Treatment (DDCAT) Index. *Journal of Dual Diagnosis, 3*, 111–123.

McGovern, M.P., Xie, H., Acquilano, S., Segal, S.R., Siembab, L., & Drake, R.E. (2007). Addiction treatment services and co-occurring disorders: The ASAM-PPC-2R Taxonomy of program dual diagnosis capability. *Journal of Addictive Diseases, 26*(3), 27–37.

McHugo, G.J., Drake, R.E., Teague, G.B., & Xie, H. (1999). Fidelity to assertive community treatment and client outcomes in the New Hampshire dual disorders study. *Psychiatric Services, 50*, 818–824.

McHugo, G.J., Drake, R.E., Whitley, R., Bond, G.R., Campbell, K., Rapp, C.A., Goldman, H.H., Lutz, W.J., & Finnerty, M.T. (2007). Fidelity outcomes in the national implementing evidence based practices project. *Psychiatric Services, 58*(10), 1279–1284.

Meisler, N., Blankertz, L., Santos, A.B., & McKay, C. (1997). Impact of assertive community treatment on homeless persons with co-occurring severe psychiatric and substance use disorders. *Community Mental Health Journal, 33*, 113–122.

Mercer-McFadden, C., Drake, R.E., Brown, N.B., & Fox, R.S. (1997). The community support program demonstrations of services for young adults with severe mental illness and substance use disorders, 1987–1991. *Psychiatric Rehabilitation Journal, 20*(3), 13–24.

Mercer-McFadden, C., Drake, R.E., & Clark, R.E. (1998). *Substance abuse treatment for people with severe mental disorders.* Concord, NH: New Hampshire–Dartmouth Psychiatric Research Center.

Mertens, J.R., Yun, W.L., Parthasarathy, S., Moore, C., & Weisner, C.M. (2010). Medical and psychiatric conditions of alcohol and drug treatment patients in an HMO. *Archives of Internal Medicine 163*(20), 2511–2517.

Miller, B.J., Paschall, C.B., & Svendsen, D.P. (2006). Mortality and medical comorbidity among patients with serious mental illness. *Psychiatric Services 57*(10), 1482–1487.

Miller, W. & Rollnick, S. (2002). *Motivational interviewing (2nd ed.): Preparing people for change.* New York: Guilford Press.

Minkoff, K. (1989). An integrated treatment model for dual diagnosis of psychosis and addiction. *Hospital and Community Psychiatry, 40,* 1031–1036.

Mueser, K.T., Bennett, M., & Kushner, M.G. (1995). Epidemiology of substance use disorders among persons with chronic mental illnesses. In A.F. Lehman & L.B. Dixon (Eds.), *Double jeopardy: Chronic mental illness and substance use disorders* (pp. 9–25). Chur, Switzerland: Harwood Academic Publishers.

Mueser, K.T., Drake, R., & Miles, K. (1997). The course and treatment of substance use disorder in persons with severe mental illness. In L. Onken, J. Blaine, S. Genser, & A. Horton, Jr. (Eds.), *Treatment of drug-dependent individuals with comorbid mental disorders* (NIDA Research Monograph 172, Publication No. 97–4172, pp. 86–109). Rockville, MD: National Institutes of Health.

Mueser, K.T., Drake, R.E., & Noorsdy, D.L. (2004). Integrated mental health and substance abuse treatment for severe psychiatric disorders. *Journal of Practical Psychiatry and Behavioral Health, 4,* 129–139.

Mueser, K.T., Drake, R.E., & Wallach, M. (1998). Dual diagnosis: A review of etiological theories. *Addictive Behaviors 23,* 717–734.

Mueser, K., Drake, R.E., & Wallach, M.A. (2005). Psychosocial interventions for adults with severe mental illnesses and co-occurring substance use disorders: A review of specific interventions. *Journal of Dual Diagnosis, 1*(2), 57–82.

Mueser, K.T., Noorsdy, D.L., Drake, R.E., & Fox, L. (2003). *Integrated treatment for dual disorders: A guide to effective practice.* New York: Guilford Press.

Mueser, K.T., Yarnold, P.R., Levinson, D.F., Singh, H., Bellack, A.S., Kee, K., Morrison, R.L., & Yadalam, K.G. (1990). Prevalence of substance abuse in schizophrenia: Demographic and clinical correlates. *Schizophrenia Bulletin, 16,* 31–56.

Mueser, K.T., Yarnold, P.R., Rosenberg, S.D., Swett, C., Miles, K.M., & Hill, D. (2000). Substance use disorder in hospitalized severely mentally ill psychiatric patients: Prevalence, correlates, and subgroups. *Schizophrenia Bulletin, 26,* 179–192.

Office of Applied Studies, Substance Abuse and Mental Health Services Administration (2002). *The DASIS Report: Facilities offering special programs for dually diagnosed clients.* Rockville, MD: U.S. Department of Health and Human Services.

Osher, F.C. & Kofoed, L.L. (1989). Treatment of patients with psychiatric and psychoactive substance use disorders. *Hospital and Community Psychiatry, 40,* 1025–1030.

Parks, J., Pollack, D., & Mauer, B. (2005). *Integrating behavioral health and primary care services: Opportunities and challenges for state mental health authorities.* Alexandria, VA: National Association of State Mental Health Directors.

Penn, P.E. & Brooks, A.J. (2000). Five years, twelve steps, and REBT in the treatment of dual diagnosis. *Journal of Rational-Emotive and Cognitive-Behavioral Therapy, 18,* 197–208.

Pepper, B., Krishner, M.C., & Ryglewicz, H. (1981). The young adult chronic patient: Overview of a population. *Hospital and Community Psychiatry, 32,* 463–469.

President's New Freedom Commission on Mental Health (2003). *Achieving the promise: Transforming mental health care in America.* Rockville, MD: Department of Health and Human Services.

Prochaska, J.O. & DiClemente, C.C. (1984). *The trans-theoretical approach: Crossing the traditional boundaries of therapy.* Homewood, IL: Dow-Jones/Irwin.

235

Prochaska, J.O., DiClemente, C.C., & Norcross, J.S. (1992). In search of how people change: Applications to addictive behaviors. *American Psychologist, 47*, 1102–1114.

Public Law 111–118 (2010). The Patient Protection and Affordable Care Act. Washington, DC: 111th U.S. Congress.

Rapp, C.A., Etzel-Wise, D., Marty, D., Coffman, M., Carlson, L., Asher, D., Callaghan, J., & Whitley, R. (2008). Evidence-based practice implementation strategies: Results of a qualitative study. *Community Mental Health Journal, 44*, 213–224.

Regier, D.A., Farmer, M.E., Rae, D.S., Locke, B.Z., Keith, S.J., Judd, L.L., & Goodwin, F.K. (1990). Comorbidity of mental disorders with alcohol and other drug abuse. *Journal of the American Medical Association, 264*, 2511–2518.

Ridgely, M.S., Goldman, H.H., & Willenbring, M. (1990). Barriers to the care of persons with dual diagnosis: Organization and financing issues. *Schizophrenia Bulletin, 16*(1), 123–132.

Roberts, L.J., Shaner, A., & Eckman, T.A. (1999). *Overcoming addictions: Skills training for people with schizophrenia.* New York, Norton.

Rosenberg, S.D., Goodman, L.A., Osher, F.C., Swartz, M.S., Essock, S.M., Butterfield, M.I., Constantine, N.T., Wolford, G.L., & Salyers, M.P. (2001). Prevalence of HIV, Hepatitis B and Hepatitis C in people with severe mental illness. *American Journal of Public Health, 91*(1), 31–37.

Sacks, S. (2000). Co-occurring mental and substance use disorders: Promising approaches and research issues. *Substance Use and Misuse, 35*(12–14), 2061–2093.

Sacks, S., Chandler, R., & Gonzales, J. (2008). Responding to the challenges of co-occurring disorders: Suggestions for future research. *Journal of Substance Abuse Treatment, 34*, 139–146.

Shollar, E. (1993). The long-term treatment of the dually diagnosed. In J. Solomon, S. Zimberg, & E. Shollar (Eds.), *Dual diagnosis: Evaluation, treatment, training and program development.* New York: Plenum Publishing Corporation.

Short, R., Hurst, M.A., Lofton, V., Neuzil, G., Gordish, L., Raia, J., Sherman, M., & Ignelzi, J. (2010). Adaptation and implementation of the integrated dual diagnosis treatment model into a psychiatric inpatient facility: A 12-year perspective, *Psychiatric Times*, June 25.

Singer, M.I., Kennedy, M., & Kola, L. (1998). A conceptual model for co-occurring mental and substance-related disorders. *Alcoholism Treatment Quarterly, 16*(4), 75–89.

Smeltz, J. (2007). *Setting the stage: Conducting tobacco treatment with clients with substance use disorders.* Cambridge: Institute for Health and Recovery: Tobacco, Addictions Policy and Education (TAPE) Project.

Steadman, H.J., Mulvey, E.P., Monahan, J., Robbins, P.C., Appelbaum, P.S., Grisso, T., Roth, L.H., & Silver, E. (1998). Violence by people discharged from acute psychiatric inpatient facilities and by others in the same neighborhoods. *Archives of General Psychiatry, 55*(5), 393–401.

Straussner, S.L.A. & Nemenzik, J.M. (2007). Co-occurring substance use and personality disorders: Current thinking on etiology, diagnosis and treatment. *Journal of Social Work Practice in the Addictions, 7*(1/2), 5–24.

Substance Abuse and Mental Health Services Administration (2002). *Report to Congress on the prevention and treatment of co-occurring substance abuse disorders and mental disorders.* Rockville, MD: Substance Abuse and Mental Health Services Administration.

Swanson, A.J., Pantalon, M.V., & Cohen, K.R. (1999). Motivational interviewing and treatment adherence among psychiatric and dually diagnosed patients. *Journal of Nervous and Mental Disease, 187*, 630–635.

Swofford, C., Kasckow, J., Scheller-Gilkey, G., & Inderbitzin, L.B. (1996). Substance use: A powerful predictor of relapse in schizophrenia. *Schizophrenia Research, 20*, 145–151.

Tiet, Q.Q. & Mausbach, B. (2007). Treatments for patients with dual diagnosis: A review. *Alcoholism Clinical and Experimental Research, 31*(4), 513–536.

Timko, C., Dixon, K., & Moos, R.H. (2005). Treatment for dual diagnosis patients in the psychiatric and substance abuse systems. *Mental Health Services Research, 7*(4), 229–242.

Torrey, W.C., Drake, R.E., Cohen, M.C., Fox, L.B., Lynde, D., Gorman, P., & Wyzik, P. (2001). The challenge of implementing and sustaining integrated dual disorders treatment programs. *Community Mental Health Journal, 38*(6), 507–521.

Tracy, E.M. & Biegel, D.E. (2006). Personal social networks and dual disorders: A review of the literature and implications for practice and future research. *Journal of Dual Diagnosis, 2*(2), 59–88.

Walsh, E., Buchanan, A., & Fahy, T. (2002). Violence and schizophrenia: Examining the evidence. *British Journal of Psychiatry, 180*, 490–495.

White, W. (2008). *Recovery management and recovery-oriented systems of care: Scientific rationale and promising practices.* Pittsburgh, PA: Northeast Addiction Technology Transfer Center, Great Lakes Addiction Technology Transfer Center, Philadelphia Department of Behavioral Health, & Mental Retardation Services.

Wieder, B.L. & Kruszynski, R.A. (2007). The salience of staffing in IDDT implementation: One agency's experience. *American Journal of Psychiatric Rehabilitation, 10*(2), 103–112.

Williams, J.M. & Ziedonis, D.M. (2006). Snuffing out tobacco dependence: Ten reasons behavioral health providers need to be involved. *Behavioral Healthcare, 26*(5), 27–30.

Woltmann, E. & Whitley, R. (2007). The role of staffing stability on the implementation of integrated dual disorders treatment: An exploratory study. *Journal of Mental Health, 16*(6), 757–769.

Ziedonis, D.M., Smelson, D., Rosenthal, R.N., Batki, S.L., Green, A.I., Henry, R.J., et al. (2005). Improving the care of individuals with schizophrenia and substance use disorders: Consensus recommendations. *Journal of Psychiatric Practice, 11*(5), 315–339.

Zornberg, G. & Weiss, R. (1997). Substance-related disorders. In *Acute care psychiatry: Diagnosis and treatment.* Baltimore, MD: Williams & Wilkins.

Chapter 15

Neuropsychiatric Perspectives for Community Mental Health

Theory and Practice

William H. Wilson

INTRODUCTION AND OVERVIEW

Our abilities to perceive, to move, to reason and understand, to love and hate, to work, to have moods and emotions, and to take action are based in the structure and function of our brains. To appreciate this truism, one has only to observe the slow decay of these abilities in someone with Alzheimer's dementia or the frighteningly sudden loss of such abilities following a significant brain injury. The brain, like other organs, is vulnerable to congenital defects and damage from illness or injury. When similar problems affect the heart, the result is an impairment of blood flow. When problems affect the brain, the result is likely to be an impairment in thinking, feeling, and/or behaving.

Many people who are served by the community mental health system have identifiable problems with perception, emotion, cognition, and behavior that can be traced to brain dysfunction. Accurate assessment of these problems, followed by proper neuropsychiatric treatment, is an essential element of care. Medications for these disorders are rarely curative, but often decrease symptoms and increase social function. The person is then more capable of participating in psychological treatment and in making better use of social resources. The diagnosis and treatment of mental illness are intended to enable people to live more fully, more effectively, and more meaningfully.

The success of neuropsychiatric treatment depends, not only on medical science, but also on the social context in which treatment is given, and the values of the people giving the care. In the context of adequate social support and culturally sensitive, "person-centered" services, neuropsychiatry provides powerful tools for helping people with mental illnesses to live more stable, more fulfilling lives. In settings of social neglect or authoritarianism, such results cannot be expected; diagnosis and treatment may at best be ineffective. The development and deployment of neuropsychiatry have not occurred in an ideal manner, but rather have been confounded by the major societal issues of our times, such as stigma against the poor and ill, economic factors, the politics of gender, race, and culture. Clearly, an understanding of neuropsychiatric disorders and pharmacotherapy is essential for any provider of community mental health care, and for administrators of community mental health services.

HISTORICAL AND THEORETICAL BACKGROUND

In the 1950s, chlorpromazine became the first medication prescribed to reduce the hallucinations, delusions, and thought disorder of schizophrenia; lithium was the first medication to reduce the mood swings of bipolar affective disorder. The fact that these medications were chemically quite different and that each affected only a particular set of mental symptoms indicated that distinct biological factors caused the symptoms of major psychiatric disorders.

The success of these early medications spurred research into the brain and the development of new medicines. Technological advances in brain imaging, molecular genetics, and cell biology led to an increasingly sophisticated appreciation of the neurological basis of major psychiatric disorders, and to the development of more effective medications. Nonetheless, knowledge remains partial, and treatments are only somewhat effective.

"Mental illnesses," more accurately referred to as "psychiatric disorders" or "neuropsychiatric disorders," are now considered to be long-standing errors in brain function, caused by both genetic and environmental factors. Environmental factors are both physical and psychosocial. Genetics determine the potential for a brain's development. The physical and social environments shape how this potential unfolds over a lifetime. There is no longer a sharp distinction between "nature" and "nurture," but rather an appreciation of the continuous give and take between the brain's biological potential and the effects of being in the world. Physical factors that shape brain development include nutrition, infections, injury, and the like. Psychological and interpersonal experience also alters brain structure and function, for better or worse. Changes in the brain that accompany PTSD are a dramatic example of the deleterious and lasting effects of negative experiences. There is growing recognition of the influence of positive social experience in healthy brain development and in the treatment of neuropsychiatric disorders. A perspective of brain plasticity based on genetics and environment allows for a realistic, comprehensive, and hopeful view of neuropsychiatric disorders (Baroncelli et al., 2010).

Classification of Psychiatric Disorders

Neuropsychiatry assumes that recognizable patterns of disturbances in thought, emotion, and behavior can be traced to particular problems in brain structure and function. Treatment is assumed to be most effective if it is directed toward this specific brain malfunction. Hence, a key activity of biological psychiatry is to parse the large historical category of "madness" or "insanity" into distinct syndromes, on the basis of symptoms, age of onset, course of the illness, and similar factors. In psychiatry, as in other branches of medicine, the description of a syndrome is followed by a scientific search for the cause of the disorder, the associated physiological abnormalities, ways to ameliorate the symptoms and, occasionally, to cure the illness. For example, at the beginning of the 20th century, German psychiatrist Emil Kraepelen drew the important distinction between what we now call "schizophrenia" and what we term "bipolar affective disorder." A hundred years later, we know that these disorders do in fact differ in genetics, in their response to various medications, and in a variety of aspects of brain function.

239

Once the cause of a "mental illness" has been traced to a particular process in the brain, society tends to consider the illness "physical" rather than "mental," even though the symptoms and duration of the illness are, of course, unchanged, and psychiatric intervention may be necessary. Examples of "mental" illnesses that are now regarded as "physical" illness include epilepsy, psychosis caused by syphilis, and mood problems caused by thyroid dysfunction. There is now enough scientific evidence for the medical community to regard psychiatric disorders as "physical." Nonetheless, insurance companies, the government, and the public continue to regard these illnesses as "mental."

The "official" definitions of psychiatric syndromes are articulated and periodically updated by the American Psychiatric Association in its *Diagnostic and Statistical Manual* (*DSM*). The current version is the 4th edition, with text revision, the *DSM-IV-TR* (American Psychiatric Association, 2000). Classification in the *DSM-IV-TR* relies, for the most part, on descriptions of symptoms and the natural history of the illness. The upcoming revision, *DSM-V*, is scheduled for publication in 2013.

The Biopsychosocial Model, Person-Centered Care, and Recovery

The goal of neuropsychiatric treatment should be to improve an individual's life, not simply to "fix" a brain. To accomplish this goal, neuropsychiatric interventions should be integrated into a comprehensive treatment plan. The biopsychosocial model provides a framework for developing such a plan. Each person is assumed to have needs based on biology; these needs may require psychiatric medications or other interventions to optimize brain function. Similarly, each individual has psychological needs related to his or her level of emotional development, coping skills, learning styles, spirituality, etc. Each of us is profoundly affected by our environment, and we have social needs—in a broad sense—that should be considered in evaluation and treatment. Such needs include extracting necessary supplies from the environment (e.g., food, shelter, transportation, money) and optimizing relationships with key individuals (e.g., family, friends, landlords, police), with social institutions, and with cultural constructs (e.g., health-care system, vocation, religious organizations, ethnic identity).

Consideration of each individual as having a unique mix of biological, psychological, and social strengths and deficits leads to a "person-centered" approach to neuropsychiatric treatment (Beck & Gordon, 2010; Talerico, O'Brien, & Swafford, 2003). The person-centered approach values the growth, development, dignity, and success of the individual person. Competing types of approach include institution-centered and population-based care. The former allows an institution to run smoothly by offering a generic treatment, which may or may not meet each person's needs. The latter focuses on overall public health, but may have little regard for individuals whose needs differ from those of the general public.

Given the current limitation of neuroscience-based medicine, successful treatment usually results in "recovery," not cure. An individual is said to be in recovery when psychiatric symptoms no longer keep him or her from pursuing meaningful life goals, such as a vocation, and meaningful interpersonal relationships. Ongoing treatment and social support are often required to maintain this degree of function.

PRACTICE ISSUES AND CONSIDERATIONS

Interdisciplinary Team Work

Most care for neuropsychiatric disorders is delivered by teams of professionals from a variety of disciplines, usually including a social worker, a "prescriber" (i.e. doctor or advance practice nurse licensed to prescribe medication), and often other case workers, therapists, vocational trainers, and housing specialists. Because of fiscal constraints, the prescribers are often called upon to make complex decisions about medication treatment on the basis of brief, infrequent contact with the client. In this situation, a prescriber's decisions are highly dependent on information provided by social workers and other team members regarding the client's ongoing behavior, response to treatment, and social situation. Prescribers also rely on the team to help the client understand, implement, and continue the prescriber's recommendations.

Principles of Psychopharmacology

Most psychiatric medications work by modulating the activity of neurons (i.e., nerve cells) in the brain (Stahl, 2008). Neurons send messages to adjoining neurons by releasing chemicals (neurotransmitters) into the specialized junctions between cells (synapses). The chemical message is received when the neurotransmitter attaches to a large molecule, termed a "receptor," on the next nerve cell, changing the shape of the receptor and thereby turning on a cascade of chemical processes within the cell. Alternatively, a neurotransmitter may cause another type of receptor to open or close a channel through which electrically charged particles can move in and out of the neuron, altering the cell's likelihood of sending on an electrochemical message to other cells.

Many psychiatric medications either inhibit or boost the action of particular neuro-transmitters. Most antidepressant and antipsychotic medications affect the "monoamine" neurotransmitters (dopamine, nor-epinephrine, and serotonin). These small molecules are found in bundles ("tracts") of nerves that run from the brain stem (where the brain meets the spinal cord) to structures throughout the brain. These tracts can be thought of as volume controls for the different parts of the brain. Release of neurotransmitter molecules increases or decreases the activity level of the nerve cells in the areas they innervate. The therapeutic effects of some medications are immediately evident. More often, symptomatic improvement accrues gradually, over weeks or months, as the brain slowly adjusts to changes in neurotransmission. Anti-anxiety medications in the benzodiazepine family modulate activity of the neurotransmitter gamma-amino butyric acid (GABA). Lithium and mood stabilizers such as divalproex affect neuronal activity in complex ways that are not directly related to neurotransmitters and receptors.

The classes of psychiatric medications (antipsychotics, antidepressants, mood-stabilizers, and the like) are named for the clinical action that is most pronounced or that was first studied. Many medications have broader clinical utility than their name implies. For example, "antidepressants" are also used to treat certain types of anxiety, and "antipsychotics" are also used to treat mood symptoms.

Disorders and pharmacological treatments

Neuropsychiatric syndromes are grouped into several larger categories: psychotic disorders, mood disorders, anxiety disorders, personality disorders, and dementias, along with several other categories that have less relevance to community mental health. Substance abuse often complicates these types of disorder (Black & Andreasen, 2011; Yudofsky & Hales, 2010).

Psychotic Disorders

The characteristic symptoms of psychotic disorders are hallucinations (abnormal sensory experiences, such as hearing voices), delusions (patently unrealistic ideas), and disorganized thoughts. Schizophrenia is the prototypical psychotic disorder, a devastating illness found in approximately 1% of the population worldwide. Individuals with schizophrenia usually have unremarkable childhoods, although in retrospect they may seem to have been awkward when compared with their siblings. Symptoms usually emerge in late adolescence or early adulthood, following some months of decline in social role performance. If these symptoms are fully present for 6 or more months, the duration of the illness is likely to be long lasting, often lifelong.

Schizophrenia is not caused by a single neurological abnormality or "chemical imbalance." Rather, there are diffuse problems in a number of brain areas that result in problems in "connectivity," that is, in the complex communication among networks of neurons and among regions that is necessary for sensory processing and cognition. Anatomically, there is usually an overall decrease in the amount of brain tissue, due in part to degeneration during adolescence. Often, nerve cells are not ordered properly within the layers of the cerebral cortex, reflecting abnormal development during pregnancy. Schizophrenia is thought to be caused by an interplay of genetic vulnerability and environmental stressors. The genes associated with schizophrenia normally guide development and maintenance of brain cells and tissues. Having only one defective gene is unlikely to lead to illness. Having several defective genes causes the brain to be more vulnerable to damage by environmental factors such as maternal viral infection, birth complications, or perhaps physiological stressors later in life. The combination of genetic vulnerability and physiological stress leads to the brain damage that causes the lifelong illness.

Treatment of schizophrenia is designed to relieve symptoms and restore normal social function. Antipsychotic medications are the mainstay of biological treatment, along with social support and comprehensive psychiatric rehabilitation. With proper treatment and social support, many people with schizophrenia are able to make substantial recovery. Too often, however, few resources for treatment and social support are available, leading to repeated hospitalization and poor social functioning.

The therapeutic action of antipsychotic medications is due to the blockade of dopamine transmission in particular areas of the brain (i.e., mesolimbic tracts). The first-generation antipsychotic medications ("typical" antipsychotics), which became available in the 1950s, are as effective as newer medications in decreasing hallucinations and delusions and increasing thought organization. However, these benefits are usually accompanied by motor-system side effects, such as tremors, muscle stiffness ("pseudo-parkinsonism"), and muscle cramps ("acute dystonia"). When taken for months or years, muscle tics and writhing movements

242

("tardive dyskinesia") are likely to occur and to persist, even if the medication is discontinued. The new-generation antipsychotic medications ("atypical antipsychotics"), which became available in the 1990s, are largely free of these motor-system side effects. However, some of the newer medications, particularly olanzapine and clozapine, are likely to cause weight gain, diabetes, and increase levels of cholesterol and lipids in the blood (Pramyothin & Khaodhiar, 2010). These factors increase the risk for heart disease and stroke, and require diet and exercise regimens along with medical care. Changing to medications that infrequently cause these metabolic side effects (such as ziprasidone and aripiprazole) can minimize the problem.

Antipsychotic medications reduce symptoms during acute episodes of psychosis. If the medications are continued, further symptomatic improvement may occur, and there is much less likelihood of relapse. Many people with schizophrenia do not take their medication as prescribed, for a number of reasons. The medication may be expensive or difficult to obtain. The person may not sense the benefits provided by medication, or may prefer psychosis to dealing with everyday reality. The person may feel coerced to take the medication and prefer autonomy. Ideally, the person may come to regard medication as an aid in achieving personal goals, such as maintaining friendships, being able to work, or simply avoiding hospitalization. Long-acting injectable medication is an option for individuals who have difficulty taking daily medication, and for patients who simply prefer to receive medication in this manner. Two of the older "typical" antipsychotics (haloperidol, fluphenazine) are available as monthly injections. Three of the newer antipsychotics are available as long-acting injections (risperidone, paliperidone, olanzapine).

Mood Disorders

Depression and bipolar affective disorder are serious public health concerns that are frequently encountered in community mental health practice. Periods of elation and depression are part and parcel of normal life. Clinical mood disorders are diagnosed when problems with mood are so severe and so long lasting as to interfere with daily functioning. Serious depression affects approximately 5% of the population. Nearly twice as many women as men report suffering from depression. Biological and social factors help to explain this disparity. For women, the hormonal changes associated with puberty, pregnancy, childbirth, and menopause increase the risk for major depression. The stress of being both caregiver and breadwinner, limited educational, economic, or professional opportunities, and the tendency to be more expressive of emotion and more willing to seek help also have been suggested as explanations for the prevalence of depression in women.

Depression affects more than a person's mood. Along with feeling sad, worthless, or irritable, a person with depression is likely to be lethargic, inattentive, and to have irregular patterns of eating and sleeping. The neurological underpinnings of depression seem to involve improper regulation of the neurotransmitters serotonin and nor-epinephrine. Medications for depression stimulate the action of these neurotransmitters. As with schizophrenia, complex genetic factors are associated with depressive disorders. Major depressive episodes tend to recur: among individuals who have one depressive episode, three-quarters of them will have at least one more during their lifetime. In severe depressions, psychotic symptoms similar to those seen in schizophrenia may occur (hallucinations, delusions). These symptoms remit as depression resolves.

243

Bipolar affective disorder (formerly known as "manic depression") affects about 1.2% of the population. Manic episodes, the hallmark of bipolar disorder, are periods of days or weeks during which a person has marked elation or irritability and increased energy and is unrealistically optimistic, perhaps even delusionally so. During such episodes, a person may take on grandiose projects, travel excessively, and engage in destructive social activities, such as spending sprees and sexual adventurism. At times, manic episodes may occur without any depressions; however, most individuals tend to cycle between mania and depression, with some intervening intervals of fairly stable moods. The incidence of bipolar disorder is similar in women and men, although women tend to exhibit more rapid cycling between depression and mania.

Particular psychotherapeutic interventions (e.g., interpersonal psychotherapy, cognitive therapy) are useful for depressed patients who retain sufficient function to engage in treatment. These may be used in conjunction with antidepressant and/or mood-stabilizing medications. Antidepressant medications tend to alleviate the physical aspects of depression and to normalize mood over a period of 6–8 weeks. Continued use of antidepressants is protective against the recurrence of depressive episodes. The older medications (monoamine oxidase inhibitors (MAOIs), tricyclic antidepressants (TCAs)) are highly toxic in overdose and thus are rarely prescribed. The newer antidepressants (selective serotonin reuptake inhibitors (SSRIs), serotonin/nor-epinephrine uptake inhibitors (SNRIs), and other newer antidepressants) are far less dangerous in overdose and are now the preferred agents. All of these medications can have undesirable side effects, including mania, and, at times, intensified depression, even to the point of inducing suicide. Worsening of depression and new suicidal behavior are most common in adolescents (Bridge, Salary, Birmaher, Asare, & Brent, 2005). Thus, treatment with antidepressant medications needs to be carefully monitored.

Bipolar disorder is treated with "mood stabilizers," such as lithium, divalproex, and carbamazepine. The latter two medications were initially developed to treat epilepsy. The "antipsychotic" medications used to treat schizophrenia are also effective in treating and in reducing the recurrence of mania. Medication treatment reduces the length and severity of manic and depressive episodes. Continued treatment lengthens the intervals between episodes and reduces the severity of subsequent episodes.

Severe depression does not always respond to medication, and may be life-threatening. A person suffering from depression may attempt or complete suicide, or become incapable of self-care. In any case, severe depression inflicts tremendous suffering. Electro-convulsive therapy (ECT) is the single most effective treatment for depression, at least in the short term. It is usually reserved for refractory cases, in part because of lingering public distrust of the treatment. In the mid 20th century, ECT was administered indiscriminately, without sufficient attention to the patient's safety and comfort. At present, ECT is administered under general anesthesia in an operating room. A small electrical current is applied to the scalp, causing the brain to have a brief epileptic-type seizure. There is no seizure activity in the body, because of muscle-relaxing medication that is given along with the anesthetic. Following the treatment, an individual will have temporary confusion and memory disturbance. Memory disturbance is usually mild and transient, but can be problematic and persistent. Between 6 and 10 treatments are usually given over the course of 2–3 weeks. The therapeutic effects are likely due to the high levels of neurotransmitters released during the seizure.

Transcranial magnetic stimulation (TMS) is a newer form of brain stimulation that is used to treat depression. TMS is done in awake, unanesthetized patients, seemingly with few adverse

NEUROPSYCHIATRIC PERSPECTIVES

effects. It is not yet widely available, and, as yet, TMS is rarely used as a community treatment. Vagus nerve stimulation (VNS), which involves stimulation of the vagus nerve in the neck by implantation of a device similar to a cardiac pacemaker, was approved for clinical use by the Food and Drug Administration (FDA) in 2005; however, it is rarely used owing to the high cost of the device and surgical implantation, as well as the overall low rate of therapeutic response (Grimm & Bajbouj, 2010).

Suicide is the 11th leading cause of death in the United States. Approximately 60% of people who commit suicide meet criteria for a mood disorder, and approximately 15% of people with serious depressions eventually kill themselves. Suicide is also common among people with schizophrenia, although the rates are lower than with depression. Three times as many women attempt suicide, but four times as many men as women complete suicide. Firearms are involved in 55% of completed suicides. The use of alcohol and street drugs increases suicide risk. Low levels of the neurotransmitter serotonin have been found in the brains of people who have committed suicide.

Anxiety Disorders

Anxiety is an unavoidable part of life. Anxiety disorders are only diagnosed when anxiety cripples the ability of an individual to function socially, and these disorders are thought to be due to over-activity of regions such as the amygdala that normally assess risks and that activate the "fight or flight reaction." The neurotransmitters serotonin and GABA are involved in the mediation of anxiety.

The various anxiety disorders differentiate the types of anxiety that people experience. Generalized anxiety disorder is a condition of virtually unremitting anxiety. In panic disorder, anxiety is sudden and intense. People with this disorder often believe that they are literally dying, and may seek emergency medical treatment. Agoraphobia complicates panic disorder, as people learn to avoid having attacks in public by staying in the relative safety of their own homes.

PTSD is a recurrent anxiety disorder. First described in combat soldiers, and then in disaster victims, it also occurs in survivors of rape and domestic violence, automobile accidents, and other civilian trauma. Individuals with PTSD experience a variety of emotional and behavioral symptoms, including emotional withdrawal and decreased ability to be intimate, vivid emotional recollection of traumatic events triggered by sights or sounds that are reminiscent of those events, and nightmares. There are clear structural and functional brain abnormalities in PTSD. Children who have endured repeated sexual or physical abuse may develop a particularly pervasive and disabling form, which is termed "complex PTSD."

Obsessive–compulsive disorder (OCD), which occurs in more than 2% of the U.S. population, is marked by the seemingly unnecessary repetition of mental and physical activity in order for an individual to ward off anxiety. For example, a woman may wash her hands until the skin is raw. Yet, if she does not wash her hands for even a few minutes, she begins to worry that there are germs on her hands. She may know that her hands are not covered with dangerous germs, and yet she still feels compelled to wash them for this reason.

There are two main types of medication for anxiety disorders. The benzodiazepine medications quickly relieve anxiety. These drugs are often useful in the short term, but tend to be considerably less useful when used for longer periods of time. In addition, they can lead to physical dependence and are often abused. The SSRI and SNRI antidepressants are now treatments of choice for many types of anxiety. These medications are often used in conjunction with cognitive behavioral psychotherapy.

Personality Disorders

Certain long-standing patterns of thought and behavior have been termed "personality disorders." The *DSM-IV* lists a number of distinct disorders, noting that an individual may have traits from more than one disorder. *DSM-V* is likely to allow a more individualized description of personality function. Initially, personality disorders were taken to be learned patterns of behavior, with less of a neurological component than other disorders. More recently, this notion has been challenged. For example, "schizotypal personality disorder" appears to be a mild form of schizophrenia. "Borderline personality disorder" (BPD), characterized by chronically unstable mood, volatile interpersonal relationships, extremely low tolerance for being alone, and repeated self-harm, appears to be a catchall for disorders that may lead to similar presentations. Among the causes of BPD are complex PTSD and variants of bipolar affective disorder, a lack of progression of normal emotional development analogous to mental retardation, and learned behavior. Medications are useful for some individuals with "personality disorders." For example, antipsychotic medications reduce mildly delusional thoughts in an individual with schizotypal personality disorder. Mood stabilizers, SSRIs, and atypical antipsychotics can be useful in reducing impulsive actions and facilitating realistic thinking for people with BPD (Bellino, Paradiso, & Bogetto, 2008).

Dementias

Dementias are problems with cognition and behavior that are caused by the destruction of brain tissue, primarily in the elderly. The most familiar of these is dementia of the Alzheimer's type (Alzheimer's Association, 2011), which is caused by a gradual loss of brain tissue accompanied by deposition of abnormal materials (amyloid plaques and neurofibrillary tangles) within brain cells. The prevalence of Alzheimer's dementia increases with age. At age 65, 1 person in 10 is affected; nearly half of people above the age of 85 are. The onset of symptoms is quite gradual, with a slow decline in memory, orientation, problem solving, and language skills. As the illness progresses, personality change, anxiety, depression, delusions, and hallucinations are common. At present, there is no cure, and the illness eventually leads to death.

The anticholinesterase medications (donepezil, rivastigmine, galantamine) slow the expression of symptoms in mild to moderate dementia, but do not affect the actual progression of the illness. Memantine, a medication that blocks a particular receptor for the neurotransmitter glutamate, is similarly useful in more advanced illness. Although Alzheimer's dementia is usually thought of as a "neurological" as opposed to a "psychiatric" illness, the emotional and behavioral symptoms require institutional care.

Other common forms of dementia are "vascular dementia," which results from strokes, and the dementia that follows head injury (Brain Injury Association of America, 2011). Approximately 5.3 million Americans are disabled as the result of traumatic brain injury; 80,000 new cases of disability occur annually in civilians. Disability is likely to be permanent. Vehicular accidents are the leading cause of such injuries in civilians. Such injuries due to explosions are relatively common in disabled veterans of the wars in Iraq and Afghanistan. Cognitive problems (memory, attention, difficulty shifting from one task to another, problem solving) and emotional problems (anxiety, depression, and impulsivity) are also common. Medications may ameliorate the emotional symptoms, while having little effect on cognitive symptoms.

Substance Abuse

Psychiatric disorders are often complicated by concurrent substance abuse (Thylstrup & Johansen, 2009). At least half of the individuals with schizophrenia misuse or abuse alcohol or street drugs. The interaction of street drugs and alcohol with the biology of neuropsychiatric disorders is complex. At times, psychiatric disorders follow as a direct consequence of substance abuse, as, for example, in the long-term psychosis caused by prolonged amphetamine abuse. At other times, individuals may "self-medicate" with street drugs and alcohol to relieve depression or to ease the suffering from psychiatric illness. Nicotine may help people with schizophrenia to think more clearly. At other times, individuals may have substance abuse and neuropsychiatric illness as two separate problems. Programs that address one problem and not the other are often much less effective for these individuals than integrated, "dual diagnosis" programs, which treat the substance abuse and mental health problems simultaneously.

POLICY ISSUES AND CONSIDERATIONS

To this point, neuropsychiatry has been discussed in medical and biological terms. However, neuropsychiatry does not exist in a rarefied atmosphere of pure scientific thoughts, but, rather, is interwoven into the fabric of society. All of the large social issues of the day impinge on neuropsychiatry. In order to understand and apply neuropsychiatry, one must understand its social context.

Consumerism, Advocates, and Critics

People who use neuropsychiatric services and their family members are advocates and critics of neuropsychiatric research programs and service delivery systems. Consumer perspectives run the gamut from enthusiastic support of research and treatment to intense opposition to psychiatry as a whole. Empowerment seems to be the common theme. People want to be in charge of their own lives and to have a say in the services they access. The Internet now gives voice to people who would previously have gone unheard; there is a plethora of blogs and support groups on professionally maintained, educational sites (e.g., NAMI.org, dbsalliance.org, schizophrenia.com), sites by concerned celebrities (e.g., Glenn Close's bringchange2mind.org), sites arising from the community (e.g., twloha.co), commercial sites organized or supported by the pharmaceutical and health-care industries, and informal discussions on social media sites. The anti-psychiatry movement within academia of the 1970s has largely collapsed, as evidence has accumulated for the neurological basis of psychiatric disorders; there are, however, strong voices supporting consumer self-determination (Rissmiller & Rissmiller, 2006). Policymakers can foster empowerment by including consumers in the design, implementation, and monitoring of mental health services and research projects. Consumer and family perspectives should be integrated into the educational curricula for all mental health professions.

Stigma

Our society finds many ways to stereotype, denigrate, discredit, and marginalize people who have neuropsychiatric disorders. This societal stigma reflects fear, ignorance, and a desire to exclude anyone who is different. From a medical point of view, psychiatric diagnoses appear free of stigma. A diagnosis simply describes a problem so that appropriate treatment may be given. However, neuropsychiatric diagnoses often become denigrating social labels, both inside and outside the health-care system. For example, a landlord may not take a tenant's complaints seriously simply because he knows that the tenant has schizophrenia. Medical and social professionals need to be aware of the distinction between "diagnosis" and "labeling," and to avoid the pernicious effects of stigma.

A scientific diagnosis may turn into a social label that causes the individual to be prejudged as damaged, dangerous, and insignificant. Individual practitioners and program planners can avoid this dark side of neuropsychiatry by conscious attention to the biopsychosocial model, to person-centered care, and to the value of each individual's recovery.

Economics

Psychiatric medications are developed, manufactured, and sold through the system of global capitalism. Governmental research agencies such as the National Institute for Mental Heath do not fund research into drug development. Lacking such support, university researchers are not able to develop medications or to independently assess the benefits and risks of existing medications. Thus, medication development is driven by the profit motive at the corporate level. Globalization has effected the protection of subjects in clinical studies of new medications. These studies were traditionally carried out in the United States and in Europe, where there are fairly strict rules regarding informed consent and other safeguards for subjects in the studies. Increasingly, new drugs are being tested in developing nations, where ethical guidelines are lax.

The potential for financial gain from psychiatric medications led to a number of unfortunate consequences in the past decade. Several prominent academic psychiatrists have been exposed as having misrepresented data regarding the effectiveness of drug studies for their own financial gain and career advancement. Pharmaceutical companies have been found to have withheld data that did not have the desired results and to have withheld information about serious side effects. A relative lack of information coupled with advertising directly to consumers has, to an extent, reduced physicians from independent scientific practitioners to purveyors of consumer products (Spielmans & Parry, 2010).

The burden of paying for psychiatric treatment and medications falls largely on governmental insurance programs, as people with psychiatric illness are often vocationally disabled and so are unable to obtain insurance through employment. These costs strain already overburdened government budgets for mental health care. Newer medications are often considered to be more effective and less toxic than older medications, and yet the validity of these assumptions and the true benefits of using newer medications can be difficult to assess. Efforts to reduce medication costs continue (Lu, Ross-Degnan, Soumerai, & Pearson, 2008; Lu, Soumerai, Ross-Degan, Zhang, & Adams, 2010), but may have less impact than comprehensive reform of the relationship between the government and the pharmaceutical industry.

Gender

The biological differences between the sexes are easily accommodated within a biomedical framework (Kohen, 2010). For example, differences in hormonal fluctuations between men and women are measurable, as are the correlations of these fluctuations with the symptoms of various disorders. The hormonal variations in women during the menstrual cycle, following childbirth, and at menopause are associated with increased risk for mood disorders at these times. During pregnancy and breastfeeding, medications need to be tailored to the needs of the fetus and infant as well as to the mother.

The social dimensions of gender, however, are more problematic. Definitions of a neuropsychiatric disorder almost always include a statement to the effect that the disorder must be severe enough to impair social functioning. The definition of "social functioning" is itself a social construct, based on what may be questionable norms of expected behavior. Once one moves beyond discussion of the ability to perform basic self-care, the qualities of "functional" social behavior become murkier. One observer may attribute non-normative behavior to illness, where another observer may see the behavior as an adaption to oppressive social pressures. When social function is equated with social conformity, neuropsychiatric interventions can easily be invoked to legitimize social rigidity, rather than to foster individual growth and achievement.

In the 1950s, anti-anxiety medications, which were then called "tranquilizers," were liberally prescribed to women to make them more compliant with their roles as wives and mothers. This pathologizing of women's discontent, and the use of medication to suppress it, may have stood in the way of women's efforts to reshape gender roles in post-war America. The rhetoric and symbolism may have changed over the years; however, the pathologizing of women's lives and the promotion of profitable psychotropic medication as treatment of these supposed psychiatric problems continue. A recent example is the controversy over whether lack of sexual desire in women should be considered a psychiatric disorder (Jutel, 2010).

Race and Ethnicity

Race and ethnicity are important factors in the recognition of psychiatric disorders and in giving neuropsychiatric care (Department of Health and Human Services, U.S. Public Health Service, 2001). As with gender, both straightforward biological factors and much more problematic cultural factors are associated with race and ethnicity. The incidence of major mental illnesses is similar across ethnic and racial groups. No known differences in brain functions are attributable to race or ethnicity. There are differences in the frequency of particular genes that regulate breakdown and elimination of medications by the liver drug metabolism within particular populations. For example, many Asians metabolize certain drugs more slowly than do most people of European extraction. Asians may therefore need lower doses of these drugs than are recommended by the manufacturer.

Although human brains are similar regardless of ethnicity, the expression of brain disorders varies with culture. For example, members of cultures in which the expression of emotion is discouraged are likely to manifest depression in terms of physical illness rather than emotional distress. Some culturally determined expressions of psychiatric distress appear only within particular populations (e.g., "*susto*" among indigenous people in Latin America, "*koro*" in Southeast Asians). These "culture-bound" syndromes are thought to be culturally fostered manners of expression of more universal problems (for example, anxiety), rather than being unique neurological abnormalities.

Cultural competency is central to the provision of neuropsychiatric care to people who are not part of the dominant culture. Members of racial and ethnic minorities in the United States have less access to psychiatric care and to medical care in general than do non-minority individuals. The care that minority individuals receive is inferior to that which is available to the general population. Given the long history of institutionalized racism in the United States, it is not surprising that it has been identified, at times, as a factor influencing neuropsychiatric care. Caregivers and system planners need to ensure that ethnic bias is not clouding neuropsychiatric diagnosis and treatment.

SUMMARY

Neuropsychiatry provides a useful perspective on what has been termed "mental illness" and a powerful set of tools to improve mental and social functioning. The scientific findings of neuropsychiatry must be used in the context of the person. The goal of treatment is not to fix a brain; it is to improve a particular person's life. As with any large-scale social undertaking, neuropsychiatry is profoundly influenced by the economic system, as well as by cultural issues. Neuropsychiatry offers a perspective and a set of tools. What we do with this perspective and these tools depends upon our values and our commitment to putting those values into practice.

DISCUSSION QUESTIONS

1. Discuss the following sentence: "The goal of neuropsychiatric treatment should be to improve an individual's life, not simply to 'fix' a brain." What does this mean? How does this relate to community mental health?

2. The chapter draws a distinction between "diagnosis" and "labeling." Why is this difference important to avoiding the stigmatization of mental illness?

3. Discuss the following assertion: "Schizophrenia is thought to be caused by interplay of genetic vulnerability and environmental stressors."

LEARNING ASSIGNMENT

As a class project, find as many examples as you can of advertising for psychiatric medication in the media (print, TV, etc.). What techniques do you think these ads use to market their products? How do you think consumer advertising impacts the development of psychiatric medications?

SUGGESTED READINGS

Black, W.B., & Andreasen, N.C. (2011). *Introductory Textbook of Psychiatry*, 5th ed. Arlington, VA: American Psychiatric Publishing, Inc.

Stahl, S.M. (2008). *Stahl's Essential Psychopharmacology: Neuroscientific Basis and Practical Applications*, 3rd ed. New York: Cambridge University Press.

Talerico, K.A., O'Brien J.A., & Swafford, K.L. (2003). Person-centered care. An important approach for 21st century health care. *Journal of Psychosocial Nursing & Mental Health Services, 41*(11), 12–16.

INTERNET RESOURCES

National Institute of Mental Health: www.nimh.nih.gov

National Alliance of the Mentally Ill: www.nami.org

U.S. Psychiatric Rehabilitation Association: netforum.avectra.com/eweb/StartPage.aspx?Site=USPRA&Web Code=HomePage

REFERENCES

Alzheimer's Association (2011). Home page. Retrieved from: www.alz.org/index.asp

American Psychiatric Association (2000). *Diagnostic and statistical manual of mental disorders, 4th ed., Text revision*. Washington, DC: Author.

Baroncelli, L., Braschi, C., Spolidoro, M., Begenisic, T., Sale, A., & Maffei, L. (2010). Nurturing brain plasticity: Impact of environmental enrichment. *Cell Death & Differentiation, 17*(7), 1092–2003.

Beck, B.J., & Gordon, C. (2010). An approach to collaborative care and consultation: Interviewing, cultural competence, and enhancing rapport and adherence. *Medical Clinics of North America, 94*(6), 1075–1088.

Bellino, S., Paradiso, E., & Bogetto, F. (2008). Efficacy and tolerability of pharmacotherapies for borderline personality disorder. *CNS Drugs, 22*(8), 671–692.

Black, W.B., & Andreasen, N.C. (2011). *Introductory textbook of psychiatry,* 5th ed. Arlington, VA: American Psychiatric Publishing, Inc.

Brain Injury Association of America (2011). Home page. Retrieved January 10, 2011, from: www.biausa.org

Bridge, J.A., Salary, C.B., Birmaher, B., Asare, A.G., & Brent, D.A. (2005). The risks and benefits of antidepressant treatment for youth depression. *Annals of Medicine, 37*(6), 404–412.

251

Department of Health and Human Services, U.S. Public Health Service (2001). *Mental health: Culture, race, and ethnicity. A supplement to mental health: A report of the Surgeon General*. Washington, DC: Department of Health and Human Services, U.S. Public Health Service.

Jutel, A. (2010) Framing disease: The example of female hypoactive sexual desire disorder. *Social Science & Medicine, 70*(7), 1084–1090.

Kohen, D. (Ed.) (2010). *Oxford textbook of women and mental health*. New York: Oxford University Press.

Grimm, S., & Bajbouj, M. (2010). Efficacy of vagus nerve stimulation in the treatment of depression. *Expert Review of Neurotherapeutics, 10*(1), 87–92.

Lu, C.Y., Ross-Degnan, D., Soumerai, S.B., & Pearson, S. (2008). Interventions designed to improve the quality and efficiency of medication use in managed care: A critical review of the literature—2001–2007. *BMC Health Services Research, 8*, 75. www.biomedcentral.com/1472–6963/8/75

Lu, C.Y., Soumerai, S.B., Ross-Degan, D., Zhang, F., & Adams, A.S. (2010). Unintended impacts of a Medicaid prior authorization policy on access to medications for bipolar illness. *Medical Care, 48*(1), 4–9.

Pramyothin, P., & Khaodhiar, L. (2010). Metabolic syndrome with the atypical antipsychotics. *Current Opinion in Endocrinology, Diabetes & Obesity, 17*(5), 460–466.

Rissmiller, D.J., & Rissmiller, J.H. (2006). Evolution of the antipsychiatry movement into mental health consumerism. *Psychiatric Services, 57*(6), 863–866.

Spielmans, G.I., & Parry, P.I. (2010). From evidence-based medicine to marketing-based medicine: Evidence from internal industry documents. *Journal of Bioethical Inquiry, 7*(1), 13–29.

Stahl, S.M. (2008). *Stahl's essential psychopharmacology: Neuroscientific basis and practical applications*, 3rd ed. New York: Cambridge University Press.

Talerico, K.A., O'Brien J.A., & Swafford, K.L. (2003). Person-centered care. An important approach for 21st century health care. *Journal of Psychosocial Nursing & Mental Health Services, 41*(11), 12–16.

Thylstrup, B., & Johansen, K.S. (2009). Dual diagnosis and psychosocial interventions—introduction and commentary. *Nordic Journal of Psychiatry, 63*(3), 202–208.

Yudofsky, S.C., & Hales, R.E. (2010). *Essentials of neuropsychiatry and behavioral neurosciences*. Arlington, VA: American Psychiatric Publishing, Inc.

Chapter 16

Case Management Strategies that Target High-Risk Homeless Subpopulations

Philip E. Thomas

This chapter provides an overview of the effectiveness of the diverse case management (CM) models and approaches for homeless individuals with substance use and mental health disorders (SUMHDs), in addition to some historical background and policy considerations. Empirically identified risk factors for homelessness continue to include individuals with SUMHDs (Rosenheck, Bassuk, & Salomon, 1999; Stein & Santos, 1998). Although mainstream resources such as rental subsidies and poverty assistance play essential roles in the care of the homeless, it is becoming increasingly evident that CM is now also seen as one of the cornerstones of intervention for achieving residential stability (Austin & McClelland, 1997; Kanter, 1989; McMurray-Avila, Gelberg, & Breakey, 1999; Stephens & Dennis, 1991). Based upon the updated evidence, "best practice" models for CM services will be presented in hopes to enable practitioners to become aware of the empirically supported knowledge relative to work with homeless.

OVERVIEW

The diversity of people who are homeless continues to increase worldwide. Homelessness has been well documented in European nations as well as Canada and the United States and is now an entrenched phenomenon in the modern world (Apicello, 2010).

The 2009 Annual Homeless Assessment Report (AHAR), sponsored by the U.S. Department of Housing and Urban Development (HUD), reveals that, on a single night in January 2009, there were an estimated 643,067 sheltered and unsheltered homeless people nationwide; 110,917 of these people were experiencing chronic homelessness, of which 75–80% were men (United States Department of Housing and Urban Development, 2009). The 2009 figure is a decrease of 11% from the 2008 count (124,135). Nearly 1.56 million people used an emergency shelter or a transitional housing program during the period from October 1, 2008 through September 30, 2009. Two-thirds were homeless as individuals, and one-third was homeless as members of families (United States Department of Housing and Urban Development, 2009). This is a reduction from earlier conservative estimates that 2.3 million adults and children were likely to experience an episode of homelessness at least once during

1996 (1996 National Survey of Homeless Assistance Providers and Clients). However, it is important to keep in mind that some declines may be due to changes in counting methodology, and that family homelessness has been on the rise most likely owing to the recent recession and ongoing poverty risks (United States Department of Housing and Urban Development, 2009).

Among the homeless, SUMHD are common, accounting for approximately 50% of those in emergency shelter (Culhane, Chang-Moo, & Wachter, 1996). According to Burt, Aron, Lee, & Valente (2001),

> The proportion of clients who had one or more [SUMHD] was high (66 percent) for the past month (that is, 34 percent did not report any problems), and reached 86 percent for their lifetimes. As the time increases, the proportion of clients reporting only one problem decreases, and the proportion reporting combinations increases. For lifetime problems, 47 percent reported mental health problems accompanied by alcohol problems, drug problems, or both.
>
> (pp. 102–105)

Substance abuse is one of the most common comorbidities among individuals with severe mental illness (SMI), including those who are homeless (Adams, Rosenheck, Gee, Seibyl, & Kushel, 2007; Brunette, Mueser, & Drake, 2004). Approximately half of all individuals with SMI, such as schizophrenia and bipolar disorder, have lifetime substance use disorders, with 30% of those individuals also meeting the diagnostic criteria for a current substance use disorder (Essock, Mueser, Drake, et al., 2006; Regier, Farmer, & Rae, 1990). Clearly, people with SUMHD are overrepresented among the homeless (five to six times more than in the general population), as only 4% of the U.S. population has SUMHD problems (Rosenheck, Bassuk, & Salomon, 1999).

THEORETICAL BACKGROUND

The reasons why people become homeless are as complex as the individuals experiencing homelessness. Many of the factors leading to homelessness are highly correlated with one another, and most do not have an independent impact on the risk of homelessness (Rosenheck, 1996). Adding to the complexity, there is no clear direction of causation, as homelessness is both a cause and an effect of other serious problems, such as poverty, mental illness, and poor physical health. However, for sake of simplicity, most researchers agree there are interrelated functional and structural causal perspectives (Burt et al., 2001; Koegel, Burnam, & Baumohl, 1996; Rosenheck, 1996).

Structural Explanations

Structural explanations of homelessness often focus on inequitable distribution of societal resources causing at-risk individuals to be systematically underserved (Koegel et al., 1996).

Examples include poverty, racial discrimination, prejudice, reduced public support, deinstitutionalization, and fragmentation of society's social safety net programs (Koegel et al., 1996; Rosenheck et al., 1999). Two of the more frequently cited structural causes of homelessness are that incomes and industrial jobs have declined since 1973. In addition, there has been an 18% decline in the real value of the minimum wage, leaving many without a livable income (Rosenheck, 1996). The combination of these two factors puts a greater burden on those with the least education and fewest transferable skills.

The HUD estimates that 5 million households in the United States have incomes below 50% of the local median. These individuals pay more than half of their income for rent on housing that is substandard. Moreover, there has been a 5% decline in the number of low-cost housing units, with federal rental assistance programs not being able to fill the gap owing to long waits for Section 8 vouchers (United States Department of Housing and Urban Development, 2001). The equation is simple: too few low-cost housing units for too many low-income people during a climate of declining public support for the poor result in increased prevalence of homelessness (Koegel et al., 1996).

Functional Explanations

On the other hand, functional explanations tend to find the locus of homelessness within the individuals themselves (mental illness, substance abuse, poor adjustment). By focusing on these functional causes and effects of homelessness, proponents of the "functional argument" believe policies have a greater chance of providing individuals with the needed treatment and rehabilitation that will enable them to take advantage of housing that they otherwise could not secure or maintain (Koegel et al., 1996).

Given the complex web of causation discussed above, it follows that homelessness is both a cause and an effect of structural and functional factors. If homelessness is thought of as a game of musical chairs, the structural factors are the ones responsible for the removal of chairs (e.g., low-cost housing), whereas functional factors determine who loses their seats (Koegel et al., 1996; Rosenheck, 1996). Those affected most profoundly are often the most vulnerable owing to their SUMHD (Stein & Santos, 1998).

PRACTICE ISSUES: CASE MANAGEMENT

The origins of CM as a means of linking clients to needed services in the community lie in the late 19th century and derive primarily from social work traditions (Rapp & Chamberlain, 1985). Traditionally, CM has been provided to the seriously mentally ill to replace and coordinate the many services provided in state hospitals. Over time, CM has become a more refined intervention, used differentially among diverse populations such as children, the elderly, and public welfare recipients (Sullivan, Wolk, & Hartmann, 1992). Since the 1980s, CM has proved to be the cornerstone for serving homeless populations (Lam & Rosenheck, 1999) and has derived its prominence owing to increasing concern with service effectiveness (Rapp, 1998a) and managed care (Solomon & Draine, 1995).

Definitional Issues

Despite its importance as a service component in the area of mental health and homelessness, the diversity of CM tasks and approaches has reinforced the lack of consensus regarding its definition. Although there is little consensus on a definition of CM or a single approach, a few common themes and core components have emerged: (1) outreach and engagement; (2) assessment; (3) development of a case plan; (4) procurement of services; (5) monitoring and advocacy; and (6) tracking and evaluation (Mueser & Bond, 2000; Sullivan et al., 1992). These components have contributed to a broad definition of CM: a pragmatic and collaborative approach to offering practical assistance (i.e., housing, finances, medications, access to services) and enhancing the social functioning of persons with mental illness through assessment, counseling, teaching, modeling, and advocacy (Mueser & Bond, 2000; Sullivan et al., 1992).

Practice Approaches

Without consensus on a definition of CM, the development of a wide variety of CM approaches and models is not surprising. The terms models and approaches are at times used interchangeably. However, "models" can be defined as a complex set of interventions designed to achieve specific goals, whereas the term "approach" often refers to a treatment philosophy that is not formally specified in all details (Morse, 1999).

Solomon (1992) identifies four types of model: assertive community treatment, strengths CM, rehabilitation, and generalist CM. Other researchers have distinguished six types: brokered, clinical, strengths, rehabilitation, assertive community treatment, and intensive CM (Mueser, Bond, Drake, & Resnick, 1998).

Rather than models or approaches, others have defined dimensions along which CM programs might differ. These include: type of staff; emphasis on outreach; client–staff ratios; shared versus individual caseloads; time and duration of availability (24 hours, lifetime, time-limited); medication delivery; type of care (direct care versus brokerage of services); target population; locus of contact (setting); and inclusion of payee services (Marshall & Lockwood, 1998; Ziguras & Stuart, 2000).

Also gaining popularity are "hybrid and tiered" approaches (stage-wise CM), where different levels of service intensity are matched with different levels of client need (Mueser & Bond, 2000). Bedell, Cohen, and Sullivan (2000) reviewed eight published literature reviews of CM and determined that three categories of CM approach existed: full service (attempt to provide directly all clinical and support services needed), hybrid (some services provided directly and some brokered), and brokered (provide very little direct service). Let us take a closer look at these approaches.

Full Service

Assertive Community Treatment (ACT): ACT was originally established as an effective community-based intervention for the non-homeless severely mentally ill. Proponents of ACT eschew the notion that it is a type of CM (Morse, 1999). Nevertheless, it shares many elements of other CM models and will be considered here for purposes of this article. Elements of the original model (Stein & Santos, 1998) include: a multidisciplinary-staff team approach, often directed by a psychiatrist; a low client–staff ratio (10:1); shared caseloads; 24-hour availability, time-unlimited services; locus of contact in the community. Goals often focus on help with symptom management, relapse prevention, enhancing supportive social and family systems, meeting basic needs, enhancing quality of life and social functioning, preventing hospitalization, and assistance with locating and maintaining work. Research is now looking toward its implementation with various subpopulations of persons with severe mental illness, such as the homeless (Dixon, Krauss, & Kernan, 1995; Morse, Calsyn, & Allen, 1992). Other examples of full service approaches include Training in Community Living, Assertive Outreach and the Bridge Program (Bond, McGrew, & Fekete, 1995; Test, 1992).

Hybrid Approaches

Continuous treatment teams (CTTs)

CTT is often considered a variation of ACT (Morse et al., 1992). It refers to a multidisciplinary team approach to serving the seriously mentally ill. Program components include: multidisciplinary team of mental health workers, including a psychiatrist; outreach; ongoing responsibility for providing and coordinating treatment, whether in the hospital or not (i.e. 1-year duration); shared and relatively small caseload size (15:1); locus of care in the client's natural setting.

Although presented as distinct from ACT, a review of the literature suggests some ambiguity surrounding specific ways in which the CTT model departs from the ACT model, and some make little or no distinction between ACT and CTT (Johnsen et al., 1999, p. 330).

Intensive case management (ICM)

ICM gets its name from the conceptualization of being more intense than usual, brokered CM. ICM is a CM approach, as it has emerged from the field in absence of an extensive theoretical or research base (Morse, 1999). Caseload ratios are often 10:1 or 15:1. It has many of the same admission criteria and goals as ACT, but is less clearly defined and often operationalized differently across programs. It typically does not use a shared-client team approach.

The strengths model

The Strengths Model is yet another hybrid model of CM used to address the needs of the seriously mentally ill. As the name of the model suggests, it is based on the humanistic and pragmatic principle of focusing on individuals' strengths rather than pathology (Rapp, 1998b). The case manager's role blends functions of therapist and broker toward the dual purpose of identifying and then securing and sustaining resources that are both internal and external to the client (Rapp, 1998b; Rapp & Chamberlin, 1985). The model's components are: (1) focus on the person-in-environment; (2) use of paraprofessionals or consumers; (3) strengths assessment; (4) heavy emphasis on outreach, engagement, and relationship; (5) resource acquisition; (6) emphasis on self-determination (i.e., high degree of responsibility given to the client) (Rapp, 1998b). Client–staff ratios are often 20:1, and clients have 24-hour access to staff. Time of services to clients is indefinite, and case managers have individual caseloads, which are shared for purposes of backup. However, the strengths model does utilize a group supervision/team approach for case planning and review (Rapp, 1998b). Although often used

257

with a broad, non-homeless population of persons with severe mental illness, it has been implemented in the ACCESS demonstration project for the homeless (Johnsen et al., 1999; Morse, 1999).

Clinical case management (CCM)

CCM is an aggressive approach to assisting the mentally ill that stresses the importance of formal clinical training and services (individual and group therapy). Case managers take a longitudinal perspective of the course of an illness, and they strive for the maintenance of the client's physical and social environment, with the goals of enhancing the client's basic survival, personal growth, community participation, and recovery. The typical client–staff ratio of CCM is 1:15. However, case size should be flexible, based on the type and intensity of clinical services provided (Kanter, 1989).

Critical time intervention (CTI)

Early research has indicated some promise for the CM approach known as CTI. This approach is designed to prevent first episodes of homelessness, as well as recurrent homelessness, by augmenting the continuity of care for individuals being discharged from institutions to community living (Susser et al., 1997). CTI is time-limited and focuses on the time of overlap before and after discharge. A primary element of CTI is that post-discharge services are delivered by staff who have established a relationship with the client while hospitalized. CTI is similar to ACT in that its focus is on *in vivo* support. However, more emphasis is placed on the critical transitional time of discharge to the community. Once the client is situated in the community, the primary responsibility of care is transferred to existing supports in the community. CTI staff do not have to be professionals, but they are supervised by a psychiatrist or mental health professional (Herman et al., 2000).

Brokered Approaches

Brokered case management (BCM)

BCM includes the traditional CM functions of assessment, planning, referral, and monitoring. However, the case manager provides little to no direct service or outreach to the client and has no responsibility for ensuring that the brokered services are completed. Brokered case managers are often bachelor-level professionals based in an office, from where they coordinate caseloads of 30 or more. Other brokered approaches of CM are Specialist, Generalist, and Supportive (Bedell et al., 2000). Although common, these approaches are not recommended for homeless populations (Morse et al., 1997).

CONSIDERING THE EVIDENCE

ACT Studies

ACT is one of the best-researched CM models, with over 25 randomized controlled trials evaluating its effectiveness, along with a number of quasi-experimental and non-experimental studies. Recently, a meta-analysis of studies that employed an ACT intervention for homeless populations with mental illness supports the efficacy of this model. The meta-analysis, which included six randomized trials and four observational studies, totaling over 5,775 subjects, found that ACT was significantly associated with a greater reduction in homelessness and greater improvement in mental health symptoms, compared with individuals receiving standard CM services (Coldwell & Bender, 2007).

Lehman et al. (1999) and Lehman, Dixon, Kernan, DeForge, and Postrado (1997) tested the efficacy of a modified ACT model for homeless persons with severe and persistent mental illness. Clients are referred to a "miniteam," consisting of a case manager, psychiatrist, and consumer advocate. However, the entire team works together in decision-making and is knowledgeable about most of the clients. In addition, the modified ACT model assumes a time-limited, rather than a time-unlimited, framework for service delivery. Finally, a family outreach worker and consumer advocate was added to provide services to a subgroup of families and clients. However, many other original ACT components remain, such as 24-hour coverage and low client–staff ratios (9:1).

Through stratified random assignment, half the participants received ACT services, and the other half received services as usual (community mental health centers). Preliminary findings showed that the ACT clients spent more days stably housed, used fewer crisis-oriented services, and had more outpatient visits than did the comparison group. ACT clients also had greater symptom reduction and greater improvements in life satisfaction and health. No differences were found in areas of employment and interpersonal relations. Overall, the authors concluded that it is possible to modify the ACT model for homeless subgroups.

Herinckx, Kinney, Clarke, and Paulson (1997) randomly assigned homeless persons with severe mental illness to one of two ACT teams or a usual-care (UC) control condition. Results showed that the ACT teams retained 68% of their clients, versus 43% in UC. UC clients were more than twice as likely to drop out owing to dissatisfaction with treatment as ACT clients were. For each additional night homeless during the 6-month period prior to enrollment in the study, there was a 14% increase in the probability of dropout. The authors concluded that ACT has a greater ability to engage and retain formerly homeless clients in mental health care than does care as usual.

Korr and Joseph (1995) studied a group of clients in a state hospital who were randomly assigned to ACT or routine services. At 6-month follow up, 36 ACT clients were housed, compared with 15 receiving routine services. None of the ACT clients had returned to the streets or to shelters. The authors concluded that ACT was an effective means to house the mentally ill homeless.

Morse et al. (1997) conducted an experimental study comparing three types of CM (ACT versus ACT plus community workers versus BCM) for the mentally ill who were homeless or at risk of homelessness and in acute crisis. Clients were primarily recruited from emergency rooms and inpatient units. The ACT-only treatment group conformed to the standard ACT treatment principles described above, with the exception of a few modifications to meet the special needs of the homeless: (1) there was assertive outreach to shelters and specialized training in engaging the homeless; (2) the team did not have a psychiatric nurse; (3) the psychiatrist was available for only 2 hours a week; and (4) medication services were obtained primarily through linkages with private or clinic-based psychiatrists. The ACT plus community worker treatment group was the same as the ACT-only group. However, clients were also assigned a paraprofessional who assisted with activities of daily living (ADLs) and leisure, primarily in

259

the later stages of treatment. The BCM treatment group followed standard CM principles described in the CM models section.

Results indicated that clients in the two ACT groups were more satisfied with their treatment and had fewer symptoms in the areas of thought disorder and unusual activity. Clients in the ACT-only group averaged more days stably housed than clients in both the ACT plus community worker and BCM groups. No significant treatment group differences were found between the treatment groups on income, anxiety–depression, hostility–suspicion, and self-esteem and substance abuse variables. The authors concluded that ACT is a more effective intervention for mentally ill persons at risk of homelessness or homeless than BCM. In a very similar study, Morse and colleagues conducted an experimental study that randomly assigned clients to ACT versus a community mental health clinic versus a drop-in center. Once again, ACT proved to be the most effective service for the same population (Morse et al., 1992).

In another publication of the above-mentioned study, Wolff et al. (1997) reported on the cost-effectiveness of three approaches to CM for the homeless or at risk of homelessness mentally ill described above. They found that there was no statistically significant difference between the treatment conditions in terms of total costs. However, the ACT conditions spent less money on inpatient services than did BCM, but more on CM services and meeting basic needs (food stamps, housing, SSI). The authors concluded that, overall, ACT achieves better outcomes, at no greater cost, than BCM.

Shern et al. (2000) tested a psychiatric rehabilitation approach of services for the homeless and severely mentally ill. Participants were randomly assigned to the experimental Choices program or offered information on "standard treatment." The Choices program was described as being similar in structure to the ACT program described above, with the addition of respite housing and a low-demand drop-in center. Results indicated that members of the Choices experimental program were more likely to attend a day program, meet their basic needs more often, spend less time on the streets, and spend more time stably housed than those in the control group. The experimental group also reported greater life satisfaction and had fewer psychiatric symptoms compared with the control group. The authors concluded that, with a comprehensive service model based on psychiatric rehabilitation principles, it is possible to engage homeless persons and improve their use of human services, housing conditions, quality of life, and mental health status.

Calsyn, Morse, Klinkenberg, Trusty, and Allen (1998) studied the impact of ACT on the social relationships of people who are homeless and mentally ill. Using two randomized experiments, they compared the effectiveness of ACT versus outpatient therapy, drop-in centers and BCM. Clients receiving ACT services reported having more professionals as part of their support network. However, they did not report significant differences among treatment conditions on most of the other social relationship dimensions.

ICM Studies

Braucht et al. (1995) studied a group of homeless individuals with substance abuse problems. Half of the clients randomly received comprehensive substance abuse services, while the other half received ICM in addition to the substance abuse services. Clients improved on average regarding their substance abuse, housing, mental health, employment, and quality of life status.

CM marginally increased client contact with counselors and was found to have little to no effect on outcomes.

Cox et al. (1998) studied homeless substance abusers to test the effectiveness of ICM in improving finances, residential stability, and reducing alcohol use. Subjects were randomly assigned to ICM or a control group and given follow-up measures at 6-month intervals for a period of 2 years. Results showed significant group differences for those receiving ICM in all three outcome areas. The authors concluded that ICM had a beneficial affect for alcohol abusers.

Hurlburt, Hough, and Wood (1996) were interested in studying the effects of substance abuse on housing stability of homeless mentally ill persons receiving supported housing. Using a two-factor longitudinal design, clients were randomly assigned to four experimental conditions. Half the clients were given Section 8 vouchers, enabling access to independent housing. All clients received traditional CM, but half were provided ICM. Results revealed that clients were more likely to end up in independent housing if given the opportunity to obtain a Section 8 voucher. No differences emerged across the two different levels of CM. Housing stability was significantly mediated by several factors, primarily the use of drugs or alcohol. The authors concluded that supported housing can be very effective in helping the homeless achieve stable housing, regardless of the associated CM model (ICM versus traditional).

Stahler, Shipley, Bartelt, DuCette, and Shandler (1995) studied alternative treatments for homeless, substance-abusing men. The treatments included (1) integrated comprehensive residential services; (2) on-site shelter-based ICM with referrals to a community network of services; and (3) UC shelter services with CM. Results indicated that all three treatment groups were associated with significant improvement, as evidenced by reduced substance use, increased employment, and increased stable housing. However, no differential improvements were found among the treatment groups.

Toro et al. (1997) randomly assigned homeless clients to ICM or a control group. Results indicated that, regardless of the intervention, clients reduced the nights spent homeless, as well as adverse physical health symptoms and stressful live events. However, clients receiving ICM had better quality of housing, fewer stressful life events, and less psychopathology compared with the control group.

Willenbring (1997) studied the (cost-) effectiveness of three intensities of CM (intensive = caseload of 12; intermediate = caseload of 45; or episodic care only) with homeless substance abusers. Participants were recruited from a public detoxification center and randomly assigned to the treatment conditions. Results indicated that both CM treatments were associated with significant reductions in costs, use of detoxification, and emergency services, compared with episodic care. However, the two CM interventions did not differ. The authors concluded that there was no real advantage to a caseload of 12 over a caseload of 45. Overall, CM is a cost-effective treatment for homeless substance abusers.

Sosin, Bruny, and Reidy (1995) studied graduates from a short-term inpatient substance abuse program who were homeless and randomly assigned to one of three treatment conditions: (1) CM only; (2) CM plus supported housing; (3) normal aftercare in the community (control). The two treatment groups use a "progressive independence" approach, which targets obtaining basic needs and improving clinical status. Results showed that participants in both treatment groups had lower levels of substance abuse and higher levels of housing stability compared with the control group. Retention and residential stability were increased owing to the targeting of immediate, tangible resources (income maintenance and housing), and substance abuse was reduced with the assistance of supportive services and behavioral training in relapse prevention.

Lapham, Hall, and Skipper (1995) studied project H&ART, a randomized intervention trial for homeless substance abusers. CM plus peer-supervised housing was compared with peer-supervised housing only and with a housed and non-housed control group. Results revealed graduation rates of about 25% for all three housed groups. The authors concluded that client personal motivation factors of recovery were more salient in determining outcomes than were program-related factors.

CTI

Herman et al. (2000) and Susser et al. (1997) studied the effectiveness of CTI in preventing recurrent homelessness. Ninety-six men with psychotic disorders who were discharged from a homeless shelter were randomly assigned to receive either CTI or usual services (US) (mental health and rehabilitation referrals) only after their housing placement had been selected (ranging from board and care homes to single room occupancy (SRO)). The CTI involved two primary components, the worker supporting the client's long-term ties to services, family, and friends, as well as providing emotional and practical support during the time of transition. Practical support also included medication and money management. The men in the CTI intervention received 9 months of CTI plus US and then usual services only (USO) for the remaining 9 months. The number of nights homeless was measured during monthly face-to-face interviews, and psychiatric symptom severity was measured with the Positive and Negative Syndrome Scale (PANSS). Results showed that CTI was associated with a significant and lasting reduction in post-discharge homelessness (CTI had a mean of 30 nights versus USO with a mean of 91). The primary effect of CTI was reducing extended homelessness (episodes over 54 days): 21% of clients receiving CTI experienced extended homelessness, versus 40% of the clients in the comparison group (Rog, 2004; Susser et al., 1997). In addition, CTI was associated with a significant decrease in negative psychiatric symptoms at the 6-month follow-up. There was no significant effect on positive or general psychopathology symptoms. The primary study limitation, as with any experimental studies that test a "package" of services, was the difficulty in differentiating the specific mechanisms through which the treatment produced the observed results (Herman et. al., 2000; Susser et al., 1997).

Jones et al. (2003) investigated the costs associated with the comparison groups. Cost variables included acute care services, outpatient services, housing and shelter services, criminal justice, and entitlement income. Over the 18-month study period, the CTI program cost $52,374, versus $51,649 for services as usual. Although the cost difference between groups was not statistically significant, the CTI group had significantly greater net housing stability. The overall results showed that, if a program is willing to spend an additional $152 per non-homeless night, critical time intervention is cost-effective.

A second generation of CTI outcome studies has begun to test the effectiveness and adaptability of the model for different populations and service settings. For instance, a modified CTI demonstration project for mentally ill homeless veterans following discharge from inpatient psychiatric care in eight VA sites was recently published (Kasprow & Rosenheck, 2007). The study used a non-randomized pre–post cohort design with a 1-year quarterly follow-up to study housing and mental health outcomes. A comparison cohort (phase 1) of 278 participants was recruited before CTI was implemented, and a treatment cohort (phase 2) of 206 participants was recruited after implementation and offered CTI. Veterans in phase 2 on average had 19% more days housed in each 90-day reporting period over the 1-year follow-up ($p < .002$) and 14% fewer days in institutional settings ($p = .041$). Veterans in phase 2 also had 19% lower Addiction Severity Index (ASI) alcohol use scores ($p < .001$), 14% lower ASI drug use scores ($p = .003$), and 8% lower ASI psychiatric problem scores ($p = .001$). A shortcoming of this evaluation is that clients were not randomly assigned to receive CTI or US. As a result, it cannot be certain that outcome results are entirely attributable to the program intervention, because differences in the groups at baseline also may have contributed to differences in study outcomes at follow-up.

Brokered CM

Marshall, Lockwood, and Gath (1995) conducted a randomized controlled trial to evaluate a social services CM approach (brokered) for the chronically mentally ill who were homeless or at risk of being homeless. Forty clients were each randomly assigned to social services CM and to services as usual (care provided them before the study, but not receiving another CM service). Results after 7 months revealed no clinically or statistically significant differences between the treatment and control groups. At the 14-month follow-up, the CM group showed lower levels of deviant behavior compared with the control group. The authors concluded that social services CM (brokered) did not improve the quality of life or the social behavior of chronically mentally ill homeless and commented that it was unfortunate that social services CM had been widely implemented in the United Kingdom.

POLICY ISSUES AND HISTORICAL BACKGROUND

Homelessness is not a new problem, and governmental policies have frequently changed focus in order to manage the problem. During the depression eras (1873, 1885, 1893, and 1929), "skid rows" often consisted of a transient male homeless population that included the physically disabled, mentally ill, and elderly who were served by volunteers and clergy in rescue missions (Johnson & Cnaan, 1995). They congregated in large urban areas where poverty, illness, and substance abuse were an accepted way of life (Johnson, 1995).

In 1933, the federal government began efforts to ameliorate homelessness. One such effort involved the Federal Transient Bureau's agreement to pay cities for the shelter and meal costs of non-locals at established tent camps and "Main Stems" (Snow & Anderson, 1993). In addition, "Roosevelt proposed what became the National Housing Act of 1934, which created the Federal Housing Administration program of insuring home mortgage loans" (Roisman, 2005, p. 118).

The approach of a residential continuum of care (COC) emerged in the 1970s and has been utilized to address the rapidly rising homeless problem. The McKinney Act of 1987 (Public Law 110–77) initially involved 20 programs targeting housing assistance, health, mental health, food assistance, substance abuse, education, and job training, in order to address the complex needs of homelessness.

263

The COC approach emphasizes that people with SUMHD need specialized residential programs managed by mental health entities as an answer to deinstitutionalization (Carling & Ridgway, 1987). These have taken many forms, such as quarter-way houses, halfway houses (Budson, 1981), three-quarter-way houses (Campbell, 1981), family foster care (Carling, 1984; Linn, Klett, & Caffey, 1980), crisis alternative models (Stein & Test, 1980), Fairweather Lodges (Fairweather, 1980), apartment programs (Carling, 1978), boarding homes (Kohen & Paul, 1976), nursing homes (Carling, 1981), and homeless shelters (Bachrach, 1984), all intended to make up a residential continuum.

The COC approach is traditionally based on a medical or clinical model where people are trained to manage symptoms and dysfunctions of SUMHD prior to being placed in independent living arrangements (Corrigan & McCracken, 2005). The approach, sometimes referred to as "Train–Place," assumes that high-risk clients have difficulty succeeding in independent housing and thus can have their clinical needs better met through segregated, congregate-style transitional housing, with onsite services that are professionally staffed. Often, housing access and tenure are linked to clinical status and treatment compliance with drug and alcohol abstinence, psychiatric assessments, and medication (Carling & Ridgway, 1987; Fitzpatrick, 2005; Hopper & Barrow, 2003; Rog, 2004). As the client progresses, they move through a range of housing options, with decreasing intensity of services and demands along with differing locations and structures designed to help clients progress to more independent housing (Ridgway & Zipple, 1990). Failure to receive these step-wise services in safe environments may lead to stress that exacerbates symptoms and disabilities that fuel a limited sense of self-efficacy (Corrigan & McCracken, 2005).

The COC has been identified as an integral component of the comprehensive response to homelessness (Barnard-Columbia Center for Urban Policy, 1996; United States Department of Housing and Urban Development, 1995). From 1987 to 1990, HUD awarded hundreds of Transitional Housing Program grants to nonprofit organizations and state and local governments for acquiring and/or rehabilitating housing facilities and supportive services to help homeless individuals transition to independent living in 24 months (Washington, 2002).

Approximately 10–15 years ago, another approach emerged in response to criticisms about the COC approach. Government started to place more of an emphasis on ending chronic homelessness through the use of supportive housing or housing first. Consumers felt the residential continuum did not meet their varying needs, and that often parts of the continuum were not available and that the clinical model was paternalistic and did not honor individuals' preference and choice (Rog, 2004). In addition, each transition along the continuum is a significant adjustment that leads to chronic dislocation. Ultimately, housing readiness is a subjective judgment, which both increases the discretion of staff and generates a systematic disattention to the individual economic issues that are fundamental to an exit from homelessness (Dordick, 2002).

Supported housing/housing first is based on the "Place–Train" psychiatric rehabilitation model and harm reduction principles (Corrigan & McCracken, 2005). This approach involves placing people in independent community housing first, with sufficient housing subsidies available to enhance the affordability of housing choices. Independent living arrangements are based on consumer preferences (for type of housing, roommates, location, etc.) and are later augmented with the appropriate level of professional and nonprofessional support necessary for the individual to manage independent living skills (Carling, 1993). Housing is not contingent on treatment compliance for the most part. Supported housing's primary function is to prevent homelessness and its reoccurrence among individuals with a history of homelessness or those at risk, including the chronically mentally ill, disabled, and persons in recovery for substance dependence (Cohen, Mulroy, Tull, White, & Crowley, 2004). This approach has received great attention and is endorsed by the U.S. Interagency Council on Homelessness as an approach to end chronic homelessness.

Finally, governmental policy has started to focus on prevention. The inclusion of the Homelessness Prevention and Rapid Rehousing Program (HPRP) as part of the American Recovery and Reinvestment Act of 2009 signals a paradigm shift in the government's approach to addressing housing and homeless services (Apicello, 2010). Instead of preserving the status quo of providing assistance to individuals and families only after they have become homeless, the HPRP takes a prevention-oriented approach to avoid a large influx into homelessness of persons who otherwise may have become homeless owing to the ongoing recession and affordable housing crisis (Culhane & Byrne, 2010). CM plays a crucial role in the implementation of HPRP in order to help at-risk individuals negotiate the often fragmented service delivery system and gain access to programs and funding. However, the practice of homelessness prevention is just at its inception, and there is a need for rigorous evaluation, as there is no consensus about the most appropriate approaches (Apicello, 2010).

SUMMARY

The benefits of CM services for persons who are homeless with SUMHD seem promising. Evidence suggests that ACT, CTI, and ICM reduce the number of days homeless compared with the BCM or other standard approaches. In addition, some studies have shown an increase in service utilization, better engagement and retention, reduced symptoms, greater satisfaction with services, improved income, and increased quality of life (Blankertz, Cnaan, White, Fox, & Messinger, 1990; Morse, 1999). ACT remains the best-researched CM model, even when modified for homeless populations. However, CTI is one of only a few homelessness prevention interventions to be featured in SAMHSA's National Registry of Evidence-Based Programs and Policies (Herman & Mandiberg, 2010) and has been examined in a number of studies supporting its effectiveness in improving outcomes among homeless adults with mental illness following discharge from an institutional facility (Dixon et al., 2009; Herman & Mandiberg, 2010; Kasprow & Rosenheck, 2007; Susser et al., 1997). As a result, it seems that the research strongly supports ACT and its modifications (CTI) for the homeless as an "evidenced-based practice" and "best practice" among the current literature for homeless persons with SUMHD. However, more research is needed on comparing CM between housing first and the COC approaches, as well as its effectiveness when working with those with an active or severe addiction and its role in prevention.

DISCUSSION QUESTIONS

1. What factors cause homelessness? How are these factors interrelated?

2. How can case management play a role in preventing or helping a person to no longer be homeless?

3. Identify and explain the underlying principles that inform Housing First versus the linear Continuum of Care?

LEARNING ASSIGNMENT

After reading the chapter, volunteer in a local food bank or shelter and discuss your experiences in class, contextualizing what you have learned in connection with the reading.

SUGGESTED READINGS

Burt, M.R., Aron, L.Y., Douglas, T., Valente, J., Lee, E., & Iwen, B. (1999). *Homelessness: Programs and the People They Serve*. Washington, DC: Interagency Council on Homelessness.

Hopper, K. (2002). *Reckoning with Homelessness (The Anthropology of Contemporary Issues)*. Cornell University Press.

National Alliance to End Homelessness (2000). *A Plan Not a Dream: How to End Homelessness in Ten Years*. Washington, DC: Author.

Rapp, C. (1998). *The Strengths Model: Case Management with People Suffering from Severe and Persistent Mental Illness*. New York: Oxford University Press.

Rossi, P.H. (1991). *Down and Out in America: The Origins of Homelessness*. University of Chicago Press.

Stein, L.I. & Santos, A.B. (1998). *Assertive Community Treatment of Persons with Severe Mental Illness*. New York: W.W. Norton.

U.S. Department of Health and Human Services and U.S. Department of Housing and Urban Development (2007). Toward Understanding Homelessness: The 2007 National Symposium on Homelessness Research. Washington, DC: Author.

U.S. Department of Housing and Urban Development (2009). Opening Doors: The Federal Strategic Plan to Prevent and End Homelessness. HUD's Annual Homeless Assessment Report (AHAR) for 2009.

INTERNET RESOURCES

Corporation for Supportive Housing: www.csh.org

National Association to End Homelessness: www.endhomelessness.org

U.S. Interagency Council on Homelessness: www.ich.gov

U.S. Department of Housing and Urban Development: portal.hud.gov/portal/page/portal/HUD

2007 National Symposium on Homelessness: aspe.hhs.gov/hsp/homelessness/symposium07/caton/index.htm

REFERENCES

Adams, J., Rosenheck, R., Gee, L., Seibyl, C., & Kushel, M. (2007). Hospitalized younger: A comparison of a national sample of homeless and housed inpatient veterans. *Journal of Health Care for the Poor and Underserved, 18*(1), 173–184.

Apicello, J. (2010). A paradigm shift in housing and homeless services: Applying the population and high-risk framework to preventing homelessness. *The Open Health Services and Policy Journal, 3*, 41–52.

Austin, C.D. & McClelland, R.W. (1997). Case management in human services. Reflections on public policy. *Journal of Case Management, 6*, 119–126.

Bachrach, L.L. (1984). The homeless mentally ill and mental health services: An analytical review of the literature. In H.R. Lamb (Ed.), *The homeless mentally ill* (pp. 11–53). Washington, DC: American Psychiatric Press.

Barnard-Columbia Center for Urban Policy (1996). *The continuum of care: A report on the new federal policy to address homelessness.* Washington, DC: U.S. Department of Housing and Urban Development.

Bedell, J.R., Cohen, N.L., & Sullivan, A. (2000). Case management: The current best practices and the next generation of innovation. *Community Mental Health Journal, 36*, 179–194.

Blankertz, L.E., Cnaan, R.A., White, K., Fox, J., & Messinger, K. (1990). Outreach efforts with dually diagnosed homeless persons. *Families in Society, 71*, 387–396.

Bond, G.R., McGrew, J.H., & Fekete, D.M. (1995). Assertive outreach for frequent users of psychiatric hospitals: A meta-analysis. *Journal of Mental Health Administration, 22*, 4–16.

Braucht, G.N., Reichardt, C.S., Geissler, L.J., Bormann, C.A., Kwiatkowski, C.F., & Kirby, M.W. (1995). Effective services for homeless substance abusers. *Journal of Addictive Diseases, 14*(4), 87–109.

Brunette, M.F., Mueser, K.T., & Drake, R.E. (2004). A review of research on residential programs for people with severe mental illness and co-occurring substance abuse disorders. *Drug and Alcohol Review, 23*, 471–481.

Budson, R.D. (Ed.) (1981). *New directions for mental health services: Issues in community residential care.* San Francisco, CA: Jossey-Bass.

Burt, M., Aron, L.Y., Lee, E., & Valente, J. (2001). *Helping America's homeless: Emergency shelter or affordable housing?* Washington, DC: The Urban Institute Press.

Calsyn, R.J., Morse, G.A., Klinkenberg, W.D., Trusty, M.L., & Allen, G. (1998). The impact of assertive community treatment on the social relationships of people who are homeless and mentally ill. *Community Mental Health Journal, 34*(6), 579–593.

Campbell, M. (1981). The three-quarterway house: A step beyond the halfway house toward independent living. *Hospital and Community Psychiatry, 32*, 500–501.

Carling, P.J. (1978). Residential services in a psychosocial rehabilitation context: The Horizon House model. In J. Goldmeir, F.V. Mannino, & M.E. Shore (Eds.), *New directions in mental health care: Cooperative apartments* (pp. 52–64). Adelphi, MD: Mental Health Study Center, National Institute of Mental Health.

Carling, P.J. (1981). Nursing homes and chronic mental patients: A second opinion. *Schizophrenia Bulletin, 7*, 574–579.

Carling, P.J. (1984). *Developing family foster care programs in mental health: A resource guide.* Rockville, MD: National Institute of Mental Health.

Carling, P.J. (1993). Housing and supports for persons with mental illness: Emerging approaches to research and practice. *Hospital and Community Psychiatry, 44*, 439–449.

Carling, P.J. & Ridgway, P. (1987). Overview of a psychiatric rehabilitation approach to housing. In W.A. Anthony & M. Farkas, *Psychiatric rehabilitation: Turning theory into practice* (pp. 28–80). Baltimore, MD: Johns Hopkins University Press.

Cohen, C.S., Mulroy, E., Tull, T., White, C., & Crowley, S. (2004). Housing plus services: Supporting vulnerable families in permanent housing. *Child Welfare, LXXXIII*(5), 509–528.

Coldwell, C.M. & Bender, W.S. (2007). The effectiveness of assertive community treatment for homeless populations with severe mental illness: A meta-analysis. *American Journal of Psychiatry, 164*(3).

Corrigan, P.W. & McCracken, S.G. (2005). Place first, then train: An alternative to the medical model of psychiatric rehabilitation. *Social Work, 50*(1), 31–39.

Cox, G.B., Walker, R.D., Freng, S.A., Short, B.A., Meijer, L., & Gilchrist, L. (1998). Outcomes of a controlled trial of the effectiveness of intensive case management for chronic public inebriates. *Journal of Studies on Alcohol, 59*(5), 523–532.

Culhane, D. & Byrne, T. (2010). *Ending chronic homelessness: Cost-effective opportunities for interagency collaboration.* United States Interagency Council on Homelessness—FSP Supplemental Document #19.

Culhane, D., Chang-Moo, L., & Wachter, S. (1996). Where the homeless come from: A study of the prior address distribution of families admitted to public shelters in New York City and Philadelphia. *Housing Policy Debate, 7*(2), 327–365.

Dixon, L., Goldberg, R., Iannone, V., et al. (2009). Use of a critical time intervention to promote continuity of care after psychiatric inpatient hospitalization for severe mental illness. *Psychiatric Services, 60*, 451–458.

Dixon, L.B., Krauss, N., & Kernan, E. (1995). Modifying the PACT model to serve homeless persons with severe mental illness. *Psychiatric Services, 46*, 684–688.

Dordick, G.A. (2002). Recovering from homelessness: Determining the "quality of sobriety" in a transitional housing program. *Qualitative Sociology, 25*(1), 7–33.

Essock, S., Mueser, K.T., Drake, R.E., et al. (2006). Comparison of ACT and standard case management for delivering integrated treatment for co-occurring disorders. *Psychiatric Services, 57*, 185–196.

Fairweather, G.W. (1980). *The Fairweather Lodge: A twenty-five year retrospective.* San Francisco, CA: Jossey-Bass.

Fitzpatrick, C. (2005). Housing first becoming the standard model for homeless populations. Special reports: Innovations in behavioral health. From the editors of *Alcoholism & Drug Abuse Weekly*, 16(41), and *Mental Health Weekly*, 14(41), 1–3.

Herinckx, H.A., Kinney, R.F., Clarke, G.N., & Paulson, R.I. (1997). Assertive Community Treatment versus usual care in engaging and retaining clients with severe mental illness. *Psychiatric Services, 48*(10), 1297–1306.

Herman, D. & Mandiberg, J. (2010). Critical time intervention: model description and implications for the significance of timing social work interventions. *Research on Social Work Practice, 20*, 502–508.

Herman, D., Opler, L., Felix, A., Valencia, J.D., Wyatt, R.J., & Susser, E. (2000). A critical time intervention with mentally ill homeless men: Impact on psychiatric symptoms. *The Journal of Nervous and Mental Disease, 188*(3), 135–140.

Hopper, K. & Barrow, S.M. (2003). Two genealogies of supported housing: Implications for outcome assessment. *Psychiatric Services, 54*, 50–54.

Hurlburt, M.S., Hough, R.L., & Wood, P.A. (1996). Effects of substance abuse on housing stability of homeless mentally ill persons in supported housing. *Psychiatric Services, 47*(7), 731–736.

Johnsen, M., Samberg, L., Calsyn, R., Blasinsky, M., Landow, W., & Goldman, H. (1999). Case management models for persons who are homeless and mentally ill: The ACCESS demonstration project. *Community Mental Health Journal, 35*(4), 325–346.

Johnson, A.K. (1995). Homelessness. In *Encyclopedia of social work*, 19th ed. (pp. 1338–1346). Washington DC: NASW.

Johnson, A.K. & Cnaan, R.A. (1995). Social work practice with homeless persons: State of the art. *Research in Social Work Practice, 5*(3), 340–382.

Jones, K., Colson, P., Holter, M., Lin, S., Valencia, E., Susser, E., et al. (2003). Cost-effectiveness of the critical time intervention to reduce homelessness among persons with mental illness. *Psychiatric Services, 54*, 884–890.

Kanter, J. (1989). Clinical case management: Definition, principles, components. *Hospital and Community Psychiatry, 40*(4), 361–368.

Kasprow, W.J. & Rosenheck, R.A. (2007). Outcomes of critical time intervention case management of homeless veterans after psychiatric hospitalization. *Psychiatric Services, 58*, 929–935.

Koegel, P., Burnam, M.A., & Baumohl, J. (1996). The causes of homelessness. In J. Baumohl (Ed.), *Homelessness in America* (pp. 24–33). Phoenix, AZ: The Oryx Press.

Kohen, W. & Paul, G.L. (1976). Current trends and recommended changes in extended-care placement of mental patients: The Illinois system as a case in point. *Schizophrenia Bulletin, 2*(4), 574–594.

Korr, W.S. & Joseph, A. (1995). Housing the homeless mentally ill: Findings from Chicago. *Journal of Social Service Research, 21*(1), 53–68.

Lam, J.A. & Rosenheck, R. (1999). Street outreach for homeless persons with serious mental illness. *Medical Care, 37*(9), 894–907.

Lapham, S.C., Hall, M., & Skipper, B.J. (1995). Homelessness and substance use among alcohol abusers following participation in project H&ART. *Journal of Addictive Diseases, 14*(4), 41–55.

Lehman, A.F., Dixon, L., Hoch, J.S., Deforge, B., Kernan, E., & Frank, R. (1999). Cost-effectiveness of assertive community treatment for homeless persons with severe mental illness. *British Journal of Psychiatry, 174*, 346–352.

Lehman, A.F., Dixon, L., Kernan, E., DeForge, B.R., & Postrado, L.T. (1997). A randomized trial of assertive community treatment for homeless persons with severe mental illness. *Archives of General Psychiatry, 54*(11), 1038–1043.

Linn, M.W., Klett, C.J., & Caffey, E.M. (1980). Foster home characteristics and psychiatric patient outcome: The wisdom of Gheel confirmed. *Archives of General Psychiatry, 37*, 129–132.

Marshall, M. & Lockwood, A. (1998). Assertive community treatment for people with severe mental disorders (a Cochrane review). Oxford, England, Update Software (for the Cochrane Library).

Marshall, M., Lockwood, A., & Gath, D. (1995). Social services case management did not improve behaviour or quality of life in persons with long-term mental disorders. *Evidence-Based Medicine, 1*, 30–39.

McMurray-Avila, M., Gelberg, L., & Breakey, W.R. (1999). Balancing act: Clinical practices that respond to the needs of homeless people. In L.B. Fosburg & D.L. Dennis (Eds.), *Practical lessons: The 1998 National Symposium on Homelessness Research* (pp. 8/1–8/44). Washington, DC: U.S. Department of Housing and Urban Development, U.S. Department of Health and Human Services.

Morse, G. (1999). A review of case management for people who are homeless: Implications for practice, policy and research. In L.B. Fosburg & D.L. Dennis (Eds.), *Practical lessons: The 1998 National Symposium on Homelessness Research* (pp. 7/1–7/34). Washington, DC: U.S. Department of Housing and Urban Development, U.S. Department of Health and Human Services.

Morse, G.A., Calsyn, R.J., & Allen, G. (1992). Experimental comparison of the effects of three treatment programs for homeless mentally ill people. *Hospital and Community Psychiatry, 43*, 1005–1010.

Morse, G.A., Calsyn, R.J., Klinkenberg, W.D., Trusty, M.L., Gerber, F., Smith, R., Tempelhoff, B., & Ahmad, L. (1997). An experimental comparison of three types of case management for homeless mentally ill persons. *Psychiatric Services, 48*(4), 497–503.

Mueser, K.T. & Bond, G.R. (2000). Psychosocial treatment approaches for schizophrenia. *Current Opinion in Psychiatry, 13*, 27–35.

Mueser, K.T., Bond, G.R, Drake, R.E., & Resnick, S.G. (1998). Models of community care for severe mental illness: A review of research on case management. *Schizophrenia Bulletin, 24*, 37–74.

Rapp, C. (1998a). The active ingredients of effective case management: A research synthesis. *Community Mental Health Journal, 34*(4), 363–380.

Rapp, C. (1998b). *The strengths model: Case management with people suffering from severe and persistent mental illness.* New York: Oxford University Press.

Rapp, C. & Chamberlain, R. (1985). CM services to the chronically mentally ill. *Social Work, 30*, 417–422.

Regier, D.A., Farmer, M.E., Rae, D.S., Locke, B.Z., Keith, S.J., Judd, L.L., et al. (1990). Co-morbidity of mental disorders with alcohol and other drug abuse. *Journal of the American Medical Association, 264,* 2511–2518.

Ridgway, P. & Zipple, A. (1990). The paradigm shift in residential services: From the linear continuum to supported housing approaches. *Psychosocial Rehabilitation Journal, 13,* 11–31.

Rog, D.J. (2004). The evidence on supported housing. *Psychiatric Rehabilitation Journal, 27*(4), 334–344.

Roisman, F.W. (2005). National ingratitude: The egregious deficiencies of the United States' housing programs for veterans and the "public scandal" of veterans' homelessness. *Indiana Law Review, 38*(103), 103–176.

Rosenheck, R.A. (1996). Research on homelessness among veterans: Causes and treatment outcomes. VA National Conference on Services for Homeless Veterans: September 10, 1996; Dallas, TX.

Rosenheck, R., Bassuk, E., & Salomon, A. (1999). Special populations of homeless Americans. In L.B. Fosburg & D.L. Dennis (Eds.), *Practical lessons: The 1998 National Symposium on Homelessness Research.* Washington, DC: U.S. Department of Housing and Urban Development and the U.S. Department of Health and Human Services.

Shern, D.L., Tsemberis, S., Anthony, W., Lovell, A.M., Richmond, L., Felton, C.J., Winarski, J., & Cohen, M. (2000). Serving street-dwelling individuals with psychiatric disabilities: Outcomes of a psychiatric rehabilitation clinical trial. *American Journal of Public Health, 90*(12), 1873–1878.

Snow, D.A. & Anderson, L. (1993). *Down on their luck: A study of homeless street people.* Berkeley, CA: University of California Press.

Solomon, P. (1992). The efficacy of case management services for severely mentally disabled clients. *Community Mental Health Journal, 28*(3), 163–180.

Solomon, P. & Draine, J. (1995). The efficacy of a consumer case management team: Two-year outcomes of a randomized trial. *Journal of Mental Health Administration, 22,* 135–146.

Sosin, M.R., Bruni, M., & Reidy, M. (1995). Paths and impacts in the progressive independence model: A homelessness and substance abuse intervention in Chicago. *Journal of Addictive Diseases, 12*(4), 1–20.

Stahler, G.J., Shipley, T.F., Bartelt, D., DuCette, J.P., & Shandler, I.W. (1995). Evaluating alternative treatments for homeless substance-abusing men: Outcomes and predictors of success. *Journal of Addictive Disease, 14*(4), 151–167.

Stein, L.I. & Santos, A.B. (1998). *Assertive community treatment of persons with severe mental illness.* New York: W.W. Norton.

Stein, L.I. & Test, M.A. (1980). An altenative to mental health treatment: I. Conceptual model, treatment program, and clinical evaluation. *Archives of General Psychiatry, 37,* 392–397.

Stephens, D. & Dennis, E. (1991). The diversity of case management needs for the care of homeless persons. *Public Health Reports, 106*(1), 15–20.

Sullivan, W.P., Wolk, J.L., & Hartmann, D.J. (1992). CM in alcohol and drug treatment: Improving client outcomes. *Families in Society: The Journal of Contemporary Human Services, 73*(4), 195–203.

Susser, E., Valencia, E., Conover, S., Felix, A., Tsai, W., & Wyat, R.J. (1997). Preventing recurrent homelessness among mentally ill men: A critical time intervention after discharge from a shelter. *American Jouranl of Public Health, 87*(2), 256–262.

Test, M.A. (1992). Training in community living. In R.P. Liberman (Ed.), *Handbook of psychiatric rehabilitation* (pp. 153–170). New York: Macmillan.

Toro, P.A., Passero Rabideau, J.M., Bellavia, C.W., Daeschler, C.V., Wall, D.D., Thomas, D.M., & Smith, S.J. (1997). Evaluating an intervention for homeless persons: Results of a field experiment. *Journal of Consulting and Clincal Psychology, 65*(3), 476–484.

United States Department of Housing and Urban Development (2001). *A report on worst case housing needs in 1999.* Washington, DC: Economic Policy Institute.

United States Department of Housing and Urban Development (1995). *Review of Stewart B. McKinney homeless programs administered by HUD. Report to Congress.* U.S. Department of Housing and Urban Development.

United States Department of Housing and Urban Development (2009). *The 2008 annual homelessness assessment report: A report to the US Congress*. Washington, DC: Author.

Washington, T.A. (2002). The homeless need more than just a pillow, they need a pillar: An evaluation of a transitional housing program. *Families in Society: The Journal of Contemporary Human Services, 83*(2), 183–188.

Willenbring, M.L. (1997). Case management for homeless public inebriates conference abstract. 150th Annual Meeting of the American Psychiatric Association. San Diego, CA. May 17–22, 1997.

Wolff, N., Helminiak, T.W., Morse, G.A., Calsyn, R.J., Klinkenberg, W.D., & Trusty, M.L. (1997). Cost-effectiveness evaluation of three approaches to case management for homeless mentally ill clients. *American Journal of Psychiatry, 154*(3), 341–348.

Ziguras, S.J. & Stuart, G.W. (2000). A meta-analysis of the effectiveness of mental health case management over 20 years. *Psychiatric Services, 51*, 1410–1421.

Part Six

Community Mental Health

Organizational and Policy Issues

Chapter 17

Community Mental Health
Policy and Practice

Eileen Klein

Community aftercare has been an integral part of mental health service provision since 1906, when the first outpatient program opened in New York State (Trattner, 1994). Providing effective services to the mentally ill in an outpatient setting has become even more important since the deinstitutionalization movement began in the late 1960s. At this time, the emphasis was on treatment provision in the least restrictive setting to preserve patients' rights. However, despite policy and program changes, there is still a huge gap in the social worker's ability to provide essential services to clients in a community mental health program, and the professional role of the social worker has been in a continual state of flux. New initiatives have begun in an effort to provide adequate, coordinated care for the mentally ill in the community.

Providing services that effectively meet the needs of the seriously mentally ill in the community has been challenging in response to initiatives that include limiting the number of visits for treatment in managed care programs and an increased focus on moving patients through a continuum of care. Care providers are continually measuring outcomes of treatment in terms of moving to less intensive service provision, both in outpatient and residential settings. This provides challenges to those in care to progress into more independent living and to continually develop new skills with fewer services. This has been positive in terms of clearly defining treatment goals and objectives; however, pressure to move forward is a delicate balance for both provider and client. Reduced episodes of inpatient hospitalization and shorter authorizations for outpatient treatment do contain the costs of managed care programs, but, does this mean that services are being provided more efficiently, or that there is a risk to any long-term treatment for complex mental disorders (Clemens, 2010)?

HISTORICAL BACKGROUND

As far back as the 1700s, the mentally ill, referred to as "lunatics," were observed by the population as in need of asylum. The early institutions in Europe were known for their mistreatment of patients. In 1794, Philippe Pinel is credited with the beginnings of moral treatment of mentally ill patients. He worked to release them from the chains and shackles that they had been kept in while in psychiatric institutions, or asylums (Isaac and Armat, 1990).

Moral treatment recognized the environmental causes of mental illness, and there was an effort to move the patients to a more beneficent place, outside of the stresses of urban life. Often, administrative and medical staff lived on the hospital grounds, so that patients could be involved in shared meals and activities with them on a regular basis. Staff spent time educating the community about mental illness and worked on plans that resulted in sending the patients to live and work in community settings. Many of the ideas that followed in mental health treatment have their roots in further interpretation of moral treatment (Sands & Gellis, 2001).

The success of moral treatment did not bear out as institutions became more crowded. These asylums for the mentally ill included a population of alcoholics, violent offenders, and immigrants who did not fit into society. As a result, treatment began to revert to use of restraints to control the population, and custodial care became the norm. There was a pervasive feeling that mental illness was the result of genetic defects, and that patients may be unfit for survival, using some of the ideas of Darwin. Therefore, medications and treatment were seen as irrelevant (Sands & Gillis, 2003).

Not much changed in how patients were treated until the 1930s, when new methods of treatment were initiated. These treatments helped to improve some patients' conditions, reduced agitation, and allowed many patients to return home, but they also had damaging effects on the faculties of memory, cognition, and personality (Isaac and Armat, 1990). Some of these modalities included various types of shock therapy and other dramatic techniques used to keep patients under control.

Inpatient hospital censuses' continued to grow, without much public interest in the treatment or welfare of this population, until the 1940s. There was a growth of public interest in how mental health services were provided after World War II, as a result of concern for the large number of draftees being screened and found to have a mental illness and veterans returning home with psychiatric problems. At the same time, a series of exposés on state hospitals appeared in the media (Landsberg and Rock, 2009).

In response to this growing and visible problem, under the National Institutes of Health, the National Institute of Mental Health was founded in 1946 under the National Mental Health Act (Stubbs, 1998). This was the beginning of one of a series of mental health initiatives by the federal government. These included a Joint Commission on Mental Illness and Health being established in 1955, and legislation in 1963, the Mental Retardation Facilities and Community Mental Health Centers Construction Act, usually referred to as the Community Mental Health Centers Act. Throughout the United States, in the 1950s, there were about 550,000 residents in state hospitals, which were very costly to run.

This legislation, along with other factors in the 1960s, which included the passage of the Medicaid and Medicare bills, led to a downsizing of the state institutions. These funding initiatives allowed the states to share costs with the federal government and move patients into federally subsidized programs (Landsberg and Rock, 2009). The mentally ill were released from inpatient settings into the community, but many did not have adequate preparation for life outside of an institution and did not have the ability to get enough supports on the outside. By 1975, the term "deinstitutionalization" was used to describe the release of patients from the state hospitals into the community. State hospital censuses were reduced to 90,000 during this period.

In the past few decades, inpatient treatment and providing custodial care of the mentally ill changed as a result of litigation, which produced philosophical, administrative, and programmatic changes. Current thinking indicates that the communication by the hospital staff of a feeling of hope and efficacy will lead to recovery more than more sophisticated forms of treatment and the introduction of drug therapies (Mechanic, 1999). Staff conveying a positive attitude to a patient was at the center of the patient feeling he will be able to cope in the community and function outside of the hospital. This continues to be the current philosophy in mental health practice.

Because mental illness is a multidimensional problem with a lack of clear definition, causality, level of disability, and impact on the person and the community, there have always been great policy debates as to the purpose and direction of mental health policy and treatment initiatives. The Substance Abuse and Mental Health Services Administration [SAMHSA] (1993) established criteria in an attempt to develop federal criteria for severe mental illness. It includes those persons who have had a diagnosable mental, behavioral, or emotional disorder, as defined within the *DSM-III-R*, and this disorder has resulted in functional impairment that interferes with or limits one or more role functioning.

It is difficult to develop new programs that are effective when there are competing ideas about causes, cures, and responsibility. The Community Mental Health Centers Act began a drive toward deinstitutionalization, but, since then, there have been many other mental health programs, and laws have been instituted with the purpose of returning the mentally ill to the community.

PRACTICE CONSIDERATIONS

Academic literature has begun to define mental heath treatment fundamentally within the concept of recovery. This orientation gives a more positive connotation to treatment efficacy and refutes the idea that severe mental illness is unremitting and untreatable. Recovery is a process whereby a person with mental illness can return to a life that is useful and meaningful by establishing their own goals and working toward achieving them (Anthony, 1993). It was developed by a group of psychiatric consumers who felt they had survived and coped successfully with symptoms of their mental illness. This concept, also used in addiction, has the goal in both cases to work with those affected by these illnesses "by reducing the impairment and disability, and improve quality of life" (Gagne, White, & Anthony, 2007, p.34).

Recovery helps to give hope that there can be the establishment of a meaningful life, with a positive identity and meaningful connections and roles in the community. This concept has been embraced by family members and social service providers and has become a guiding principal in public mental health policy. Fundamental components of recovery include self-direction, respect, responsibility, and peer support, using person-centered, individuals' strengths (Sands and Gellis, 2001).

Evidence-Based Practice

Evidence-based practice (EBP) has emerged in the social work field in an effort to use knowledge and interventions that have been validated by research. Rubin (2009) suggested that EBP is a "process for making practice decisions in which practitioners integrate the best research evidence available with their practice expertise and with client attributes, values, preferences, and circumstances" (p. 7). There has been a great deal of research that indicates that there are positive outcomes using EBP approaches, including assertive community treatment, illness management and recovery, family education and involvement, medication management, supported employment, and integrated approaches to treating dually diagnosed individuals (Sands and Gellis, 2001).

Although EBP has been able to contribute a great deal to the advancement of prevention, treatment, and greater knowledge of mental illness, Aisenberg (2008) states that not enough ethnic and minority populations have been included in the samples. As funding and services are often limited for mental health services, it is crucial that programs and treatments are initiated that have demonstrated effectiveness in cost-effective ways. It is equally important that interventions of certain treatments and modalities include how these effect people of color and other ethnic minority populations. It has been shown that different cultural, social, and ethnic groups may respond differently to specific treatments and interventions. There are differences in the use and delivery of mental health services to these populations that should be acknowledged when studying treatment efficacy (Aisenberg, 2008).

Cultural Competence in Mental Health Treatment

According to the President's New Freedom Commission on Mental Health (2003),

> the mental health system has not kept pace with the diverse needs of racial and ethnic minorities, often underserving or inappropriately serving them. Specifically, the system has neglected to incorporate respect or understanding of the histories, traditions, beliefs, languages and value systems of culturally diverse groups.
>
> (p. 49)

Since the United States is a multicultural society, it is important that the services we provide to the mentally ill account for this diversity, and that mental health treatment be equally accessible to all. However, it has been found that there are disparities in access to mental health services, and poorer quality of services delivered to African–Americans, many Latino groups, Asian–Americans, and American Indians, as compared with those offered to their white counterparts (Sands and Gellis, 2001). In order to attempt to address this issue, there has been extensive training available to mental health providers to help them increase awareness of the need to provide culturally competent services.

The National Association of Social Workers (2008) has deemed cultural competence to be crucial to an ethical social work practice. Clinicians have to be knowledgeable about different ethnic practices and traditions, and aware of issues related to discrimination and oppression. They must be able to adapt their interventions to build relationships, make assessments, and provide social work services that acknowledge differences in racial and ethnic communities. Cultural identity refers to a system that a person uses to understand what is happening in his or her life according to values, symbols, and the customs of his or her specific culture, and perceptions are often learned and passed on to others (Sands and Gellis, 2001). There are sometimes barriers to seeking treatment, such as language, cultural mistrust, stigma, or lack of insurance.

The *DSM-IV* has noted that culture has an impact on the expression of mental illness, and that norms must be established taking into account a person's culture, experiences, and beliefs before a diagnosis is determined (American Psychiatric Association, Committee on Nomenclature and Statistics, 1994, 2000). In addition, how a person is treated, i.e. talk, cognitive, or behavioral therapy, should be determined with an acknowledgement of ethnic and cultural variations in response to these interventions (Sands and Gellis, 2001).

Therapeutic interventions can only be provided if the patient attends outpatient treatment or seeks mental health services. The results of a study conducted in Connecticut of 4,184 community residents indicated that attitudes toward the use of mental health services are affected by age, sex, race, education, and socioeconomic status (Leaf, Bruce, Tischler, & Holzer, 1987). They found that people with the fewest financial resources and the least education are the least likely to seek mental health services if they identify a problem, and they are more likely to use clergy, or the family doctor, as a source of mental health treatment. Non-whites in their study shared this view, as well as those between ages 18 and 24, or those over 64. Older respondents, as well as those with less education and income, also had a great deal of concern about their family's reaction to their seeking mental health care.

In a study by Howard et al. (1996), it was found that sociodemographic factors, as well as the stigma of help-seeking, are a barrier to mental health treatment. Help-seeking behavior has also been found to be affected by ethnicity and socioeconomic class (Gallo, Marino, Ford, & Anthony, 1995; Mechanic, 1975). In addition, Neighbors and Howard (1987) found that gender was a significant factor in seeking help for black women in one study, but this difference was eliminated when income was accounted for (Neighbors & Howard, 1987).

Programmatic Initiatives

As problems were identified, a variety of programs were initiated to help mental health professionals serve those with severe mental illness. Case management and advocacy services were developed to engage individuals and link them to community services. Programs for assertive community treatment (PACT) or assertive community treatment (ACT) and intensive case management (ICM) were developed to keep these individuals in care and safely in the community. The programs were developed to keep patients in treatment, teach them life skills, and limit hospitalizations. Many of these programs have emergency funds to provide for urgent client needs that come up, for transportation, clothing, food, or housing.

Assertive Community Treatment

ACT is now considered an EBP that offers supportive services and treatment to individuals in the community to help them achieve meaningful goals and life roles. PACT was originally developed in 1972 in Wisconsin, after researchers noted that skills developed while in hospital were often lost when a person was discharged. They developed a program to provide support, treatment, mobile interventions, rehabilitation, skill development, and collaboration with family in the person's home, on an individual basis (Moniz and Gorin, 2007). The treatment is provided

279

by a multidisciplinary team, including psychiatrist, nurse, social worker, and case managers, using a person-centered, recovery-oriented approach that includes education, vocational development, peer support, and medication, using assertive outreach.

There have been studies that cite ACT programs resulting in fewer hospitalizations, increased housing stability, and improved quality of life for individuals experiencing serious impairment from mental illness (Chandler and Spicer, 2002). Dixon, Weiden, Torres, and Lehman (1997) studied medication compliance in a group of homeless mentally ill and found that compliance rates were significantly higher after they entered an ACT program, and this was associated with fewer psychiatric symptoms, but not with better housing or fewer hospital days.

Case Management

Case management is a method of a single person delivering care to an outpatient individual with serious mental illness. The case manager will coordinate supportive services to the assigned client, including all mental health and medical care necessary. ICM began in the late 1980s and has an emphasis on a small caseload (fewer than 20) and on providing services to those severely mentally ill individuals who are hard to treat, have frequent hospitalizations, and usually have a high number of inpatient days. The provision of ICM services is expensive, and contacts with clients are more frequent, requiring more case managers to provide services to fewer patients. Numerous studies have been undertaken to determine if smaller caseloads produce better outcomes than case management provided for severely mentally ill with higher case loads. The results vary by study.

Holloway and Carson (1998) found that there was no difference in patient symptoms, or social functioning, with case managers who had 8 cases versus case managers with 35 cases. However, they found an improved quality of life and satisfaction with services from those with an ICM. On the other hand, Dieterich, Irving, Park, and Marshall (2010) found that ICM was effective in reducing hospitalization, improving social functioning, and increasing retention in care. They were unable to determine, however, if there was an effect on the clients' quality of life, mortality, or mental state.

A study conducted by Byford et al. (2000) did not find any difference for case management versus ICM for 508 clients in their study for the outcome of days in hospital, quality of life, or patient satisfaction. In addition, they found no significant differences in outcome according to ethnic group (African-Caribbean versus other) or social functioning.

POLICY CONSIDERATIONS

Some of the more recent laws have led to the requirement that mentally ill individuals must be treated in the least restrictive treatment setting possible, and that placements in the community should accommodate the affected individual, rather than the person being kept in an institution. In 1975, Donaldson v. O'Connor reinforced the idea of treatment in the community and emphasized the patient's civil rights (Landsberg and Rock, 2009). This ruling mandated that states could not confine individuals to an institution unless they were a danger to themselves or others. It also required that, if confined to an inpatient setting, the patient had to be provided with treatment (Moniz and Gorin, 2007).

280

In 1990, President George Bush signed the Americans with Disabilities Act (ADA) into law. It is a civil rights law that prohibits discrimination based on disability and affords similar protections against discrimination as the Civil Rights Act of 1964. A disability is defined by the ADA as "a physical or mental impairment that substantially limits a major life activity." It was amended in 2008 to give broader protection and provide accommodations for disability in the workplace.

In the Olmstead decision of 1999, L.C., a mentally retarded individual with mental illness, sued the Commissioner of Georgia and alleged that the state violated the law in failing to place her in a community-based program, once the treatment team determined that such placement was appropriate. She had been voluntarily admitted to Georgia Regional hospital and was deemed ready to move into the community, but no "resources" were available. The Supreme Court determined that the state must find an accommodation because it was discriminatory to keep her in an isolated and institutional setting.

While these decisions shifted the focus of care to the community, unintended problems developed as a result. The movement into the community and the downsizing of mental health institutions involved cost shifting from the state to the federal government. At times, patients were discharged into the community without adequate skills or preparation, or they were sent to other institutions, such as nursing homes. By the mid 1970s, the term deinstitutionalization was being used, and it began to have negative connotations, as there were often not enough funds or programs in the community to supervise and treat those released (Landsberg and Rock, 2009). Karger and Stoesz (2002) stated the "legal decisions favoring the mentally ill often proved illusory," and often offered "nothing more than the right to be insane" (p. 263).

Mental Health Parity Laws

As the cost of insurance for mental health services is high, and the public has historically lacked an understanding of mental illness and addiction, some insurers placed limits on the use of mental health benefits to make insurance costs more affordable. Changes have come about in response to new health insurance regulations that require mental health treatment to be provided in health insurance plans.

In September 1996, the president signed the Mental Health Parity Act. This Act ruled that companies that provided medical insurance to their employees could not put ceilings on mental health benefits that were more restrictive than those of medical and surgical benefits (Otten, 1998). This did not include benefits for substance abuse treatment. In 2008, the United States passed a federal parity law that extended mental health and substance abuse insurance benefits coverage to be on a par with treatment provided for physical conditions.

It is important that we understand both the purpose of these initiatives, as well as some of the issues that have arisen in their implementation. There is a fear that there will be an increase in the cost of health insurance benefits and that this cost will be passed along to workers in the form of higher insurance premiums (Fronstin, 1997). Another concern is that insurance companies will lower their annual or lifetime ceiling for medical and surgical benefits to avoid an increase in the mental health ceiling. There also might be an increase in the deductible or copayments, or a reduction in the number of hospital days allowed. In addition, some providers indicated that, as only certain mental health diagnoses were included, an unintended

281

consequence was that there was an incentive to assign a more severe diagnosis, so that it would be covered by the plan (Rosenbach, Lake, Williams, & Buck, 2009).

Managed Care

Managed care arrangements have been used since the 1990s to provide health benefits to those who need routine care by charging a set fee for a defined set of benefits. Mechanic (1999) describes managed care as a process or strategy in an organizational and financial structure that is designed to monitor and influence treatment decisions so that care can be provided in the most cost-effective way. Mechanic (2008) indicates that the provision of services to persons with a diagnosed mental disorder is from general medical doctors, who provide about 25% of the care. It is estimated that 12% receive care from a psychiatrist, and 16% from some other mental health specialty provider. About one-third of mental health visits of any kind are provided by practioners who specialize in alternative and complementary medicines.

For the treatment of mental illness, there is concern that managed care will influence clinical discretion and that services may be changed, or access may be limited, by the motivation to reduce costs. Although primary physicians may want to limit their scope of practice, patients with mental health issues will still make up a significant cohort of those in their care. As it may not be most economical to shift care for mental illness to more specialized sources, there should be an effort to improve the ability of primary care physicians to recognize common problems and improve their knowledge of psychoactive drugs and effective psychotherapeutic interventions (Mechanic, 2008).

There is a fear that managed care is too rigid for implementing mental health treatment services, and that treatment has to be individualized to be effective. Insurance companies vary in their managed care plans for mental health services. Often, these services are carved out to specialty companies that provide services, after referral by primary care doctors, as they have expertise in this area. It is important that there be communication between the medical and behavioral health providers. This shared information can prevent prescribed drug interactions, as well as physical health issues that have an impact on mental health and wellness.

Many states have adopted managed care in light of the new parity laws, which can reduce the person's freedom to use whichever mental health provider he/she chooses (Otten, 1998). There is great variation in state, city, and county implementation, making the risk–benefit analysis difficult for generalization.

HIPAA

The National Association of Social Workers' Code of Ethics (National Association of Social Workers, 1996/1999/2008) indicates that social workers' documentation should protect clients' privacy and should only include information in the record that is directly relevant to the delivery of services. It is the duty of a social worker to protect client privacy and protect client records, both written and electronic, and other sensitive information. This was further supported when the U.S. Department of Health and Human Services (HHS) issued the Privacy Rule to implement the requirement of the Health Insurance Portability and Accountability Act of 1996 (HIPAA).

This law was developed to set a standard for individuals' privacy rights to understand and control how their health information is used:

> A major goal of the Privacy Rule is to assure that individuals' health information is properly protected while allowing the flow of health information needed to provide and promote high quality health care and to protect the public's health and well being. The Rule strikes a balance that permits important uses of information, while protecting the privacy of people who seek care and healing. Given that the health care marketplace is diverse, the Rule is designed to be flexible and comprehensive to cover the variety of uses and disclosures that need to be addressed.

> (www.hhs.gov)

A practitioner covered under HIPAA may disclose patient health information (PHI) to facilitate treatment, payment, or health care operations (or if they have obtained authorization from the individual). However, when a practioner discloses any PHI, he or she must make a reasonable effort to disclose only the minimum necessary information required to achieve its purpose. There may be times, however, when a social worker or medical provider must breach confidentiality as required by law to protect someone from harm. An example of this is the necessity by mandated reporters to report child abuse or neglect immediately.

Duty to Warn or Protect

Although confidentiality is a critical part of a therapeutic relationship, there are times when the social worker is obligated to violate this agreement, if there is a compelling professional reason to do so (National Association of Social Workers, 2008). A case in California, Tarasoff v. Regents of California, 1974, became a landmark decision when a graduate student told his therapist that he intended to kill Ms. Tarasoff when she returned from vacation and proceeded to do so. The family sued the therapist and stated that Ms. Tarasoff should have been warned of the danger. The ruling stated that the therapist could be culpable if reasonable care was not provided to protect the victim when such a disclosure was made in the course of a session (Sands and Gellis, 2001).

This ruling has often posed an ethical dilemma for social workers. The social worker is compelled to make a judgment based on the assessment of an individual's dangerousness, select a course of action, and implement an action plan when such issues arise. It is important that, in such cases, the social worker should consult other professionals in the agency and be aware of the interpretation of the Tarasoff rule in each state, as it differs in interpretation.

SUMMARY

When working with the mentally ill, Goering and Stylianos (1988) describe the need for a "real" and "human" relationship to take place within a therapeutic environment. They refer to the need for a patient and therapist to work together collaboratively, in combination with genuine trust and liking. There is also a greater emphasis on client satisfaction in mental health service delivery (Elbeck & Fecteau, 1990). This chapter has attempted to define key concepts in community mental health treatment and provide a guide for social workers engaged in this field of practice. There are many issues to consider when providing services to the severely mentally ill in the community, and these encompass practical and ethical considerations that were briefly touched on in these pages. It is important to note that there are both risks and benefits in the provision of mental health care that impact on the individual, the family, the community, and society. Many of these have competing priorities for funding, and have significant impact on those affected.

DISCUSSION QUESTIONS

1. Compare and contrast the custodial model of care for the mentally ill with the recovery model.

2. Identify the factors that lead to deinstitutionalization.

3. Discuss the Health Insurance Portability and Accountability Act of 1996 (HIPAA).

LEARNING ASSIGNMENT

Debate Duty to Warn: As a class, research the landmark case Tarasoff v. Regents of California, 1974. Have a class discussion on the ruling. What ethical dilemmas can be identified?

SUGGESTED READINGS

Moniz, C. and Gorin, S. (2007) *Health and Mental Health Care Policy: A Biopsychosocial Perspective*, 3rd ed. Boston, MA: Allyn & Bacon.

Mowbray, C. and Holter, M. (2002). Mental health and mental illness: Out of the closet. *Social Service Review*, 78(1), 135–179.

Smith, T. & Sederer, L. (2009). A new kind of homelessness for individuals with serious mental illness? The need for a "mental health home." *Psychiatric Services, 60*(4), 528–533.

INTERNET RESOURCES

Mental Health: A Report of the Surgeon General: www.surgeongeneral.gov

Mental Health America: www.nmha.org

National Alliance on Mental Illness: www.nami.org

Samhsa's National Mental Health Information Center: www.samhsa.gov

REFERENCES

Aisenberg, E. (2008). Evidenced-based practice in mental health care to ethnic minority communities. *Social Work, 53*(4), 297–306.

American Psychiatric Association, Committee on Nomenclature and Statistics (1994). *Diagnostic and Statistical Manual of Mental Disorders, IV Edition (DSM-IV)*. Washington, DC: American Psychiatric Association.

American Psychiatric Association, Committee on Nomenclature and Statistics (2000). *Diagnostic and Statistical Manual of Mental Disorders TR, IV Edition (DSM-IVTR)*. Washington, DC: American Psychiatric Association.

Anthony, W.A. (1993). Recovery from mental illness: The guiding vision of the mental health service system in the 1990's. *Psychosocial Rehabilitation Journal, 11*, 11–19.

Byford, S., Fiander, M., Torgenson, D.J., Barber, J.A., Thompson, S.G., Burns, T., van Horn, E., Gilvarry, C., & Creed, F. (2000). Cost-effectiveness of intensive v. standard case management for severe psychotic illness. *The British Journal of Psychiatry, 176*, 537–543.

Chandler, D. & Spicer, G. (2002). Capitated assertive community treatment program savings: System implications. *Administrative and Policy in Mental Health, 30*(1), 3–19.

Clemens, N.A. (2010). New parity, same old attitude towards psychotherapy? *Journal of Psychiatric Practice, 16*(2), 115–119.

Dieterich, M., Irving, C.B., Park, B., & Marshall, M. (2010). Intensive case management for severe mental illness. *Cochrane Data Base System Review*, Oct. 6, 10.

Dixon, L., Weiden, P., Torres, M., & Lehman, A. (1997) Assertive community treatment and medication compliance in the homeless mentally ill. *American Journal of Psychiatry, 154*(9), 1302–1304.

Elbeck, M. & Fecteau, G. (1990). Improving the validity of measures of patient satisfaction with psychiatric care and treatment. *Hospital and Community Psychiatry, 41*(3), 998–1001.

Fronstin, P. (1997). Issues in mental health care benefits: the costs of mental helath parity. *EBRI Issue Brief*, Feb.(182), 1–14.

Gagne, C., White, W., & Anthony, W.A. (2007). Recovery: A common vision for the fields of mental health and addictions. *Psychiatric Rehabilitation Journal, 31*(1), 32–37.

Gallo, J.J., Marino, D., Ford, D., & Anthony, J.C. (1995). Filters on the pathway to mental health care, II. Sociodemographic factors. *Psychological Medicine, 25*, 1149–1160.

Goering, P.N. & Stylianos, S.K. (1988). Exploring the helping relationship between the schizophrenic client and rehabilitation therapists. *American Journal of Orthopsychiatry, 58*(2), 271–280. www.hhs.gov/ocr/privacy/hipaa/understanding/summary/index.html

Holloway, F. & Carson, J. (1998). Intensive case management for the severely mentally ill. Controlled study. *The British Journal of Psychiatry, 172*, 19–22.

Howard, K.I., Carnill, T.A., Lyons, J.S., Vessey, J.T., Lueger, R.J., & Saunders, S.M. (1996). Patterns of mental health service utilization. *Archives of General Psychiatry, 53*, 696–703.

Isaac, R.J. & Armat, V.C. (1990). *Madness in the streets*. New York: The Free Press.

Karger, H.J. & Stoez, D. (2002). *American Social Welfare Policy: A Pluralist Approach* (4th ed.). New York: Addison Wesley Longman.

Landsberg, G. & Rock, M. (2009). *Social Policy and Social Work: The Context of Social Work Practice*. Pearson Custom Publishing.

Leaf, P.J., Bruce, M.L., Tischler, G.L., & Holzer, C.E. (1987). The relationship between demographic factors and attitudes toward mental health services. *Journal of Community Psychology, 15*, 275–284.

Mechanic, D. (1975). Sociocultural and social psychological factors affecting personal responses to psychological disorder. *Journal of Health and Social Behavior, 16*, 393–405.

285

Mechanic, D. (1999). *Mental Health and Social Policy: The Emergence of Managed Care*. Boston, MA: Allyn & Bacon.

Mechanic, D. (2008). *Mental Health and Social Policy: Beyond Managed Care*. Boston, MA: Pearson.

Moniz, C. & Gorin, S. (2007). *Health and Mental Health Care Policy: A Biopsychosocial Approach*, 3rd ed. Boston, MA: Allyn & Bacon.

National Association of Social Workers (2008). *Code of Ethics of the National Association of Social Workers*. www.socialworkers.org

Neighbors, H.W. & Howard, C.S. (1987). Sex differences in professional help seeking among adult black Americans. *American Journal of Community Psychology, 15*(4), 403–417.

Otten, A.L. (1998). *Mental Health Parity: What Can it Accomplish in a Market Dominated by Managed Care*? New York: Milbank Memorial Fund.

President's New Freedom Commission on Mental Health (2003). *Achieving the Promise: Transforming Mental Health Care in America*. Rockville, MD: Department of Health and Human Services.

Rosenbach, M.L., Lake, T.K., Williams, & Buck, J.A. (2009). Implementation of mental health parity: Lessons from California. *Psychiatric Services, 60*(12), 1589–1594.

Rubin, A. (2009). *Practitioner's Guide to Using Research for Evidence-Based Practice*. Hoboken, NJ: John Wiley.

Sands, R. & Gellis, Z.D. (2001). *Clinical Social Work in Behavioral Mental Health: An Evidenced-Based Approach*. Boston, MA: Allyn & Bacon.

Stubbs, P.M. (1998). Broken promises: The story of deinstitutionalization. *Perspectives in Mental Health*. Oct.–Dec.

Substance Abuse and Mental Health Services Administration (1993). Definition of adults with SMI and children with SED. *Federal Register, 58*(96), 29422–29425.

Trattner, W.I. (1994). *From Poor Law to Welfare State: A History of Social Welfare in America*. New York: The Free Press.

Chapter 18

"The Times They Are a Changin'—Again"

More Turbulence—Even Greater Challenges

W. Patrick Sullivan

Soon after shots rang out in Tucson, Arizona, on January 8, 2011, the state of mental health care in America was, once again, back under the microscope. As the life of Congresswoman Gabrielle Giffords hung in the balance, any number of pundits and armchair psychiatrists had already offered a diagnosis of the perpetrator and touted simple remedies for a troubling and complex situation. For those who have spent their careers in the field, this was but another chapter in a sad, but oft repeated tale. Mental illness is an out-of-sight, out-of-mind phenomenon for most policymakers and only seems to enter the consciousness of the general public when it is jolted by such tragedies. What follows is painfully predictable. There is the normal hunt for a scapegoat, those challenged by mental illnesses will be largely painted with a broad brush, and the purported inadequacies of the system and commitment laws will be, for a moment, a popular radio and television topic. Yet, time will pass, the crisis will fade from memory, and mental health concerns will recede into the background once more.

Regardless of the ebb and flow of public attention, each day mental health providers are tasked with a nearly impossible job. The actual work is difficult enough, but when one considers the contextual factors that shape direct practice it becomes clear that decision-making from the micro to the macro level reflects Herbert Simon's theory of satisfying (Brown, 2004). When making satisfying choices, it is recognized that one may not have the luxury or the ability to pursue an ideal course of action, but, rather, must be content with what "is good enough, rather than the absolute best" (Brown, 2004, p. 1241). Consider this. The primary function of public policy is to allocate social resources, and, in the case of human services, more often than not, these resources are earmarked to ameliorate conditions defined as social problems (see Chambers & Wedel, 2009). In community mental health, and other like realms, it is exceedingly rare when the level of available resources matches any reasonable definition of need. Compounding this conundrum is the ever-present necessity to delicately balance the competing demands of key stakeholders and thereby preserve the sanction needed to operate. This is far more difficult than it seems. For example, the public expects practitioners to treat people with mental illnesses effectively while simultaneously shielding the public from those whose behavior is disturbing. Yet, as the Giffords tragedy illustrated anew, respecting and preserving individual rights and liberties, a bedrock principle of our democracy, produce any number of thorny dilemmas that cannot and should not be simplified nor ignored. Ironically, the efforts of policymakers, mental health professionals, and advocates to educate the public about mental illness, and to reduce the stigma surrounding seeking help have been so effective that the demand for services continues to rise (Mauer & Druss, 2010). In 2004, Bob Williams, who has now spent over three decades in the field, took the time to offer astute observations on the dilemmas endemic to mental health leadership (see Sullivan, 2006), including this one:

> A more sophisticated public demands the kind of outcomes that they read about on the internet while a declining level of stigma results in ever increasing numbers of individuals and families seeking help. In short, we face a greater demand for more effective and sophisticated services at a time of fewer dollars, and fewer professionals available with the necessary skills to provide those services at the salaries we can afford to pay them.

Suffice to say that the issues outlined by Williams just a few years ago have not abated. In truth, there was a time when clinicians could remain relatively detached from the realities of the business side of helping. Those days are largely over. Productivity requirements, concern about billable units, and restrictions and limits imposed by third-party payers can no longer be ignored—or are ignored at personal peril. This evolving clash of cultures impacts every aspect of organizational life and requires the most sensitive of balancing acts—and at the vortex of these powerful countervailing forces are those in leadership positions.

Leadership has never been an easy proposition in community mental health, but, as will be detailed in the pages that follow, never has the task been more difficult and, concomitantly, more crucial. Five years ago it was argued that, to be effective, leaders in community mental health must successfully negotiate a highly turbulent world (Sullivan, 2006). It comes as little surprise that such turbulence, particularly given how rapidly things change in an information-saturated world, is now a way of life (Mason, 2007). Speaking directly to leaders in business, Heifetz, Grashow, and Linsky (2009) asked: "Are you waiting for things to return to normal in your organization? Sorry. Leadership will require new skills tailored to an environment of urgency, high stakes, and uncertainty—even after the current economic crisis is over" (p. 64).

LEADING IN TURBULENT TIMES: THEN . . .

The words of Heifetz and associates (2009) certainly resonate for those in human services. In late 2004, a sample of community mental health leaders, many with long tenures at the helm, were asked to reflect on how their jobs had changed over the course of their careers, and what the future seemed to hold in store (Sullivan, 2006). Their observations confirmed what most already knew: this was a challenging time for community mental health and, by default, for the stewards entrusted to make wise decisions. So what has changed in just a few short years? To flesh out the trends and dilemmas that confront community mental health today, the wisdom of veteran leaders in the State of Indiana will again be tapped and compared with observations and predictions generated in the original study. Accordingly, one of the central goals of this work is to explore what core concerns and foci remain (most respondents were in the original sample), what new issues have emerged, and what, at least from the perspective of this group of leaders, we can expect in the future. In some instances, the observations of informants for the report *Mental Health Leadership in a Turbulent World* (Sullivan, 2006) are presented anew, but, given the task here, select material from the initial data set is also presented for the first time. If there was one thing these experts could agree on in 2004, it was that the road before them was a rocky one. Now, with health-care policy and costs on every agenda and the economy fractured, it seems far from certain if community mental health, at least in its current configuration, will survive.

It is important to acknowledge that, aside from the primary mission, there is little uniformity in how community mental health services are structured from state to state. In Indiana, the primary providers are private, not-for-profit entities that must rely on a wide range of funding mechanisms and revenue-generating activities to remain solvent. As with individuals and families, there is danger in leaning too heavily on one source of income, and therefore diversification of funding streams is essential. Unfortunately, the more successful providers are in this enterprise, the more tradeoffs there will be. Suddenly, serious attention must be devoted to usable management information systems, appropriate accounting software, records and rules, compliance issues, and accreditation standards. Certainly, attending to these items reflects good business practices, but, with the advent of proprietary behavioral health-care providers, managed care contracts, and the demise of the public health model that served as an initial blueprint for community mental health decades ago, such activities moved quickly to the front burner. For old-school leaders, it is hard not to wax poetically about a time when their primary focus was on clinical matters. These kinds of concern were certainly very much on the minds of mental health directors when surveyed in 2004.

Ann Borders, who has now spent 35 years in mental health and over half of that as a CEO of a community mental health director, remarked,

> The challenge today is to somehow manage to deliver good care while maneuvering through a seemingly impenetrable maze of external laws, regulations, and requirements governing behavioral health care. Today, the job of behavioral health leaders is two-fold. First, they must devote a significant amount of their time to organizational risk management, ensuring that accreditation, fraud and abuse, antitrust, antikickback, local/state/federal contract, human resources, HIPPA, and other state and federal laws and requirements are met. Second, leaders must somehow create a culture that puts the principles, purposes and guiding beliefs of the organization first. When the legal-regulatory axe is at the neck, it is very easy for an organization to develop a culture where the rules become the end.
>
> (Sullivan, 2006, pp. 250–251)

In a similar vein, Galen Goode, who has spent over 40 years in mental health, noted:

> Thirty-five years ago all of the funding was State dollars so in many ways the system was easier to influence and less complicated. Today our revenue streams are multiple and we have to balance programs that make a profit with those where we donate services so as to cover total expenses and have enough money for program expansion. With multiple payor sources comes multiple expectations and audits.
>
> (Sullivan, 2006, p. 253)

It was becoming clear then, and it is undeniable now, that the worlds of business and clinical care had collided. Indeed, no one can escape this trend. As noted above, today, clinical practice is under greater scrutiny by all who help pay the bills, adding more layers of documentation and demanding practitioners to justify the care plans they so carefully constructed. Furthermore, to ensure that those in direct practice do even more to keep the office lights on, productivity requirements have become commonplace.

The impress of these changes in day-to-day operations may have been subtle at first, but in the long run the impact cannot be overstated. Increased demands to capture and interpret a wide range of information required agencies to recruit and retain employees with the requisite technical, managerial, and actuarial skills this brave new world demanded. In the blink of an eye, overhead skyrocketed, the organizational chart became a confusing matrix, and leaders suffered an endless string of headaches and acid reflux. Slowly, language germane to the insurance world permeated the boardrooms and hallways of community mental health. Providing care somehow became intertwined with risk management, the notion of a catchment area gave way to a concern with covered lives, and old friends were suddenly openly competing or discussing the necessity of forming a strategic alliance to stay afloat.

Now retired, in 2004, Jim Jones served as the Director of the Indiana Council of Community Mental Health Centers, and, as he pondered the emerging state of affairs, remarked,

> Most providers are forced to consider trying to take market share from one of their peers in order to keep on growing. To quote a bestselling author, it's not the big that eat the small . . . it's the fast that eat the slow.

For years, Jim led a trade organization that represented 30 freestanding community mental health centers (CMHCs). At this time, there are just 25 CMHCs—a reflection of strategic mergers and a result of one provider being dropped from the role. Mergers and alliances accomplish many things. Administrative functions, including information management, legal services, and the like, can be centralized to reduce overall costs, while the consolidated program now casts a wider service net. In 2004, Bob Krumweid, then serving as a director of a standalone CMHC noted,

> Although the size of the agency isn't remarkably larger today than it was 15 years ago, I feel more like the conductor of an orchestra toady where I used to feel like the front man for a four member band.

(Sullivan, 2006, p. 250)

Consistent with the trends noted above, today Krumweid serves as the CEO/director for a relatively new organization created via a merger of longstanding community mental health centers. Krumweid's job, it stands to reason, just got even harder. As Mason (2007) notes:

> As complexity increases, the ability to understand and use information to plan and predict becomes more difficult. As all systems increase in complexity over time, the increasing complexity leads to more change. As the system becomes more complex, making sense of it becomes more difficult, and adaptation to the changing environment becomes more problematic.

(pp. 10–11)

No matter how futile the cause may be, all businesses attempt to predict the future and plan accordingly. Prediction is far easier when the surrounding environment is relatively stable, and the ability to successfully adapt to a changing environment is a function, in part, of one's span of control. In the world of traditional business, if consumer tastes change, new product lines can be offered, or existing products can be modified accordingly. In this scenario, the litmus test for success is easy to ascertain by simply scanning the balance sheet at the end of the day. Here, failure to respond to the changing environment can result in a significant loss of market share or even one's demise. Guided by a mission of public service, community mental health operates under a vastly different set of rules. Even the laws of supply and demand hold little sway if revenue generation per units of service cannot offset the cost of delivering them. Thus, in this scenario, far too common in community mental health, increased volume of services delivered results in a loss of revenue, not increased profits. In addition, although new service lines can be created, and the efficacy of these new interventions can be demonstrated, the widespread adoption of these innovations is still predicated on the willingness of a third party to pay for them. The irony here is that survival can depend more on the alignment of common practice with the fiscal parameters dictated by an external party, and less on what the consumer needs or demands, or even empirically derived guidelines.

Lane and Down (2010) define turbulence as "a state of unpredictable change that was not foreseen" (p. 514). Likewise, Mason (2007) focuses on the "dynamism in the environment, involving rapid, unexpected change in the environment and sub-dimensions," and further argues that, "Turbulence is the natural state of the world" (p. 10). Few mental health leaders would disagree, and so often the turbulence that is experienced is the result of policies developed by those external to the organization. Likewise, these same policies are often the consequence of significant macro-level trends, such as the near total economic collapse experienced at the end of the first decade of the 21st century.

It is clear that this is no time for mental health leaders to be caught asleep at the wheel —not only are these treacherous times for public providers, but, like their brethren in the trenches, those at the top of the organization chart must continually update their skill set as well. Given her tenure in community mental health, Ann Borders has rarely enjoyed a moment where she could sit back and catch her breath; in fact, looking through the lens of history, she observes,

> At almost any point during the history of community mental health, "change and challenge" would aptly describe the times. From the initial infrastructure building, to the evolution of the care continuum, to the near escapes from public policy and funding disasters, to the throes of managed care, and now to health-care reform and beyond—the behavioral health leader has always required an expansive array of skills cemented by an abundant dose of fortitude. This has never been an endeavor for the faint of heart.

Few Indiana community mental health leaders could have predicted the economic mayhem that would come, or foreseen that the nation would soon be in the grips of an emotionally charged debate about health-care coverage. However, the footprint for today's challenges could certainly be discerned at the midpoint of the decade, and many of the leaders surveyed presaged the road ahead. At the sharp end of the prediction queue, many pondered if community mental health would survive (Sullivan, 2006).

By the early 1990s, concerned about rampant increases in spending for health care, states began exploring a wide range of options to retard the rate of growth. Any number of arrangements would be executed across the land, from the development of public managed care models, to entering into contracts with proprietary behavioral health-care organizations. It was also not a time when state mental health authorities could approach their general assembly for more funds, or expect an appreciable increase in federal block grant funding. There was only one way to expand the public safety net, and that was to leverage Medicaid. With the possibilities offered by various option and waiver programs, programs such as case management could be expanded, and an *adequate* system of services for the most seriously ill could be established. As always, any course of action comes with consequences, and there was fear that the entire mental health system had now become a house of cards that could be toppled at any time. Beyond this, as more and more funds were expended to provide the match needed to draw down Medicaid dollars, program flexibility was reduced. Likewise, as more services were dedicated to Medicaid-eligible clients, the working poor and the uninsured remained underserved (Mauer & Druss, 2010). As the principles of managed care (risk-based contracts, capitation, and prior authorization) penetrated public mental health, and Medicaid reimbursement became increasingly important, community mental health strayed even farther from its historical roots. In 2004, Terry Stawar, then in his 20th year in the field observed,

> With Medicaid funding assuming such a crucial role in center finance, there is less time spent with community development and social changes aspects of the center's mission and much more time devoted to health-care policy and issues. In the past there was more of balance between the social services/poverty agency aspect of the organization and the health-care provider aspect.

The good old days of community mental health were slipping further and further away, and it was with obvious regret that a veteran like Jim Jones, whose organization served as a state and national advocate for community mental health, admitted that, "Providers are increasingly being forced to choose to focus their mission away from trying to be a comprehensive safety net for all, and either provide less service to all or exclude some in favor of not compromising quality" (Sullivan, 2006, p. 252).

No mental health leader has had the luxury to remain inward facing for long, as it has always been important to remain attuned to the mood of stakeholders whose cooperation was essential. As the winds of change picked up speed a decade ago, it also became increasingly necessary to develop an entrepreneurial mindset. Paul Wilson was closing in on his first decade as the director of a CMHC in Fort Wayne, Indiana, when first asked about the challenges of leadership, and at that time he surmised that it was essential to keep "one eye on the very difficult environment and the shrinking resources, yet also staying open to new possibilities and being entrepreneurial in finding ways to support the mission. It is tricky, but rewarding."

It was a time when some agencies began taking their first shaky steps outside their traditional comfort zone. As Bob Dunbar said, "In the past few years, I have spent much more time developing and nurturing a number of strategic affiliations formed as a result of 'public managed care' and increasing competition" (Sullivan, 2006, p. 254). Luckily, even at this juncture, Dunbar could claim that important gains had been made in these new ventures, which appeared to be resting on solid ground. The danger, of course, is that, in adapting to the new realities, the core mission, the *raison d'être* of community mental health, could be lost (Kane, 1993; Ryan, 1999). Larry Burch would devote four decades to community mental health, the majority of that time in a leadership position, and long before he retired he foresaw one of the central dilemmas that his predecessors would face: "Our industry is going through revolutionary change," he noted, "and an organization must be able to make market adjustments without compromising its mission. Likewise, setting the moral/ethical climate for the organization is most critical" (Sullivan, 2006, p. 253).

There was no denying the obvious: community mental health was in the midst of a sea-change, and, putting her finger on the pulse while peering into the crystal ball, Ann Borders suggested,

> I think that successful organizations will be less distinctly recognizable as "the community mental health center." Increasingly, leaders will be developing alliances that will allow for the delivery of more and more services in natural settings such as schools, homes, community centers, and the workplace. The clinician will not serve as "the mental health expert" so much as an equal partner on a larger multi-organizational community team. Similarly, our organizational status as a "carved out," independent entity will diminish. We will be expected by policy makers, funders, and consumers to integrate behavioral health services with primary care, public health, child welfare, justice, educational, and other systems.

. . . AND NOW

While mental health leaders watched another decade peel off the calendar, any hope for a temporary respite from the tumult that had ruled their lives was quickly dashed. As noted above, in the course of a few short years, the sheer number of Indiana CMHCs was reduced, primarily owing to mergers, and interested observers were left to ponder if the rollercoaster ride would ever end. Years ago, center director Larry Ulrich believed, "Indiana will have to reduce the number of CMHC's in the state by 10 to 15. There would be reduced administrative costs and services would not suffer." Also of note, Medicaid, once the sole purview of a state-level department, is now managed by several intermediary agencies, while one of the backbones of community-based care, the Medicaid Rehabilitation Option, has come under greater scrutiny. In practice, this has increased the emphasis on prior authorization and concurrent review activities, to the chagrin of those on the frontlines. These developments would be cause for concern at any point in time, but, given the fiscal crisis experienced at all levels of government, and the tendency for human services to be the first to be placed on the chopping block, high anxiety is pervasive.

Mergers and alliances, the move to evidenced-based practice, and diversifying revenue streams were much on the mind of mental health leaders in 2004. Yet, even then, some leaders believed that, to really ensure their organization's long-term prospects, it was time to explore new horizons. Although it is certain that not all subscribed to this vision of the future then, evidence abounds that CMHC director Eric Crouse's contemporary assessment rings true: "The times they are a changin'—again."

Not surprisingly, living on the edge can become wearisome, but, when you consider Paul Wilson's summary of the current state of affairs, his words reflect the unbending resilience commonly found in leaders who have devoted their life to a cause they deem a worthy one:

> Traditional sources of funding have and will continue to erode, pushing us to re-think how we provide and pay for services. The percentage of health care dollars going to behavioral health continues to decrease, and of that decreased amount, more is going to meds, less to treatment. We as an industry have failed to prove our worth. We are generally seen as a burden rather than an investment. Medicaid is currently the largest source of funds for mental health centers, but it has grown so complex and burdensome that it takes a lot more administrative effort and expense to bring in those dollars. The days of mental health centers as standalone facilities, supported financially to a reasonable amount by the State are dwindling. Those Mental Health Centers will continue to shrink. Leaders need to be much more creative, need to link with physical health care, need to look to affirmative businesses, so essentially they need to be entrepreneurs. It is not the contract we assumed we signed when we got into the field, and many days it does not feel fair. Yet, if we can move past our despair, there will be some neat opportunities.
>
> (Personal communication)

When Indiana CMHCs first braced for the changes that the managed care revolution seemed to portend, some quickly embraced the concept of managed competition, while others linked arms to stave off the threats that appeared imminent. In 2010, it seemed certain that, to thrive, community mental health must be reinvented.

One sign that the tireless work of advocates was beginning to make headway in the battle against stigma was the passage of insurance parity legislation. Finally, the idea that mental illness and physical illness were not distinct worlds was gaining significant traction, and, today, many are anxious to see how the field will fare in whatever version of health-care reform survives. As community mental health has grown in the ability to manage risk-based contracts, use actuarial analysis in allocation decisions, and benefit from the judicious use of evidence-based practice and medication management, the idea that mental and physical health care can be successfully integrated is no longer a pipedream.

Yes, there are exciting possibilities, but, as the uncharted territory is navigated, there is an equal measure of angst. It would seem that Eric Crouse, who leads a mental health center embedded within a hospital system, would be more at ease in an integrated model. Yet he too has an extensive list of questions:

> How do CMHC's integrate themselves into the physical health-care system and/or vice versa? Will this spell the end of CMHC's? What is our relationship to the Health Care Center's movement? Do CMHC's become health care centers, or do health care centers become CMHC's? What is the relationship of CMHC's to primary care's "health care home" model? Will health care centers and CMHC's continue to exist when and if we move to Accountable Healthcare Organizations (ACO)? What are CMHC's relationships to ACO's if hospitals become the nexus of that movement? How will the broader focus of CMHC's on the social well being of our consumers (e.g. housing, employment, etc.) be incorporated in the traditional medically focused health care model? Will insurance companies continue

to exist in their current form? How will the transition from a service based health-care system, to an outcomes based health-care system effect behavioral health?

(Personal communication)

Ann Borders echoes her peer's concerns, and explicit in her remarks is the additional fear that the fate of community mental health may well lie in the hands of others:

There are any number of ways that community mental health stands to lose its heretofore protected status within the new health-care environment: if we fail to be recognized as the health-care home for persons with chronic behavioral health conditions; if we are slow in adapting to the new health information and technology requirements; if lawmakers decide that it's time to fully integrate health care—and to achieve that through public health entities; or if we are too slow to redesign systems, structures, and processes to meet the fiscal and public policy challenges of the future.

(Personal communication)

When heavy environmental turbulence places human services on the "edge of chaos," danger may indeed be at the door. However, these same moments of vulnerability may provide the stage for creative responses that allow organizations to seize opportunities and elevate their performance (Mason, 2007). Managing chaos may well be the primary task for mental health leaders in the next decade. While some may approach this test with trepidation, others relish the prospect of rolling up their sleeves and getting to work. Significantly reengineering the organization may become a necessity, and those in key positions may need to alter their leadership style to match the demands of a new health-care paradigm.

As the calendar turned to 2011, no one could predict the fate of the Patient Protection and Affordable Care Act, better known simply as Healthcare Reform. Nonetheless, how behavioral health would be impacted and what would emerge as a result of some high-profile demonstration projects and federal initiatives were on many minds. Front and center is the reemergence of calls for the integration of physical and behavioral health care. Accordingly, new words have entered the lexicon of mental health leaders, and among them are Accountable Care Organizations (ACOs), and Patient-centered Medical Homes—concepts that will be described below.

On the surface, this marriage has always made sense. Primary care physicians have been treating mental illnesses for years, and, while the record may have been mixed in the past, better protocols for common conditions such as depression and anxiety, plus further advances in psychopharmacology have unquestionably moved the needle in a positive direction. In the case of those with the most serious mental illnesses, long the purview of community mental health, physical health is often neglected. The prevalence of serious physical illnesses, some the result of lifestyle, some—such as diabetes—ironically a consequence of treatment, is staggering, and the rate of premature death among this population is sobering (Alakeson, Frank, & Katz, 2010; Mauer & Druss, 2010).

Previous attempts to draw these two systems together, particularly in the early days of the managed care movement, were spotty. Many mental health advocates were concerned that benefit packages offered in most arrangements did not match the needs of the most seriously ill, and they also argued that the expertise to serve these individuals still resided in the public mental health safety net. Likewise, given the challenge and unpredictability of serious and persistent mental illness, many programs anchored in the physical health care and insurance world were more than happy to be excused serving this population. As a result, behavioral health care was often considered separately or "carved out" from traditional managed care or system of care arrangements. So, the question looms, are circumstances different, and, if so, how will community mental health be impacted? On the positive side of the ledger, a productive integration between the world of physical health care and behavioral health can be viewed as the cumulative result of years of work to produce an enlightened understanding of mental illness and another salvo in an attempt to reduce stigma and enhance the quality of care. However, the fear is that current trends will result in another bifurcation of the system, with the most seriously ill relegated to seek care in an underfunded and isolated system of public providers. The stakes are high.

In the minds of Indiana's veteran leaders, the handwriting is on the wall: some form of integration is inevitable. Two stalwarts of community mental health, Bob Williams and Bob Dunbar, have already taken steps to position their organizations to take advantage of new fiscal policies and opportunities that lie in store. Williams, now a leader in a behavioral health concern that was created via alliances within Indiana and also crosses state lines, observes:

> With the significant (startling!) growth in funding for Federally Qualified Health Centers (FQHCs) there is a deliberate effort to increase access to mental health and dental services for clients of these community health centers. As a result many community providers of mental health and addictions services are collaborating and partnering with FQHCs to help ensure that the whole person receives treatment in one location. At the same time, SAMHSA is supporting medical homes for CMHC consumers at the location where they may be most comfortable receiving medical services—i.e. at the CMHC where they receive their mental health and addictions services.
>
> (Personal communication)

Dunbar has also pointed his organization in this direction, and predicts that other community mental health centers will

> attempt to increasingly integrate services with primary care/FQHCs and other health-care providers, and to position their agencies for inclusion in Accountable Care Organizations. Many will also directly offer primary care services, serving particularly as medical homes for people with serious and persistent mental illnesses.
>
> (Personal communication)

Terry Stawar, with over a quarter-century of experience in the field, understands that big changes may be just around the corner, suggesting that,

> Community Mental Health leadership will need to effectively plan for the evolution of behavioral health as a component of Accountable Care Organizations that are driven by large health-care systems. We will need to understand the culture of large health care organizations and how to work effectively in such organizations.
>
> (Personal communication)

It is impossible to know for certain how sweeping the changes in the landscape may be: at one end of the spectrum, there will be concerted efforts at co-location of staff, either through bringing physical health-care specialists inside mental health, as noted above, or the inclusion of behavioral health services in primary medical settings. At the other extreme will be fully integrated arrangements, possibility under the rubric of ACOs. If there is one thing that many experts agree upon, it is that structural integration does not guarantee clinical integration, although the stronger and more formal the ties, the greater the odds that optimum care is delivered. Not surprisingly, the most important consideration is the fiscal arrangements that tie the system together, with proper incentives and quality standards needed to ensure that the final arrangement is, in fact, consumer-centered (see Druss & Mauer, 2010; Mauer & Druss, 2010; Rittenhouse, Shortell, & Fisher, 2009).

As noted above, for many, the quest has already begun to partner with Federally Qualified Health Centers (FQHCs), which, an effort currently underway in Missouri suggests, would strengthen the basic safety net for many in need (Schuffman, Druss, & Parks, 2009). At present, there are some financial incentives to forge such partnerships, and significantly, after a decade of horizontal integration with peer agencies marked by loose alliances and mergers, aligning with an FQHC represents an important step toward vertical integration with partners that may be important allies should survival depend on becoming relevant in a larger system of care such as an ACO.

Another popular model that is piquing the interest of today's leaders, and one that actually has roots decades deep, is the patient-centered medical home (Alakeson et al., 2010; Druss & Mauer, 2010; Kilo & Wasson, 2010). This model, which was designed for children with chronic illness, is "not a specific place but rather an approach with a range of processes and attitudes toward care" (Smith & Sederer, 2009, p. 529). Designed with primary care at the core, the medical home concept emphasizes relationship-centered, comprehensive care along with increased accountability and the proper alignment of incentives (Kilo & Wasson, 2010; Smith & Sederer, 2009). None of the concepts or ideas central to this model is foreign to community mental health, and it is significant that, under the Patient Protection and Affordable Care Act, those with a serious mental illness and covered by Medicaid can designate a provider as a health home (Druss & Mauer, 2010).

So, in the case of those with the most serious mental illnesses, should the CMHC be designated as the medical home rather than a primary care provider? Some think so. Alakeson and associates (2010) noted that a foundation principle of medical homes is to serve people where they traditionally interface with the health-care system. While recognizing that great strides have been made treating mild and moderate mental illnesses in primary care, these authors argue that serious and persistent mental illnesses present a special situation and tout the idea of the specialty care medical home:

People with severe and persistent mental disorders are a primary population for these organizations, which are largely supported by public funds. These specialty providers have a commitment to serving this group. The results have been the establishment of trusted relationships between clinicians and individuals with severe and persistent mental disorders within specialty care. Such relationships increase the likelihood that treatment will be accepted and followed and should result in health improvement.

(Alakeson et al., 2010, pp. 869–870)

297

The implications here are noteworthy. Given recent trends, including the priorities of state mental health authorities and the increasing role of Medicaid for organizational survival, CMHCs have increasingly focused services on the most ill. Therefore, it is conceivable that serving as the medical home for this specific population will be the niche that allows theses agencies to flourish.

In the absence of claiming this piece of the health-care turf, CMHCs may opt to become players in ACOs. DeVore and Champion (2011) report that, "an ACO generally describes groups of providers who are willing and able to take responsibility for improving the overall health status, care efficiency, and health care experience for a defined population" (p. 41). Although elements of the ACO model seem to be a simple restatement of many principles of managed care, some note that the emphasis on outcomes management and the overall experience of the consumer makes this model different (DeVore & Champion, 2011). As some Indiana leaders offered above, there are more questions than answers at the moment, and central to these concerns is if community mental health will have a seat at the table. As behavioral health is central to care for a designated population, community mental health services would appear to be vital—but becoming fully integrated will require providers to adapt to a new environment, one potentially dominated by the medical model.

Needless to say, the decisions faced by today's mental health leader are weighty. In these topsy-turvy times, long-range planning is virtually useless, and, unless leadership has the power of a soothsayer, one must be prepared to fashion an organization that is quick and nimble. Hierarchical organizations will give way to those that are more decentralized and flat, staffed by people with advanced generalist skills, particularly when new and different health-care partners are secured (Lane & Down, 2010; Mason, 2007). Old methods of solving problems, and even how one manages and leads, must be changed to match the demands of an unpredictable environment and a newly configured workforce. Lane and Down (2010) provokingly suggest, "How leaders contend with turbulence and uncertainty in the external world is partly a function of how they deal with uncertainty within themselves. Anxiety and fear can lead to retrenchment; conversely, confidence and courage can lead to new opportunities" (p. 513).

Ann Borders can see the emerging trends as well, and she instinctively realizes that the old ways of doing business must be toppled:

> I believe that executives must begin by reimagining the entire concept of organizational leadership. Successful organizations of the future will tap the leadership potential of each employee. We must also reexamine our organizational structures. Community mental health centers have traditionally operated in a fairly centralized manner, often propelled forward by the vision of a longstanding leader. This needs to change, I believe. Top-down, layered organizational structures and traditional notions about leadership aren't enough to succeed—or possibly to survive—in this new world. Successful organizations will redesign their structures and move toward flatter and more fluid systems that fully engage staff and mine the talents of all employees. It's a no-excuses environment marked by personal accountability and broader individual authority than can be found in traditional systems.
>
> Future leadership competencies include employee and team engagement skills, the ability to increase efficiency (probably to a greater degree than any of us think possible today), the capacity to develop internal and external alliances, a talent for promoting innovation and

organizational learning, and the ability to apply new technologies to every aspect of operations. The successful leaders of the future will create passion for the mission and sustain a culture marked by personal accountability and achievement. It can be done, but it will require us to rearrange our thinking about best practices for managing the ever-present challenges of change.

(Personal communication)

While Indiana experiences the retirement of the pioneers of the community mental health movement, a new group of leaders will carry the baton forward. Some, like Bob Dunbar, wonder if CMHCs "are at or very near their business cycle." Galen Goode sees promise in new developments on the national and state scene, and even feels there is mutual understanding about the task at hand, but also notes,

The discussions are positive and the need for change is accepted by both sides. However, the resulting decision by the public funders falls short of providing the means for change. The resulting change process tweaks the system around the edges rather than the heart of the issue.

(Personal communication)

Once again, those who care deeply about the future of community mental health find themselves peering into a murky crystal ball, and, in spite of years of experience, they deal with the uncertainty as well. As Ann Borders says:

We are experiencing a "change of personality" within our industry. Those CEO's who joined community mental health as young clinicians in the 1960's and 70's are retiring almost en masse. These leaders set the vision, articulated the values, shaped the cultures, and in many ways defined the organizations that they led. Entering the scene are new CEO's who weren't even *born* at the time of the 1963 enabling legislation. So, where will these new leaders take us? What leadership constructs, structures, and competencies will define future success?

(Personal communication)

DISCUSSION QUESTIONS

1. This chapter describes a new health-care model: Accountable Care Organizations. Discuss its components. How do you think it might affect community mental health services?

2. Define and discuss the differences between structural integration and clinical integration of services.

3. Discuss the following sentence: "Providers are increasingly being forced to choose to focus their mission away from trying to be a comprehensive safety net for all, and either provide less service to all or exclude some in favor of not compromising quality."

LEARNING ASSIGNMENT

Mental health-care services are dependent on a shrinking funding stream. Within that context, discuss the assertion that it is axiomatic that painful choices, ranging from who receives care, how much care can be delivered, and if the most efficacious services can be liberally offered, must be routinely made.

SUGGESTED READINGS

DeVore, S., & Champion, R.W. (2011). Driving population health through accountable care organizations. *Health Affairs, 30*(1), 41–50.

Kane, T. (1993). Reflections on the community mental health movement: Implications for the administrator. *Administration and Policy in Mental Health, 21*, 101–105.

Smith, T., & Sederer, L. (2009). A new kind of homelessness for individuals with serious mental illness? The need for a "mental health home." *Psychiatric Services, 60*(4), 528–533.

INTERNET RESOURCES

FAQ On ACOs: Accountable Care Organizations, Explained: www.kaiserhealthnews.org/stories/2011/january/13/aco-accountable-care-organization-faq.aspx

REFERENCES

Alakeson, V., Frank, R., & Katz, R. (2010). Specialty care medical homes for people with severe, persistent mental disorders. *Health Affairs, 29*(5), 867–873.

Brown, R. (2004). Consideration of the origin of Herbert Simon's theory of "satisficing" (1933–1947). *Management Decision, 42*(10), 1240–1256.

Chambers, D., & Wedel, K. (2009). *Social policy and social programs*, 5th Ed. Boston, MA: Pearson.

DeVore, S., & Champion, R.W. (2011). Driving population health through accountable care organizations. *Health Affairs, 30*(1), 41–50.

Druss, B., & Mauer, B. (2010). Health care reform and care at the behavioral health—primary care interface. *Psychiatric Services, 61*(11), 1087–1092.

Heifetz, R., Grashow, A., & Linsky, M. (2009). Leadership in a (permanent) crisis. *Harvard Business Review, 87*(7/8), 62–69.

Kane, T. (1993). Reflections on the community mental health movement: Implications for the administrator. *Administration and Policy in Mental Health, 21*, 101–105.

Kilo, C., & Wasson, J. (2010). Practice redesign and the patient-centered medical home: History, promises, and challenges. *Health Affairs, 29*(5), 773–777.

Lane, D., & Down, M. (2010) The art of managing for the future: Leadership of turbulence. *Management Decision, 45*(2), 512–527

Mason, R. (2007). The external environment's effect on management and strategy. *Management Decision, 45*(1), 10–28.

Mauer, B., & Druss, B. (2010). Mind and body reunited: Improving care at the behavioral and primary healthcare interface. *The Journal of Behavioral Health Services & Research, 37*(4), 529–542.

Rittenhouse, D., Shortell, S., & Fisher, E. (2009). Primary care and accountable care—two essential elements of delivery-system reform. *The New England Journal of Medicine, 361*(24), 2301.

Ryan, W. (1999). The new landscape for nonprofits. *Harvard Business Review*, January/February, 127–136.

Schuffman, D., Druss, B., & Parks, J. (2009). Mending Missouri's safety net: Transforming systems of care by integrating primary and behavioral health care. *Psychiatric Services, 60*(5), 585–588.

Smith, T., & Sederer, L. (2009). A new kind of homelessness for individuals with serious mental illness? The need for a "mental health home." *Psychiatric Services, 60*(4), 528–533.

Sullivan, W.P. (2006). Mental health leadership in a turbulent world. In J. Rosenberg & S.J. Rosenberg (Eds.), *Community mental health: Challenges for the 21st century* (pp. 247–257). New York: Routledge.

Glossary

Advocacy groups	Groups dedicated to addressing social problems and advocating for change.
Antidepressants	Medication designed to address and treat depressive symptoms.
Antipsychotic	Medication designed to stabilize and reduce psychotic symptoms.
Assertive community treatment	Interdisciplinary teams that manage consumers outside in the community and provide a wide variety of psychiatric and psychosocial support.
Asylums	An institution for the care of the seriously mentally ill. Many persons with severe mental illness lived the majority of their lives in asylums in the years preceding deinstitutionalization. Such persons often received minimal treatment.
Biopsychosocial	A framework to assess and support functioning that addresses needs and resources at a biological, psychological, and social level.
Bipolar disorder	Major mental illness characterized by a disturbance in mood. Symptoms can include mania and psychotic depression.
Bullying	Intentionally physical, verbal, and/or emotional aggressive behavior, often between adolescents, that involves an imbalance of power or strength.
Capitation	A method for asserting financial control for health-care services. A capitation strategy asks the organization to provide a specified service package to a target population and pays a pre-arranged fee for each member of the population, regardless of whether or not they use the service.
Case management	Treatment programs that utilize outreach services and may include working with clients in their homes or on the streets. Services typically provided include housing assistance, financial entitlements, linkages with general health-care and social services providers, and transportation to community services or meetings.

Child and Adolescent Services Program	Federal initiative in the early 1980s that focused on developing and supporting "systems of care" in the community for children with mental illness, and their families.
CIT	Crisis intervention team.
Clinical case management	Case management that includes counseling and psychodynamic therapy. Services are provided by a case manager who is trained as a therapist.
Clinician bias	Personal opinions and attitudes held by clinicians that interfere with being able to refrain from judgments; non-scientific and subjective perceptions about a client.
Coercive	To be forced to do something against one's will. Persons with serious mental illness who are hospitalized involuntarily are coerced.
Cognitive behavioral training	A treatment approach wherein cognitive techniques are used to modify problematic behaviors.
Co-occurring mental and substance disorders	Consumers who are dually diagnosed with mental illness and substance abuse. Such persons are often referred to as mentally ill chemical abusers (MICAs).
Community aftercare	Community treatment provided to persons with serious mental illness post discharge from an inpatient unit.
Community-based services	Services provided in the community and designed to support successful adaptation to community life.
Community housing	Residences in the community that provide a variety of living arrangements and services for the seriously mentally ill; can include supported living, community residences, group homes, and independent living apartments.
Community Mental Health Act of 1963	Legislation that provided funding for the development of community-based mental health care programs. The Act called for a shift from an institution-based public mental health system to a community-based system and ushered in the period of deinstitutionalization.
Community mental health centers	Entities that address mental health needs that are located in neighborhoods and counties and provide services to the local population.
Consumers	Persons who both utilize and often participate in treatment provision for the serious mentally ill. The term "consumers" represents a philosophical shift from a traditional medical model that views the mentally ill as patients to a perspective based on principles of empowerment and treatment collaboration.
Consumer-operated services	Therapeutic or social services run by consumers.
Continuous treatment teams	Often considered a variation of ACT teams, the use of a multidisciplinary team approach to serving the seriously mentally ill is generally used to treat the client in his/her community.

Cross-culture	The discourse concerning cultural interactivity, sometimes referred to as cross-culturalism. The term "cross-cultural" emerged in the social sciences in the 1930s, largely as a result of the Cross-Cultural Survey undertaken by George Peter Murdock, a Yale anthropologist. Initially referring to comparative studies based on statistical compilations of cultural data, the term gradually acquired a secondary sense of cultural interactivity. The comparative sense is implied in phrases such as "a cross-cultural perspective," "cross-cultural differences," "a cross-cultural study of," etc.
Cultural adaptation	Eliciting from the community members' concept of culture, the values of the group, and their ideas about the best approaches to reaching various people within their community.
Culturally competent	An approach wherein an understanding of the client's background (cultural, gender, sexual orientation, etc.) informs the therapeutic relationship and treatment.
Deinstitution-alization	The large-scale discharge of persons with severe mental illness to the community, emphasizing the use of the least restrictive treatment settings and rehabilitation programs in the community. Deinstitutionalization has often been criticized as falling short of its promise to provide adequate community services.
Disaster	An overwhelming event/circumstance that tests the adaptational responses of a community or individual beyond their capacity, temporarily leading to massive disruption of functioning for the community or individual.
DSM-IV-TR	*The Diagnostic and Statistical Manual*, the standard classification of psychiatric disorders.
Empowerment	A key concept of the recovery model, empowerment emphasizes the consumer's self-determination in treatment and life-style choices.
Environmental barriers	Barriers in the environment, such as lack of adequate housing, that impede successful community adaptation.
Eurocentric	A perspective that interprets reality and history solely from the experience of European civilization.
Evidence-based practice	Treatment that is based on research that demonstrates its efficacy.
Family therapy	Psychotherapeutic intervention that treats the entire family as a unit.
Fotonovela	A health education tool that uses posed photographs with simple text bubbled to portray a soap opera narrative that conveys an educational message.
Fee for service	A system of payment for services based on individual visits.
Fidelity scale	An instrument that attempts objectively to measure and assess whether a program is being faithful to the intended model.

Fountain House	A clubhouse in NYC for persons with serious mental illness, Fountain House is one of the earliest programs dedicated to the recovery of men and women with mental illness by providing opportunities for its members to live, work, and learn, while contributing their talents through a community of mutual support.
Gender stereotyping	Myths and stereotypes based on gender.
Health literacy	The ability to obtain, process, and understand basic health information.
Illness-based management	Treatment based on the premise that persons with serious mental illness are "sick."
Immigrant paradox	A population-based finding in which foreign-born people report less physical health and psychiatric morbidity than their United States-born counterparts, despite the stressful experiences and poverty associated with immigration.
Individuals with Disabilities in Education Act (IDEA)	A 1990 federal law that ensures that children with physical and mental disabilities receive appropriate care through early intervention, special education, and related services.
Intensive case management (ICM)	A case management approach that typically has a low caseload ratio of 10 or 15:1. It has many of the same admission criteria and goals as ACT, but is less clearly defined and often operationalized differently across programs. It typically does not use a shared-client team approach.
Internalized oppression	The process of adopting negative attitudes perpetuated in the dominant culture; for example, persons of color who adopt racist stereotypes and internalize oppressive attitudes.
Labeling	Assigning characteristics to persons based on stereotypes and without taking into account individual variation.
Limited English proficiency	Individuals for whom English is not their primary language and who have a limited ability to read, speak, write, or understand English.
Major depression	Mental illness characterized by severe depressive episodes.
Managed care	Refers to a variety of techniques packaged as unique strategies aimed at marshaling appropriate clinical and financial resources to ensure needed care.
Measures of fidelity	Methodologies that replicate an original research design.
Mental health-care disparities	Racial and ethnic inequalities in the access, use, engagement, and quality of mental health care.
Mood stabilizers	Medication designed to address mood disorders, such as bipolar disorder.
Medical necessity	Access to treatment is based on medical considerations and restricted. Often, the condition has to be deemed sufficiently serious for treatment to be provided and generally excludes emotional and psychological factors.

305

MHC	Mental health center.
Motivational interviewing	Interventions such as "motivational interviewing" are intended to assist clients in understanding the impacts of their illness and drugs and alcohol on their lives. Techniques are utilized to help the client identify discrepancies between current behaviors and future goals, and to develop strategies to begin to achieve them.
Multi-systemic therapy (MST)	An intensive family- and community-based program designed to address serious antisocial and/or delinquent behaviors in children and adolescents.
National Alliance for the Mentally Ill (NAMI)	Founded in 1979, NAMI is a nonprofit, grass-roots, self-help support and advocacy organization of consumers, families, and friends of people with severe mental illnesses.
National Committee on Mental Hygiene	Founded in 1909 by Clifford Beers, the National Committee for Mental Hygiene, the precursor to today's National Mental Health Association, was dedicated to improving mental health care and combating stigma. Often called the founder of the modern mental health movement, Clifford Beers himself struggled with major mental illness and subsequently he devoted his life's work to advocacy on behalf of persons with mental illness.
National Institute of Mental Health	A federal agency charged with the task to transform societal understanding of mental illness through research and education.
Neuropsychiatry	A medical framework that incorporates both neurology and psychiatry.
Neurotransmitter	A substance in the brain that transmits nerve impulses across a synapse.
Not-for-profit organizations	Although the distinction between private and not-for-profit (voluntary) agencies is increasingly blurred, traditionally, not-for-profit agencies do not seek to make a profit and are supported by public funding.
Outcomes evaluation	An increasingly popular focus on evaluating efficacy of treatment approaches through systematic review of outcomes.
Organizational networks	Social structures that allow organizations to interact, exchange information, work together on joint projects, and plan regional service.
Parity	Providing for health insurance benefits for mental health and substance abuse services at a level equal to that for health-care conditions.
Partnership model	Sometimes used to describe peer or group support in which people with a common concern voluntarily come together to help one another.
Peer	A substitute term for consumer, it refers to the equal and supportive actions of persons with a disability to each other.
Peer case management services	The practice of peers (or consumers) who function as case management providers for persons with serious mental illness.

Peer support	An increasingly popular treatment model, the use of peers to provide therapeutic and social support.
Pharmacotherapy	Treatment of mental illness using medication.
Play therapy	Form of psychotherapy for children that utilizes play behaviors for diagnosis and treatment.
Prevalence	A measure that refers to the number of people who have a particular disease.
Psychosocial rehabilitation	A recovery model based on stages of consumer development toward independent living and productive social functioning.
Psychotic disorders	Mental illness characterized by psychosis, including schizophrenia and bipolar illness.
Psychotropic medications	Prescription drugs taken to affect mental state or treat mental disorders.
Recidivism	A tendency to relapse, to return to a previous condition of illness.
Recovery	A treatment philosophy based on wellness and recovery.
Schizoaffective disorder	Major mental illness characterized by both a disturbance in thinking and a disturbance in mood; often one of the most severe forms of mental illness.
Schizophrenia	A major mental illness characterized by severe thought disorders, including delusions and psychosis.
Scientific racism	Epidemiological studies that reflect and perpetuate racism; for example, studies that served to provide a rationale and justification for slavery and discrimination against blacks after emancipation.
Self-determination	A central concept of the recovery model, self-determination emphasizes the consumer's ability and right fully to participate in treatment planning.
Self-stigma	The process of internalizing negative social stereotypes; for example, gays and lesbians identifying with homophobic attitudes.
Sheltered workshops	A vocational rehabilitation treatment where persons with serious mental illness were trained to perform simple functions such as mail room and stock.
SIM	Sequential intercept model.
Social integration	To integrate oneself into the community and into social groupings.
Staff downsizing	A pattern of reducing employment in agencies; often a response to funding restrictions.
Stigma	The assignment of negative characteristics to individuals, based on non-objective and unscientific criteria.
Supported employment	A component of the psychosocial rehabilitation model, an intervention designed to assist consumers successfully to navigate the world of work.

Symptomatically   Presenting with the characteristics (symptoms) of an illness.

Synapse   The point at which a nervous impulse passes from neuron to neuron.

Telepsychiatry   The practice of utilizing secure computer and video linkages to enable interviews and treatment between clients and psychiatrists who are in geographically separate locations.

Total institution   These facilities "warehoused" persons with serious mental illness, divorcing them from contact with the "outside" world and providing for all their daily needs.

Transinstitution-alization   The process of going from one institution to another; for example, a psychiatric inpatient who is transferred to a prison.

Trauma wound   A term for either physical injury caused by some direct external force or psychological injury cause by some extreme emotional assault.

Voluntary   Engaged in willingly and by choice.

We Are Not Alone (WANA)   In the 1940s, a group of former mental patients formed WANA. Their goal was to help others make the transition from inpatient hospitalization to community living. These efforts led to the establishment of Fountain House.

Wellness-based management   Part of the recovery philosophy, emphasizing the consumer's strengths and potential for wellness.

Index

317

racism: African–Americans 135–136, 139–140, 143; conclusion 143; and identity development 140–142; institutionalized 138, 142–143; internalized 139; and Latinos 169; manifestations of 138–139; in mental health services 135–136, 143; and stereotyping 139; white 139, 141

Rainbow Heights Club 22, 23; conclusion 30; consumer input 26; consumer survey 27–30; demographics 28; and economic crisis 26; hospitalization rates 27; program description 25–27; sense of hope 28; tenets 27; treatment compliance 27; vignettes: Laura 29–30; vignettes: Steven 30

RAND Corporation 50

recovery 277; addictive disorder 277; and assertive community treatment (ACT) 205, 208–209; and evidence-based practices (EBPs) 8–10; illness management and 9–10; and neuropsychiatry 240; older adults 114; and outcomes 3, 4; as a process 3, 4–5; schizophrenia 4; summary 15–16

Red Cross 181–182

reflective listening skills 10–11

relapse prevention 11, 13

Robert Wood Johnson Foundation 9, 200, 226

Rogers, C. 11

Rosen, A., Mueser, K.T., & Teesson, M. 198

Rubin, A. 277–278

Sacramento Bee 149

Salyers, M.P. et al. (1998) 206

Salyers, M.P. et al. (2010) 205

satisfying, theory of 287

Schell, T. & Tanielian, T. 55

schizoaffective disorder 207–209

schizophrenia 9, 239; anti-psychotic medications 242–243; and assertive community treatment (ACT) 198, 200; and co-occurring mental and substance abuse disorders 217–218; Crisis Intervention Team (CIT) 66; environmental factors 242; and family experience 94–95; genetic factors 242; and Latinos 171–172; a life-shortening disease 228; medication for 239; and neuropsychiatry 242; older adults 109, 113–114; and recovery 4; social isolation 97; specialized police response 66; and substance abuse 215, 247, 254; and suicide 245; treatment of 242–243; UCLA Social and independent Living Skills Program 171–172

Schizophrenia Patient Outcomes Research Team (PORT) 96, 200, 217–218

schizotypal personality disorder 246

"Screening, Brief Intervention, Referral, and Treatment" (S-BIRT) 123

secondary post-traumatic stress disorder 54

Section 8 vouchers 255, 261

selective serotonin uptake inhibitors (SSRIs) 79–80, 244, 246

self-determination 36

self-esteem 36

self-help 37–39

self-stigma 7–8, 14–15

self-stigmatizing cognitive schemata 14–15

Sequential Intercept Model (SIM) 63–64, 65, 67–68, 70–71, 72

serious mental illness (SIM): and assertive community treatment (ACT) 197, 203; and developmental (intellectual) disability 203; statistics 203

serotonin 243, 245

serotonin/nor-epinephrine uptake inhibitors (SNRIs) 244, 246

shared decision-making (SDM) 12

Shern, D.L. et al 260

Sierra Leone 188–189

Simon, Herbert 287

Simpson, S.M. et al. 148

smoking 223

Snowden, L.M., Masland, M.C., Peng, C.J., Wei-Mein Lou, C., & Wallace, N.T. 149

social integration 39

social isolation 208; and anxiety 121; and depression 121; older adults 121, 124; schizophrenia 97

social justice 36, 180

social services CM approach 263

social workers 205, 275, 282–283

Solomon, P. 256

South Cove Community Health Center, Boston 153

Spagnolo, A.B., Murphy, A.A., & Librera, L.A. 13

specialized police response 63, 64, 65–66, 68–69, 71, 72

Sphere Project: The Humanitarian Charter and Minimum Standards in Disaster Response Handbook 181, 183

Stahler, G.J., Shipley, T.F., Bartelt, D., DuCette, J.P., & Shandler, I.W. 261

Stawar, Terry 292, 296

Steadman, Henry 68

Stein, Leonard 199